12

H. M. DAUGHERTY
AND THE POLITICS OF EXPEDIENCY

H.M. Daugherty as Attorney General (*Ohio Historical Society*)

H. M. Daugherty
and the Politics of Expediency

JAMES N. GIGLIO, *1939-*

The Kent State University Press

Library of Congress Cataloging in Publication Data
Giglio, James N 1939-
    H.M. Daugherty and the politics of expediency.

    Based on the author's thesis, Ohio State University.
    Bibliography: p.
    Includes index.
    1.   Daugherty, Harry Micajah, 1860-1941.   2.   Politicians—United States—Biog-
raphy.   3.   Lawyers—United States—Biography.   4.   United States—Politics and
government—1865-1933.   I.   Title.
E664.D23G53   973.91'092'4   [B]   78-17106
ISBN 0-87338-215-3

For My Parents Frank and Mary
and My Wife Fran

Contents

Preface

HARRY Micajah Daugherty (H.M., as he always signed his name and advertised his law practice) was one of the most durable and controversial Republican politicians of the twentieth century. He is remembered today chiefly for his role in helping Warren G. Harding attain the presidency in 1920, for his service as Attorney General during the Harding administration, and for his association with the scandals attendant upon that era. Historians writing on the Harding-Coolidge period have relegated him to a minor role, first worthy of attention in 1918, shortly before the Harding presidency, and passing into obscurity after his forced resignation in 1924.

But there is much more to the man than his political association with Harding and his troubled attorney generalship. Daugherty began his career eighteen years before the turn of the century, during one of the most tumultuous eras of American politics—the heyday of John Sherman, Joseph Foraker, and Marcus Hanna, who made Ohio politics synonymous with national political power. It was to be a career checkered with notable successes and equally notable failures. Daugherty was one of William McKinley's most important political managers in the early 1890s, and took part in his presidential campaign in 1896; he was a leading political adviser of William Howard Taft in the latter's presidential campaign of 1908; and he successfully managed Harding's preconvention campaign in 1920. But he also was involved in Taft's losing campaign in 1912, when the Republican party suffered a disastrous split, which was further exacerbated in Ohio by Daugherty's fanatical persecution of the progressives who had bolted to the cause of Theodore Roosevelt. So intense were the enmities spawned by that campaign that bitterness and divisiveness persisted among Ohio Republicans into the 1920s.

Although he had served in local government early in his career, Daugherty's efforts to obtain elective office in the twentieth century were repeatedly frustrated. He made his mark instead as a party organizer, manager, and state factional leader. His Republicanism was commonplace and conservative, dictated by pragmatism rather than ideology. He was dedicated above all to the advancement of party, as well as personal, interests, and he regarded the attorney generalship as a just reward for his years of party loyalty and his service in the Harding campaign.

It is on his attorney generalship that history has judged him. Both his fitness for the office and his performance while in it came under heavy criticism. His resignation in 1924 during the storm of scandal that swept the Harding administration and his subsequent acquittal on a charge of conspiring to defraud the government of his honest services were the source of acute humiliation for Daugherty, and he spent the remainder of his life trying to answer the charges against him and vindicate his career. In his efforts to do so, he played a part in creating some of the myth that has surrounded the tragedy of the Harding presidency.

It is the purpose of this study to examine Daugherty's life more fully than has previously been done. A study of his career can tell us much about the Republican politics of the late nineteenth and early twentieth centuries, a time in which the Republican party for the most part maintained its post-Civil War supremacy in presidential politics. Such a study can also shed light on the motivations of Harry Daugherty, on his aspirations and methods, and on the nature of his political associations, especially those with William Howard Taft and Harding.

"Anyone who wants the truth has ample facilities for finding it out," Daugherty asserted in 1939.[1] In reality, I found it difficult to obtain pertinent manuscript material for this study. Daugherty apparently destroyed his papers, a loss that seems irreplaceable, as no close family survives. In addition, material on Daugherty is lacking in several other potentially useful manuscript collections, compounding the difficulties. Consequently, I have given little attention to the details of Daugherty's personal life, and there are some gaps in the record of his early political development. Nevertheless, related documents, newspapers, and other sources make it possible to reconstruct the main outlines of Daugherty's career. It is my hope that this book will serve to further the understanding of a significant political figure and the years in which he lived.

Acknowledgments

THE idea for this study originated in early 1964, just after the Harding Memorial Association dramatically turned over the Harding Papers to the Ohio Historical Society, which quickly opened the collection for historical research. At the time I was an M.A. candidate at Kent State University in search of a thesis topic in twentieth-century American history. Because of the new opportunities which the Harding Era presented, I, like so many other researchers, flocked to the old society library on the campus of Ohio State University. The result of my investigation was a thesis on the attorney generalship of Daugherty, for which I owe much to Professor William F. Zornow for his patient guidance. I later expanded the Daugherty study into a political biography that fulfilled the dissertation requirement at Ohio State University. Professor Robert H. Bremner of the Department of History ably and conscientiously directed the project. Since then, the manuscript has undergone considerable revision to prepare it for publication. It has profited from the encouragement and criticism of many scholars, especially Victor Agruso, Jr., of Drury College, J. Leonard Bates of the University of Illinois, and Dominic J. Capeci, Jr., of Southwest Missouri State University, all of whom have read the manuscript in its entirety. This probably would have been a better book had I adopted more of their suggestions, but errors of fact and interpretation are solely my responsibility.

I am indebted to the generous assistance provided me by the staffs of many libraries and archival depositories, especially the Ohio Historical Society Library, the Manuscript Division of the Library of Congress, the National Archives, the Indiana State Library, the Cincinnati Historical Society Library, and the Western Reserve Historical Society Library. It would be impossible to mention all of the archivists, librarians, and manuscript curators who were so courteous and helpful, but a few names stand out: Conrad Weitzel of the Ohio Historical Society Library; David Larson, formerly of the Ohio Historical Society Library; Ferris Stovell of the National Archives; and Barbara Massello of the Southwest Missouri

State University Library, who promptly handled my innumerable inter-library loan requests. Special thanks go to Daugherty's nephew, H. Ellis Daugherty, for authorizing the release of Draper Daugherty's medical file from Lima State Hospital, and to Professor Clifford Whipple of South-west Missouri State University for helping me interpret it. I also thank Southwest Missouri State University for extending me a semester sab-batical and a stipend to do additional research in Washington, D.C. A debt is due the editors of *Ohio History* for granting permission to reprint material verbatim from my two articles: "The Political Career of Harry M. Daugherty, 1889-1919" in Volume LXIX (Summer-Autumn 1970) and "Lawyer as Lobbyist: Harry M. Daugherty and the Charles W. Morse Case" in Volume LXXXII (Summer-Autumn 1973).

Last, but most important, I give heartfelt thanks to my wife, Fran, who always encouraged me and did much of the typing, and to my young sons, Peter and Anthony, for being around.

Introduction to Law and Politics

IN 1881, Harry Micajah Daugherty, a young man of twenty-one, nailed his shingle to a law office door over Adams Brothers' Store on downtown Court Street in Washington Court House, Ohio. Compared to the state's urban centers, his bailiwick of 3,798 people was minuscule, yet it was the most important municipality in Fayette County because it was the commercial and governmental hub of the county. Here, farmers sold agricultural products and livestock, bought supplies, transacted legal affairs, and saw the county governed. Located in the center of Fayette and Union Township next to Paint Creek, Washington Court House is only thirty-nine miles southwest of Columbus, the state capital, and sixty-nine miles northeast of Cincinnati, the industrial and trading area of southern Ohio. Today it remains small, having a population of only 12,495; many of the old buildings still stand, including the majestic courthouse where Daugherty argued his first case in its red-carpeted courtroom.

Fayette County, named for the Marquis de Lafayette, is situated in the productive farming region of southwestern Ohio. It lies between Franklin (Columbus) and Hamilton (Cincinnati), politically the most important counties in southern Ohio. Unlike Hamilton, Fayette has always lacked the swift rivers and iron and coal deposits so necessary for significant industrial growth. Its rich soil and slightly rolling terrain, however, made it a major producer of cereals and grasses, which generated a profitable livestock business. Large farms accounted for Fayette's sparse rural population.

When Daugherty began his legal career in the early 1880s, Washington Court House was experiencing its most significant growth. Aided by a growing rural affluence and three railroads serving the area, its population increased by one-third within the decade.[1] The development of manufacturing accompanied this expansion. A major step was taken when community leaders met in January 1881 to devise plans for the purpose of "starting some kinds of manufacturing establishments in this place." At that time only a small spinning business, a tool-handle factory, and a stamping works existed. By 1890, despite the intervention of a devastating cyclone in 1885, the county Republican newspaper proudly announced in a special trade issue the many new manufacturing establishments gracing Washington Court House, including a maple-leaf gum works, a shoe factory, and a lamp and stove manufacturer. The following year provided the community with a modern waterworks, well-illuminated streets, and a large number of new buildings in the downtown area. The only "shadow," according to one observer, was the twenty-five saloons which, with their painted glass windows, lined every street of the downtown district.[2] Although the growth rate did not continue, neither the severe economic depression of the 1890s nor its accompanying populist politics affected the community.

Instead, Fayette was a hotbed of Republicanism in a state that dominated Republican national politics for the last three decades of the nineteenth century. The county gave Republican presidential candidates sizable majorities from 1872 to 1912. Fayette also consistently backed GOP candidates on state tickets. Even when state voters elected Democratic governors in 1883 and 1889, the county voted overwhelmingly for the Republican opposition. County Republicans were especially fond of Senator John Sherman from Mansfield who, as Secretary of the Treasury under Rutherford B. Hayes, had been responsible for the redemption of inflationary greenbacks. Fayette voters also supported the Republican shibboleths of protective tariffs and Civil War pensions, for many of their sons had fought in the Union army.

Harry Daugherty lived his first thirty-four years in Washington Court House, maturing in its period of significant growth. Born on January 26, 1860, he was the son of John H. and Jane Draper Daugherty.[3] His father, a farmer and merchant tailor, was the son of Scotch-Irish immigrants. He spent his childhood in Lancaster, Pennsylvania, coming to Ohio while still a young man, first to Zanesville, then to Washington Court House. Little else is known about him. The *Washington Court House Herald*, in reporting his death in 1864, noted only the time of expiration and the approximate age at death, a sad commentary that he had left no mark in the community. Daugherty's mother, Jane Draper, came from a prominent local family, her Virginia ancestors having migrated to Ohio in 1810, a generation after the first Virginians had settled the area under the provisions of the Virginia Military Survey of 1783. In her youth, she had eloped with a young man, only to have their parents annul the marriage.

Daugherty's maternal grandfather, Micajah Draper, had been one of the original Drapers to settle the area. A respected man, he had been township trustee in 1839 and later held several important county positions. He was also a grain merchant and owned one of the most successful farms in the area—141 acres, located two miles west of the village. By the time of his death in 1887, Micajah had accumulated a comfortable estate.

Nevertheless, Harry's childhood was afflicted with hardships. His father died of diphtheria when Harry was four years old. One of Harry's two remaining brothers also died in the epidemic (one had died earlier), and Harry himself was left in a weakened condition. With the father's estate amounting to only $1,800, and with apparently little assistance from grandfather Micajah, Jane and her sons found life a struggle.[4] They managed to survive because of Jane's self-reliance and resourcefulness, traits she passed on to her children. Eventually, the energetic but frail Harry and his brother Mally S. undertook an assortment of jobs to help out at home. From the beginning the two brothers were inseparable even though Mal later became a Democrat, at least until the party nominated William Jennings Bryan in 1896. Mal was taller and more powerfully built, but Harry more than made up for the disadvantage by his stronger drive. Harry's mother later recalled that he was so little when he worked in the neighborhood grocery store on Court Street that he had to stand on a box to reach the cash drawer.[5] But he learned to take care of himself.

Daugherty became so independent that even his strict mother could not control him. Jane wanted him to become a Methodist minister after the completion of his secondary education, and his family doctor, who had almost completely restored Harry's health, counseled him to become a physician. He studied under the doctor for one year, but neither medicine nor religion interested him. After a brief sojourn as a cub reporter for the *Cincinnati Enquirer*, Daugherty decided to enter law school without undergraduate preparation. His aggressive, outgoing, and resourceful nature attracted him to a legal career. He also probably chose law because of the meager resources of his youth. Alexis de Tocqueville once observed that the closest thing to an American aristocracy was to be found in the legal profession. Aside from status, successful lawyers became wealthy. Daugherty wrote four years before his death that he had turned down federal judicial appointments as a younger man because he wanted to make more money.[6]

In 1878, Daugherty chose the University of Michigan Law School because, as he later reminisced, Michigan had a colder climate than Ohio. Weighing only one-hundred pounds, he hoped the harsher weather would increase his resistance and strengthen him from the after effects of diphtheria. More to the point, Daugherty's independent spirit perhaps required that he be farther away from his mother and friends than the nearby Ohio State University Law School. Michigan's excellent reputation and reasonable tuition also influenced him. He was able to supplement his meager finances by betting on election contests, boasting later that his wager on James Garfield in the 1880 presidential election enabled him to finish school in "good style."[7] But the young law student's occasional desire for easy money also embarrassed him. During one of his recesses from Ann Arbor, Harry and Mal set up a device in a culvert outside of Washington Court House to tap telegraph wires to obtain sporting news in advance. Their betting success puzzled the local gamblers, but Harry M. Weldon, later a sports editor of the *Cincinnati Enquirer*, soon exposed them.[8]

Harry graduated from law school in 1881 and returned home to accept a junior partnership with A.R. Creamer, the former county prosecuting attorney, and to prepare for the bar examination. In less than a year, Daugherty became the senior associate of Daugherty and Gregg, despite Nye Gregg's being slightly older and having greater experience and a more prominent social background. The ambitious young lawyer quickly turned to politics—a predictable choice, as politics was one of the few ways to gain exposure in nineteenth-century rural society. Exposure, together with political connections, promoted legal business. Politics also provided an almost singular competitive stimulus in much the same way that activities like golf, tennis, or football do today. Unquestionably, politics appealed to Daugherty's intensely competitive nature. For all of these reasons, most attorneys in Fayette—as elsewhere—played an active role politically, especially in the Republican party.[9] Daugherty later commented that "law and politics, you know, go hand in hand."[10]

As early as 1881 he attended Republican meetings in Washington Court House. That summer he was chosen a delegate from Union Township to the county judicial convention held later that year. In the spring of 1882 the county Republican central committee made him its secretary. His participation within the party organization increased when he became secretary of the county executive committee in 1883. Despite his youth, Daugherty's aggressiveness and organizational ability served him well.

Party organizational work was not his only political effort. In 1882, to use Daugherty's later self-description, "a beardless and probably brainless boy," was elected Union Township clerk. He served one two-year term, earning an annual salary of $1,500. The clerkship provided him with exposure and experience, enabling him to augment his law practice.[11] Upon the completion of his tenure, he was elected to the city council for a two-year period.

Daugherty received his first introduction to state politics in 1883 as one of five delegates appointed at the Fayette Republican convention to represent the county at the Republican state convention in Columbus. His selection was not made without a fight. After previously associating with the older Sherman politicians who controlled the county, Daugherty committed himself to the support of a young Republican clique that wanted representation on the proposed county delegation to the state convention. They tried to obtain the consent of the old crowd for the selection of two young Republicans. When the organization balked, Daugherty served notice that he and his young associates would forcibly reorganize the executive committee at the county convention. The "young turks" were successful, and Daugherty became secretary of the delegation representing Fayette at Columbus.[12]

The primary objective of the Republican state convention in 1883 was the nomination of a gubernatorial candidate. Charles Foster, twice Republican governor, was unwilling to run for an unprecedented third term. Joseph B. Foraker, a judge on the superior court of Cincinnati and Foster's personal choice, was nominated. He represented the young Republicans, who wanted a more responsible role in state politics, and greater participation for all on the local levels. Young, charismatic, and a captivating speaker whose spread-eagle style won him the titles of "Fire Alarm Joe" and "Boomtara," Foraker was the antithesis of Sherman, who continued to dominate the Ohio party and seek the presidency. Pompous, crusty, and no orator, the bearded and white-haired Sherman was of the old Republican leadership of the Civil War era. He was accustomed to controlling the state organization from Washington and keeping out young blood.[13] Inevitably, these two men would clash.

Daugherty, of course, strongly supported Foraker's nomination. In return, Foraker assisted Daugherty's later political ambitions. Daugherty's rejection of the Sherman leadership was not altogether clear, however, because he did receive local party positions. There is no evidence that he acted out of principle or out of any strong admiration for Foraker, although the latter's magnetism did attract many followers. It may be that he was dissatisfied and sought more than the party leadership would allow. Perhaps his impatience stemmed from memories of his early hardships and his father's premature death, both of which made him determined to move quickly.

In addition, his fiancée, Lucy Walker, was a cousin of Foraker's wife, and this may have helped move him closer to Foraker. Lucy Walker, of Wellston, Ohio, had first come to Washington Court House in February 1883. She came to organize classes in vocal music and quickly made an overwhelmingly favorable impression, especially as a vocalist in the Methodist church choir and at community functions. So sweetly did she sing "Jesus Lover of My Soul" and "Love's Old Sweet Song" that one of the newspapers resorted to poetry about her. Lucy's attractiveness increased her popularity among the town's eligible bachelors, few of whom were as handsome as the mustachioed, slender Harry. Dapper in dress, with brown hair neatly parted in the middle, he also had slightly protruding eyes, one of which was brown and the other blue. He and Lucy quickly fell in love and were married in Richmond, Indiana, on September 3, 1884. In the early years it was a happy marriage, and they often traveled and entertained. Daugherty's legal work was primarily local, enabling him to spend time at home, something he did not often do by the next decade.

Neither did he play an active role at that time in state politics. His defiance of the county organization in 1883 proved costly. He was not selected as a delegate to the 1885 Republican state convention, when Fayette sent a delegation pledged against Foraker's gubernatorial candidacy. In the next three years Daugherty served one term as city councilman (1886-1887) and as chairman of the county central committee (1886), but he focused almost entirely on a law practice that profited from the community's growth. After practicing alone for three years he formed a partnership with Colonel Horatio B. Maynard, a Civil War veteran and a prominent attorney. Maynard and Daugherty soon became one of the leading law firms in the county. As a result, Daugherty invested in real estate and became one of the principal stockholders of the *Cyclone and Fayette Republican*, the Republican organ. A few years later, Daugherty's brother Mal, by then a local bank president, became a stockholder of the *Fayette Record*, another Republican weekly.[14]

Harry Daugherty's political opportunity came in 1889, when Republican David Worthington decided not to seek reelection as Fayette's representative in the Ohio General Assembly. Daugherty ran for the nomination in the county primaries and defeated his Republican rivals by less than two-hundred votes. He then conducted a vigorous campaign against Joshua Mahan, his Democratic opponent. He was, of course, fully endorsed by the *Cyclone and Fayette Republican* as one who would best serve the interests of the business classes and the farmers because "there is no more levelheaded or industrious gentleman in Fayette."[15] The battle was intense, for reaction against "Forakerism" was almost as strong among some Sherman Republicans as it was among Democrats. Daugherty, a Foraker supporter in the governor's quest for a third term, wrote to Foraker's campaign manager Charles Kurtz of Columbus that "our friends are pretty scarce." He suggested that "some money might be used to good advantage in getting out the vote."[16] The Foraker organization did what it could to help.

On November 5, Daugherty was elected to the Ohio House of Representatives by a 2,979 to 2,145 vote. Foraker, however, failed in his bid for a third term, and the Democrats gained control of the state legislature. According to several local newspapers, Daugherty had an excellent record during his first year as a member of the minority party.[17] He did reflect the sentiment of his county. His bill in February made farmers "special constables" to arrest hunters who trespassed upon their land; he opposed the repeal of the Owen Sunday Bill, which prohibited the sale of liquor on the Sabbath; and he initiated a bill authorizing the Washington Court House council to borrow money to improve its streets.[18]

The Republican state convention of 1890 further enhanced Daugherty's reputation. Not only was he elected chairman of his county delegation, but convention delegates selected him for the state central committee as a representative of the tenth state congressional district. This gave him some influence in formulating statewide policies. Daugherty continued to impress party leaders in his first legislative term. He was friendly, a staunch partisan, and an excellent organizer. He was also regarded as an expert on parliamentary law and a good speaker. On several occasions he occupied the speaker's chair, where his strong, high-pitched voice became familiar. Daugherty was considered a possible choice as speaker of the house in the event the Republicans gained a majority in the fall elections. The *Cyclone and Fayette Republican* considered his reelection "reasonably sure."[19]

If Daugherty's contemporaries had been more perceptive, they might have focused on his other characteristics, for he was also combative and clever, pragmatic and amoral, ambitious and courageous. These characteristics accounted for his later political successes, but they also explain some of his defeats and disappointments. Reverses came whenever he employed these traits without restraint, when combativeness turned into vindictiveness, ambition into greed, amorality into unethical behavior, pragmatism into unprincipled action, and courage into recklessness. His background had much to do with the shaping of his character and personality. His father's early death and his mother's strong personality had played a part in forming his ambition for early success, and had been part of the motivation for his seeking a career in politics. In addition, memories of his childhood hardship had already, as has been noted, led him into some ethical lapses. This type of behavior was further encouraged by his entry into politics in the social milieu of the Gilded Age, when self-aggrandizement was characteristic of so many political figures. Daugherty too would have his share of questionable involvements, but not every charge of unethical activity made against him was true, nor was financial gain his sole motivation in politics. Indeed, he often engaged in political battles apart from any consideration of financial gain, and sometimes at a personal loss as well. Nevertheless, the world in which he found himself in the 1890s, with all its frustrations and defeats, served only to reinforce patterns of behavior already begun.

Frustration and Defeat
1891-1899

THE 1890s brought Harry Daugherty some political success, but mostly they represented a period of frustration and defeat that temporarily damaged his political career and left a few scars as well. Daugherty's difficulties began in the summer and fall of 1891, when the revival of factionalism within the Ohio Republican party complicated his reelection bid, eventually ensnarling him in the feud between the aging Senator Sherman and ex-Governor Foraker—the leading Republicans of the state. Their organizations had fought each other intermittently since the Republican national convention of 1888, when Foraker had been accused of deserting Sherman for the presidential candidacy of James G. Blaine. Afterward, intraparty battles emerged over the perennial issue: Who would control state politics—Sherman or Foraker?

The fight intensified in 1891 because of Foraker's desire to unseat Sherman in the senatorial contest of January 1892. The ex-Governor's friends—Charles Kurtz, A.L. Conger of Akron, and Asa S. Bushnell of Springfield—began campaigning for him the spring of 1891. In the interest of party harmony, Foraker agreed to nominate William McKinley of the Sherman-Hanna contingent for governor before announcing his own candidacy for senator. At the Republican state convention in Columbus in June, McKinley of Stark County benefited from one of Foraker's most successful orations. In turn, Foraker's record as governor won an endorsement in the party platform. To the casual observer, intraparty differences seemed momentarily resolved.

But in the weeks that followed, Foraker renewed his rivalry with Sherman. He informed associates that Sherman could not be reelected because of opposition in the party and the Farmers' Alliances. He also resented the manner in which the Sherman crowd sought his promise not to contest the senator's reelection. On July 19, Murat Halstead, the publisher of the *Cincinnati Gazette*, publicly disclosed Foraker's candidacy.[1]

Since Ohio senators were elected by the General Assembly, Foraker needed not only a Republican legislature, but also one that contained a majority of Foraker supporters. Consequently, he sought the support of Republican assemblymen like Daugherty, who had rendered Foraker useful service in the past and was sympathetic to his senatorial ambitions, no doubt because of the past assistance from Foraker's organization. Local political conditions, however, put Daugherty on the fence. Republican leaders in Fayette County, who were overwhelmingly for John Sherman, tried to pressure Daugherty to endorse their candidate. Joe Gest, editor and business manager of the *Cyclone and Fayette Republican*, in which Daugherty continued to hold stock, published an article in the *Cincinnati Enquirer* on August 1, declaring that Daugherty would "be unceremoniously shelved" as representative unless he ended his neutrality.[2] Upon reading Gest's article, Foraker wrote Daugherty, explaining that he would rather lose the support of his friends than have them suffer; regardless, he told Daugherty he needed his vote. He then called the Sherman forces cutthroats, who had knifed him in 1889 and who would do so again if he were now nominated as senator.[3] "Sherman men are many and active here," Daugherty replied, admitting that Gest and others would guarantee his renomination and reelection to the General Assembly in return for his pledge to Sherman.[4]

Nevertheless, Daugherty's renomination was unopposed at the Fayette County Republican convention in mid-August, which endorsed the candidacies of Sherman and McKinley. After Daugherty's nomination, party leaders appointed three delegates to escort him to the convention hall, where he delivered a short address in which he pledged that if reelected he would "support the candidate for United States Senator who may be the choice of the Republicans of Fayette County." That evening Daugherty assured Foraker's campaign manager, Charles Kurtz, of his allegiance to Foraker.[5]

In the ensuing weeks, Daugherty stumped Fayette for his own candidacy, while Foraker campaigned in behalf of the state ticket. They did not see each other until October 31, three days before the state elections. At that meeting, Foraker asked Daugherty if it were permissible for the *Cincinnati Commercial Gazette*, which was publishing senatorial preferences, to indicate that he was for Foraker. As Foraker wrote Kurtz the following day, Daugherty "at once hemmed and hawed, and said that was a matter he ought to keep quiet about for the present." Foraker then asked Daugherty whether he had made any pledges to the Sherman people. Daugherty replied that he had not, that he would be all right when the time came, but that he had a difficult county to handle and was much embarrassed by the situation there. Foraker then spoke frankly. Realizing that the Sherman forces had probably already promised to provide for

Daugherty in the organization of the legislature in January, he told Daugherty that "we had not forgotten him in considering these matters; that on the contrary, we had kept him in mind, with a view to making for him a suitable and satisfactory provision." Foraker further related to Kurtz that Daugherty "may be alright, but my confidence in him is not very strong."[6]

In the November election Daugherty was swept into the General Assembly for another two-year term after defeating Abner Swope by a 2,787 to 2,110 vote. William McKinley was elected governor, and the Republicans captured the Ohio legislature by nearly a two-thirds margin, insuring the election of a Republican to the Senate that January when the legislature reconvened. Given the legislature's composition, Foraker appeared to have the initial advantage in the senatorial contest. Two days after the election, he claimed a majority of eleven over Sherman.[7]

"Uncle Jawn's" friends now took Foraker more seriously. Campaign manager Mark Hanna, the portly, heavy-jowled Clevelander who was emerging as a prominent state party leader, raised thousands of dollars in Sherman's behalf, which William Hahn, the pro-Sherman Republican state executive committee chairman, put to good use. Agents were selected to enter doubtful districts to generate public pressure against Foraker-leaning legislators. Daugherty remained one of Sherman's prime targets, for his name often appeared on Foraker lists as a Foraker supporter in the postelection period.[8] The senator's lieutenants worked in conjunction with the *Cyclone and Fayette Republican* to pressure Daugherty. The newspaper reminded him of the county's overwhelming support of Sherman and predicted his reelection by a large majority.[9] Leading Fayette Republicans also cooperated by conducting a canvass to overwhelm Daugherty with the sentiment of the county Republicans.[10]

In the face of increased pressure, Daugherty's intentions still remained uncertain. Privately sympathetic to Foraker, he failed to reaffirm his August pledge to support "the choice of the Republicans of Fayette County," which happened to be John Sherman. Foraker, meanwhile, began to lose patience with Daugherty. He confided to Kurtz that Daugherty neglected to answer his correspondence, and he saw other signs he did not like.[11] Foraker's suspicions were justified. On December 11, Hahn arranged to have Daugherty visit Sherman in Washington, D.C. He assured the senator that Daugherty would travel on an evening train so that "no one would know anything about him being there." He also predicted Daugherty's vote for Sherman. In almost the same breath, he warned Sherman that it "will require considerable money to carry on our work," although "nothing will be done at these headquarters that will in anyway compromise your personal honor."[12] No record exists as to what transpired in Daugherty's consultations with Hahn and Sherman. He most likely assured them that he would honor his August pledge and signed a statement to that effect.[13]

Daugherty finally arrived in Columbus on December 29, four days before the speakership and nine days before the senatorial contests. That evening he went to Foraker's hotel room to tell him that sentiment for Senator Sherman was so strong in Fayette County that he would have to vote accordingly. He then showed Foraker the "card" on which he declared for Sherman. Foraker requested Daugherty to delay making his announcement until the day before the senatorial caucus.[14]

In the party caucus on January 2, 1892, Lewis C. Laylin (Sherman's candidate) defeated John F. McGrew (Foraker's choice) for speaker of the house by four votes. Much to Sherman's concern, Daugherty voted as pledged for McGrew, a close friend who resided in nearby Clark County. This preliminary setback placed Foraker at a disadvantage for the senatorial contest to be held on January 6.

As promised, Daugherty publicly reaffirmed his pledge to Sherman the day before the senatorial caucus. He justified his protracted silence by stating that he had wished to hear "fully and fairly" from friends and supporters of both candidates before deciding. On the following day he presided over the caucus. After his opening remarks, a debate ensued among the delegates on whether to use an open or secret ballot to nominate a senatorial candidate. Foraker favored a secret vote because he had more to gain in not forcing legislators to stand by their pledges. He perhaps reasoned that Daugherty, among others who had favored a secret ballot, could then dishonor his pledge to vote for Sherman.[15] By a forty-seven to forty-four vote, however, the open ballot prevailed. The nomination followed, and Sherman became the party's choice, obtaining fifty-three votes, including Daugherty's, to Foraker's thirty-eight. This vote insured Sherman's election, since the Republicans dominated the General Assembly. Immediately afterward, Sherman expressed his deepest gratitude to Mark Hanna "that our canvass was made without the expenditure of a single dollar for boodle, with no bitterness to our adversaries, and with no appeals for our candidate to the interested cupidity or ambition of the senators and members."[16]

The Democratic *Columbus Post*, in several editorials following the caucus, did not agree with Sherman's statement and, in fact, accused Daugherty and fourteen other legislators of changing their pledges from Foraker to Sherman because of "intimidation, threats, promises and actual purchase." The *Post* claimed that Hahn had paid Daugherty for his vote.[17] A grand-jury investigation of the charges ended without indictments. Foraker, who would have made an interesting witness, refused to cooperate with the inquiry. "As to the Grand Jury business," he wrote Kurtz, "I sincerely hope that no friend of mine will have anything to do with it." He made it clear that he would not accept responsibility for the disclosure of any charges. The contest, according to Foraker, had ended with the caucus.[18] Intraparty unity had developed to prevent exposure by any outside force.

The grand jury's withdrawal enabled Daugherty to act. In a speech in the house on January 26, he asked for a bipartisan committee to investigate the *Post* charges.[19] Daugherty expected full vindication of the accusations, for he had letters from both Sherman and Foraker attesting to his honorable activity during the senatorial contest.[20] The select house committee of two Republicans and two Democrats conducted the investigation. The *Columbus Post* manager, Charles Q. Davis, failed to substantiate his charge that Daugherty had accepted a bribe. Davis's accusation was partly based upon an alleged conversation he had overheard between Daugherty and an unidentified person near a cigar stand in the Neil House sometime before the caucus. Daugherty, according to Davis, had commented that Sherman would not receive his vote unless he "put up for it." Davis had no witness to confirm Daugherty's supposed statement. The *Post's* charge that Hahn had withdrawn seven $500 bills from the Deshler National Bank of Columbus on the day of the caucus and had given the money to Daugherty also collapsed, for insufficient evidence.[21]

Neither Daugherty nor Sherman, however, was completely honest in his testimony at the committee's hearings. Daugherty amazingly testified that he had consistently supported Sherman's candidacy since the August resolutions of the Fayette County convention. Sherman's testimony was also misleading. Choosing to ignore Daugherty's trip to Washington in mid-December, he said that he did not know anything about Daugherty's senatorial choice aside from what he had heard from Fayette Republicans. Indeed, Sherman claimed that he had never seen Daugherty in the entire preliminary caucus. It was not, according to Sherman, until two or three days before the speakership contest that he had first talked to him about the campaign.[22]

Daugherty was unanimously exonerated by the house committee in April. After several house members congratulated him, he leaned his head on the desk and sobbed. To Daugherty the matter now "was so well settled that there is no one believing any of the charges against me or any of the other gentlemen mentioned by the paper."[23] He was right in one respect. The *Post's* inability to substantiate its charges damaged the paper's reputation, and it shortly suspended publication without any compensation to its staff for salaries due them. According to one account, Daugherty distributed $1,800 among the hard-pressed staff with the wry remark that there were no "crisp $500 bills" in the disbursement. He then successfully sued the *Post* for the staff salaries and made no charge for legal services.[24]

The senatorial contest altered Daugherty's political career. He became a member of the Sherman-Hanna-McKinley wing of the party after having previously associated himself with Foraker. Upon the convening of the General Assembly in January 1892, House Speaker Laylin appointed Daugherty chairman of the important corporations committee and placed him on the judiciary committee. Meanwhile, Foraker representatives were excluded from all chairmanships. The Sherman faction also selected Daugherty as chairman of the house caucus, entrusting him with the responsibility of organizing legislative support for Governor McKinley's programs.[25]

Despite the immediate favors the Sherman wing provided, Daugherty's behavior in the senatorial contest had important adverse effects. Some distrust of him continued within the Sherman organization because of his hesitant vote. He also lost the support of Foraker and his many followers. Kurtz remarked sarcastically that he saw little of Daugherty after their last meeting in 1891, when Daugherty had promised to support Foraker.[26] Subsequently, Daugherty would fail in his challenge of Hanna's leadership because Foraker refused to help. Above all, Daugherty's conduct cast a shadow on his later career as critics often alluded to his alleged duplicity. As late as 1920 the New York *World* opposed Daugherty's appointment as Attorney General in part because it questioned his behavior in 1892.[27]

Such repercussions were not so apparent when Daugherty became Governor McKinley's floor leader in the house. The square- and smooth-faced McKinley, known for his kind and dignified manner and his dark frock coats, worked closely with Daugherty in the next two years. The two often breakfasted together in their hotel near the state house and shared many evenings. During the legislature sessions, as Daugherty later recalled, all the congenial McKinley had to do was to inform him, and he put the program through, always with alterations acceptable to the governor.[28] Daugherty engineered the joint resolution empowering McKinley to appoint a commission to codify the state tax laws and to recommend new provisions eventually providing for more equitable excise and corporate tax statutes.[29]

As legislative leader, Daugherty was also an extreme partisan who created considerable agitation in January 1892 when he introduced a bill to alter Columbus's form of government. His ripper was a typical reorganization bill used by both parties to place control of the city administration into the hands of those initiating the legislation. Such bills were introduced under the pretext of reform to disguise the real intent.

Daugherty's bill proposed to revoke a previous Democratic-inspired ripper by transferring appointive power from a Democratic mayor to a Republican control board. Republican Probate Judge L.D. Haggerty was to select the four-member board, members of which would be elected in succeeding years.[30]

Opposition to Daugherty's bill quickly emerged. Washington Gladden, minister of the First Congregational Church, spoke out against it. Even the Republican *Columbus Dispatch* balked, suggesting that the legislation "was prepared with a view of getting the most possible out of the city government for the few schemers who are pushing it for personal aggrandizement."[31] The bill remained buried in the house municipal committee until it appeared in March in an amended form. Despite a committee recommendation for passage, it was defeated by thirty-seven votes. The Foraker opposition strongly backed the Democrats partly because Daugherty sponsored the bill. On March 22 a disappointed Daugherty referred to the Forakerites' obstruction in a house speech attacking the Democrats: "I notice your [Democratic] appreciation by the smiles and applause which greets the remarks of those Republican members who oppose the measure."[32]

Daugherty's defeat was only temporary. The crippled bill reappeared in the house and was finally accepted after the attachment of Foraker amendments. It passed the senate in April 1892. After the Columbus mayor refused to implement several provisions of the new law because he thought them unconstitutional, Daugherty and his associates applied for a writ of mandamus from the Ohio supreme court, compelling the mayor to do so. Ironically, Daugherty was employed as one of the counsel in the court proceedings. In June 1893 the court allowed the writ, thus upholding the constitutionality of the bill.[33]

Daugherty's municipal reorganization schemes were not limited to Columbus. His home town suffered the same fate in April 1893 when a Daugherty bill passed the state legislature, placing the positions of chief of police, street supervisor, and corporation counsel under the appointive power of the city council instead of filling them by popular vote. Daugherty was elected to the city council in November, where he personally put the new charter into effect.[34] It was not surprising that factionalism increased within the Fayette Republican party as a result of his strong-arm methods.

Resentment against Daugherty had actually intensified in mid-1892 after his peculiar behavior in the Sherman-Foraker contest. In March, the *Cyclone and Fayette Republican* had considered him either a likely choice for United States Congress or secretary of state of Ohio. Daugherty sought the former, but he met opposition in the county when a Republican faction led by Mills Gardner backed A.R. Creamer, Daugherty's former law partner and a recent Fayette state senator. Because of an impending county convention battle in June, the newspaper suggested a primary to resolve the intraparty squabble. Creamer assented, but not Daugherty, who used his influence with county chairman Ace Gregg to have the Republican county convention settle the issue, thinking he could get its support.[35] After a bitter fight at the convention resulted in a party split, two Fayette Republican delegations went to the seventh district congressional convention held at Washington Court House—one favoring Daugherty, the other Creamer. The committee on credentials decided to split Fayette's vote evenly between the two delegations. This hurt both candidates, and on June 23 dark-horse George Wilson of Madison County was nominated after three days of balloting. The *Cyclone and Fayette Republican* blamed Daugherty for this predicament.[36]

Soon after his congressional defeat, Daugherty rejected Senator Sherman's offer of an assistant district attorneyship at Columbus.[37] He instead opened a law office there in early 1893 while still residing and retaining a practice in Washington Court House, where he ran for city council in March and was elected that November. In June he had been instrumental in the renomination of McKinley. Supported by the young Republicans of the party, he was chosen chairman of the Republican convention at Columbus, which endorsed McKinley for a second term.

Daugherty privately insisted after the gubernatorial campaign in November that he was through with politics.[38] He was completing his last term in the state legislature with only a councilmanic seat at Washington Court House to look forward to the following year. Still considered a young and promising political leader, he could afford to wait. Some newspapers even thought him a likely choice to succeed McKinley in 1896.[39]

Daugherty in fact strengthened his domination of county politics during his "retirement," but not without criticism. In August 1893, an outspoken Republican minority accused him of bossism when he selected his friend Ace Gregg for a common pleas judgeship.[40] Gregg died the following spring, and Daugherty's law partner, Horatio B. Maynard, replaced him. Daugherty came under fire when he again used his political power to obtain Maynard's nomination at the district judicial convention. His dominance of the Fayette executive committee enabled him to choose delegates who favored Maynard, and his political association with the party leader of Pickaway County provided Maynard with the additional support to win.[41]

The same opposition that denounced Daugherty's political control questioned his integrity as an attorney. In September 1894, Daugherty and two other attorneys were charged with unprofessional practice for allegedly extorting over $2,500 from an estate.[42] Daugherty asked Judge

Maynard for an investigation of the charges. Maynard quickly appointed a three-member committee of the bar, which exonerated them after an inquiry. They were probably justly absolved, but, as in the case of Daugherty's involvement in the 1892 senatorial election, the air remained clouded afterward. This time skeptics, who thought Maynard's committee a "whitewash," pointed to the need for a grand-jury investigation.[43]

Daugherty's eventual legal involvement in the Washington Court House riot of October 1894 contributed to his unpopularity in the county, although he later exaggerated its impact.[44] The incident that led to the riot occurred on October 9, when a Negro raped a prominent white woman at Parrett's Station. After apprehending the assailant, the sheriff requested national guard troops to prevent an angry mob from lynching him. On October 17, Governor McKinley sent two companies of troops under the command of Colonel Alonzo Coit to guard the prisoner, who was removed to the courthouse following a sentence of twenty years at a trial held the previous day. The prisoner was to be taken to the Columbus penitentiary on the day the troops arrived. At that time the mob tried to lynch him, and Coit instructed the militia to fire upon them as they were hammering down the doors of the courthouse. The shots killed seven and wounded fifteen. McKinley ordered a court of inquiry to investigate Coit's actions; it subsequently indicted the colonel for manslaughter.

Daugherty was in Cincinnati the day of the shooting and so did not hear about it until the train trip home. There he found people in a terrible state of anger. He accepted McKinley's invitation to be one of the attorneys to defend Coit despite the opposition he knew it would evoke in the county. The issue soon became political. Months after Coit's acquittal on March 5, 1895, Democrats and anti-Daugherty Republicans both criticized Daugherty for deserting Fayette to defend Coit.[45] The opposition Daugherty faced caused him to fight harder.

In fact, sometime in late 1894, Daugherty decided to become a candidate for public office again. The time seemed auspicious, for McKinley was serving his final term as governor. The task of choosing a successor fell upon the 1895 Republican state convention. Daugherty thought himself its worthiest prospect. Indeed, he had rendered McKinley enormous service while he had been Republican floor leader in the house. In 1893, as chairman of the state convention, he had backed his gubernatorial renomination and had introduced a resolution endorsing his administration at the Fayette County convention the following spring. Even so, Hanna made it known that he would favor Judge George K. Nash of Columbus, a long-time administration man, for governor.

Daugherty secured the allegience of the Hanna faction for the attorney general nomination upon realizing that he lacked their support for governor. But he had to win the endorsement of the county Republicans, which he had not been able to do in 1892. At the Fayette County convention in May, amid opposition, his law partner David Worthington and other loyal supporters dictated its permanent organization. They obtained an endorsement of Daugherty and authorized him to select Fayette's delegation to the May state convention at Zanesville. Daugherty happily announced to his friends that the "mugwump" opposition had "been laid on the shelf in politics here and I have assisted in the job with much delight."[46] His friends chartered a special Pullman sleeper for the entourage. On the side of the car as it left Washington Court House on the evening of May 27 was a large streamer, "For Attorney General, Harry M. Daugherty of Fayette." The train first stopped at Bloomington in Paint Township, where Republican women presented Daugherty with a huge floral bouquet. He was the recipient of additional boosting before the train pulled into the Zanesville station.

Zanesville was a compromise site between the Foraker faction, who had wanted Cincinnati, and the Hanna-Sherman forces, who had favored Columbus. As it turned out, this was one of the few convention compromises Foraker made. Sitting on stage, a familiar figure with his piercing eyes and drooping mustache, Foraker watched his floor managers carry out his carefully prepared strategy. His clever tactics surprised the opposition so completely that he was able to dominate the convention. He received endorsement of the delegates for senator in 1896, wrote the party platform, and chose almost the entire state ticket, including the gubernatorial nominee, Asa S. Bushnell. Since Foraker controlled the key committees and many of the large delegations, Sherman and Hanna were both rendered powerless. Their only consolation was McKinley's endorsement for the presidency in 1896.[47]

Foraker's convention strength weakened Daugherty's chances for nomination. William L. Parmenter of Lima, not Daugherty, was Foraker's choice for attorney general. On the first two ballots, however, Daugherty and Frank S. Monnett of Bucyrus were the leaders with Parmenter a poor third. On the following ballot, Hamilton County boss George B. Cox gave his delegation's eighty votes to Foraker's alternate choice, Monnett. The result was inevitable; Monnett defeated Daugherty by 486 to 236.[48]

The newspapers blamed Daugherty's defeat on geographic factors. Bushnell came from southern Clark County, and many nominees who preceded Monnett's selection were from southern Ohio. Logic dictated that the ticket be balanced by nominating a northern Ohioan for attorney general. Thus, Monnett and Parmenter were more suitable choices.[49] Actually, it probably mattered little to Foraker and Kurtz where Daugherty resided, for he had offended Foraker in 1892 and was considered a strong Hanna-Sherman man. Ironically, Foraker's political comeback paralleled Daugherty's rising political ambitions. Although losing a tough fight, Daugherty made a good impression among delegates from other counties, many of whom were or would become loyal friends. No headquarters was as crowded as Daugherty's with well-wishers and allies.[50]

By mid-February 1896, Daugherty again aspired to public office. He announced he was a candidate for United States Congress, provided that Fayette held a Republican primary preceding the congressional convention and that a majority of the county Republicans voted for him.[51] Daugherty stated later that the 1896 primary was his most bitter fight in politics. Blaming his participation in the Coit trial as the cause, he claimed that feeling against him was so great that the harness was removed from his horse while he was addressing a rally.[52] Nevertheless, on March 14 Daugherty defeated A.R. Creamer by 109 votes in the Republican primary county election. Editorials of the *Cyclone and Fayette Republican* helped Daugherty, since they surprisingly blamed Creamer for the weakened Republican county organization since 1892. That a Democrat nominated Creamer for mayor partly explains the anti-Creamer posture. Moreover, Creamer had not indicated that he would support the Republican nominee for congress if his congressional nomination attempt failed.[53] All of this might explain Daugherty's rare primary commitment. He could now challenge his boss image while campaigning against a candidate whose loyalty was in doubt.

To win the congressional nomination, Daugherty also had to receive party endorsement at the seventh United States congressional district convention at Springfield. Mark Hanna asked him, just prior to the convention, to use his position as chairman to select delegates to support McKinley for president at the Republican national convention in St. Louis. This was incompatible with Daugherty's nomination strategy for congress. His plan centered upon Madison County, one of five counties in the seventh congressional district. Pickaway and Miami sent anti-McKinley delegations to the Springfield convention while Fayette and Clark were both for McKinley. The remainder rested with Madison, which dispatched two delegations, each contesting for the right to be seated. George F. Wilson, the incumbent McKinley-Hanna congressional candidate, headed one, and John Locke led the anti-McKinley group. Locke had promised Daugherty that he would commit his county's twenty votes to him, provided that Fayette voted to recognize his rump delegation. This would have given Daugherty fifty-nine votes, more than enough for the nomination.[54]

Daugherty felt compelled to change his plans upon hearing from Hanna. He wired Hanna that he would "seat the Wilson delegation from Madison [even] if they cut my throat a moment later." After the pro-McKinley delegation had been selected and Daugherty had lost the nomination to Walter L. Weaver of Clark County, he again telegramed Hanna that he had "seated the Wilson delegation, and they have cut my throat."[55] Daugherty's only consolation was that he had been selected as a delegate to the Republican national convention in June, his first of five such conventions.

That fall Daugherty worked hard in behalf of the national ticket. The McKinley-Bryan fight was a crucial contest, for the Democrats' acceptance of free silver threatened to crystalize over twenty years of farm and labor dissatisfaction with Republicanism. Daugherty traveled over nine-thousand miles in the campaign. At the request of the Republican National Committee, he spoke in Ohio, Illinois, Indiana, Wisconsin, Minnesota, Nebraska, Kansas, and South Dakota. Generally, he focused his attack on the unfairness of free silver. Daugherty spoke at Howard, South Dakota a few hours after Populist Mary Lease to contest her denunciations of McKinleyism and the gold standard. The *Cyclone and Fayette Republican* claimed that Daugherty, at the conclusion of his speech, received "rousing cheers."[56]

In 1897, Daugherty gained some recognition for his work for McKinley. At the June Republican state convention in Toledo, he was selected chairman of the Republican state central committee, the most important party office in Ohio.[57] The Hanna forces dominated the convention itself as the Foraker faction had done in 1895. The only success Foraker and his lieutenants managed was the gubernatorial nomination for Bushnell. The bald-headed and walrus- mustachioed George K. Nash replaced Kurtz as chairman of the state executive committee, putting the pro-Hanna Nash in charge of the campaign.

The fall contest indirectly led to Daugherty's first altercation with Hanna. The Red Boss of Cleveland (so named for the red smoke of that industrial city) had been appointed to the Senate in February 1897 after Sherman became McKinley's secretary of state. Anxious to be elected in his own right, Hanna, for the first time in his career, went on the stump in an effort to insure the election of pro-Hanna legislators at the November polls. He appeared to have secured enough pledges to win despite the opposition of the Foraker faction and Democrats. Nevertheless, Foraker's lieutenants collaborated with Democrats in the postelection period in an effort to win over some of the Hanna pledges. Led by such pro-Foraker leaders as Kurtz and Republican Mayor Robert E. McKisson of Cleveland, they seemed to have enough support to defeat Hanna at the convening of the General Assembly in early January. Hanna, however, won by the narrowest of margins. James Otis, an anti-Hanna Republican, thought Hanna bought votes to win and accused a Hanna agent of bribery even before the final vote was tallied. On the morning of the Assembly contest, state senator Vernon Burke introduced a resolution calling for a Senate investigation of the bribery charges. The United States Senate also appointed a committee of investigation, which was to submit a report to the Senate Committee on Privileges and Elections on whether Hanna should be reseated or expelled.[58]

Hanna's friends thought it imperative that he be represented with counsel. His most loyal aide, Charles Dick, Secretary of the Republican National Committee, employed Daugherty and Cyrus H. Huling, a Columbus attorney-politician, for this purpose.[59] This seemingly routine incident contributed to a rift between Daugherty and Hanna which continued almost without interruption until Hanna's death in 1904.

Disagreement began in May 1898 after the Committee on Privileges and Elections failed to find enough evidence to implicate Hanna or his friends. On May 16, Daugherty wrote Hanna, enclosing bills to the Republican National Committee totaling $7,500 which was to be divided among Daugherty, Huling, and G.L. Marble, an attorney from Paulding County, for legal services in Hanna's behalf. Daugherty justified these charges for the "constant and careful work" that he and his associates had performed throughout the investigation, claiming that he had practically set aside his other legal work from January to May because of his extensive surveillance of the committees. He believed the National Committee should pay the expense since Hanna was its chairman and the attack was indirectly centered upon the Republican party.[60] Secretary Dick, who first read the letter, quickly replied that Daugherty's services were not a National Committee matter and, even if they were, the Committee did not have sufficient funds. He concluded his letter to Daugherty by questioning various aspects of the bills:

> It appears to me the bills are exorbitant and entirely out of proportion and I am sure they will so impress the Senator. I know nothing of the employ-meny [sic] of Mr. Marble; by whose authority or for what purpose he was retained in the matter. I don't think the matter ought to be presented to the Senator in this shape and I believe after you have had an opportunity to consider it you will thank me for speaking frankly.[61]

Daugherty refused to make revisions in the fee. He replied that Dick's "conduct in regard to our communications to Senator Hanna is a great surprise and an insult to us"; he informed the secretary the trio was coming to Washington to speak to Hanna personally. Daugherty ended the letter forcefully: "We are as unwilling to impose on Senator Hanna as you are, and we are also equally unwilling to be imposed upon."[62]

There are two accounts of Hanna's reaction to Daugherty's insistence that he or the Republican national committee pay the $7,500. Dick stated the following year that when he had asked Hanna what he should do, Hanna had replied: "Do? Do nothing, that's what the fellows have done—

nothing. Put it all in the hands of Andy Squire [Hanna's personal attorney] and let him settle." George A. Myers of Cleveland, a black barber and a local Hanna politician, in his correspondence with historian James Ford Rhodes over twenty years later, elaborated upon the senator's retort. Myers claimed that Hanna had said: "pay the——and let him go."[63] Whatever his specific response, Hanna was annoyed, even though he eventually paid Daugherty.

The difference between Daugherty and Hanna subsided within a month. In fact, no disagreement appeared to have occurred. At the June Republican state convention at Columbus, Daugherty became chairman of the state executive committee, and his friend Huling replaced him as state committee chairman. Hanna men were instrumental in these selections. Busily occupied in Washington, Hanna did not attend and, therefore, played no part in the convention proceedings. It is doubtful, however, that Daugherty was Hanna's choice, though he did not feel strongly enough about the outcome to prevent it. As chairman, Daugherty engineered the successful Republican campaign that fall. Secretary of State Charles Kinney, the head of the ticket, easily won reelection.[64]

Daugherty broke with Hanna the following year. The break came over Daugherty's desire to seek the gubernatorial nomination. Deterred in 1895, Daugherty had decided in the summer of 1898 that he must make the race in 1899.[65] Bushnell was approaching his last year of two terms. There might not be another opportunity until 1903 if Bushnell's successor were a Republican. Besides, Daugherty felt that the administration owed him an open field for he had worked extensively for the McKinley organization since 1892.

Both Ohio senators rejected Daugherty's candidacy. On January 5, 1899, Senator Foraker sarcastically said in an interview that it was "natural" for him to be for Daugherty, since Daugherty had provided such loyal support in the 1892 senatorial contest. A day later the *Cincinnati Enquirer* predicted that Nash was Hanna's choice for the nomination, although Hanna had not as yet openly supported any candidate.[66] Daugherty visited Hanna in Washington later that month to tell him "that a free field and no favor would be a desirable thing in Ohio." In early March, however, Hanna told him that is was not his year to make the race. Nevertheless, Daugherty announced that Hanna favored his nomination.[67]

Daugherty and his followers attempted to create the impression that the administration regarded him as favorably as it did Nash. On May 10, this strategy came into question when either Charles Dick or one of his lieutenants released a statement, elaborating upon how Daugherty "held up" Hanna in the bribery investigation the previous year. In a rebuttal the following day, Cyrus Huling claimed that the fee was reasonable and justified because of the extent of the work. Daugherty and Huling then proceeded to attack Dick in the various newspaper exchanges that week. They accused Dick of jealously resenting Daugherty's elevation as chairman of the state Republican executive committee. Dick, they said, was deliberately using his position with Hanna to curb Daugherty's influence in the party.[68]

Because of the publicized fight with Dick, Daugherty was no longer able to insist that Hanna approved of his candidacy. It was evident that the "puppet" Dick and other Hanna men would not have generated the anti-Daugherty publicity without Hanna's approval. All had not ended for Daugherty, however; his control of the Republican state executive and central committees enabled him to dominate the nominating convention organization. The Republican convention's temporary and permanent chairmen both would be Daugherty men. He also had the support of those who were dissatisfied with Hanna's leadership in the Ohio party. James W. Holcomb, who had fought the pro-Foraker McKisson and the Hanna forces in Cleveland to a standstill, was in constant communication with Daugherty before the Republican convention. In addition, Daugherty had his own organization of loyal followers, which included Huling; Charles Kinney, Ohio secretary of state; and Howard Mannington, former Ohio assistant secretary of state and now Daugherty's campaign manager. Daugherty's strategy precluded any attempt to align with the hostile Foraker crowd. He planned to present his case before the delegates as a deserving McKinley-Hanna man who sought an open convention in which Hanna would not dictate. His fight, however, was not as much one of principle as he claimed.[69] He believed in the same boss-oriented party system as Hanna.

In the week before June 1, the date of the state convention in Columbus, Daugherty appeared to have the backing of most of the delegates selected at the various Republican county conventions, including, potentially, Boss Cox's Hamilton County delegation. The skillful Cox, a blubbery, cigar-smoking bon vivant of 225 pounds, had been a major force in the party since the 1880s, when he aligned with Foraker. Some of Daugherty's managers had journeyed to Cincinnati for a meeting with Cox where, it was claimed afterward, an agreement had been made regarding the committee on credentials. This assured the seating of the contested Holcomb and Cox delegations and created the possibility of Cox's eventually swinging his delegation to the support of Daugherty. David Walker, Daugherty's brother-in-law, later said that Cox at least had promised not to use his votes in Nash's behalf. On May 27, Daugherty announced at his Neil House headquarters that at least 350 delegates were pledged to him, while Nash—Hanna's choice—claimed about 275 votes and Lieutenant Governor Asa Jones—Foraker's candidate—followed, a poor third. On the following day President McKinley said in Washington that "Daugherty is a good fellow and would make a good governor" but refrained from endorsing any particular candidate.[70]

On the day before the opening of the convention, Daugherty left his headquarters and walked down the Neil House corridor to Hanna's rooms, even though Hanna had earlier failed to recognize the Daugherty group as he passed by their headquarters. The men shook hands, whereupon Hanna said, "Well, Harry, this is a great fight that you have been putting up." Daugherty retorted that it was not a fight but a contest. He went on to say that he did not relish being denounced as an antiadministration man. Hanna politely replied, "That is wrong, Harry, I consider . . . you . . . as good an Administration man as I am."[71] This was Daugherty's last conversation with Hanna until after the "contest." To the end, Hanna's legendary charm had concealed a ruthless streak.

Daugherty's chances faltered in the early hours of convention morning as a result of decisions made in several conferences held from the previous evening until the convention met the next day. The most important resulted from a Cox-Hanna meeting just after midnight. Cox, who privately despised Daugherty for his past disloyalty and had preferred a compromise candidate from Hamilton County, agreed to favor Nash until the third ballot in exchange for Hanna's promise to nominate Cincinnati ex-mayor John A. Caldwell for lieutenant governor.[72] Cox's eighty-six votes from Hamilton gave Nash a tremendous advantage.

James Holcomb nominated Daugherty on the second day of the convention. According to the *Cleveland Plain Dealer*, the cheering that followed Holcomb's speech meant very little, as the very men who cheered were soon to cut his throat. Nash led Daugherty at the end of the first ballot, 289 to 211. On the second vote, Nash was nominated as Cox swung his eighty-six delegates to the Hanna side, encouraging other delegations to follow. Nash received 461 to Daugherty's 205 votes on the final ballot. Amid the demonstration, Daugherty walked to the platform where he spoke briefly:

> This is a good deal like a man dancing a jig at his own funeral, nevertheless there is a great deal of pleasure in doing it. I thought it might be becoming . . . [to] cheerfully ratify the choice of this convention. To my friends . . . I have nothing to offer but sincere thanks. To those who have supported the victor in this contest, I bear no malice.
>
> I will remain a private citizen—not, perhaps, because of my own choice, because that is a privilege that no man dare deny me. I am determined to have my own way about something.[73]

Daugherty waged a good fight in spite of being opposed by the Hanna and the Foraker factions—the two major wings of the Ohio party. His smooth organization surprised both Hanna and Nash. He failed to win not only because of the duplicity of Cox, but also because Hanna was adamant in his refusal to allow an open convention. Although many pro-Hanna delegates had favored Daugherty, they were reluctant to vote for him when it became clear that Nash was Hanna's choice.[74] They had their state jobs, patronage, and political influence to weigh against a candidate who was unable to assure them of certain success.[75]

Harry Daugherty's political career was temporarily frustrated after his defeat.[76] He was never included in the party councils as long as Hanna lived, or Charles Dick (Hanna's senatorial successor), Joseph Foraker, and George Cox remained powerful. Their opposition persisted because Daugherty had been judged disloyal, a cardinal sin for those who lacked sufficient power in the Foraker-Hanna era. Because of his betrayal of Foraker in 1892, and Hanna later, he was no longer to be trusted by the party hierarchy despite his extensive party service in the 1890s. But for the time being Daugherty ignored these bitter realities as he retired to French Lick, Indiana, for a vacation before returning to campaign for Nash in the fall.

On the Fringes of Power
1900-1910

DAUGHERTY'S elimination as a significant political influence began immediately after the 1899 Republican state convention. Dick replaced him as chairman of the state executive committee, and Myron Norris of Youngstown succeeded Cyrus Huling as state central committee chairman. Hanna's program of intraparty harmony in the fall campaign curtailed any further action. In the gubernatorial race, Nash faced the strong opposition of John R. McLean, the *Cincinnati Enquirer* magnate, and Samuel "Golden Rule" Jones, the independent mayor of Toledo. Consequently, Hanna sought maximum support for Nash and the remaining state ticket. Even Daugherty energetically campaigned for his reelection.

But Daugherty refused to accept a secondary role in the postelection period. In January 1900, his candidate, Burgess McElroy of Knox County, supported by other anti-Hanna Republicans, won the clerkship fight in the house, and John P. Maynard, the son of his former law partner, was appointed assistant chief clerk. No longer serving in the legislature, Daugherty still had some power there. His supporters, however, collaborating with the Democrats, failed to defeat the Nippert reorganization bill, which had been introduced by the governor's friends to repay Boss Cox for his 1899 support. The Cincinnati ripper enabled Cox to control the municipal government after a fusion group had overturned him in 1898.[1]

Daugherty's actions induced the Hanna-Cox organizations to collaborate temporarily with the anti-Hanna Kurtz forces against him.[2] As a result, Daugherty found himself politically checkmated. This was most evident in April: the Republican state convention at Columbus was so controlled by the Hanna organization that some observers claimed Dick himself had brought the party platform with him from Washington to be rubber stamped by the delegates. In fact, Howard Mannington had faced so much opposition in his quest to be nominated for secretary of state that he withdrew three days before the convention met. Hanna's men also stripped Daugherty of power in the reorganization of the state central committee, conceding him only the twelfth congressional district.[3] Daugherty was conspicuously missing from the Ohio delegation, which went to the Republican national convention that June to renominate William McKinley as the party's standard-bearer.

The Hanna organization contested Daugherty's control of Fayette in the following year. Dick worked with the anti-Daugherty Republicans to establish a separate county organization. In June, the Fayette County convention failed to settle the issue, for two delegations emerged to represent Fayette at the Republican state convention held in Columbus, one led by Daugherty and the other by Grant and Thomas W. Marchant.[4] By rejecting any compromise with Daugherty, the Marchants expected the committee on credentials to vote on the acceptance of their delegation. On June 25, the pro-Dick committee voted twenty to one against seating the Daugherty contingent.[5] This marked the first year that Daugherty was not a delegate since 1888; his political influence had reached its lowest ebb.

In the next five years, Daugherty sought to bolster his political position by courting the leaders of both factions. Always a practical politician, he outwardly harbored no animosities now that he lacked political power. He honored requests from Chairman Dick's office to speak in behalf of state Republican candidates and paid homage to the party leadership. At a Republican rally in Washington Court House on October 23, 1902, for example, he shared the platform with Governor Nash and Senator Hanna. He introduced Nash by saying that "no one could have served better or more wisely." He then complimented Hanna and the party, contending that "no organization except the schools and the churches has done so much good for the country." Daugherty also privately assured party leaders of his support. He told Foraker, whom he courted most, not to worry about the congressional district comprising Fayette because Congressman J.M. Willis "will vote for you as his instructions and inclinations are both that way." In congratulating Foraker on his splendid campaign, Daugherty continued to do what was politically necessary as he awaited the opportunity for a comeback.[6]

One of his most perplexing problems was obtaining patronage. He wrote both Dick and Foraker for consideration in the appointment of friends to federal positions. On one occasion Daugherty reiterated to Dick that he "had a talk with poor old Charlie Kinney . . . and he is really in need of some help if it can be given to him."[7] In 1905 he sought the appointment of Mannington as surveyor of customs in Columbus. Foraker was willing to favor Mannington despite one Columbus businessman's claiming that he "was one of the most profane men that ever struck the town; everybody was glad when he left and they surely don't want any more of him."[8] The senior senator dropped the matter, however, when

Senator Dick, who was entitled to name the surveyor, refused to endorse him. Undeterred, Daugherty immediately wrote Dick that he had certain suggestions regarding the collectorship which were of "great benefit to the party and yourself."[9] He received better treatment from Nash, who assured the Daugherty leader of Paulding County that patronage would be provided to all loyal Republicans regardless of faction.[10]

Throughout this period Daugherty retained enough of a foothold in the party to assert himself later. Even after the setbacks of 1901, he still influenced several Republicans in the legislature who had known him since his first term in the General Assembly. They saw a dimension of his personality that often lay hidden to adversaries. Besides being combative, ambitious, and cunning, he was congenial and witty. He imbibed and swapped stories with the best of them.[11] Daugherty was also considerate—and practical—enough to look out for friends. Rarely did he fail to honor their many resquests. He was persuasive and courageous, and many still greatly admired him for his stand against the goliath Hanna in 1899. Some legislators saw him as an alternative to party domination by Hanna or Foraker whom for varying reasons they disliked.[12] Consequently, they were again prepared to support him for high office. Others, despite loyalty to existing leaders, were occasionally willing to favor Daugherty because they thought well of him. In February 1902, George Myers asked Daugherty to use his connections to defeat a proposed state measure that placed Negro barbers in an inferior position within the profession. Daugherty played a major part in its defeat.[13]

By 1902, Daugherty appeared to have recovered politically. He won an important victory in January when William S. McKinnon, an Ashtabula friend Daugherty strongly supported, was selected speaker of the Ohio house. Since this position carried the power to appoint all house committees, Daugherty men would again receive recognition.[14] The victory was made possible because Hanna, who disapproved of Foraker's choice and lacked the votes to elevate his own man, reluctantly threw his support to the more independent McKinnon. Later that year Daugherty regained control of the Fayette Republican organization and came to the May Republican state convention in Cleveland at the head of his delegation.[15]

Almost immediately talk resumed of his elevation to the governorship as Nash's successor in 1903. Securing headquarters at the Hollenden Hotel, he sought out old friendships that might deliver him the nomination. Hanna later made it clear, however, that he preferred Myron T. Herrick, a Cleveland banker and a long-time underwriter of party deficits. This caused Daugherty to postpone any announcement of candidacy until after the 1903 spring election in Cleveland. He decided to challenge only if the Democrats carried the municipal contest, thereby tarnishing Herrick. As it turned out, the Republicans swept the election. In June, Daugherty again was the chairman of the Fayette delegation to the state convention, which was still dominated by the Hanna faction. His appointment to the Rules and Order of Business Committee was a meager consolation for the elusive gubernatorial nomination.[16]

The following year the Marchant group in Fayette again challenged Daugherty's control of the county, charging that his brother Mal, the county chairman, obstructed the implementation of a primary. After a heated fight, two delegations went to the state convention, where Daugherty managed to obtain the recognition of the credentials committee. He also became a delegate to the June Republican national convention in Chicago, serving on the Rules Committee that assisted in Theodore Roosevelt's nomination.[17] His assignment undoubtedly occurred because of the backing of Roosevelt's influential Ohio friend, James R. Garfield, another anti-Dick Republican. For the first time, in 1905, he became chairman of the Franklin County delegation at the Republican state convention, which met in Columbus.

While he had regained some political power, Daugherty was never an important cog in the Ohio Republican party as long as Hanna, Foraker, or Cox ruled. Hanna died on February 15, 1904, one month after his reelection, but Dick, the Hanna workhorse, replaced him in the Senate. An alliance of Dick, Cox, and Governor Herrick ran state politics in 1904. The four delegates-at-large to the Republican national convention included that triumvirate, along with Foraker, whose organization failed to place even one man on the new state central committee.

In 1905, the Dick-Cox-Herrick leadership faltered. Herrick proved an unpopular governor, especially with the temperance and church groups, because of his failure to pass the Brannock liquor law favoring local option in residential districts. The sporting crowd also detested him for vetoing a measure legalizing the sale of pools at race tracks. Cox had problems as well. Inspired by Lincoln Steffens's "Ohio: A Tale of Two Cities," muckrakers made Cox synonymous with the evils of urban bossism. Even Secretary of War William Howard Taft spoke out against the Hamilton County boss in an October speech at Akron. Since Dick and Foraker also were the custodians of the existing order in Ohio, they too were vulnerable to the progressive impulse sweeping the nation. As long as they controlled, reform was impossible.

After the revelations of "Coxism" and Herrick's defeat in November, several state Republican leaders grew more intolerant of the state machine, which retrenched under a newly-formed Dick-Foraker-Cox alliance. By 1906, Harry Daugherty was one of the leaders of a budding insurgent movement that included Theodore Burton, seven times congressman from Cleveland, the opportunistic Herrick, and Robert Wolfe, who later became one of Daugherty's chief protagonists. Twenty-eight years old when he came to Columbus, Wolfe was one of the founders of the Godman Shoe Company. Afterward he and his brother, Harry P., borrowed $300 to form a shoe manufacturing business, which by the 1920s evolved into the "Wear-U-Well" company with 3,000 outlets. In 1903, they also acquired the *Ohio State Journal* and two years later, the *Columbus Dispatch*. As publisher, the stocky Robert was active in community affairs and dedicated to honest and efficient government. After 1912 his progressivism and independence caused him to support the Wilson Presidency and several state Democrats, thereby antagonizing staunch Republicans like Daugherty.[18]

In 1906, Wolfe subscribed to the same progressive principles that were toppling political machines and boss-rule throughout the country. And it was only natural for Daugherty to wish to lead the insurgency in Ohio. In 1899, he had strongly opposed one-man control in the selection of political candidates. This brought him considerable support, alarming party leaders who attempted to deal with him without eradicating the sources of his popularity. But given Hanna's opposition to his gubernatorial candidacy, Daugherty's antibossism was pragmatic. In 1906, he responded similarly because the Dick-Foraker-Cox combination had nearly relegated him to political obscurity. That they and Herrick had indirectly contributed to the Democratic landslide of 1905 only strengthened his anticombination opposition. He loftily explained to one supporter that "I am so thoroughly saturated with Republicanism that I must always take a hand to some extent in assisting the party. I want to see it kept clean and see it give every man a show."[19]

Daugherty's experience reinforces recent scholarship on the Progressive era that stresses the diverse motivations of its participants.[20] Daugherty's insurgency represented neither conscience, principle, nor fear of the masses. His interest instead seemed to be primarily power for personal rather than for social ends, setting him apart from progressive bosses like Tom Johnson of Cleveland. In this respect he was no different from any of the old guard. To succeed, however, he had to adopt the guise of the reformer. For this reason he also supported such progressive principles as primary election laws, stronger railroad regulation, and tariff revision.[21] Nevertheless, in 1912 he would oppose the progressive work of the Ohio Constitutional Convention and would fight the progressive rebellion in Ohio. Unlike most insurgents in this decade, Daugherty's progressivism was shortlived, for it ended after the abortive effort of 1906.

The other major leader of the insurgency, Congressman Theodore Burton, complemented Daugherty. Where Daugherty was persuasive, occasionally hot-headed, and impulsive, Burton was dispassionate, cautious, and dull. Aside from serving capably in the Congress since 1888 where he occasionally showed flashes of being independent-minded, he had published several books, including one on John Sherman. Indeed, the tall, slightly-built and quiet-mannered Burton looked more like a college professor than a politician. Like Daugherty, Burton was a progressive for a season.[22] Exactly what his motives were is not really clear. He did, however, covet Foraker's senatorial seat, which he obtained in January 1909 with Roosevelt's blessings. By then his reform zeal had cooled considerably; he became in time a strong defender of Taft and the old guard, thereby alienating progressive elements. Next to Burton and Daugherty in active leadership, Herrick clearly acted opportunistically. The Democratic antibossism campaign of 1905, which crippled the Republican ticket severely, made a believer of the defeated Herrick. But after the 1906 insurgency failed, he too returned to a conservative position, eventually backing Taft, who rewarded him with an ambassadorship to France.

Daugherty's criticism of state Republican leadership began at the close of the state campaign of 1905.[23] On March 30, 1906, he moved into a more insurgent position in a speech at the Lincoln Club banquet at Toledo. His talk focused on the Hepburn amendment to the Interstate Commerce Act, which best expressed the conflict between President Roosevelt and the conservative Foraker. Daugherty, following the progressive sentiment of the time, enthusiastically supported Roosevelt's regulation proposals, arguing that "railroads have not been as just in their dealings with the people during the past twenty-five years as they might have been." The interests of the people, according to Daugherty, must take precedence over those of the railroads. His speech was an indirect slap at Foraker, who disagreed with the President's desire to strengthen the regulatory powers of the Interstate Commerce Commission.[24]

By mid-August, Daugherty had already aligned himself with Burton, Herrick, and Wolfe in an effort to fight the state machine. They openly revealed their dissent in the month preceding the Republican state convention. On August 16, Burton, in a speech before the Cleveland Tippecanoe Club, denounced the clique within the Ohio Republican party for exploiting personal interests instead of advancing the party welfare. He directed his attack at Dick and Foraker who controlled the state organization. Since they were "at variance with the President and the Republican party of Ohio," Burton proposed that the approaching Republican state convention endorse them "less cordially" than it did the administration.[25] Later that month Daugherty repeated Burton's statements and then added several of his own in an address at the Cleveland Cuyahoga League of Republican Clubs. Daugherty insisted that, for the success of the party, Dick must not again be chairman of the Republican state executive committee. "The Republican party," according to Daugherty, "needs no bosses, and all the semblance of bossism should be avoided by its representatives." The only pro-Dick leader who spoke out at the meeting was Forakerite Warren G. Harding of Marion, who favored the continuance of Dick as state chairman and who also supported a strong endorsement of the two senators.[26]

By the end of August, Daugherty, the field marshal of the insurgent preconvention campaign, contested Dick's strength in both the county and congressional district organizations. The latter selected the state central committee, which in turn elected the chairman of the state executive committee. To remove chairman Dick, Daugherty needed a central committee dedicated to his objectives. That meant the priming of an insurgent candidate for central committeeman in each congressional district with the hope that a majority of the candidates were elected in the various district caucuses at the state convention. When the anti-Dick Arthur Garford of Elyria indicated a desire to be central committeeman from the fourteenth congressional district, he immediately asked Daugherty to get "in touch with some of your confidential friends and supporters in Richland, Morrow, and Knox Counties and request them to support me for the position." It was in this way that Garford and others secured the allegiance of their district organization. On September 9, three days before the Republican state convention at Dayton, Daugherty claimed that he had the support of a majority of the districts.[27]

The Daugherty-Burton challenge was also active at the county Republican conventions in obtaining delegate support in the week preceding the state convention. Daugherty's success was often remarkable. At one of the first meetings, the Republicans of Portage County, comprising a segment of Dick's congressional district, declared against a policy of permitting United States senators to act as state chairman as it invited "the grave charge of bossism." Allen and Richland Counties also quickly selected anticombine delegations. The greatest blow to the Dick forces, however, came on September 8, when Cuyahoga and Summit Counties chose anti-Dick delegations. The latter, Dick's home county, refused to endorse him unequivocally. That day seven other counties declared against Dick for state chairman. In an evening interview Daugherty predicted that Charles Dick would not be the chairman of the state executive committee.[28]

The Foraker and Dick forces did not play dead in the face of the insurgent groundswell. Both defended their senatorial records in the press. On August 26, Foraker stated that he favored Dick's reelection as state executive chairman. Dick also embarked upon a vicious counterattack in which he claimed that Daugherty was only after the party organization as a prelude to seeking the gubernatorial nomination in 1907.[29] On the day preceding the convention, Dick and his lieutenants cornered many of the county leaders in a campaign for more votes.

The Republican state convention, held September 11-12 in Dayton, at the convention hall of the National Cash Register Company, witnessed two significant encounters between the Daugherty-Burton-Herrick insur-

gents and the Dick-Foraker supporters. The first centered on the chairmanship of the Republican state committees. On the first day of the
convention, each congressional district delegation held a caucus to elect
its central committeeman. The insurgent cause weakened when the Dick
men won thirteen out of twenty-one congressional caucuses. The newly
organized central committee then proceeded to elect officers to the state
central and executive committees. Walter Brown, the pro-Dick political
boss of Toledo, became the central committee's new chairman on a twelve
to seven vote, and Dick retained the executive chairmanship by a fourteen
to seven vote, which meant that party control would remain with the
incumbent group. Daugherty, however, refused to accept Dick's chairmanship victory as conclusive. On the morning of September 12, he issued
a statement that the chairmanship issue would be brought before the
convention that same day. He blamed the previous day's defeat on the
hundreds of federal and state employees who spent their money in Dick's
behalf.[30]

True to his word, Daugherty contested Dick's reelection when the
convention met again. James Holcomb, a Daugherty delegate from Cleveland, introduced a resolution calling for Dick's removal. As the junior
senator gritted his teeth, Daugherty and Burton ascended the rostrum to
argue against his continuance as chairman. Daugherty first answered
Dick's accusation that personal ambitions accentuated his motives by
asking the convention to "write in its platform . . . the proposition that I
shall never aspire to any office, appointive or elective." After explaining
that his opposition to Dick was impersonal, he demanded that Dick
withdraw for the welfare of the party. But Foraker's compelling address
resurrected the names of the immortal McKinley and Hanna, for whom
Dick had served as chairman. He wondered who could discard Dick now?
Not most of the delegates; they endorsed Dick's reelection by a 573-285
vote. The two senators also received the delegates' unqualified endorsement and their votes in defeating Burton's resolutions for tariff revision
and an immediate United States senatorial nomination primary.[31] Although conceding some moderate reform proposals, Foraker and Dick
proved too formidable for the insurgents. It did not help that the aloof
Burton was uninspiring and that Daugherty and Herrick played such
leading roles, providing credence to Dick's accusations that it was a revolt
to supplant machines. Warren G. Harding, the platform committee
chairman, wrote in his Marion *Daily Star*: "The amiable and talented Mr.
Daugherty shuddering about bossism is a spectacle to amuse all of
Ohio."[32]

Even though disappointed, Daugherty and Burton optimistically
looked to the future. Burton assured his friends that he was awaiting the
movement's fight at the next state convention in 1908. Daugherty prom-

ised that the "fire has just been kindled, and it will not be speedily quenched."[33] The rhetoric of the moment soon passed after the Dick-directed Republican ticket emerged victorious in the fall campaign. In 1907, Daugherty and Burton aligned with the William Howard Taft organization, where they continued their opportunistic fight against the Foraker and Dick forces, which weakened under the mounting opposition that included President Roosevelt and his heir apparent, Taft. Roosevelt detested Foraker for having opposed his progressive programs and for having criticized his handling of the Brownsville affair in 1906, which involved the President's unjust dismissal of three black infantry companies. Foraker's announced presidential ambitions for 1908 convinced Roosevelt and Taft that he should retire from politics entirely. In July 1907, Taft unhesitantly rejected suggestions that he endorse Foraker's reelection in return for the senator's presidential endorsement. Roosevelt had already begun to transfer federal patronage in Ohio from Foraker and his ally Dick to Taft and Burton.

Taft was a hefty, amiable man of over 300 pounds who came from a distinguished Cincinnati family. Upon graduation from Yale and the completion of his studies at Cincinnati Law School, he had entered Ohio politics and was soon appointed to the state Superior Court to conclude an unexpired term. The next year, 1888, he was elected in his own right. He never sought another elective office until he campaigned for the presidency in 1908. Instead, in succession, Taft became Solicitor General of the United States, a judge of the Federal Circuit Court, the president of the Philippine Commission, Governor General of the Philippines, and Roosevelt's Secretary of War and his unofficial assistant president. As both judge and administrator, Taft had impressed. Consequently, Roosevelt's selection of Taft as his successor would come as no great surprise.

Through the hulking and politically inexperienced Taft, Daugherty hoped to recapture influence in Ohio politics and bag the governorship or a senate seat for himself. His initial encounter with Taft had come at the 1905 Republican state convention in Columbus, where the Secretary of War served as temporary and permanent chairman. Unable to attend the evening reception for Taft, Daugherty extended his hand the following day. Soon after the convention, he wrote Taft, congratulating him on his address and for his services to the country. "Perhaps," he concluded, "you may be working too hard Mr. Secretary and I trust you will be careful of your health."[34] The Taft Papers reveal that until 1908 their scant correspondence included mostly patronage requests from Daugherty, which Taft did not fulfill.

Daugherty was first mentioned as a Taft supporter in January 1907, but he said nothing publicly until March when he delivered a speech at the W. Aubrey Thomas Club banquet in Cleveland. There, he strongly implied that he favored Taft's candidacy, which quashed rumors that he would back Vice President Charles W. Fairbanks, a personal friend.[35] By the following year, Daugherty would play a major part in Taft's campaign. At the March Republican state convention in Columbus, he was a leading figure in initiating a resolution endorsing Taft's presidential nomination.[36] Neither Foraker nor Dick attended to witness the Taft steamroller that was so reminiscent of the Hanna, Dick, or Foraker-controlled sessions. In June, Daugherty went to the Republican national convention at Chicago as a delegate and as vice chairman of the committee on credentials. So diligently did he function in that capacity that he was called the "chief chauffeur of the Chicago steamroller."[37] Taft received 702 votes to Foraker's sixteen, a devastating defeat for the senator.

The most damaging blow to Foraker came in September, when William Randolph Hearst of the *New York Journal* revealed a series of letters between the senator and John D. Archbold, vice president of the Standard Oil Company. The 1900-1903 correspondence indicated that Foraker had been the legislative agent of Standard Oil, receiving retainer fees of $29,500. This revelation so damaged Foraker that his candidacy was in question months preceding the election in January 1909.

That fall a cluster of candidates jostled into position for Foraker's seat. A certain contender as early as the preconvention campaign and friendly to Taft's lieutenants Arthur Vorys and Carmi Thompson, Daugherty more than likely had backing from the Taft organization immediately after the convention. The situation changed in the fall when Taft's older half-brother, Charles P. Taft, owner of the *Cincinnati Times-Star*, indicated that he too had senatorial aspirations.[38] With the support of President Roosevelt, Congressman Theodore Burton had also entered the race.

Perhaps because of the competition, Daugherty never publicly announced his candidacy. He covertly solicited the help of political friends like Arthur Garford, whom he wrote on November 9 for "open and active support." Garford replied that, while he had always admired Daugherty, he had been committed to Burton since November 1907.[39] Daugherty presumably received similar replies, for by December 2 Burton was informed by James Cassidy, his clerk on the House Committee on Rivers and Harbors, that Daugherty was "ready for a deal." Daugherty apparently wanted Burton's support in 1911 for senator or governor in return for his backing of Burton now.[40] On December 4, the *Ohio State Journal* reported that he was withdrawing from the senate contest.

In the closing weeks, the senate race developed into a three-way battle among Burton, Taft, and Foraker. Taft subsequently withdrew on December 31, announcing that a united party was more important than personal ambitions. This induced Boss Cox, who had deserted Foraker, to maneuver from Taft to Burton, causing Foraker to announce his retirement. Burton was selected by the Republican caucus on January 2, 1909, and elected to the Senate on January 12. In reviewing the election, Burton's biographer, Forrest Crissey, wrote that "probably no other supporter of the Cleveland Congressman contributed more to the success of his campaign than did Mr. Daugherty."[41]

In the next two years, Daugherty played a nominal role in politics. There was a compelling reason for this. Eagerly seeking Dick's seat in the Senate since Burton's victory, he found his ambitions shattered in the 1910 gubernatorial race, when Democratic incumbent Judson Harmon defeated Harding in a landslide 100,000 vote plurality. Enough Democrats came in on Harmon's coattails to give the party a substantial majority in both houses of the state legislature. The Democrats really won the senatorial race in November, even though the General Assembly did not conduct the election until January 10, 1911. At that time Atlee Pomerene, the Democratic nominee, gathered eighty-six votes in the legislature to Daugherty's seventeen.[42] Daugherty led the other Republican aspirants, although he had not campaigned for the office after Harmon's victory.

Despite another disappointing defeat, Daugherty could find some consolation in that he had contributed to the demise of the Foraker-Dick dominance. The old party system largely remained, but he was now more a part of it. His political future depended on whether the Taft organization, in the crucial contests of 1912, could overcome the Democratic success in Ohio and the progressive opposition that existed within the party. In the interim, Daugherty devoted his attention to a successful practice that had begun to focus increasingly on corporate law after his arrival in Columbus.

Family, Law, and Lobbying
1893-1922

POLITICS was at the center of, but never completely dominated, Daugherty's life. His legal career and family also absorbed his time. In one way or another, each was interrelated and affected the other. Of the three, domestic matters received the least attention.

In early 1894, the Daugherty family moved to Columbus. By then, it included Emily, seven, and Draper, six. In the next ten years, the Daughertys lived in four Columbus residences. It was not until 1904 that Daugherty purchased a three-story red stucco house on East Town Street, an exclusive area occupied by professional people like himself. The top floor was Daugherty's study, which he later boasted contained one of the finest libraries in Columbus. Besides a fashionable home, the family had other material comforts such as new automobiles and membership in one of the local country clubs. The children had the opportunity to attend exclusive schools.

Emily graduated from the National Park Seminary in Washington, D.C. In October 1908, in what the local papers described as one of the largest weddings that fall, she married Ralph, the lawyer son of Dr. F.S. Rarey of Columbus. After a honeymoon of two weeks, they were entertained at a reception at the Daugherty home attended by 250 guests. After his dismissal from Culver Military Academy for hazing, Draper completed his high school education in Columbus. Despite his father's urgings, he had no desire for college. Instead his parents bought him a half interest in a clothing store on South High Street. In 1910, he married Dessa Gibson of New York City with whom he lived less than a year because of incompatibility. Following a divorce, he wed Jean Bowers in 1917, the daughter of West Virginia Congressman George Bowers.

Despite material and social advantages, the family had more than its share of trouble. The children's mother, Lucy, was so afflicted with arthritis that it crippled her by 1915. Her widowed sister lived with the family in order to help out. By 1919, she too became so ill that she was unable to care for herself. While Daugherty remained genuinely devoted to Lucy (no philandering was ever associated with him), his frequent absences restricted his usefulness. Emily meanwhile was physically and often emotionally ill. Because of various female disorders, including a hormone imbalance which caused a profuse menstrual flow, she was unable to bear children and was frequently on medication. The drugs the physicians prescribed eventually turned her into an addict. Early in her marriage, Emily found herself in and out of sanitariums. In the spring of 1917, for example, she spent a number of weeks at Dr. Charles E. Sawyer's Sanitarium near Marion. Her condition did not improve, however, and an increasing dependence on alcohol only compounded the problem. In August 1918, on the way to visiting Draper's wife in Martins-ville, West Virginia, she "blew into" Washington, D.C., drunk. She never did see Jean. In subsequent years, her physical and mental problems became even more critical, the latter bordering on psychosis.[1]

Even more tragic was Draper's life. Undisciplined as a youth, he was irresponsible and unstable as an adult. As a handsome, dapper bachelor, Draper had spent much time chasing governors' daughters and other socialites. He also developed a drinking problem, for which he was committed to sanitariums in 1913 and 1915. Consequently, the clothing store failed, as did his other business ventures, all of which caused his father constant concern. Draper's second marriage and brief military career, in which he served under General John Pershing in the Mexican campaign and as an officer in the Third Division during the World War, represented temporary stability. But in France he was gassed and wound-ed and suffered from double pneumonia. As a result, his alcoholism was acute in the postwar period. He failed to retain steady employment, got into financial difficulties, and kept company with pleasure seekers. By 1923, the decline was precipitous.[2]

Harry Daugherty's frequent absences from home undoubtedly had contributed to Draper's instability. Surely family life in general suffered. During Draper's childhood his state legislator father had lived mostly in Columbus, while the family remained in Washington Court House. From that time on politics was to occupy Daugherty's evenings and even holi-days. Moreover, an expanding law practice eventually carried him, for weeks at a time, to such distant points as El Paso, Charleston, Atlanta, New York City, Washington, D.C., and Alaska. Only on rare occasions did his family accompany him, and only in periods of serious family illness did he reduce his workload. It is not surprising that Draper later complained of his father's neglect. Never having had a father model himself, Daugherty did not know how to be a father. Being an over-achiever only intensified the problem. Consequently, he often spoiled Draper to compensate for his frequent inattention. On countless occa-sions after his son had fallen into financial or other personal difficulties,

Daughety came to his assistance, always protecting him from legal or criminal actions. As late as 1926, when Draper was thirty-eight years old, Daugherty still repeatedly referred to him as "boy" and provided him with nearly $4,000 to purchase a half interest in an insurance business, which quickly failed.[3] Apparently Daugherty never realized that Draper's alcoholism and his irresponsible actions that brought him attention might have been related to paternal mishandling. Nor did he understand why Draper resented him while still depending on his support.

What effect Daugherty's family life had on his political and legal careers is of course conjectural. Daugherty's occasional impulsive political behavior, however, might well have been related to the frustration he obviously felt from the family situation. There is little doubt that Daugherty was drawn even more into political and legal activities because of family difficulties which he felt powerless to resolve. The considerable family-related expenses also necessitated more attention to money making. This occupied much more of his time after he shifted his law practice to Columbus.

Daugherty made the move in 1893, though he still retained an office and his home in Washington Court House. The following year, after moving the family to Columbus, he formed a partnership with David Worthington, a former state senator from Fayette. Worthington accepted a judgeship in 1898, leaving Daugherty unattached until he joined John E. Todd in 1903. The firm of Daugherty and Todd expanded in 1910 when Daugherty's son-in-law entered the partnership, which continued until Daugherty's appointment as Attorney General in 1921. Also a fixture was the efficient and discreet secretary, Katherine M. Carroll, whom Daugherty employed in 1910 and retained until his death in 1941. From 1903 to 1917, the firm had its offices in the bay-windowed and steel-framed Wyandotte building, conveniently located adjacent to the state capital on West Broad Street. The law offices were moved to the Huntington National Bank Building in 1917 when the Wyandotte was purchased by the state to handle the bureaucratic overflow.

Although Daugherty handled criminal cases in his earlier legal career, he was primarily a corporation lawyer.[4] In the 1890s, he became the attorney for the B & O Railroad and by 1899 he was also the attorney and a major stockholder of the Scioto Traction Company. Living in a period when small telephone, gas, and electric plants were being merged into larger systems, Daugherty became especially adept at obtaining new charters from the legislature, winning concessions from regulatory bodies, or negotiating compromises with minority groups of stockholders. Aside from an occasional criminal case, he rarely appeared in court. His zeal for action and restless temperament precluded his poring over lawbooks. He obtained results by contacting acquaintances occupying positions of leverage at the statehouse, on administrative commissions, or in the

Republican party. Technical legal problems he delegated to Todd, who was a scholarly attorney.[5]

Daugherty's legal forte was the role of lobbyist. His clients included the American Tobacco Company, Armour and Company, the American Gas and Electric Company, the Western Union Company, and the Ohio State Telephone Company. A 1911 vanity book, *Club Men of Columbus in Caricature*, portrayed him walking down the street protectively leading a little trolley car and telephone with each hand.[6] That year he represented J.P. Morgan's telephone interests when the Democratic legislature proposed amendments to a public utilities bill, giving the public service commission power to regulate utilities in the peoples' interest. Daugherty appeared before legislative committees in an effort to prevent their passage.

His career as a politician obviously complemented his legal work. His service from 1892 to 1894 as chairman of the house committee on corporations, where he made a special study of corporate activities, helped him considerably.[7] Overall, four years in the legislature enabled him to learn the intricacies of lawmaking and provided him with valuable contacts. Indeed, lobbyists' pay depended upon their ability to persuade clients that they could fix people and things. That was one reason Daugherty fought to retain power after Hanna defeated him in 1899. His active interest in politics at the time was in part related to his legal activity.

He managed to cultivate enough legislators who were ready to perform a favor. During 1911-12 his law partner, Todd, was able to assist him as a state senator. Todd, in fact, was notorious in his support of utility interests.[8] But Daugherty also exaggerated his influence so that he appeared more powerful than he actually was. After the organization of the General Assembly in 1900, Daugherty, as James Cox later related, wrote a number of insurance companies, asserting that his friends controlled both branches of the legislature. He suggested that they should have "someone on the ground" to protect their interests against unfriendly legislation. He allegedly offered his services for $1,500, but unfortunately one of his letters fell into unfriendly hands, causing considerable discussion around the state capital. Various "milker" bills, introduced to extort money from the threatened interests, were also identified with Daugherty. One of the last of these bills was an anticigarette measure proposed in 1905 by L.M. McFadden, a representative from Fayette.[9]

The house speakership, the leader of the senate, and the clerkships of the Assembly became strategic positions for Daugherty. Influence with the house speaker or senate leader gave him a hand in the organization of the legislature as well as in the disposition of bills to committees. That was one reason he cultivated close relations with them. House Speaker William S. McKinnon, who owed Daugherty a debt of gratitude for his appointment in 1902, was especially cordial. Friendly Assembly clerks, meanwhile, kept Daugherty informed on proposed bills and the progress of legislation. He especially succeeded in influencing the selection of house clerks. A *Columbus Dispatch* reporter, during the 1900 contest, saw Daugherty anxiously viewing the race from the gallery. His candidate won, and promptly appointed John P. Maynard, the son of Daugherty's former law partner, as assistant clerk.[10] In 1908, Maynard became house clerk, where he quickly alienated Senator Theodore Burton by promising the assistant clerkship to three different people. Daugherty found Maynard useful as an informant who reported bills to him as soon as they were introduced. According to James Cox, Daugherty then indicated to Maynard the committees to which they were to be referred. Cox accused Maynard of burying bills that were unfriendly to Daugherty's clients.[11]

By 1908, however, Democratic Governor Judson Harmon made it difficult for Republicans like Daugherty to use public office for their personal advantage. Even though Harmon was a conservative in the mold of Grover Cleveland, he was, like the former President, also a strong advocate of honest and efficient government. Consequently, he won the support of Democratic progressives. One of his first actions was to investigate the treasurer's office, which was long suspected of corruption. The investigation determined that former house speaker McKinnon, as state treasurer in 1906-07, had placed state funds at low interest rates in banking institutions in which he held stock. It appeared that state money had gone into his own pocket. Eventually Harmon's attorney general brought suit against McKinnon and other Republican officials. Even though McKinnon had died, the state recovered $114,506 of the misappropriated public monies from his estate.

McKinnon's deputy, Charles Green, and another former treasurer, Isaac B. Cameron, were indicted for embezzlement and subsequently went to jail.[12] Cameron was exposed after the bankruptcy of the Columbus Savings and Trust Company in 1913, at which time he served as its president. Nonetheless, the state got access to the bank records, which revealed that in 1904, as state treasurer, Cameron deposited $100,000 of embezzled state funds in his personal account at the Columbus Savings and Trust. At that time Cyrus Huling was president. Some evidence indicated that Huling had known about Cameron's wrongdoing and had permitted the bank to be improperly used in other ways. Along with a few other financial institutions, it had served as a depository for state revenues. The interest on such monies went to the state treasurers and bank officials rather than to the state. Bank records were falsified to conceal such questionable activities. Huling was indicted for aiding and abetting Cameron. His friend Daugherty—a director, the bank's legal counsel, and former vice president—also came under investigation for the misuse of depositors' funds.

By this time, James M. Cox had succeeded Harmon as governor. His administration decided not to file charges against Daugherty because of insufficient evidence. The indictment against Huling also failed on the ground that knowledge on his part was not conclusively shown.[13] Even though Daugherty escaped indictment, his association with the Columbus Savings and Trust Company did not help him politically. His connection with a bank failure that deprived depositors of part of their savings (they were subsequently paid 68 1/2 percent) invited criticism.[14]

Progressive legislation to regulate lobbyists appeared to have little effect on Daugherty. In 1913, three years after Governor Harmon failed to obtain an antilobby measure, Cox successfully encouraged the legislature to pass a regulatory law. Lobbyists were now required to register the name of the firm that employed them and to indicate the bills in which they were interested. They also were to make available their receipts and expenditures. Only then could they appear before the committees of the General Assembly. But the law was never strongly enforced, and Daugherty never even registered.[15] Moreover, he was too influential and clever to be circumscribed. He still requested meetings with Governor Cox regarding legislation affecting companies which he served. On one occasion, when a street railway regulatory measure passed the Assembly, he boldly wrote Cox: "When this bill reaches you for consideration I shall be glad if you will call my office and if I am in town I will come over and talk with you very briefly about it. If I am not here, . . . Mr. Todd will do so. I do not want in anyway to embarrass you in the performance of your duty . . . . I just think that you ought to know the step taken by this particular legislation."[16] Although always polite, Cox never acceded to Daugherty's requests.

Indications are that such lobbying activities hurt Daugherty politically. The label "corporation lawyer" or "lobbyist" was especially unpopular during the Progressive era. In 1912, the progressive press referred to Daugherty as attorney for the J.P. Morgan telephone interests and as lobbyist for the "Beef Trust." Such publicity had prevented him from becoming chairman of the Republican National Committee. When he sought a Senate seat in 1916, critical reference to his legal work again emerged. Similar criticism developed prior to his Attorney General appointment.[17]

Conversely, Daugherty's political influence often aided his law practice. Because of his legal success in Ohio, he was by 1900 more in demand nationally. That Ohio Republicans frequently dominated the national spotlight contributed to his popularity in corporate circles outside the state. Daugherty made it known that he was intimately acquainted with Hanna, Foraker, Dick, Garfield, and Taft. In that way he found employment in cases where political influence mattered.

In February 1906, one such case involved Daugherty and Thomas B. Felder, Jr., a Democratic politician and attorney from Atlanta. They had first met at the turn of the century while representing mutual interests, beginning a friendship that would continue into Daugherty's Attorney Generalship. They now were employed by Armour and Company to oppose certain provisions of the proposed Hepburn bill. Specifically, they were against a clause that would enable the Interstate Commerce Commission to prevent meatpackers like Armour from using their private refrigerator car lines to extort or discriminate against other shippers.[18] Nevertheless, Daugherty and Felder argued that fruit growers and other shippers disliked the clause. Daugherty consequently asked Senator Dick to appear before the Committee on Interstate Commerce: "You need only say that constituents of yours who are interested in large farms in the South have requested you to ask the Committee not to report a bill" that included the objectionable feature. He concluded by flattering Dick for the attention he received in his maiden senatorial address.[19]

Because Dick was apparently too busy to make an immediate appearance, Daugherty wrote Senator Foraker, requesting him to urge the junior senator to find the time. That spring he also asked Foraker, who opposed the Hepburn bill, to offer a floor amendment, eliminating the refrigerator clause. On May 4, Foraker told the Senate that he was proposing the revision because of the great number of letters he received from constituents in Ohio and fruit growers elsewhere.[20] Republican Senator Jonathan Dolliver of Iowa, who led the floor fight for the bill's passage, rejected Foraker's amendment. He argued that fruit growers strongly favored the clause because private refrigerator car lines like Armour exploited such shippers. The clause, according to Dolliver, would not deter Armour from contracting with the railroads. It instead required that refrigeration charges to the shippers be computed as part of the transportation cost and be published as part of the railroad rate.[21] The bill subjected Armour to the jurisdiction of the Interstate Commerce Commission—precisely why Armour wanted it amended. The Senate defeated Foraker's amendment, to the chagrin of Daugherty, who watched from the gallery. He expressed disappointment to Foraker that "parties who had promised to support it took no interest in it."[22]

Although his efforts to amend the Hepburn act failed, Daugherty, with Felder's assistance, succeeded five years later in the Charles W. Morse case. No matter how one might evaluate Daugherty's role in that case, it provides some of the best insights into his character and his utilization of political influence to enhance his law practice. The victim was the President of the United States, William Howard Taft. Later Daugherty himself would also be victimized by his own deception in this episode.

The beneficiary clearly was the chunky and unattractive Morse, who had become one of the most daring promoters and speculators in the United States at the turn of the century. Born in Bath, Maine, in 1856, he quickly exhibited a talent for capitalizing on opportunities. At age seventeen Morse was employed by his father as a $30-a-week bookkeeper, but the youngster soon hired someone else to do the work for $10 a week. He used the remainder to pay his way through Bowdoin College. By graduation he already had made a small fortune in the shipping business. He then joined with his father and cousin in an extensive ice-shipping and lumber-transporting operation. By 1897, Morse gravitated to Wall Street as he began to dominate the New York ice market. Two years later the "Ice King" created the American Ice Company, an overcapitalized merger that quickly doubled the price of ice, causing a tremendous public outcry. An investigation followed, disclosing that Morse had received important docking privileges from Tammany Hall after bribing Mayor Robert Van Wyck and Tammany Boss Richard Croker with shares of American Ice Company stock. The inquiry forced Morse's retirement from the business with profits estimated at $12,000,000.[23]

Morse's next ventures were in shipping and banking. In six years he had a virtual monopoly of coastal shipping from Bangor to Galveston. He succeeded as handsomely in financial circles. In a few years of collaboration, Morse, with F. August Heinze, a leading copper speculator, and E.R. Thomas, a young man of inherited wealth, controlled almost a dozen New York banks, including the Bank of North America. Such control permitted them to speculate with depositors' funds. They also organized a profitable copper pool which collapsed in 1907, contributing to that year's panic. Both Morse and Heinze were forced to retire from banking during the scare. As a grand jury proceeded to look into Morse's illegal activities, which the panic fully exposed, United States District Attorney Henry Stimson gathered enough evidence to send him to prison on fifty-three counts of criminally misapplying the funds and making false entries in the books of the Bank of North America.

In November 1908, he was sentenced to a stiff fifteen year term in the Atlanta Penitentiary. An unsuccessful appeal followed during which time Morse spent ten months in the Tombs of New York City. Finally, in January 1910, he began his Atlanta imprisonment. Confinement temporarily ended the career of one who had spent an appreciable part of his life narrowly skirting fraud and crime. Yet, Morse lamented that "there is no one in Wall Street who is not daily doing as I have done." To Morse, the indictment occurred because the Theodore Roosevelt administration had wanted a scapegoat.[24]

Less than one year after Morse's imprisonment, requests for pardon began to reach President William Howard Taft. The prisoner's family initiated a number of these appeals. Gilbert Pevey of Boston, representing Morse's wife, even managed to obtain a hearing with Taft. Public officials were also active in Morse's behalf. In December 1910, Senator Eugene Hale of Maine, respecting Mrs. Morse's request, presented a petition to the White House. Four months afterwards, New York attorney James M. Beck, later President Warren G. Harding's Solicitor General, recommended that Taft pardon Morse. Thousands of other requests for a pardon, commutation of sentence, and reinvestigation followed, bearing signatures of many prominent public officials. Undoubtedly, the encouragement and efforts of Mrs. Morse had much to do with the rather remarkable demonstration.[25]

In May 1911, however, Taft refused to grant a pardon, although he consented to a review after January 1, 1913. By then Morse would have been in better position for at least a commuted sentence, since Henry Stimson, the former prosecuting attorney, now advised that the sentence might be shortened to five years. Stimson had succumbed to a feeling shared by many conservative lawyers, politicians, and businessmen: Morse's sentence had been inordinate. Their sentiment was partly influenced by the 1909 judgment of the Circuit Court of Appeals, which had concluded that the sentence was "excessive and unusual." Stimson also conceded that his approval of the original sentence had come at "the close of the most difficult case that I have ever tried, where the work of prosecution had been done under extreme pressure, and where the investigation . . . had brought into my mind a large number of collateral facts bearing unfavorably upon Morse's character." He, however, favored no less than a five year incarceration for Morse because of the seriousness of his crimes, and the Circuit Court of Appeals generally affirmed his opinion.[26] As it turned out, Morse's release would come much sooner than anyone thought possible.

That it did come so quickly was in part due to the efforts of Harry Daugherty. He first became involved with the Morse case in the early summer of 1911, when Felder requested his legal assistance. To this day the circumstances of this initial involvement are unclear. Daugherty would later claim that they only sought Morse's testimony so as to resolve several civil actions concerning investors of the dissolving Metropolitan Steamship Company, which Morse once headed. Under no circumstances were they initially interested in securing Morse's freedom. By 1917, however, Felder did admit that Fred Seely, the proprietor of the Atlanta *Georgian*, had asked him to pursue Morse's release because of Seely's "benevolent and charitable interest in the fate of Mr. Morse." Felder then related that he had requested help from his friend Daugherty because Daugherty "stood as close to the President as any other lawyer or citizen in the United States."[27]

With whatever initial intent, Daugherty and Felder sought to visit Morse. On July 25, 1911, Warden William H. Moyer of the United States Penitentiary at Atlanta received notification from the Attorney General's office that they wished to see Morse "upon a matter related to a civil proceeding" involving the Metropolitan Steamship Company. Moyer was ready to comply until Daugherty requested an unprecedented private interview.[28] When the warden and the Department of Justice refused to waive regulations, Daugherty on July 28 telegraphed a political cohort, Charles Hilles, who was also Taft's private secretary, that he was unable to "secure facts necessary to handle Morse matters properly and professionally without such an interview." He asked Hilles to obtain the consent of the Attorney General for a "reasonable request." Because this did not materialize, the persistent Daugherty wrote the secretary again on August 2 that his "blood is somewhat riled about this matter" and that he would commit "every drop of blood and every pound of energy . . . to the issue until right prevails." He did not at the time relate to Hilles that he wished to procure Morse's release. By August 29, 1911, however, Daugherty told him that it was impossible to transact civil litigation without the full-time cooperation of Morse. Apparently, his restricted visits with Morse were not at all adequate. He then indicated that he must also explore the criminal aspect of the case because of the grave change in the prisoner's health. Daugherty painted an extremely dark picture:

> His life is speeding away with increased . . . rapidity day by day. His right side, as you know, is paralyzed and shriveling at a great deal faster rate than when sent here. He has Bright's disease and his confinement is making him worse so fast that I can see a change in each returning visit here. He has fainting spells and in fact, I do not believe he is likely to live eighteen months in prison.[29]

Daugherty supported his contention with a statement from Dr. Alfred L. Fowler of Atlanta, "one of the most eminent physicians in this part of the country." A former prison physician, Fowler had concluded after his examination of Morse in January 1911 that he suffered from Bright's disease, an inflammation of the kidneys. Certain that the President would pardon Morse if he knew the facts, Daugherty told Hilles that he and Felder must see Taft as soon as possible. He concluded with a patronizing postscript: "Please congratulate the President upon his speech and position and upon the general approval of the public."[30]

President Taft, about to depart on a western tour, had no time for a conference. He instead recommended that Daugherty refer the Morse matter to Attorney General George W. Wickersham. Daugherty and Felder not only saw the Attorney General, but also interviewed Stimson, the district attorney in the prosecution of Morse, as well as the trial judge and the pardon attorney. Daugherty even arranged a meeting with Theodore Roosevelt, the President at the time of Morse's trial. Daugherty's and Felder's letters, meanwhile, continued to flow into the White House. Daugherty constantly badgered Hilles regarding the urgency of the case.

On at least two occasions he cornered him for lengthy conferences, one of which Daugherty arranged after learning that Hilles was coming to Ohio to attend his father-in-law's funeral.[31]

A few weeks after Taft's return, Daugherty and Felder wired Hilles, requesting an appointment with the President. Hilles promptly fixed a tentative time.[32] The following day, on November 22, the penitentiary physician, Dr. J. Calvin Weaver, notified Wickersham of Morse's condition after a consultation with Dr. Fowler:

> Morse is drowsily apathetic and sleeps continuously: pulse sharp . . . ; his lower eyelids are chronically swollen . . . . . his urine is markedly hematuric bloody, and the quantity for the last twenty-four hours amounts to only twelve ounces and which normally should be fifty ounces; microscopic examinations of his urine discloses red blood cells, granular casts and blood casts; diagnosis that of Bright's disease; patient is surely and rapidly losing ground and there can be no doubt but that his time is now drawing to a close and that liberation only will prolong his life and even that not for a long period.[33]

Daugherty's telegram that same day made the diagnosis appear conservative. He cautioned that Morse might not live another twenty-four hours.[34]

Morse's condition concerned Taft enough that he conferred with Wickersham and the Surgeon General of the Army on November 24 before meeting with Daugherty and Felder. The President told the latter two that he had decided to transfer Morse to the Fort McPherson hospital at Atlanta for thirty days of observation. There, the President explained, Morse would be well treated and could employ his own physicians. Taft's humane action, however, was hardly in Daugherty's and Felder's interests. Morse, as it was later revealed, had handsomely retained them to secure his release. According to an August 4 agreement, Daugherty was to receive a $5,000 retainer from Morse, and if Morse was set free, Daugherty and Felder were to be paid $25,000. Morse could terminate the agreement after January 1, 1912, by giving ten days written notice. A few weeks later, he had promised an additional $100,000.[35] Consequently, Taft probably stunned the two attorneys when he disclosed his decision to have Morse transferred instead of released.

Daugherty's first impulse was to telephone Hilles after the meeting with Taft. Failing to make connections in Washington, he wrote to Hilles upon returning home that he had been very conservative in presenting Morse's condition due to his "high regard for the President." One week later Daugherty came more to the point, arguing that "Morse was excessively sentenced and his life is hanging in the balance." Morse "will never be well," Daugherty pleaded; "he is liable to die any day and yet he may live a short time if he were to be released and allowed to take treatment peculiar to his disease." Daugherty explained that he did not want to influence Taft but asked Hilles to inform the President that he was seeking a pardon on the basis of Morse's condition.[36]

The medical reports on Morse's progress in mid-December did not completely corroborate Daugherty's assertions, but they did promote Morse's eventual release from prison. On December 21, J.A. Fowler, the Acting Attorney General, informed Taft that civilian physicians at Fort McPherson agreed with the post surgeon's diagnosis the previous week— that further imprisonment would shorten Morse's life. Taft, who had requested the examinations, hardly felt that these reports justified his immediate release. He wrote Wickersham on December 24 that "what is certified is that he is suffering from an incurable disease which may not terminate his life for years, but that imprisonment is likely to shorten his life." Taft judiciously concluded that he would commute Morse's sentence if the doctors verified that he would die in two weeks.[37] He recommended the detention of Morse at the post hospital along with a monthly summation of his medical condition.

Daugherty and Felder were very active in the final weeks of December 1911 in persuading the administration to come to a more favorable decision. Daugherty pressured Wickersham, Hilles, and the prison officials to expedite reports and recommendations involving Morse.[38] Both attorneys were instrumental in the selection of Dr. Fowler to act with the post surgeon in the examinations and treatment of the ailing prisoner. Although Taft refused to see Felder, the latter asked Hilles on December 26 to deliver a letter to Taft, outlining what he had proposed to say in an interview. Three days later Daugherty telephoned from the New Williard Hotel in Washington to indicate that he would be "very glad to see the President on the Morse matter."[39] Their leverage was the declining health of Morse.

On December 30, a board of medical officers at Fort McPherson revealed its findings after a careful examination of the convict. The report stated that Morse suffered not only from Bright's disease, but also from a chronic valvular disease of the heart and a slight arteriosclerosis (hardening of the arteries). The board was of the opinion that Morse was not in any danger of dying but that because of his despondent condition, continued confinement would hamper any improvement. George Torney, Surgeon General of the Army, who wrote the cover letter to the report, nevertheless, concluded that Morse would die unless he were removed from the depressing influence of imprisonment. Ten days later Daugherty and Felder relayed Dr. Fowler's diagnosis, which confirmed Torney's conclusion. According to Major David Baker, the post surgeon, in still another report on January 12, Morse's health was so grave that he could not be transferred to Hot Springs for further treatment. Finally on

January 17, Torney reported that Morse had deteriorated to the point that he would probably live less than one month if he remained confined and no longer than six months even if his sentence were commuted. Particularly alarming to Torney was the heart blockage that Morse had suffered two days earlier.[40]

The concerned Wickersham submitted Torney's report to the President with the recommendation that he terminate Morse's sentence. On the following day, January 18, Taft reiterated Torney's conclusions in announcing Morse's commutation of sentence even though the Surgeon General had not placed the prisoner's life expectancy within the two-week period. What Taft did not reveal was that he had received a telephone call from a close friend of both him and Daugherty. Daugherty had asked John McLean, the publisher of the *Cincinnati Enquirer* and the *Washington Post* to urge Taft to go ahead with the commutation. McLean, who briefly looked into the Morse matter, did exactly that.[41]

Taft's action is perplexing because it seems out of character. Historians have often alluded to his uncompromising attitude, especially toward corporations suspected of violating antitrust policies. To Taft the law was the law; antitrust action was initiated regardless of the firm and individuals involved.[42] That approach brought him into a confrontation with Theodore Roosevelt in October 1911 over the U.S. Steel Corporation, which Roosevelt as President had excluded from antitrust action. Taft clearly wished to apply that same legalistic policy toward pardons. In March 1910, he said that one need not "be afraid that pardons will be granted too readily in this administration." This statement was in line with one he would make in October that he "sought in every way to avoid interfering with the administration of justice by yielding to maudlin sentimentality."[43] The implication was that he would continue to be strict and opposed to favoritism of any sort.

Unlike many seriously ill convicts, Morse did not die in prison. As had been stated, his affluence attracted Daugherty and Felder, and his notoriety led to a number of appeals for a pardon by prominent and conservative people who generally supported administration policy. Others challenged Morse's fifteen-year sentence. The pardon attorney, James A. Finch, and the former prosecuting attorney, Stimson, had suggested a reduction to five years. On January 15, 1912, Finch would finally recommend an immediate commutation because Morse was allegedly near death.[44] The trial judge, Charles Hough, also advised a commutation of sentence conditional upon Morse's ill health because "he is no longer that danger to the [commercial] community which in health I believe him to be."[45]

Apparently, these expressions and the medical reports overwhelmed Taft into acquiescence. A most significant factor, nevertheless, was still Harry Daugherty who, with Felder, had alerted the President of Morse's deteriorating health. Daugherty had then encouraged Taft, Wickersham, and Hilles to suspect the very worst about Morse's condition, which underwent considerable medical scrutiny. In fact, no one was more persistent about Morse's release than Daugherty, who was expected to play an important part in the President's nomination in 1912. It is not too much to believe that Taft's desire to please a political friend caused him to devote more attention to the possibilities of commuting Morse's sentence than he otherwise would have done. The President's military aide, Archie Butt, best explained Taft's sometimes contradictory actions: "He is easily influenced to do what he wants to do but he is stubborn as an ox when he gets set in the other direction."[46]

If Morse had died as predicted, his commutation would have been relegated to the realm of trivia. Later events, however, made this case one of the most bizarre episodes in the history of executive clemencies. After making several trips to Germany to undergo "water cures," the now robust Morse returned to New York in early 1913 eager again to engage in business pursuits. He organized the Hudson Navigation Company, which he hoped would become the springboard of a modern United States mercantile marine that would touch all European and South American ports. That fall ex-President Taft commented in a lecture that Morse's newly found energy "shakes one's faith in expert examinations."[47]

Despite the embarrassing questions raised about Morse's recovery, Daugherty again boldly requested the retiring Taft administration to drop a bribery indictment against another client, Peter G. Thompson, a Cincinnati businessman. The reason was Thompson's alleged poor health and innocence. On February 11, 1913, Daugherty explained to Attorney General Wickersham that Thompson was

> As pure minded a man as lives in the state of Ohio [.] He is also sick and I doubt if he will ever be better unless he is relieved of the worry of this indictment. Unfortunately Mr. Thompson's wife died about ten days ago and I have no doubt but that her life was shortened on account of the worry and distress incident to the prosecution. About the only hope Mr. Thompson has of regaining his health so that he can attend to business again would be for him to go abroad, where he could be free from care and would receive proper attention.

Most assuredly, he contended, "every banking and business interest in Cincinnati would approve this course and I do not believe there would be a single criticism from anybody in the world if you were to take this action." He concluded by congratulating Wickersham on his splendid record as Attorney General. Daugherty also visited Wickersham on at least one occasion, but the administration refused his request.[48] Perhaps one Morse case was embarrassment enough.

In time the Morse episode became quite discomfiting to Daugherty too, particularly after he decided in late 1915 to seek the 1916 Republican senatorial nomination in Ohio. The press and political opponents criticized his involvement in the Morse case and his apparent deception of Taft. Feeling their sting, he wrote Taft on November 17 explaining that one "who has lived in more or less of a storm all of his life and been in the thickest of the hardest fights naturally has enemies." He complained that "disgruntled, disappointed, ambitious persons and certain yellow newspapers" were soiling his character in claiming that he had duped the administration. He then requested Taft to write him a letter to the effect that "I did not discuss the Morse case with you; that anything I did in that matter was done through Attorney General Wickersham; that I never deceived you about the matter or anything else, and that I have your confidence and respect."[49]

In other words, to further his political career, Daugherty asked Taft to be untruthful. The former President was more than willing to help, for Daugherty had been one of the staunchest Taft men in the 1912 campaign. On November 22, 1915, Taft repaid a political debt: "I write to say that in no way did you influence me in respect to the application for pardon of Charles Morse. My recollection is that you told me you were counsel for Morse, but that you declined to present the matter to me." The latter of Taft's two statements was clearly untrue. Daugherty managed to receive a less affirmative but favorable response from Wickersham.[50] Regardless of Daugherty's eventual primary defeat, the presentation of these letters momentarily silenced the critics.

In late 1920 and early 1921, the Morse case again hung on Daugherty wherever critics discussed his credentials for the Attorney Generalship. The issue received considerably more attention in February 1922 when the Department of Justice brought charges against the elusive Morse, his three sons, and twenty other persons for using the mails to defraud investors in the U.S. Steamship Company. This action followed an earlier grand jury indictment in 1920 when Morse, his three sons, and eight others were charged with having conspired to defraud the United States Shipping Board of large quantities of federal money and property. Apparently, after war was declared against Germany in 1917, governmental demand for ships provided shipping magnates like Morse with opportunities for lucrative contracts. Morse contracted to furnish the government twenty-four steel and twelve wooden vessels. He managed to deliver only two wooden ships prior to the armistice. Eventually nineteen ships were handed over. What compounded Morse's failure was the fact that the money he had borrowed from the U.S. Emergency Fleet Corporation was used to construct shipyards instead of ships. He also appropriated governmental equipment for his own purposes.[51] Yet, in 1922 Morse charged that Daugherty was prosecuting him because of a disagreement over a retainer arising out of his 1912 commutation. Morse's statement spurred Daugherty's critics to delve more deeply into the case.

On May 2, 1922, Senator Thaddeus H. Caraway of Arkansas questioned Daugherty's fitness to prosecute war-fraud cases since, as an attorney, Daugherty had specialized in getting criminals out of prison and was still associated with Felder in unethical cases. Specifically, the zealous and vitriolic Democrat accused the Attorney General of having had Morse freed for a sizable payment. In a later Senate speech on May 20, Caraway inserted into the *Congressional Record* a photostatic copy of a contract for "civil and criminal matters" that Daugherty and Felder had consummated with Morse on August 4, 1911. The compact had provided Daugherty with a $5,000 retainer, $1,000 for expenses, plus $25,000 which he and Felder would divide after Morse's release. In addition, they were to receive 25% of whatever sum they were able to recover from the Metropolitan Steamship Company matter. Caraway also managed to secure, probably from Morse, a copy of a letter from Daugherty to Morse dated April 13, 1913 which reminded Morse of his financial obligations as stated in the August 1911 contract.[52]

The most interesting revelation in the Morse case came two days later when Caraway presented a copy of an October 12, 1917 letter from Felder to Leon O. Bailey of New York. Felder had requested Bailey's help in recovering the $25,000 which Morse had neglected to pay. He explained that Morse had also promised to pay an additional $100,000 after his release. Daugherty and he, Felder continued, had attempted to collect from Morse on numerous occasions. Pleading lack of cash, Morse had tried to reimburse them with worthless stock. The disappointed Daugherty, according to Felder, had "complained very bitterly of treatment by Morse." On one occasion, he had confronted Morse in a hotel room in New York where he had denounced him in "unmeasured terms, declining emphatically to accept the stocks tendered either as collateral or payment."[53]

Morse's quick recovery after the commutation of sentence had deterred the two attorneys from filing suit against him. Felder explained that they had feared that the Wilson administration would have remanded Morse if they had agitated the matter in any way. "I have not been unmindful of the damaging evidence secured by the Department of Justice," Felder wrote, "to ascertain whether or not a fraud had been perpetuated upon the Government by Morse in his efforts to obtain his freedom." Daugherty and Felder somehow discovered that the department had evidence revealing that, after the physicians had been appointed to examine Morse and before they had arrived, "soap suds or chemicals . . . would be taken by him to produce a hemorrhage of the kidneys, and that as soon as the

examination was over . . . the patient would recuperate rapidly." Felder
assured Bailey that neither he nor Daugherty had any knowledge that
Morse had deceived the doctors. Caraway was quick to remind the
Senate, however, that Morse had given Daugherty and Felder full control
of the case. Consequently, he demanded Daugherty's resignation as Attorney General.[54]

Daugherty attempted to respond to Caraway's initial accusations by
informing his friend, Senator James E. Watson of Indiana, that he had
had no part in the criminal aspect of the Morse case.[55] Watson com-
municated that information to the Senate on May 2, where Caraway
challenged it two weeks later by producing the August 1911 contract and
other relevant correspondence, which Daugherty did not contest. In defense, Daugherty released the 1915 Taft and Wickersham letters, which
stated that he had never approached the President directly about the case.
He also denied that he had received any compensation from Morse,
although he admitted that he had accepted $4,000 from Felder, which he
claimed was about half of the expenses he incurred in the case.[56] Only
Daugherty's assertion that he had obtained $4,000 from Felder seems
correct. There is, however, no known documented evidence that substan-
tiates Caraway's claim that Daugherty and Felder had engaged in any
fraud with respect to Morse's health. Morse had a history of heart and
probable kidney disorders which incarceration might well have aggra-
vated.[57] His later recovery is not necessarily an indication that deceit had
been practiced. Some forms of Bright's disease (for example, acute nephritis) eventually heal without medication and without damage to the
kidneys. The medical profession in 1911 lacked the expertise to distin-
guish accurately the acute from the more serious chronic nephritis, which
meant certain death.[58] Morse in fact later stated that the Italian physician
who examined him in 1913 claimed that he did not have Bright's disease
but a much less serious "irritation of the duct caused by sharp uric acid
crystals."[59] The probability exists that the American doctors innocently
diagnosed Morse's kidney condition wrongly.

This is not to say that collusion was impossible. Morse could have
taken a chemical to severely irritate his weakened kidneys, as Felder had
written in 1917. That action would not be completely out of character,
particularly since there was no immediate hope for his release. Despite
Felder's disavowals, Daugherty and he could also have been involved.
Their actions in the early 1920s especially reveal an unethical, if not a
criminal, disregard for justice.[60] Moreover, their contract with Morse, as
Caraway pointed out, gave them absolute control. It also stipulated that
Morse's release was the only basis for substantial remuneration. Such a
provision can tempt the most scrupulous attorney.

Collusion might also have necessitated the cooperation of a physician. Dr. Alfred L. Fowler, the former prison physician, is a possible suspect. He had resigned under an alleged Department of Justice investigation in early 1911.[61] Prior to that resignation, it was Fowler who had first diagnosed Morse's ailment as Bright's disease. Daugherty and Felder consulted him in July 1911, quoted his diagnosis to the administration, and then employed him to stay with the hospitalized Morse during the critical weeks of December 1911. At that time, Fowler, whose practice was more specialized, exercised an influence over the diagnoses of other physicians examining Morse.[62] Interestingly, eleven years later Fowler again became prison physician at Atlanta immediately after Daugherty became Attorney General.[63] While one can make a circumstantial case for collusion, the fact remains that neither Caraway nor anyone else provided the direct evidence to prove it.

Undoubtedly, Caraway's desire to expose Republican maladministration and fraud was responsible for his undocumented charge. But the exposé of Felder in the Senate as a notorious corruptionist who had become *persona non grata* in Georgian legal and political circles further encouraged suspicion. In 1925, Felder was convicted along with Gaston B. Means for consiracy to bribe government officials in the Glass Casket fraud case. He was fined $10,000 and automatically disbarred.[64] On March 11, 1926, Felder died in a Savannah, Georgia, hotel of acute dilation of the heart and of acute alcoholism.

As for Charles Morse, he was acquitted in a long and costly trial involving government ship-building contracts. A subsequent civil suit in 1925 against Morse's business, the Virginia Shipbuilding Company, resulted in a settlement for the federal government of over eleven and a half million dollars. The second indictment against Morse and his sons, which involved mail fraud, was never tried because Morse was adjudged too ill to stand trial as a result of a recent paralytic stroke. The charges against his sons were dismissed after a jury disagreed. In January 1933, Morse died of pneumonia, almost three years after the death of the President who had commuted his sentence twenty years earlier.[65]

Daugherty also was to suffer reverses after the Morse case exposure. The culmination of charges that he was ethically unfit to serve as Attorney General led to his forced resignation in March 1924. The Morse episode itself had little to do with his dismissal, but it did reveal Daugherty to be an ambitious and resourceful lobbyist who displayed poor judgment in pursuing Morse's commutation. He surely knew that Felder sought him because of his political association with the administration. What compounded this questionable conduct was his misrepresentation of Morse. He did not inform the Taft administration that he had earlier contracted with Morse for his release. The August 4 contract was, in fact, consummated more than three weeks before Daugherty expressed grave concern about Morse's health.[66] Later, Daugherty's request that Taft and Wickersham lie in his behalf further damned his conduct. Overall, the Morse involvement reflected unfavorably on all major participants, but it also provided a revealing example of why Daugherty became such an often criticized public figure.

The Uncompromising Republican
1912

LIKE the Morse case, Daugherty's involvement in the Taft-Roosevelt feud of 1912 contributed to his controversial image. In fact, his strong defense of Taft aroused enmities that lasted into the 1920s. At the same time the campaign of 1912 also brought him back into the political limelight in Ohio. In an intraparty battle between the standpat and progressive elements, he strongly led the former, reversing a stand he had taken in 1906, when Republican insurgents first challenged the state machine. Daugherty was not the only Republican leader in the state who found himself in a different camp in 1912, for Theodore Burton exchanged positions with Walter Brown in a conflict that contained other minor realignments. The new fight in Ohio was, in some respects, similar to the earlier revolt, in which the Taft men had ended the Foraker-Dick domination. Personal ambitions as much as principles inspired both struggles.

As early as 1909, Taft's failure to follow Roosevelt's progressivism caused an outbreak of Republican insurgency on both the national and the Ohio scene. It began when the President sided with Secretary of the Interior Richard Ballinger in his altercation with conservationist Gifford Pinchot of the Forestry Service. To the insurgents, the high Payne-Aldrich Tariff of the same year also represented Taft's surrender to the old guard. The President's inconsistent attitude in the congressional insurgents' campaign to dethrone House Speaker Joseph Cannon drove yet another wedge into party unity. Moreover, as the congressional elections of 1910 confirmed, Taft's conception of government was too laissez-faire for most progressives. But perhaps the event that pushed Roosevelt actively into the campaign was the administration's decision to ignore his gentlemen's agreements by seeking to prosecute the U.S. Steel Corporation.

Anti-Taft sentiment in Ohio remained unorganized until early March 1911, when Republican insurgents held a meeting in Akron to discuss possible progressive presidential candidates for 1912. More positive action came on November 3, 1911, at a dinner meeting in Cleveland. Three-hundred insurgents established a temporary organization entitled the Ohio Progressive Republican League. It quickly expanded into twenty-four counties, with its headquarters at Columbus. The movement, however, was not without difficulties. The progressive cause was badly divided between the partisans of Senator Robert La Follette of Wisconsin and those of Roosevelt. The former, a smaller and more amateur group, included Judge Robert H. Wanamaker of Akron and John D. Fackler of Cleveland. James R. Garfield, formerly Roosevelt's Secretary of the Interior, and Elyria industrialist Arthur Garford led the latter faction. Progressives like Garfield, whom Taft chose not to retain as interior secretary, especially disdained Taft's alteration of Roosevelt's policies.

Other supporters of Roosevelt in Ohio, such as Dan Hanna, the son of the late Republican leader, and Walter Brown, joined the cause for more selfish reasons. Hanna and his firm faced indictments by the Taft administration for violating the Sherman Act. When the administration refused to drop the charges, Hanna, who was also the owner of the *Cleveland Leader*, found the Roosevelt cause more congenial. Having both money and influence, he was a welcome addition. The pragmatic Brown contributed his organizational skill to the insurrection mostly out of political expediency. Often labeled the leader of the Toledo Tammany, he hoped to use the movement's success to strengthen his hold on progressive Lucas County.[1]

The impact of the Roosevelt element began to snowball by late November, when Hanna's *Cleveland Leader* continually emphasized the necessity for the former Rough Rider's candidacy. The Roosevelt faction's growing strength in the Ohio Progressive Republican League also helped. At a meeting on New Year's Day, the League defeated a resolution endorsing La Follette for president. One month later the senator suffered from nervous exhaustion while addressing the periodical publishers in Philadelphia. His "breakdown" resolved the differences within the Ohio progressive organization, for the League quickly drafted Roosevelt. By the time Roosevelt spoke before the Ohio Constitutional Convention at Columbus in February, he had already announced his candidacy. The contest thus officially began between two former friends. It signified the greatest intraparty fight in the history of the Republican party.

One of the major battlefields was Taft's own state. There Daugherty quickly emerged as a Taft backer. At age fifty two, hair thinning and developing a paunch, Daugherty no longer resembled his sleek, mustachioed appearance of the 1890s. His political promise also seemed to be disappearing, but not his drive or ambition. He entered the preconvention campaign in Ohio against Roosevelt despite his enthusiastic support of the Roosevelt presidency. The former President's earlier challenge of

Hanna, Foraker, and Dick probably had as much to do with Daugherty's prior allegiance as did party loyalty.[2] There was, however, no inconsistency in his now aligning with Taft. He had not only favored Taft's administration, but he also found him more in tune with his conservative Republicanism, which remained fairly consistent throughout his life.[3] Besides, Taft was an Ohioan, and one who was aware of Daugherty's own political aspirations. Indeed, Daugherty expected the organization's support in any future senatorial campaign.[4] To Daugherty, then, Roosevelt's challenge sprang from personal ambition because the honest and capable Taft was entitled to the party's renomination.

In early 1912, however, the situation appeared bleak for the Taft organization in Ohio. There was little question that Roosevelt appealed to the grassroots element of the party, which was probably captivated more by his charisma than by his progressivism. There were also indications of dissatisfaction among federal employees who were under the jurisdiction of Postmaster General Frank Hitchcock, Taft's former campaign manager in 1908 and past Republican National Committee chairman. Concerned Ohio Republicans questioned Hitchcock's policies and doubted his loyalty.[5] The state Republican organization also was not immune to the Roosevelt revolt. Walter Brown was the chairman of the central committee that included Garford as well as other pro-Roosevelt members.

Prior to April, Daugherty was one of the few active Taft men in Ohio. So appreciative was the President that he wrote Daugherty a personal note in March to thank him for his work.[6] By mid-April conditions remained grim, despite Daugherty and Ohio National Committeeman Arthur Vorys devoting considerable time to organizational work. "If the President will only spend a week here and C.P. Taft will do what is necessary to be done," Daugherty assured Taft's preconvention manager, Congressman William B. McKinley, "I think we will pull it out." He also recommended that Senator Elihu Root of New York make a speech at Toledo, a progressive stronghold, and deliver two addresses at other strategic localities in the state. At Toledo, Daugherty planned to have a progressive pro-Taft judge preside at the Root meeting, "saying things that Mr. Root cannot say, which the President cannot say, which he is expected to say . . . where things are bad and newspapers are against us."[7]

To Taft's secretary Charles D. Hilles, Daugherty expressed concern about the disloyalty of Postmaster General Hitchcock, who, he claimed, had turned Ohio postmasters, railway clerks, and inspectors against the administration. The state organization needed their support to the extent that the President should ask for Hitchcock's resignation immediately. Daugherty suggested that he should be replaced before the June Republican national convention, where he would be dangerous because of his influence with southern delegates. "This is a fight to the finish," Daugherty warned; if Hitchcock left prior to the Ohio May primary, "we would have much more active and beneficial support than we are receiving."[8]

Although Taft neglected to dismiss the capable but independent Hitchcock, he attempted to pursue Daugherty's other suggestions. In early May he asked Root to campaign in Ohio prior to the crucial primary on May 21. As Roosevelt's former Secretary of State, however, Root sought a neutral position even though he was now privately opposed to Roosevelt.[9] Thus, on two separate occasions in May, Taft came to his home state without Root in an effort to salvage it from a Roosevelt victory. The stakes were high since Roosevelt had won several decisive primary victories the previous month. If Taft now lost his own state delegation, the repercussions could be tremendous.

On May 8, 1912, Taft met with his Ohio backers at a party meeting in Columbus. Daugherty, who presided at the get-together, introduced him by commenting that there was as much difference between the principles advocated by Taft and Roosevelt as there was between the American and the red flag. After the President's speech, Daugherty, Vorys, and Lewis Laylin, chairman of the state executive committee, briefed Taft on the schedule for a seven-day tour of Ohio, beginning on May 14 and concluding on the day prior to the district primaries.[10]

One day after Taft opened his state campaign, Theodore Roosevelt embarked on an Ohio excursion. In special trains, they followed each other in a canvass that degenerated into a barrage of innuendoes and personal abuse, with Taft characterizing his opponent as an "egoist," "demagogue," and "bolter"; Roosevelt retorted with "puzzlewit" and "fathead." On May 18, Daugherty joined the Taft entourage at Lima to deliver a major address which dwelt on state patriotism, a familiar tactic in Ohio campaigns, particularly since 1876. He asked the audience whether it desired that a delegate

> representing the candidacy of some man from some other state shall arise and with trembling voice announce for the first time in Ohio's recollection that Ohio, proud Ohio, famous Ohio, Ohio, the state in which was born or lived at the time of his nomination every Republican president, but two— since the organization of the party—that this great state which has written and made the greatest history among the sister states, and in the world, for leadership, for brains, in the soldiery, and for patriotism, waives her right to the presidency and yields it to any son from any state other than Ohio?

The Taft organization thought enough of Daugherty's speech to publish it in pamphlet form![11]

The campaign came to an end one day before the district primaries. Taft had traveled 3,000 miles in making fifty speeches, while Roosevelt had campaigned over half that distance in delivering seventy-five. For the President, it was all to no avail. He suffered a devastating defeat, as he obtained pledges from only eight Ohio delegates for his June renomination bid. Roosevelt, meanwhile, gathered thirty-four pledges in outdistancing Taft 165,809 to 118,362 in the total vote. Only the "big six" remained unselected. The six delegates-at-large were to be chosen at the state Republican convention of June 3 and 4. The Taft men, hoping to recover from the May 21 defeat, were determined to win that encounter. As Daugherty wrote Hilles, "the tendency of the other side is to flatter and fool and to inquire if the state convention is not going to allow the express will of the voters of Ohio to dictate the delegates-at-large. This of course is all moonshine and we ought not to have a man in Ohio weakened in the least."[12]

Indeed, the will of the voters was denied despite a majority of delegates to the state convention receiving their credentials from county primaries held prior to the June 3 meeting. Roosevelt did exceedingly well in these selections, but Taft completely dominated the county convention selections. Consequently, Taft had a narrow lead of 349 delegates to Roosevelt's 335, with 74 still uninstructed, 53 of whom comprised the Cuyahoga County delegation. On the day preceding the convention, Daugherty rallied the Taft forces in an organizational meeting at the Neil House and aided in putting together the Taft delegate-at-large slate.[13]

The selection of the "big six" occurred on June 4 after a bitterly fought contest in which hisses and catcalls interrupted speeches from both factions. The Taft contingent won the fight on a 390 1/2 to 362 1/2 vote as Daugherty became one of Taft's six delegates-at-large, along with Harding, Burton, Vorys, C.P. Taft, and David Cable of Lima. Although Daugherty and the rest played strategic roles, Maurice Maschke, the Cuyahoga County boss, was most responsible for the victory. He cast his entire delegation vote of fifty-three for Taft despite an agreement with Walter Brown to divide it in proportion to Roosevelt's decisive county primary victory. To have honored the pledge would have given Roosevelt control of the convention and thus the "big six." But Maschke changed his mind, supposedly after Burton told him that he (Burton) could not face Taft again unless the Cuyahoga County delegation voted for the President. Burton also reminded him that Taft had made Maschke Collector of Customs in Cleveland at Burton's insistence.[14]

Even though Daugherty led the Taft delegates from Ohio to the June 18-21 Republican national convention at Chicago, Roosevelt progressives controlled thirty-four out of the state's forty-eight delegates and dominated the organization of the delegation. Arthur Garford became both its temporary and permanent chairman. Ohio's representatives to the credentials and resolutions committees were also progressives. This ran counter

to Daugherty's plans to seek the chairmanship of the credentials committee so that he might help Taft control the convention.[15] But he must have
pleased the President when he delivered a speech to a partisan crowd in
the "Gold room" at the Congress Hotel. There, he called Roosevelt's
campaign a vaudeville and intimated that he was a liar. Declaring that he
came from a proud state, he then boosted the qualities of Taft.[16]

After his return, Daugherty wrote Taft in detail about Roosevelt's bolt.
His opinions are revealing since they reflect his own attitude toward
politics, which tolerated practically any indiscretion aside from a party
bolt:

> I have no doubt about his personal honesty, but no man is honest who
> enters a contest with a worthy adversary and is not willing to abide by the
> result. He carried his fight too far and both his cause and his conduct
> became vulgar. This could all be forgiven, though it was hard to stand while
> the contest was on, if he could now become reconciled to his defeat. As the
> chairman of the Taft delegation from Ohio, had you been defeated, I would
> have taken the responsibility of a motion to make your adversary's nomina-
> tion unanimous. There are only two kinds of men who get along in poli-
> tics,—the man who wins always succeeds, and the only other man who has a
> chance is the man who, when he has fought his battle and has exhausted his
> resources and strength, falls at the feet of his conqueror.[17]

By July 2, Daugherty turned his attention to the second session of the
state convention, which again met in Columbus. The main business was to
select the state candidates and to write the state party platform. Taft had
already cautioned Daugherty against nominating a Roosevelt man for
governor.[18] The Ohio progressives, still electing to remain in the party,
were equally adamant about remaining steadfast. But Burton, who represented the conservatives, suggested a compromise to win progressive
support for the Republican national ticket. He offered Brown, the progressive negotiator, the Taft organization's support of Garford for the
gubernatorial nomination, as well as concessions in the platform, provided that the insurgents agreed to endorse Taft. Refusing to bargain with
his conscience, Garford instructed Brown to reject Burton's offer.[19] He
consequently lost the nomination on the fifth ballot to a conservative dark
horse, Judge Edmond B. Dillon of Columbus. The remainder of the ticket
included only one Republican progressive—John L. Sullivan, the nominee for secretary of state. The Taft Republicans further proved that they
had recovered from the insurrection by endorsing the President by a
majority of 125. This represented an increase of almost 100 votes from the
state convention endorsement in June.

Afterward, Daugherty and Vorys departed for Washington, where
Vorys was Daugherty's most enthusiastic sponsor for chairman of the

Republican National Committee. On June 30, Daugherty had conveniently suggested that Hilles replace Hitchcock as Postmaster General so that
the chairman could work easily with him. He had insisted, however, that
he was not after the post.[20] In the following week several letters came to
Taft recommending Daugherty for national chairman. The *Ohio State
Journal* considered him a major contender, along with Congressman
Harry New of Indiana, William Barnes of New York, and Carmi Thompson of Ohio.[21] Hilles, the logical choice, did not want it.

On July 8, a subcommittee of the National Committee conferred with
Taft about the selection of a new chairman. Hilles, as Taft later related,
was the only candidate who had no enemies and no opposition. While he
was reluctant to accept the position, Hilles soon conceded that he was the
only one that the administration could select. Taft wrote his wife, Helen,
that Vorys was angry because "we did not take Daugherty, but nobody
knew Daugherty well enough to speak strongly in his behalf. Then," the
President continued, "there were some statements that he was a lobbyist
and that there might be some weaknesses in his record."[22]

After Daugherty had written several letters to Hilles complaining of his
rejection, Taft wrote him on July 17, indicating that he was "very sorry
indeed that your feelings were hurt." He explained his inclination to favor
the appointment because both Vorys and Hilles preferred it. As soon as
Taft proposed Daugherty's name to the committee, however, he "found
that sort of hesitation which comes from a lack of knowledge [of
Daugherty]." He also "found the circulation of stories in opposition . . . to
such a selection."[23] The subcommittee's disapprobation was one of
Daugherty's greatest disappointments. Stunned, he told Taft that he never
sought the chairmanship. He only desired to help in the selection of a
trusted chairman like Hilles. "I knew," Daugherty boasted, "I think first
and better than any person the game being played against you." In later
years Daugherty claimed that he had rejected the chairmanship because of
serious illness in his family.[24]

Meanwhile, Judge Dillon, the Republican gubernatorial nominee, requested that Daugherty run the Ohio campaign as chairman of the
Republican state executive committee. On July 18, Daugherty promptly
declined the offer.[25] By August 1, Dillon resigned the nomination four
days before the recently created Progressive party nominated Roosevelt
for president. The judge apparently suspected that a third party was also
in the offing to disrupt intraparty peace in Ohio, thereby narrowing his
chances of election. His resignation set the stage for another battle with
the progressives.

Taft, who refused to compromise with Ohio progressives, wanted the
aggressive Daugherty as the party's new candidate. Daugherty rejected
the overture repeatedly in the week preceding the August 10 central

committee caucus. Pleading that he "was too young 12 years ago and too old now," he also alluded to the pressure of business engagements.[26] He had rarely spurned an endorsement in the past, but the Republican chances now appeared grim in the face of a probable bolt in Ohio. In a Columbus meeting of Taft leaders on August 7, Daugherty failed in his attempt to push Harding into the race. Harding declined despite the suggestion that he was the "Moses to lead the harassed Republicans out of the Egyptian darkness."[27] As a result, three days before the central committee meeting to select Dillon's replacement, the Taft element had no likely candidate.

On August 10, most of the major state Republican leaders attended the central committee caucus. The Taft men finally rallied around General Robert Brown, an ardent pro-Taft newspaper editor from Zanesville. While the Progressives first favored Garford, they suggested Ulysses Grant Denman of Toledo, a moderate, as a compromise choice. They further proposed that Denman, if nominated, would neither declare for Taft nor Roosevelt but conduct a campaign on state issues alone. This was not what the conservatives had in mind. According to one account, Daugherty threatened to have his name placed on the ballot as an independent gubernatorial candidate in the event the committee chose Denman.[28] Holding a narrow majority, the Taft committeemen then nominated Robert Brown.

Walter Brown, Garford, and six others walked out of the central committee meeting after the conservatives' uncompromising stand. As he and his colleagues left, Daugherty remarked:

> Do you know where there are any good milk bottles for babies made here? Really I think the little children should have nourishment while they are on the way to their homes and the breasts of their mother constituency. They may cry if they are not fed—the babies.[29]

Ten days later Walter Brown and Garford formally announced their bolt.[30] Declaring their allegiance to the Progressive party, they formed part of the cadre of the Ohio party, which held its convention at Columbus on September 4. Garford became the party's gubernatorial candidate.

Daugherty managed the Republican rump in Ohio. He helped to reorganize the Republican central committee as a member-at-large and also became chairman of the Republican state executive committee on the urgings of both Taft and Robert Brown.[31] As housecleaners were putting the Republican headquarters in shape on the morning of August 14, Daugherty sat at his desk for the first time. He literally intended to follow their example, for a housecleaning was one aspect of his disciplined campaign to purge the unfaithful and to strengthen the party's hard core. Daugherty inspired such a program, which had the enthusiastic support of the President.[32]

Viewing the conflict as nothing less than war, Daugherty quickly wrote a confidential directive to each county executive chairman, asking for the names and addresses of officers and members on both the county central and executive committees. He then directed the chairman to indicate whether each member was a loyal Republican or a Bull Mooser. Daugherty proceeded to purge the committees of members who were unwilling to support Taft or who had\defected to the Progressives. In seventeen counties, he had entire committees replaced because of the large-scale desertion to the Progressive party.[33]

Daugherty's objective was to have loyal committees in each county. He did not complete the task by the end of August, as he had intended. Consequently, on October 21, he assured county executive secretaries that the process of eliminating traitors "can go on as well . . . and even more justifiably after the election." In another directive immediately following the election, Daugherty also ordered both the county executive and central committee chairmen to replace unfaithful members with loyal Republicans who could be depended upon in the future. He also suggested that the reorganization extend to the township and ward committees. Those who had been disloyal might be welcomed as supporters, but they were not permitted to reenter the party cadre.[34]

During the campaign, Daugherty followed the same disciplinary tactics with state Republican candidates who had hoped to carry "water on both shoulders." Already assured of a place on the Republican ballot, many catered to the Progressives in the expectation of a Bull Moose endorsement as well. Daugherty continually put pressure on them either to declare for Taft or be counted as belonging to the opposition. "I desire not to act precipitately," he stated, "but I am entitled to know and will learn about each candidate on the Republican state ticket, [and] whether he is a loyal Republican. This is what all loyal Republicans in Ohio want to know." He implied that candidates who did not follow his advice would find themselves financially unsupported by the state and county committees. All of this antagonized several Republican contenders, since a declaration for Taft ended any hope of securing Progressive support, which they needed to win.[35]

On September 4, the Progressive party partially resolved the issue when it selected its own candidates for the seven leading state offices. Hundreds of Republican candidates running on the district and county levels, however, could still seek the endorsement of the Progressive party and a place upon its ballot. Consequently, Daugherty worked with Secretary of State Charles H. Graves in enforcing the controversial Dana Law, which permitted a candidate's name on only one ticket.[36] Daugherty's action forced Republican candidates to retain their party identity and eliminated the Progressive party as a force on the local levels.

Closely related to Daugherty's hard-line campaign was his full use of Taft's patronage power in Ohio. His appeals for party loyalty would have had less meaning without the promise of state jobs. Daugherty believed in the old school policy of "first taking care of our friends and then if there is anything left, let the other fellows have it."[37] He quickly contacted Taft's new secretary, Carmi Thompson, when he heard that the recent civil appropriations bill permitted the employment of 300 clerks from Ohio at the Pension Office in Washington. "When will these jobs be available?" Daugherty questioned. "I understand that civil service registration has no control over them." In hoping that more had been created, he requested more specific information so that he could submit a claim for the entire number.[38]

Daugherty sometimes carried his patronage promises too far. On one occasion, he asked Thompson to write a party worker that, win or lose, the President's friends planned to take care of him. The presidential secretary reminded him that Taft would not make a pledge of that sort. If the President were elected, Thompson explained, he would have an opportunity to make "many appointments agreeable to the Ohio crowd."[39] Taft's defeat, however, enabled Daugherty to employ only a few party workers in the postelection period. Nevertheless, he fared better than his Progressive opponents.

Besides combatting the disloyalty of Ohio Republicans, Daugherty fought the infidelity of federal employees in the railway mail service. The center of their Ohio activity was in Cincinnati, where Superintendent Clyde Reed had his headquarters. Daugherty accused Reed of being a vigorous Roosevelt proponent who incited his employees to turn against the administration. Their treasonous activity, according to Daugherty, "is cutting the life out of us." Joseph Garretson, the editor of the *Cincinnati Times-Star*, corroborated Daugherty's assertions, and also pointed to the service's demoralization due to Reed's inconsiderate supervision of the work force.[40]

Daugherty's solution was simple. He wanted Reed transferred to another railway service headquarters and replaced by the assistant superintendent, the loyal W.L. Poe. But Postmaster General Hitchcock had already filled the only comparable vacancy. Since Daugherty saw the problem as simply political in nature, he refused to understand why civil service laws were not waived in either demoting someone in another area to accommodate Reed or even reducing Reed himself. That Hitchcock did not act upon his recommendations provided Daugherty with additional proof of his disloyalty. Again, he complained of his activities and on two occasions in August urged his removal as Postmaster General.[41]

On September 11, after the administration failed to act, Daugherty finally exploded: "I'll be damned if I don't propose to resign this job if

Hitchcock's conduct in putting things over on us is not stopped." He added that he spent half the time "listening to stories of the damage being done by employees of the Postoffice Department." His letter to Thompson so startled Taft that he immediately asked Hitchcock: "What under heaven is the matter with your people in Ohio?" The President suggested that the Postmaster General see that employees there were at least neutral.[42]

In the end Daugherty's persistency paid some dividends. In a letter marked personal and confidential, he told Taft that he had recently confronted Hitchcock about replacing Reed. While the Postmaster General had finally consented to moving Reed to St. Louis, Daugherty did not like the idea of transferring an aged St. Louis supervisor to Cincinnati. Daugherty, also angered that Poe did not receive the appointment, complained that Hitchcock "never desires to do anything recommended by anybody from Ohio." I have frequently told you plainly what I think should be done with Hitchcock," he wrote: "I will not repeat now my recommendation in that regard."[43] His letter convinced Taft of the necessity of replacing the questionable Reed with Poe. When Hitchcock explained that there was no vacant position for Reed elsewhere, Taft acceded to the suggestion that Reed exchange locations with a loyal New Orleans superintendent. The President then related to Daugherty that Hitchcock was no doubt anxious to do what he could. "I do not distrust him as you do," Taft added. Daugherty hesitantly accepted the situation.[44]

Daugherty also attempted to take action against disloyal postmasters. Probably the greatest defector was C.H. Bryson, the postmaster of Athens County, who Daugherty claimed had been "very offensive to our friends." Writing to Taft on October 24, he warned that he would never be satisfied until "this fellow is kicked out of the postoffice. He is deceitful, politically dishonest and ungrateful." Daugherty also wanted him removed as a warning to other "limber back" postmasters and postal employees who operated under the instructions of a disloyal Postmaster General. The slow-moving administration, however, waited several weeks before removing Bryson.[45]

Daugherty was aware that such defections jeopardized financial contributions from federal employees, one of the reasons he had fought so hard for the removal of Reed and Bryson. For sundry other reasons, he had difficulty collecting funds. For example, he ordered county chairmen not to accept money from Republicans who swayed from an "uncompromising fight against all who are opposing the national or the state ticket."[46] Party integrity and discipline had to be preserved above all else.

Sizable contributions, then, proved to be the exception rather than the rule. On one occasion, Daugherty elatedly alluded to a $1,000 donation

from an old client by warning Thompson: "Perhaps you had better lean
up against the Whitehouse or go down to the Union Station and lean up
against it, or lean up against the President."[47] The Cincinnati Prosperity
League also raised $15,000, and the President's family and friends contri-
buted substantially.[48] Beyond this, the response was disappointing. Making matters worse, major donations from Ohio went straight to Hilles at
the Republican National Committee headquarters. Such funds were
turned over to Daugherty only after some delay. He was often irritated
because of the wait, especially since he had requested that the money go
directly to him.[49] On one occasion he became so perturbed that he repri-
manded one of Hilles's workers, briefly causing friction between the two
headquarters. Vorys tried to soothe relations by justifying Daugherty's
impetuosity: "He has been frantic this week because he felt that he must
know . . . the extent of his resources . . . [to help] the different county
organizations who have been driving him crazy for money." Despite the
fact that Daugherty often "lost his head," Vorys reminded Hilles that he
found it quickly. On the following day, Daugherty apologized for his
impatience.[50]

The chairman had other reasons for sometimes losing his temper. By
often devoting sixteen hours a day to his job, Daugherty put himself into
an exhausted state.[51] In addition, he frequently found it difficult to obtain
Republican leaders to address important state rallies. In early September,
Root pleaded illness to a request to open the state campaign in Columbus
on September 20, although Senator Henry Cabot Lodge of Massachusetts
finally proved a formidable substitute. Foraker, notwithstanding Daugherty's persistent appeals, was unreceptive almost to the very end. On
September 19, Daugherty remarked to the old political antagonist:

> I will come down and spend a day with you even though I am as busy as a
> man can be and impoverishing myself in nervous and physical strength. I
> will gladly come down and try my hand on talking you into the campaign in
> your old fashioned way.[52]

Such friendly gestures prompted Foraker's one address at Columbus in
the campaign's final week.

Other old-line Republicans refused to render full support. Ambassador
Herrick, in France, could be excused for removing himself from the
campaign, but both Daugherty and Taft expected at least nominal assistance, which Herrick did not provide.[53] Even Senator Burton became
lukewarm. He not only disagreed with the way Daugherty ran the campaign, but also resented his interference in a Dayton postmaster contest.
In the campaign's last weeks, discouraging reports of political conditions
in Burton's bailiwick caused Thompson to proceed there to shore up the
organization. No wonder Daugherty privately confessed that his job had
"about broken me down and broken me up."[54]

Generally, however, Daugherty remained outwardly cocky. He initially informed the President that he would conduct an open, frank, and fearless campaign. In the succeeding weeks, he continually assured him and others of improving conditions. On October 5, Daugherty wrote Taft that "if you do not carry Ohio, I will be surprised and greatly disappointed."[55] By mid-October he completely ignored the Progressives in confidently concentrating on "Professor" Wilson and the Democrats. A Democratic victory, he warned, would ensure the radicalism of Bryan, the end of the protective tariff, and disaster to the country. Daugherty ended the campaign in a flourish. His slogans, "four weeks work in one" and "ten days work in two," were geared to inspire the state committees to a whirlwind finish. Two days prior to the election, Daugherty announced to the county executive chairmen that he had been too conservative in his statements. He predicted a sizable victory for Taft in Ohio.[56]

The election returns failed to fulfill Daugherty's predictions. Ohio gave its electoral vote to a Democratic presidential candidate for the first time in the history of the Republican party. The Democrats carried the entire state ticket and controlled the state legislature by more than two to one. Obviously, the Republican party's split was to the opposition's advantage. The G.O.P., however, did finish ahead of the Progressive party. Taft outdistanced Roosevelt 277,066 to 229,327 by receiving a decisive vote in the southern counties, while Roosevelt ran well in the northern urban areas. Robert Brown had fifty-five thousand more votes than the Progressive gubernatorial candidate, Arthur Garford. He obtained a plurality in ten counties to Garford's nine.

Despite the grim defeat, Daugherty did accomplish one objective. He succeeded in keeping the Ohio Republican party in tune with Taft and the party platforms. He accomplished this by inspiring and by imposing party loyalty. The latter was much more effective, for he rid Republican organizations of disloyal members and pressured Republican candidates to endorse the President, thereby keeping them from receiving Progressive endorsements. This may have lifted Taft and Brown into second position in the final vote. But Democrats also defeated some Republican congressional, state, and local candidates who might have otherwise won. This partly explains why the Democratic party sweep was so extensive and why acrimony prevailed among Ohio Republicans in the succeeding months.

Daugherty remarked after the election that he could not understand why the party had to give way for a Wilson experiment, although he rationalized that thousands of Republicans voted for Wilson rather than risk a Roosevelt victory.[57] Confident of his course, he continued his extermination program against disloyal Republicans afterward. His approach pleased the old-guard leaders like Foraker, Vorys, and Harding. Indeed, for Daugherty the 1912 fight resulted in a more intimate political relationship with Harding which ultimately would have a monumental impact on both. Nevertheless, Daugherty also caused ill feelings among Republicans who had opposed his uncompromising Republicanism, or who now felt that the main task should be reconciliation.[58] Even though he sometimes sensed that others could better perform the chairmanship duties, he would not brook any change wrought by concession:

> I feel that some men would come back to the party who may have a feeling against me because I was compelled to take a firm stand and not give an inch. I cannot change my ideas for all the party, I can step aside and quietly do it, for somebody who is more of a harmonizer than I am, but I will support no man who flinches or who backs down from the position and the principles we stand for.[59]

In the following year, Daugherty neither flinched nor retired. Because he did neither, the hostility against him increased. He now became an obstacle to party reunion.

An Obstacle to Party Reunion
1913-1916

ALTHOUGH the Progressive party failed in 1912, the progressive movement succeeded in revamping the political structure in Ohio. In early 1913, Daugherty pondered these changes with considerable dismay. He especially deplored the work of the Constitutional Convention of 1912, which had updated the Ohio charter. To Daugherty, the direct primary, the initiative, and the referendum were all inspired by men with socialistic attitudes who had been educated by the press to crave sensationalism.[1] Like Foraker, Harding and other old-guard Republicans, he believed in the inviolability of the party convention in which experienced political leaders held sway. "It was under that system," he asserted, that "the Republican party was built up and . . . prospered and became the most beneficial agency for the good ever organized by men in this country." The tendency of the times precluded such sensible principles. Any lawyer who challenged the Convention's work, according to Daugherty, was "promptly denounced by the press as being in the employ of the interests."[2]

Daugherty viewed the growing regulation of the state government with even more alarm, believing that the progressive programs of Governors Harmon and James M. Cox had suppressed both industry and the investor, with the result that businesses no longer thought Ohio a favorable area of investment. He pointed to the lack of public utility construction and railroad expansion. He also alluded to individual taxpayers who suffered because of the enactment of a municipal and county bond tax amendment that had been first proposed at the Constitutional Convention. Daugherty pegged the recent amendments and legislative enactments as part of a socialistic movement "detrimental to the sound sensible development and growth of the country." It was an effort on the part "of those who have been unsuccessful to take something from those who have been more successful, just as honest and more industrious." He suggested to Taft that, perhaps, this was the reason the former President had decided to leave Ohio.[3]

These progressive changes reinforced Daugherty's decision to remain politically active. He believed that under his direction, Republican party unification and resurgence could do much to reverse the tide. He was not in politics solely for self-interest. And like so many Republicans who had learned their politics in the halcyon days of Sherman and McKinley, he was conditioned to associate party well-being with that of the nation or state. For that reason, too, he had devoted himself to the cause. In the fight of 1912 he had put aside his law practice for weeks. Whatever personal gain or reward he might have expected should not obscure the fact that he made significant sacrifices for the party. He remained chairman after 1912 partly to insure that the state party recovered. But more so than most politicians, he confused party interest with self-interest. By refusing to resign he hindered amalgamation and worsened the division within the party. Undoubtedly, his decision to hang on while under fire revealed his concern that he should not be made a scapegoat for 1912 and be obliterated politically. It also reflected a combative personality and a desire for power to punish his adversaries and to serve himself and his friends.

His conservative Republicanism and his uncompromising stand made Daugherty less than an ideal state executive chairman. In early 1913, the more progressive Republican state legislators publicly criticized his retention as party leader. Other progressive Republican leaders like Franklin County prosecuting attorney Edward Turner, newspaper publisher Charles L. Knight of Akron, and former Congressman Paul Howland of Cleveland resented his domination of the party machinery.[4] All believed him an obstacle to a reunited Republican party. Daugherty, nonetheless, refused to step down. The November elections seemed to solidify his position, for Republican voters defeated several of Governor Cox's constitutional amendments, including the short ballot and the proportional representation proposals, which also had the Progressive party's support. In addition, such former Republican strongholds as Newark, Sidney, Circleville, and Mansfield now returned to the fold. Daugherty interpreted the results not only as an ending of an experimental craze "to cure an imaginary sickness" but as an indication of the reemergence of the "strongest political party in the United States."[5]

A belief persisted after the election, however, that Daugherty must resign in the interest of a Republican-Progressive amalgamation. Even some conservative Republicans expressed this conviction, although Turner and other liberal leaders were the most insistent. To Turner, Daugherty was not only too closely identified with the fight, he also represented the party-boss symbol. As long as he remained chairman, a Republican campaign against the "bossism" of James Cox, who had extended the power of the governorship, and Walter Brown could bear no fruit. On February 12, Daugherty issued a rebuttal, claiming that he "never has been a boss, never proposes to be one; never has been bossed and never will be."[6] He nevertheless announced in a carefully worded statement that he would not play any official part in the 1914 campaign, nor would he be a candidate for any political office. He further promised that neither would he accept the chairmanship nor any other position within the Republican party for the following year. Daugherty attributed his "resignation" to the loss of both money and friends. While Turner was elated that Daugherty elected not to involve the organization in the primaries, the *Ohio State Journal* shrewdly pointed out he did not formally resign the chairmanship; he temporarily quit. The anti-Daugherty newspaper implied that with Daugherty anything was possible.[7]

The drive for Republican-Progressive reconciliation followed another path. By January 1914, the Republican legislators suggested a reunion banquet in Columbus. The central committee, led by W.L. Parmenter, accepted the plan and set the date for February 26. Daugherty outwardly favored the idea and persuaded the reluctant Foraker to attend. Nonetheless, he privately said that he stood as firm as ever in his old beliefs.[8] At crowded Memorial Hall, Senator William Borah of Idaho, as a sop to the Progressives, delivered the main address. Daugherty, Burton, Foraker, and David Mead Massie of Chillicothe were among the other speakers. Introduced as "Horatius, who held the bridge in Ohio in 1912," Daugherty concluded a short presentation with "gentlemen, I am a Republican." The forget-together meeting, as Daugherty termed it, was not, however, an overwhelming success. There was only a sprinkling of repentant Progressives among the 3,000 to 4,000 who were present. Since Progressive party leaders like Garfield and Brown refused even to attend, reconciliation was remote.[9] Speakers instead focused on the need to stamp out Coxism (James M., not George B.) in November, a goal that offended no one in attendance.

A more significant step toward reunion occurred on April 6 when conservative Senator Burton announced that he would not seek reelection. The eventual nominee, genial Warren G. Harding, would with his harmonizing manner, do much to facilitate amalgamation despite his conservative inclinations. The dejected Burton, faced with the prospects of a grueling primary contest, declined to run because of a growing unpopularity spawned by his loyal defense of Taft in 1912. He was also extremely sensitive about his unpopular stand on legislative measures. He had voted for the disfavored Payne-Aldrich Tariff of 1909 and had supported President Wilson's desire to repeal the Panama Canal Toll Exemption Act of 1912, which had excluded U.S. vessels from canal levies. Finally, with deep conviction, he favored both the neutralization and the equalization of the Panama Canal—long unpopular stands among Republicans.[10] In any case, for party success in Ohio, he suggested a successor who was less involved in the factional disputes of recent years.

Burton's Senate seat was, in fact, first discussed in 1912, when Taft men considered Daugherty a possible successor. Then, at a secret conference in Cincinnati in November 1913, the aging Foraker, whose large mustache had long since turned iron gray, received little opposition from leading Republicans on his decision to enter the senatorial primary the following year.[11] By March 1914, Burton's own choice was Congressman Frank B. Willis, who had straddled the 1912 rift. Willis was first elected to the Congress from the eighth district in 1910. Educated at Ohio Northern University, where he later taught, he was a big-boned and rosy-cheeked country boy who patterned his booming oratory after Billy Sunday. Despite a vivacious personality, Willis, in a lengthy public career that ended in the United States Senate in 1928, neither drank, chewed, golfed, nor played cards. His only apparent concessions to human indulgence were a taste for bonbons and long black stogies. Several weeks before Burton announced his retirement, Willis had decided instead to commit himself to the gubernatorial race, thereby challenging former Progressive Massie, the choice of most Republican leaders.

Daugherty at first advised Burton to remain in the Senate race.[12] After his refusal and after Willis made known his plans, he momentarily revived his own senatorial ambitions at a time when Harding was also emerging as a contender. The evidence regarding Daugherty's aspirations is not conclusive, but a curious letter exists to Harding from J.S. Hampton, a Harding political aide. As Hampton recalled the episode two days afterward, on April 8 he informed William H. Miller, secretary of the state executive committee, in Columbus that Harding would enter the Senate primary against the reactionary Foraker, provided that former Progressive Dan Hanna supported Harding with his newspapers. The delighted Miller said that he would locate Harry Daugherty to win over Hanna. That same day, as Hampton recalled, "Miller finally located Daugherty in a saloon in the Harrison Building." When Miller returned,

> he said Harry had thought favorably of the matter but wanted to think it over until the next morning though he agreed to get busy over the phone at once if Bill said so. Bill answered that the next day would do. Daugherty said he was sick; that he was going to a turkish bath and then straight home and would see Bill in the morning.

The next morning (April 9) the *Cincinnati Enquirer* and the *Cleveland Plain Dealer* published stories about numerous requests that Daugherty had recently received to run in the senate primary and that he would have the backing of Dan Hanna. "It was plain why Daugherty wished to delay," wrote Hampton. He had contacted the press. "I felt like hell when

I saw those stories and at once went to Bill. He said he thought as I did—that Daugherty had usurped the whole thing." Hampton indicated that he remained in Columbus that day to better determine Daugherty's intentions. But Daugherty "had gone into hiding and Bill could not locate him."[13] Daugherty's actions were not out of character. By nature he was impulsive; no other explanation exists for some of his actions. So much did he want—and, perhaps, feel he deserved—elevation to the Senate that he acted almost irrationally to Harding's proposed candidacy. What brought him quickly back to reality was undoubtedly the realization of the many obstacles that stood before him, not the least of which were Harding's formidable candidacy, his own unpopularity among progressive and some moderate Republicans, and his recent promise that he would not be a candidate for the Senate.[14]

Daugherty's decision to back Harding came less than a week after the newspaper publicity. He sent word to a conference of Ohio Republicans at Arthur Vorys's Columbus law office that Harding was his choice for senator. Everyone present, except those from Cincinnati, favored Harding, who was deserving, a campaigner par excellence, and most adept at obscuring party differences. Most likely because of Foraker's candidacy, Burton then reconsidered his retirement. But Daugherty, Hanna, and Maschke told him that it was now too late.[15] At a Cleveland conference in mid-May, Daugherty, Burton, Hanna, and Maschke formally told Harding that he had their full support against Foraker, who was an embarrassment to many Republicans. Before announcing his candidacy, Harding first obtained Hanna's promise that he would not attack Foraker and would support him if he won. He then journeyed to Cincinnati where he told Foraker that he had decided to run. Against Harding in the primary, Foraker and the unknown Ralph D. Cole of Findlay finished second and third respectively. Daugherty's role in Harding's success was important but not crucial. The fact is that Harding was primarily responsible for his own success in 1914. Yet in the 1930s, Daugherty, struggling to rehabilitate himself, claimed that without him Harding would not have even entered the primary: "I found him like a turtle sunning himself on a log, and I pushed him into the water."[16]

In another Republican contest in 1914, Daugherty completely disregarded his promise to remain aloof by opposing Frank Willis. He considered Willis one of the "dodgers and side-steppers" of the 1912 campaign who was now antagonizing the organization by seeking the governorship.[17] Daugherty used his influence as state chairman to pit Youngstown industrialist David Tod, a former state senator, against Willis. Reports persisted that Daugherty used the state organization to assist Tod in several counties. In Fayette, not only was the Daugherty-dominated organization supporting Tod, but, according to one observer,

Daugherty's brother was circulating petitions in Tod's behalf. Other reports came to the Willis headquarters of a Daugherty-inspired campaign against him.[18]

Daugherty denied that he discriminated among the primary candidates, but the Willis clique continued to use the issue to good advantage. One Willis leader astutely suggested that they confine their attacks solely to Daugherty.[19] Their often exaggerated denunciations of Daugherty as a menacing political boss won support, especially from Republicans who wanted Daugherty replaced in the interest of a reunited party. The stand on Daugherty fitted well with Willis's broadsides on the bossism and overcentralization of the Cox administration. That Tod became a defendant in a libel trial on the day of the primary further ensured Willis's chances for nomination.

Despite Willis's primary victory, Daugherty gave some indication that he would again seek the chairmanship. One Willis supporter warned the future governor that Daugherty was already intriguing with the new committeemen. Others wrote that Daugherty was a political thorn to the once Progressive voter. They suggested choosing for chairman a loyal Republican who had progressive tendencies.[20] As the Republican gubernatorial nominee, Willis did have much to say about who should run his campaign. Thus, Edwin Jones of Jackson replaced Daugherty as Republican state executive chairman. But Daugherty retained enough influence to secure a firm hold on the new state central committee.[21] Later that year, he nearly captured the house speakership for his candidate. To disguise that effort, he made the legislative fight a wet-dry issue, in which he had the support of prohibitionist elements, including Willis and the Anti-Saloon League. Thus, he began a tenuous alliance with Willis and a commitment to prohibition which he correctly believed represented an emerging majority view in Ohio. It became for him a vehicle not only to reestablish himself more in state politics and to punish his enemies, but also to elevate the Ohio party as well. He confided to an associate, Newton H. Fairbanks of Springfield, that "I am still a policeman on the force looking after the interests of this party."[22]

Daugherty did his share of the work in the successful Republican campaign of 1914, which elevated Harding to the Senate and Willis to the govenorship. He assisted Harding in the organizational aspects of the campaign while avoiding speeches that drew "fire where none is necessary."[23] The Progressive party's crushing defeat especially pleased him. The Ohio G.O.P., indeed, seemed closer to solidification.

Despite some disappointments in 1914, Daugherty optimistically looked to the future after the Republican resurgence. In early 1915 he made up his mind to seek Pomerene's Senate seat the following year. Harding's easy victory must have given him encouragement. To avoid embarrassment and to invite backing, he wrote almost every Republican politician and newspaper in Ohio to determine how his candidacy would set in their communities. The response seemed encouraging, probably because Charles Dick and Judge D.D. Woodmansee of Cincinnati were the only active Republican candidates. He was also assured of the approval of Willis, Burton, and Harding; the latter two were under obligation to him for past senatorial campaigns. The understanding was that in 1916 Governor Willis would seek reelection; Burton would enter the presidential primary as Ohio's favorite son; and Daugherty, of course, would go to the Senate.[24]

On September 18, 1915, Daugherty announced his candidacy and appeared a possible winner. As he told Taft: "Being an old crane that has been up and down a great many streams, I wanted to be sure of my ground." He assured him that "the things we stood for are popular now, and I am surprised to be assured by the Progressives that they are friendly to me." Daugherty was quick to add that he had never taken back anything that he had said or had done relating to 1912. He attributed the Progressive support to the respect that people have in a man who has stood his ground.[25]

Daugherty received Taft's assurance that brother Charles, the owner of the *Cincinnati Times-Star*, would help.[26] He also had the allegiance of those who had belonged to the Taft organization. To Ohio Republicans who hesitated, Daugherty reminded that he had performed a party service in the war of 1912. Typical was the "stiff" letter he got Fairbanks to write Myron T. Herrick:

> I am just old fashioned enough to believe that gratitude is still a virtue, and I somehow think that this year, 1916, offers a golden opportunity for all Republicans of our old state to show they know what that admirable quality in man is, and where and how to bestow it in a generous manner—by nominating Mr. Daugherty, unopposed, and electing him to the United States [Senate]."[27]

Republicans who had questioned his posture in 1912 resented Daugherty's efforts to capitalize upon it now. Congressman Simeon D. Fess of Ada, a probable candidate himself, felt that a united party must be the only consideration for 1916. On December 23, 1915, he reminded Daugherty "that you cannot head a united party. I do not refer to the leaders," Fess explained; "they can easily compose their differences, but I fear the rank and file." He told Daugherty that, for the same reasons, he had not supported Foraker in 1914.[28]

Daugherty replied sarcastically that he appreciated the arrival of Fess's letter on Christmas morning. The only Republicans who hesitated to support him, he continued, were "a few of the same class of people who were uncertain about which side to take in 1912." Had he resisted a campaign upon party regularity and an adherence to party principles in 1912, there would now be no Republican party in Ohio. "Strange to say," Daugherty unbelievably asserted, "you are the only man today holding a responsible position accredited to any party who will not say that I was right in the position I took in 1912." He went on: "I cannot understand either, my dear Mr. Fess, the consistency of your position that you were compelled from your standpoint to support Senator Harding [in 1914]... and do not approve of my candidacy in 1916 for the same reason." Daugherty rightly indicated how outspoken and fearless Harding had been in supporting his actions in 1912. While wanting Fess's backing, Daugherty would not "stultify" himself to secure the nomination. "It is not necessary to my happiness," he added. He appreciated the Congressman's personal affection toward him, but questioned why "you are not willing to dig a little deeper into me and my cause than a surface investigation and one orginating from prejudice formed in your mind because I have seen fit to be outspoken in behalf of the party." He concluded somewhat self-righteously:

> I think it possible for a man to go along, accomplish something in this world in an honorable profession and the pursuit of life, give active and even under some circumstances strenuous support to the party and be shot at and criticized for doing so, and yet possess qualifications for this high office.[29]

To Taft and Fess, Daugherty had exaggerated his progressive support. Former Bull Moosers like Dan Hanna at first promised aid, as did Robert Nevin of Dayton, the 1912 attorney general candidate of the Progressive party, who had previously supported Daugherty's challenge of Hanna in 1899.[30] Some, no doubt, admired his courage while others leaned to him because Charles Dick was an even more undesirable choice. Those who favored him, however, were clearly the exceptions.

By early January the emerging candidacy of Myron T. Herrick cost Daugherty considerable party backing. Daugherty later claimed that Herrick had assured him of a clear field and, in fact, had encouraged him to enter the race because of Herrick's interest in running "for President or Pope and everything else."[31] Regardless, Herrick's challenge was formidable. He regained his popularity with Ohioans after his successful ambassadorship at Paris. Also, he had not been actively involved in the 1912 dispute and so was more likely to promote party harmony. Aside from his controversial position in 1912, Daugherty, meanwhile, was stigmatized as a lobbyist who now faced a "whispering" campaign as information leaked out on the Morse case. But he still remained self-assured. He boasted to friends that "more than 40 newspapers, representing as many counties, have come out for me editorially in the strongest editorials possible."[32]

Charles Taft's *Cincinnati Times-Star* constituted Daugherty's major newspaper support. Its editorials reminded readers that northern Ohio monopolized the state Republican party: Senator Harding came from there as did Theodore Burton, who was to be Ohio's favorite son at the June Republican National Convention in Chicago. The *Times-Star* rejected Herrick for geographical reasons. When Herrick claimed that his entry might help to reconcile party differences, the *Times-Star* quickly came to Daugherty's defense. Herrick's argument, according to one editorial, meant that only men who fail to take a position at critical times were worthy of office after quiet was restored. Such a rule would hardly encourage fearlessness and independence of action. But no one was in doubt where Daugherty stood in 1912. To a Taft, that was a strong argument for selecting him.[33]

Senator Harding's position in the contest was much more complex. Because of his standing, he obviously could influence the outcome. Personally, he favored Daugherty. "You know that I have some gratitude in my heart, and from this statement you will understand where my sympathies lie," Harding remarked to his friend Malcolm Jennings. He was obviously referring to Daugherty's help in the 1914 senatorial campaign. Besides that, he truly felt that Daugherty would make "five times as effective a senator" as Herrick.[34] Harding, however, realized that it would be politically inexpedient and undiplomatic to come out with an endorsement. This perturbed Daugherty, who wanted an open pledge from Harding. While conceding that Harding had done his share to help, he wrote Ed Scobey, a Harding cohort, "I don't think he would have anything to lose if he would come out and say that he wanted me to go to the Senate with him because he will be elected Senator as long as he lives if he is not elected to anything better."[35]

At a Columbus meeting on May 6, Harding leaned to Daugherty, while still attempting to retain an impartial stance:

> It can be no impropriety to say that I have been associated with Mr. Daugherty in times of great stress in the Republican party and know his worth; and in view of the splendid service he has rendered it would be a fitting recognition of his sterling Republicanism and great service, if the Republicans of Ohio would send him to the United States Senate.[36]

Daugherty's opponents did not appreciate Harding's conception of nonpartisanship. Harding himself realized that he had, perhaps, gone too far. Much to Daugherty's annoyance, he remained outwardly noncommittal for the remainder of the campaign, although there was no doubt among most Republicans whom he favored.[37]

To cultivate Burton's backing, Daugherty was a diligent worker for his unrealistic presidential ambitions. But, as Ohio's favorite son, there was a slim chance that he might be nominated. At the Republican national convention of June 1916, Daugherty attempted to exploit that possibility by lining up the West Virginia delegation for him.[38] While Harding presided over the convention, Daugherty occupied Harding's delegate-at-large seat in the Ohio delegation promoting Burton. His efforts were futile as the Ohioan received only a token vote. The party nominated the more progressive Charles Evans Hughes of New York, a much better choice for those who favored Herrick's candidacy.

Daugherty threw himself into the primary campaign after returning home. He had the support of the party machinery, which he had dominated for the past four years. By committing himself to Willis's renomination, he continued to have the backing of the governor's cronies.[39] He also solicited many of the friends who had stood by him since the 1899 fight with Hanna. Howard Mannington, Cyrus Huling, and James Holcomb all worked diligently, as did members of Taft's former Ohio headquarters. William R. Halley, clerk of the senate, was his campaign manager, while central committeeman Fairbanks proved invaluable in directing the work of other committeemen. Daugherty took great pride in his organization. In a July 28 campaign speech, he asserted that "a political party standing for great principles must have a dependable head and an organization to carry out the party's will." He considered it a misfortune that the Ohio Republican party lacked the machines of the Hanna period. He promised that if he were elected, there would be an organization in Ohio. Such statements caused the *Ohio State Journal* to accuse Daugherty of dwelling in the past.[40].

The Daugherty campaign strategy included an extensive speaking tour that comprised three to ten speeches and a 200-mile trip per day. By late July, he had already spoken in fifty counties in an effort to fulfill a pledge to visit the entire eighty-eight. Labelling himself the farmers' candidate, he endorsed the Federal Farm Loan Act. He coupled this with his advocacy of a high protective tariff. Daugherty also spoke out for greater immigration restriction, a world-peace court, and a strong merchant marine.[41] He carefully slanted his speeches to the economic condition of the county to avoid alienating any particular dominant class.

Despite his serious canvass, few political observers thought him a likely winner at any stage of the campaign.[42] Daugherty saw the situation differently. He blamed his subsequent defeat primarily on Hughes's laudatory appraisal of Herrick's ambassadorship in a July 31 speech at Carnegie Hall in New York. The address, an indirect slap at Daugherty, did reflect the antagonisms that still existed among Ohio Republicans, for there was strong suspicion that Ohio National Committeeman James R. Garfield, the former Progressive, influenced Hughes to praise Herrick excessively.[43] Daugherty and other old-line Republicans were furious after they heard of Garfield's supposed actions. Equally disturbing was the attitude of the Republican organization in Hamilton County. Led by Rudolph Hynicka, one of George B. Cox's former lieutenants, the Republican county executive committee on July 26 unanimously endorsed Herrick, despite the urgings of the *Times-Star* to remain neutral. That Daugherty was more committed to dry legislation than Herrick had some effect on the organization's attitude. Daugherty, inwardly disappointed, retorted that the endorsement would not "affect the nomination, except probably to increase my majority."[44]

After the actions of Hughes and the Hamilton County committee, the campaign became more heated and personal. Daugherty accused the Herrick organization of spending money lavishly. He then struck at the misrepresentations of the county Herrick Clubs, calling them "bald fakes." Daugherty accused them of padding their rolls to include even his most loyal supporters in their desire to portray a swelling movement for Herrick. He concluded that the "fertile mind that concocted this cheat evidently knew the value of a lie and how fast and far one travels before it is overtaken."[45] Herrick's men, meanwhile, freely circulated information on Morse's pardon. The pro-Herrick Robert F. Wolfe, owner of the *Ohio State Journal* and the *Columbus Dispatch*, was equally relentless in portraying Daugherty as an undesirable candidate.

The August 8 primary gave Herrick an overwhelming victory. Daugherty carried six insignificant counties in amassing 66,182 votes to Herrick's 155,334 and Dick's 37,183. He lost Franklin County by 4,500 and Hamilton by 7,000. Only in Fayette did he win a convincing victory.[46] To Taft afterward, Daugherty mostly blamed Herrick for his defeat:

> Mr. Herrick deceived me, as you know. I could have defeated him but for an unfortunate chain of circumstances which developed. In the first place, he spent, or others spent for him, more than half a million dollars to secure the nomination. In the second place, the wet element voted solidly for him and the dry vote was divided, giving Herrick and Dick more votes than they gave me. Then the Progressives, finding that they had a good chance to get even with me, lined up solidly behind Herrick, with the understanding that they were to be given practically control of the party. Another important factor and as big as any was the praise Mr. Hughes gave Herrick.[47]

In explaining his defeat, Daugherty might have also mentioned that he had unnecessarily alienated the rank and file and the party's progressive elements. In a well-publicized speech in Dayton in August 1915, he had called the primary a failure and a "fad" and had indicated his desire to return to "the old convention days." If this were not enough, he later called for "a strong directing hand" over the party à la Mark Hanna.[48] He might have been an unknown to some voters, while Herrick certainly was not. But to many, Daugherty was an anachronism who failed to receive support even from some conservative quarters. The Foraker-Kurtz combination, now battered and semi-retired, still bore the hostility of the 1890s. Kurtz wrote that Herrick was much better than Daugherty and openly supported the Clevelander. While "Fire Alarm" Joe sounded no public accolades, he privately favored Herrick.[49] Conversely, his endorsement of Daugherty might have reversed the situation in Hamilton County and swayed voters elsewhere.

The 1914 senatorial primary law no doubt hindered Daugherty. Had the old system still existed, he would have had sufficient organizational backing to win party legislative support for nomination. But he would not have followed Harding into the Senate, for the Democrats controlled the Ohio General Assembly. They would have cast their votes for the incumbent Pomerene. In any case, it was Harding who delivered the eulogy. To Jennings he privately commented that Daugherty's defeat meant "his complete retirement."[50]

Daugherty had no thoughts of divorcing himself from politics. He was not "a man that complains because of political results." He proposed to support the ticket. Nevertheless, "I am not pleased, and neither are the old line Republicans in the state."[51] His anger heightened when Hughes catered more to former Ohio Progressives than to "thorough-going" Republicans. Daugherty fought an attempt to place the "obnoxious" Walter Brown on the Republican state executive committee.[52] But with Garfield already national committeeman, and with Hughes and Herrick victorious in November, more concessions to former Progressives would surely follow. To Daugherty the issue was more than a desire to punish his enemies. It was a matter of power. With Herrick, Garfield, and then Brown controlling the patronage and the state organization, he was finished politically.[53]

But Senator Pomerene overwhelmed Herrick in November. The latter blamed Daugherty for his defeat. He later told Harding that Daugherty "did things to me in my campaign which I never would for a moment think of doing against an opponent."[54] There is no evidence to corroborate Herrick's complaint. But Daugherty did not forget his defeat in 1916, nor had he forgotten who had opposed him in 1912. Not only was he now more determined to prevent the amalgamation of the party to include former Bull Moose leaders, but he also became antagonistic to the wet Hamilton County Republican organization, which had contributed to his primary defeat. In November, Daugherty publicly came out for prohibition in Ohio in part because of his personal grudge against Hynicka and other Hamilton County leaders—at least that was how Harding analyzed his motives.[55] In the next three years Daugherty represented a further deterrent to an inclusive, united Republican party in Ohio. His attitudes conflicted with the beliefs of the titular leader of Ohio Republicans— Senator Warren G. Harding.

The Troubled Harding Friendship of 1918

DAUGHERTY's most important political relationship was with Harding, but by the end of 1918 the two found themselves at odds and scarcely speaking to each other. Conversely, Daugherty and Willis had grown closer politically after Willis's 1916 gubernatorial defeat by ex-Governor James M. Cox and Daugherty's senatorial primary loss to Herrick. Sometime in 1917, Daugherty committed himself to supporting Willis for renomination in 1918. Both agreed on the political soundness of backing prohibition in Ohio as a means of restoring the party and themselves to power. Although the Ohio dry referendum narrowly failed in the 1917 fall election, the movement became increasingly popular among rank and file Republicans, especially since it was associated with the success of the war effort. Daugherty and the personally dry Willis, with the help of the Anti-Saloon League, were confident of its success in 1918.

Senator Harding viewed the Daugherty-Willis accord with apprehension. While he was in close consultation with both, he doubted the wisdom of renominating Willis who, as governor, had made more patronage promises than he could fulfill. He also feared Daugherty's contempt for the party's progressive and wet factions would disrupt his efforts to restore party harmony, thereby jeopardizing his reelection as well as a possible vice-presidential bid in 1920. Daugherty, on the other hand, believed that his enemies would use Harding's unity effort to dominate the party. This meant his own political demise, which Harding might expediently accept, and possibly the end of Harding's senatorial career. The Daugherty-Harding clash then developed over the fundamental issue of party control in Ohio. It was fought between the Daugherty-Willis dominated Republican central committee and the Harding-created Republican state advisory committee. Harding had formed his committee in 1916 to aid in the further reunification of the party, as well as to give him more influence in state Republican affairs.[1] Despite Daugherty's disapproval, he now intended to increase its authority. The conflicts of 1918 threatened to end the political friendship of Daugherty and Harding.

Daugherty had first met Harding in November 1899 at Richwood, Union County. Despite his mustache, nearly black hair, and thinner physique, the thirty-five-year-old Harding still clearly resembled the distinguished-looking Harding of later years with his bronzed complexion, massive, if slightly stooped, shoulders, and handsome face. The immediate setting of the meeting was a cast-iron pump behind the Globe Hotel where Harding, the younger of the two men, was washing his boots just prior to a crossroads political rally. The tobacco-chewing Harding recognized Daugherty as one of the principal speakers and promptly introduced himself. Of the two, Daugherty was more prominent in Ohio politics. Harding, still a political novice, was campaigning for his first political office—a seat in the Ohio senate. Daugherty said later that he persuaded Harding to deliver an impromptu speech. As he recalled the incident forty years later, Harding, although somewhat embarrassed and awkward, gave a good address. A contemporary witness told Harding that his talk "was far ahead of Harry Daugherty's."[2]

There is no evidence that Daugherty and Harding were close in the succeeding years. As a lobbyist, Daugherty may have cultivated the state senator. (His congratulatory letter following Harding's senatorial victory of 1899 included a request "to call upon me any time it is convenient for you.") But his later assertions that Harding was always like a younger brother are without foundation.[3] The Harding Papers contain only three letters from Daugherty for the 1899-1911 period. Harding, in fact, was a staunch Foraker supporter who often opposed Daugherty's political ambitions. In 1901, one anti-Daugherty Fayette leader felt confident enough of Harding's attitude to request his help in ending Daugherty's hold on the county delegation.[4] When Daugherty elected to challenge the Dick-Foraker combination in 1906, Harding came to its defense. In that period a Harding cohort referred to Daugherty as "foxy Harry," hardly a label one pinned on a loyal friend.[5]

While Daugherty's political influence declined in the first decade of the twentieth century, Harding advanced rapidly in Ohio politics. He was reelected to the senate in 1901 and then appointed the Republican floor leader. He impressed Governor George K. Nash and other Hanna men with his ability to harmonize intraparty differences and with his willingness to carry out the dictates of party leaders. Even though associated with Foraker, Harding always endeavored to reconcile factionalism in the name of Republican success—and for his own political advancement. In 1903, as lieutenant governor, he functioned effectively as presiding officer of the senate. He then made a strategic—and temporary—withdrawal from politics in 1905 after the unpopular Republican governor, Myron T. Herrick, decided to seek renomination. He returned to his Marion newspaper to await a more opportune time to fulfill his gubernatorial ambitions. The opportunity came in 1910 when the divided Ohio Republican party finally agreed upon Harding as a compromise choice. Daugherty played no appreciable role in Harding's nomination. In fact Daugherty-dominated Fayette County backed a rival candidate at the Republican state convention. The Harding men retaliated by opposing Howard Mannington, Daugherty's choice for the state executive chairmanship. When Harding's campaign manager Malcolm Jennings refused the position, Harding agreed on Lewis Laylin.[6] It mattered little, for the progressive-conservative rift within the party was too divisive even for Harding to heal. He had the misfortune of suffering the worst defeat of any Ohio Republican gubernatorial candidate up to that time.

The culminating party fight of 1912 created the Daugherty-Harding partnership. Both were Taft delegates-at-large at the June Republican national convention, where Harding nominated Taft amid the progressives' jeers and hisses. Afterward, Harding became a strong defender of state chairman Daugherty's get-tough policies. The Marion *Daily Star* gave him complete backing. Daugherty sincerely thanked Harding for his "constant comfort and support during the campaign. It was only on account of such support" that he was able "to go through this terrific fight." In another letter, Daugherty claimed that "one great thing resulting from this war we have had . . . is that we are better friends than ever and understand each other thoroughly and will hang together through thick and thin."[7]

Even though they were more closely aligned and enjoyed each other's company, they were not bosom friends. It was more often political rather than social matters that brought them together. As late as 1919, Daugherty knew little of Harding's associations at Marion, while Harding then remarked that he had three genuinely devoted friends: Ed Scobey of Texas, Malcolm Jennings, and "our good friend," Colonel George Christian of Marion.[8] Harding remained politically close to Daugherty out of a sense of gratitude and out of an awareness that Daugherty was still a powerful politician who would generally favor him, provided that it did not conflict with his own political goals. Daugherty, meanwhile, stood to gain in remaining friendly with Harding. By 1914, Taft and Burton were no longer as potent in Ohio politics. Harding was in a position to aid Daugherty's ambitions, which included a seat in the United States Senate.

There is no hint, however, that Daugherty dominated the relationship, as he later asserted monotonously in his autobiographical work of 1932, *The Inside Story of the Harding Tragedy*.[9] Daugherty, in fact, was often more sensitive about retaining Harding's friendship than Harding Daugherty's. As early as March 1913, Daugherty dejectedly expressed his concern over Harding's failure to settle a misunderstanding. In a letter to Harding, he referred to a speech he had made in Harding's behalf during the gubernatorial race of 1910. "You no doubt have forgotten that you were a candidate," Daugherty wrote; "I would then remind you." He enclosed the speech which had said: "[Harding] is a self-made man. He never dodged. He never scratched. He never sulked. He is a manly man."

> I am still sorry you were not elected [Daugherty continued]. But to offset that sorrow is my joy that you are well, respected, happy, and prosperous. I am still a republican. Just old fashioned. Believing in the bridge which has carried us over the stream so many times. Willing to progress as fast as judgment, necessity, and safety will permit. Hoping I will not make such a damn fool of myself as I know others have. Wanting to be natural and normal in all things. Knowing I do not know it all but knowing a man who thinks he does and is mistaken. Not downcast because I have not been more successful nor sour because many other men have been more successful than I have. Envy nobody anything. Hate nobody. Love my friends and see more good than bad in every man who does not agree with me. Regret some things, among which is the fact that I don't see you often. With love, your friend, H.M. Daugherty.[10]

Nor did Harding always depend upon Daugherty's political advice. He banked on no one individual. The senator had an array of observers to provide him with information on Ohio matters. Daugherty was only one of several, and Harding sometimes thought him the least reliable, as he considered him the most biased. Harding was more apt to depend on Malcolm Jennings, his former newspaper editor and now executive secretary of the Ohio Manufacturers' Association, and Charles E. Hard, the assistant secretary of the Republican state advisory committee. An astute politician, Harding relied also on his own political observations. He learned how to obtain his own way without offending, which was the secret of his political success. He deemphasized personal differences so that the door might be left open for reconciliation. That he held office from 1914 made this approach all the more expedient. Hard correctly assessed the contrast between Harding and Daugherty: The latter "always 'busts up' anything he is in because he plays it too hard and is too combative."[11] Harding, in many ways, was the political antithesis of Harry Daugherty. This was, perhaps, no more evident than in 1918.

In January 1918, Daugherty made a bid for the leadership of the dry cause in Ohio. He assured Fairbanks that prohibition was "going to be a movement that has come to stay and it will be joined in by the strong men of the party."[12] Daugherty was not personally dry. "Nobody ever charged me with being a crank on the proposition," he asserted, "for a man can take a drink and yet be in favor of abolishing the business." He proved his point by sending Harding and his personal secretary, George Christian, Jr., several bottles of bourbon and rye. In order not to offend Harding's stenographer, there was a bottle "for the young lady" as well.[13] Daugherty, in championing the movement out of political expediency, not only intended to elevate Willis to the governorship, but also sought to dominate the party machinery and the state legislature. Daugherty, if he succeeded, would also have much to say about presidential politics in 1920. There was already a rumor in early 1918 that if Harding were nominated to the presidency or vice-presidency, Willis, if elected, would appoint Daugherty to Harding's unexpired term in the Senate.[14]

Willis's nomination, of course, became essential to Daugherty's political success. Daugherty devoted much time to the primary campaign. He helped to prevent a preprimary convention that would have been injurious to Willis, who was disliked by several Republican leaders. He also tried to discourage others from entering the race against Willis.[15] As expected, prohibition became one of the major issues. As early as January, Daugherty told Willis that Republicans who opposed his candidacy would attempt to obtain some concessions on that point. "My advice to you is to make no concessions to anybody," he said. This put him into conflict with Boss Cox's former lieutenant, the heavy-faced and blue-eyed Hynicka, who identified with the large brewery and distillery interests of Hamilton County. By February 15, Hynicka informed Willis that if he expected to carry Hamilton, he must alter his stand to permit a wet platform for that southwestern county.[16] Willis suggested that Hynicka meet with Daugherty to reach a satisfactory compromise. It was in Willis's interests as well as the party's that he seek an accord, for the wet-dry controversy threatened to divide the party. Harding, who straddled the prohibition issue, was especially anxious that Daugherty make concessions. He told Daugherty that his "keen political understanding and abiding interest in Republican success will contribute very largely in bringing about the desired result." Daugherty, however, was a poor choice to negotiate with Hynicka. A month earlier he had tried to persuade Harding to use his influence to remove Hynicka as national committeeman.[17] While he now had a frank talk with Hynicka, he confided to Willis that "nothing can be consented to in the platform that might be considered a make-shift or susceptible to two constructions or conducive to complications."[18] Consequently, no agreements were reached.

In the ensuing months, Harding continually urged Daugherty to meet with Hynicka, as he believed the latter had a genuine interest in party success. Daugherty, however, remained unwilling to compromise. He repeated that if it came "to a question of winning in the state and losing in [wet areas like] Hamilton, Cuyahoga, and Lucas counties, I am for carrying the state."[19] On June 3, Daugherty outlined other reasons why he could not deal with Hynicka. He pointed to Hynicka's friendship with former Progressive Walter Brown. Hynicka, Daugherty claimed, was anxious for Brown's political success, because Brown favored Hynicka's stand on the liquor question. According to Daugherty, they sought no less than control of the party organization. He stated that the progressive-wet alliance was already plotting to deliver the Ohio delegation to Roosevelt in 1920. "When that is done," Daugherty prophesied, "they expect to elect United States Senators and governors, and wipe the real Republicans off the face of the earth." He accused Columbus newspaper publisher Robert Wolfe of conspiring with them in an effort to prevent Willis's nomination. Daugherty again asked Harding to endorse Willis. "It is too bad that we haven't a stronger man running," he acknowledged, "but Willis is head and shoulders above the other two."[20]

On August 13, Willis won the primary despite a trouncing in Hamilton County. His victory forecast a dry party platform and meant a Daugherty-Willis takeover of the party machinery. Newton Fairbanks became the new Republican state central committee chairman, replacing D.Q. Morrow of Hillsboro, who had the misfortune of residing too close to Cincinnati. Edward Fullington, a Willis lieutenant, supplanted Charles Hatfield as chairman of the Republican state executive committee.[21] Only the Harding-created state advisory committee remained undisturbed. At the Republican state convention on August 27, Daugherty also dictated the party platform, which included not only prohibition, but women's suffrage, the eight-hour day for women factory workers, old-age pensions, and increased aid to schools. He inserted these progressive planks to prevent Brown or Hynicka from claiming that the party was being delivered to the Anti-Saloon League.[22]

Daugherty's plans had to be modified, however, when, despite a 25,000 majority for state prohibition, Willis had the misfortune of being the only Republican candidate not to win a state office in the November election. Losing by only a 14,000 plurality, he suffered from a 16,500 deficit in Hamilton County.[23] Immediately after the election, Daugherty wrote Harding, "I suppose you learned the whole story of the bolters' crimes. . . . Practically the whole crime was committed in Cincinnati . . . . Henceforth the fight in Ohio will be against Hamilton county, and on that issue the Republicans will never lose."[24] Daugherty was now even more convinced that Hamilton County leaders must not play any significant part in the state party's organizations.

Harding did not share Daugherty's conclusions. He believed that for party success (including his own) cooperation was essential with Hamilton. "I am getting a number of echoes of the Ohio political atmosphere," he cautioned Daugherty, "and have heard you no little discussed in such revelations."[25] Because of the outcry against Daugherty's manipulations, and because of his own desire for party unity, Harding, as chairman of the advisory committee, decided to call a joint meeting of that body and the state central committee for mid-December.[26] He hoped to reactivate, expand, and reorganize the advisory committee and to include more Republicans from Hamilton County and former Progressive leaders like Walter Brown. His authority rested on the 1918 state convention's endorsement of a revitalized advisory organization.[27] Harding seemed at that time intent on weakening the influence of the Daugherty-controlled central committee.

Daugherty, of course, strongly opposed Harding's proposal and countered with a warning that the party's real enemies, the Walter Brown and Hamilton crowd especially, wished to use the meeting and the advisory committee as vehicles to capture control of the party. He implied that their plot included the weakening of Harding as a political force in Ohio.[28] Daugherty denied that ulterior motives influenced his viewpoint; he cared only for party success and the well-being of friends like Harding and Willis. Discounting any personal grudge against Hamilton County Republicans, he retorted to Harding: "I am not in the fertilizer business and do not consider it profitable to pursue or puncture dead horses." He did feel, however, that since these "black birds" had been treacherous, he would never have confidence in them nor permit their participation in party affairs. He concluded with a word of caution. If Hamilton County had a large representation on the new advisory committee, it would put Harding in a bad light with the rank and file of the party who had supported the ticket and could also invite a renewed wet-dry conflict. Apart from the question of its expanded membership, Daugherty could not conceal his resentment toward the Harding-sponsored committee. He questioned its accomplishments; he pointed to its indebtedness, and reminded Harding that it contained disloyal persons.[29]

For his part, Harding doubted the existence of a plot against himself, Daugherty, or any other Republican leader—at least, one that was inspired by Brown or Hynicka. He sarcastically confessed to Daugherty that he was, perhaps, too innocent to suspect all the so-called schemes of those who had favored the meeting. "And I am glad I am such a mind," Harding said; "I should really dislike to think that there isn't any sincerity or genuine interest in anybody."[30] He saw clearly that the personal ambitions of Daugherty and his friends were the main obstacle to his own plans of controlling a united party for 1920. Harding confided that he would take issue with Daugherty if he insisted upon organizing the General Assembly: It "ought not to be domineered by either pinheads or bull-heads in difficult times like these."[31] He considered pushing Charles Hard into the senate clerkship contest against William Halley, Daugherty's choice. Harding reiterated to Hard that he had told Daugherty "that some things he was committed to could not be."[32] Hard had already warned Harding that "we are dealing with a lot of very thorough gentle-men, [Daugherty, Halley, and Fairbanks] who are cold of blood, who know what they want, and they are going to get it if they can."[33]

In early December, Daugherty went to Washington in an attempt to settle his differences with Harding. They agreed to a joint central-advisory committee meeting to be held before the new year. Upon his return to Columbus, Daugherty supported, or more likely influenced, Fairbanks's announcement that there would be no meeting until January; that is, not before Daugherty controlled the organization of the General Assembly. Even then Daugherty suggested that the advisory committee must be completely subordinate to the central committee and indicated that he and Fairbanks must have a hand in selecting its members. Daugherty intimated to Harding that his defiance might invite an opposition candidate for his seat in the Senate—possibly Willis or Daugherty himself.[34]

Daugherty's actions angered Harding. He told Hard that he would make no future arrangements with Daugherty. Although he considered Daugherty a brilliant and resourceful man, Harding believed that his political hatreds biased his judgment, adding, "I do not think him always a trustworthy adviser." Harding, however, decided to avoid a fight with Daugherty. He accepted Hard's conclusion that Daugherty and Willis would crystalize the dry sentiment against him. Any factional fight, Hard told Harding, might jeopardize Harding's chances for reelection or for a possible presidential nomination in 1920. "Two years from now," Hard continued,

> you will be strong on the protective tariff issue, strong with the business element, strong on the second term issue, strong with the pie-brigades who will want postoffices and federal jobs, strong with the true sentiment of the party which will want no friction in a presidential year.[35]

Consequently, Harding surrendered to Daugherty on the organization of the General Assembly and consented to the postponement of the rein-auguration of the advisory committee.

At the same time Harding also made an effort to regain Daugherty's friendship. On December 20, he wrote Daugherty that "surely you do not need to see through my poor political glasses to be cordially welcomed to my home." Resorting to flattery, he stated:

> I highly valued your keen mind, your capacity, your resourcefulness, your industry, your tenacity, your knowledge of men and your estimate of public opinion. One who has so little capacity as I know myself to possess—even confessing your poor opinion of me to be a correct one, without feeling in any way wounded thereat—craves the association and cooperation of men of your knowledge and experience.[36]

Without calling attention to Daugherty's personal ambitions, Harding's advice was that he must rid himself of any vindictiveness which hindered party unity. Party harmony could not be served by eliminating everyone who had not been one-hundred percent loyal. Republicans must look forward to 1920, not back upon 1918, 1916, or even 1912, and that the means for achieving this harmony was still a strong advisory committee. Harding then concluded:

> The trouble with you, my dear Daugherty, in your political relations with me, is that you appraise my political sense so far below par that you have no confidence in me or [in] my judgment. Pray do not think because I can and do listen in politeness to much that is said to me, that I am always being 'strung.' I cannot and will not suspect everyone of wanting to use me. I must and will believe in professed political friendship until I find myself imposed upon.[37]

Daugherty reciprocated Harding's desire to work together. He considered their differences "mere squalls" instead of "storms" and confessed that "if I cannot work with you in politics I cannot work with any of the important leaders." Daugherty again disclaimed any bitterness against Hamilton County. "I do not cry over spilled milk in politics or business ventures; I follow the plan of looking out for a fresh cow in some convenient pasture."[38] But he also cautioned Harding of the danger of giving too much power to the advisory committee and too great an influence to either the Brown or Hamilton County contingent. He restated his apprehension that they might use the organization to seek a Roosevelt candidacy in 1920. Fearing, perhaps, that Harding might exclude him in a harmony love-feast that could culminate in a Roosevelt-Harding ticket, Daugherty suggested, "I do not insist on sticking in; I just want to be nice about it and to help you and the party." At the least, he would insist "on reasonable respect and consideration" for his party service.[39]

A week prior to the joint meeting in mid-January 1919, Hard told of a proposed central committee meeting on the evening preceding the joint session. He predicted that Daugherty and his following were not going to give way easily.[40] But there was an unexpected turn of events in that first week of January; Theodore Roosevelt, the leading Republican presidential candidate, suddenly died. "This makes a big change all over the country," Daugherty immediately wrote Harding. The demise of Roosevelt projected Harding into the forefront of presidential politics in Ohio. It denied the progressive Brown faction a major candidate and removed the impending doom from Daugherty, who had fought against possible extinction. If Daugherty had still thought of squelching Harding's organizational plans, he now quickly put such inclinations aside. He saw

Harding, with his potential for restoring party unity, as a leading presidential candidate. In the January 9 letter, Daugherty told Harding that he had "some ideas about this thing now which I will talk over with you."[41] And Harding also seemed anxious to see Daugherty. Upon receipt of Daugherty's letter, Harding replied: "I am a good deal more anxious to confer with you than anyone else in Ohio, because the new political situation is one that must be talked over and we must certainly plan to cooperate in meeting the responsibility which is going to come to us."[42]

During the following week, a revitalized state advisory committee officially came into being with its headquarters at Columbus. The harmony-promoting and Harding-directed organization included Daugherty, Brown, and a large representation from Hamilton County. George H. Clark of Stark County became Harding's choice to direct its operation, but Daugherty loomed as the most outspoken proponent of the Harding presidential candidacy of 1920. He would, in fact, become Harding's campaign manager and play a leading role in the crucial weeks prior to Harding's nomination.

Launching the Harding Candidacy

BY late January 1919, Daugherty had become the self-appointed publicist of the emerging Harding for president movement. He brought to that commitment over twenty-five years of experience in state and national politics that had taught him organizational and publicity techniques, as well as how to obtain political backing. Over the years, moreover, his outgoing personality had won him a number of contacts and friends outside the state, many of whom were themselves state party leaders often active in national politics. In Ohio his ambitions had alienated many; elsewhere he had few adversaries. Daugherty's tenacity and indefatigability were also assets. No matter how futile a cause or a goal, he relentlessly pursued it. To him, defeat was always temporary. Determination of this sort proved beneficial in 1920.

Nevertheless, Daugherty, in several respects, was a handicap to Harding, particularly in Ohio, where he had more than his share of enemies. He was regarded as a negative symbol of the Foraker-Hanna era who somehow had managed to survive. While others also had endured, Daugherty seemed unrepentant. His denunciation of the primary and praise of political machines overshadowed his expedient inclusion of progressive planks in the 1918 state party platform. His reputation as a lobbyist was well known. Rumors also persisted of his past unethical conduct. In addition, he was vindictive, impetuous, and not as sagacious as was often thought.[1] All of this weakened Harding in Ohio when he sought former Roosevelt backers and other groups inimical to Daugherty. Yet the presidency might have eluded him had Daugherty not been so diligently committed to that goal.

Daugherty's initial efforts was cautiously and even surreptitiously conceived, for Harding was genuinely reluctant to seek the presidency. He was happy in the Senate, where the responsibility and the work were manageable. Furthermore, he lacked a strong enough organization at home (the new advisory committee had yet to prove itself). He also seemed aware of his intellectual and physical inadequacies. Charles Hard later recalled that Harding told him in February 1919 that "he did not feel that he was big enough to fill the office of the President." Harding himself had informed Senator James E. Watson of Indiana that his blood pressure was at 185 and that a urine sample had revealed traces of sugar. Moreover, his worrisome wife, Florence Kling Harding, was especially concerned about his health, and was content with his being in the Senate. In time Harding's reluctance receded in the face of his friends' encouragement, the tangles of Ohio politics, and a vanity that gradually persuaded him that he, indeed, was presidential timber.

Daugherty was by no means the first proponent of Harding for president. As early as 1915, several of the senator's friends had thought of him in such terms. In May of that year, George Christian, Sr., wrote that Harding's many admirers had made him a candidate of "formidable proportions." Cohort Ed Scobey of Texas, noting the comments on Harding's availability in New York papers and in the *Cincinnati Enquirer*, tried to encourage him to accept the support of friends and enter the field in 1916.[2] To all enthusiastic backers, Harding disclaimed any intention of pursuing such a course, even though he was obviously flattered. He deferred to Theodore Burton, who had Daugherty's strong support, as Ohio's favorite son at the 1916 Republican national convention. After 1916, his friends persisted, and were joined by others who thought him worthy of the presidency. Unlike Harding's other friends, Daugherty was not only an experienced and an aggressive politician with numerous contacts, but he also refused to take seriously Harding's reluctance to run.

Beginning on January 23, 1919, Daugherty hinted in an interview published in the *Cincinnati Times-Star* and the *Washington Post* that Harding was a possible presidential candidate for 1920. News traveled fast; less than a week later Nebraska Republican State Chairman Harry S. Byrne, who read the *Post* article, requested that Harding come in the spring to make several speeches. Daugherty politely replied that there would be no better place than Omaha for Harding to deliver a political address. Harding, however, was reluctant.[3] He seemed, in fact, uncomfortable about newspaper speculation on his possible presidential aspirations. Daugherty advised him neither to admit nor to deny anything. But he postponed publicizing Harding, probably at the latter's insistence. Daugherty, nevertheless, suggested to Harding's secretary, George Christian, Jr., that he file Byrne's letters and that he "remember this man."[4]

In February 1919, Daugherty undauntedly resumed his promotion of Harding. He contacted friends like National Committeeman Henry Jackson of Atlanta, Georgia, to determine his interest in a Harding for president movement. Jackson replied that he would always be with Daugherty in everything he represented and wanted. Writing to Harding, Daugherty requested that he pay "some little attention" to Jackson whenever Jackson visited Washington.[5] That same month Daugherty asked Harding to arrange a dinner-poker party for him in Washington at which he requested the attendance of Republican Senators Philander C. Knox of Pennsylvania, Harry S. New of Indiana, Joseph S. Frelinghuysen of New Jersey, Charles W. Curtis of Kansas, and Frederick Hale of Maine, as well as Harding, Representative Nicholas Longworth of Ohio, and possibly former House Speaker "Uncle Joe" Cannon of Illinois. Only New and Harding were unable to attend.[6] Also in February, Chairman Newton H. Fairbanks of the state central committee, the toastmaster at the Lincoln Day Republican Celebration in Toledo, introduced Harding as Ohio's new presidential hope. Fairbanks, who scarcely breathed without Daugherty's permission, would not have made such a move without approval. In any case, Harding was incensed. He told Charles Hard on the train back to Columbus that such promotionalism must be discontinued.[7] Undoubtedly, he told Daugherty the same thing, for again he momentarily eased off.

In the spring and summer of 1919, Daugherty seemed more intent on winning Harding's confidence. He tried to be helpful in presenting Ohio sentiment on the proposed League of Nations, the major issue of the time. When he suggested that the United States join a modified League and then possibly withdraw within two years, Harding demurred on the grounds that if the country were against the organization, it should not become a member. Daugherty readily accepted Harding's opinion with an acknowledgment that "you are more capable and in a much more advantageous position." He wrote that he would never complain because Harding saw things in a different light. Nevertheless, he would politely insist on telling Harding what he thought in the most "inoffensive, conscientious, God-fearing and man-loving way."[8] He was more helpful in dealing with the Ohio political situation, where he used his influence to combine the meetings of the central and advisory committees when the latter weakened because of a lack of finance and support. Though Clark of the advisory committee remained suspicious, Harding now thought Daugherty cooperative and "wholly sincere."[9]

Harding was equally willing to assist Daugherty. Daugherty had first sought his assistance the previous year during the midst of World War I. Despite being a "Republican and not a sneak," Daugherty lukewarmly supported the President's conduct of the war, even though Wilson disapproved of the unconditional surrender of Germany. He also wished to help in war matters. He requested that Harding recommend him for one of Wilson's war boards—preferably one that "passes on assistance in financing utilities."[10] There is no evidence that Harding could fulfill this request, but he was more helpful in the summer of 1919 when Daugherty's son, Draper, a major in the Army Transportation Corps in France, wrote to his father of poor health caused by field duty in the moist climate. The previous year he had been gassed and wounded in the Meuse-Argonne offensive. He consequently considered resigning his commission, despite the elder Daugherty's cautioning of a tight labor market at home. Daugherty, as a result, asked Harding to get Draper reassigned to the United States. Thinking this unobtainable, Harding made a personal appeal to the Army Chief of Staff to secure him a furlough. When this also failed, Draper severed his military connections and returned home. In August, Harding then helped him obtain an excellent position with the White Motor Company of New York.[11]

In late summer, the critical national issue continued to be the League of Nations. Daugherty still advised Harding on the question. After Wilson's speaking appearance in Columbus on September 4, Daugherty wrote that there was no enthusiasm for Wilson on the part of the crowd that lined the streets. He explained that he had also talked with a number of sensible and loyal people who had become increasingly opposed to a League of Nations without safeguards. He then expressed to Harding his own ideas: "There is no necessity for it as long as there is red blood in the veins of American citizens, for we have shown with our red blood our ability to respond to the requirements of the nation." He concluded that no League would save us once our red blood ran out. Daugherty's contention that Wilson's proposed League was losing favor in Ohio squared with the observations of Hard and others.[12] Harding, as a result, became more critical of the League covenant.

While Harding preoccupied himself with the League fight in the Senate that fall, political turmoil again developed in Ohio, threatening to weaken the efforts of Harding to retain a united party. On October 11, the first indication of trouble reached Harding. Daugherty hinted that he had some differences with Walter Brown over the proposed composition of the Ohio delegation to the 1920 Republican national convention. Daugherty's proposal that the preferential presidential primary be replaced by an organization-appointed delegation that could play "the game of politics" did not help matters. Brown no doubt realized that such a delegation meant little representation for him. Daugherty said as much to Harding, who rejected the entire scheme.[13] The stage was set for renewed intraparty warfare in Ohio. Much of it can be attributed to Daugerty's intrigue and his adversaries' suspicions of Harding as long as Daugherty appeared to be his spokesman.

On October 17, the Brown and Hynicka factions prevailed on Clark and the advisory committee to approve of a resolution asking Harding to state his intentions for 1920—the Senate or the presidency? According to Daugherty, if Harding declared for the former, Brown, Hynicka, millionaire soap magnate William C. Procter, and others would then begin their efforts to capture the Ohio delegates to the national convention of 1920 in behalf of General Leonard Wood, who had the support of Roosevelt Republicans. If Wood became president, the Brown-Hynicka crowd would control federal patronage in Ohio. By then, Harding would have failed at reelection because he could no longer promise jobs. "They would trade you off for a yellow dog at any time if they could go patronage hunting with the dog," Daugherty wrote Harding.[14] Harding, as Daugherty advised, announced that even though he would seek reelection, that need not rule out a possible presidential candidacy as well. He gradually believed that only by controlling the Ohio delegation as a favorite son could he protect his Senate seat. Listening more to Daugherty now, he remarked to Hard that he regretted having placed Brown on the advisory committee.[15]

Daugherty took the lead in solidifying Harding's political position in Ohio. In a meeting of the advisory committee on October 31, he had Fairbanks introduce a resolution endorsing the renomination of Harding for the Senate, and at the same time, permitted the use of his name for the presidency. Daugherty succeeded in obtaining the adoption of the resolution, even though he claimed that there was "some little squirming" by Brown and his cohorts. Immediately afterward, he released a statement that Harding's refusal to be "smoked out, knocked out or frozen out" had gratified his friends. Harding's stand, continued Daugherty, "has directed the attention of the country to him in a most favorable manner."[16]

Because Daugherty rendered such open support, Harding moved closer to him. On November 3, Harding wrote Hard that he always "felt I could depend on Daugherty, though he did give me no little annoyance during the trying period we passed through last winter."[17] But Daugherty's critics became convinced that a united party under Harding could not work as long as he remained tied down to Daugherty. Harding constantly received warnings that he must dump or curb Daugherty. Robert Wolfe, whom Harding counted on for support, explained after a Daugherty-Brown conference in December that "Mr. Daugherty picked a flaw in every proposition, none of which were insisted upon or vital, and himself would propose nothing. It is unfortunate," Wolfe maintained, that Daugherty "renders it so difficult for self-respecting friends to give their best efforts. For some unknown reason petty difficulties are magnified by him into unsurmountable obstacles and personal enmities."[18] Hynicka, meanwhile, remained justifiably convinced that Daugherty plotted to remove him as Republican National Committeeman, while Herrick detested Daugherty because of his alleged vindictiveness in the 1916 senatorial campaign. County leader William Phipps of Paulding also indicated his difficulty in working with him. Even George Christian, Sr., father of Harding's secretary, was outspoken against Daugherty. He told Harding in November that Daugherty's personal hatreds and his defiant attitude had recently provoked many former Progressives who were friendly to the senator. Finally, Jennings and Scobey advised Harding not to utilize Daugherty as manager in Ohio, where he would only disrupt things. Jennings told Scobey that, though Daugherty was a lovable chap, he had lost his early following. His friends had retired from politics, according to Jennings, but his enemies were still alive and active. He concluded that a large majority of party members thought Daugherty a political adventurer with a shady past as a lobbyist.[19]

Nevertheless, Harding refused to reject Daugherty. He found him too active a booster. To Scobey, Harding explained that while he was under no particular spell in his relationship with Daugherty, "he does have one appealing attribute, namely that he is cordially for me in the open." Consequently, "I can not and will not kill off Daugherty, nor will I humiliate him in any way." Not wanting to appear ungrateful, he accepted Daugherty's help at face value and at the same time lost patience with those who criticized Daugherty but yet were not nearly as helpful.[20] Harding, however, did not consider himself a worshipper of the latter. He told Jennings that Daugherty had "never asked anything at my hands which it was not perfectly consistent and easy to grant." Harding asserted that he was not so tied up with him that he could not terminate his association. He showed his independence in December when he wooed Walter Brown away from the opposition. Still the harmonizer, Harding realized that he needed the support of former Progressives like Brown and Arthur Garford. He was willing to promise patronage to get it.[21]

But General Wood's candidacy further weakened Harding's strength in Ohio. His entry made it easier for Hynicka and other Republicans to oppose Harding. The former commander of the Rough Riders was a respected general of high character. His campaign manager, William Procter of Cincinnati, spent lavishly in his behalf, and as Roosevelt's political heir apparent, Wood attracted former Bull Moose support in Ohio. Harding correctly perceived that part of the anti-Daugherty sentiment was really anti-Harding feeling in disguise.[22]

Daugherty worked less controversially for Harding nationally. In early November, he took the initiative in secretly canvassing the "big field." He told Secretary Christian that the senator would not have to know or do much as presidents do not run like assessors. Without informing Harding, he and Christian also made appeals for funds.[23] When money became difficult to obtain, Daugherty himself pledged one quarter of his savings. Daugherty also went to Washington later that month to feel out the sentiment of Republican senators like William Borah of Idaho and Boies Penrose of Pennsylvania.[24] While there, he tried to persuade Harding to come out for the presidency. Upon his return to Columbus, he suggested that Harding would be a candidate for the office. Convinced that Americanism and the welfare of industry were to be the two major issues, Daugherty stated that the party's choice must be safe and sensible on both propositions. Harding, he proclaimed, was the candidate of the times.[25]

Daugherty increased his tempo in December. He began sending men into other states, and went himself to Washington to attend meetings of the Republican National Committee and the state committee chairmen in mid-December. To promote Harding, Daugherty arranged for fifty Ohio Republicans to obtain rooms at the Willard Hotel during the sessions. He instructed them to impress the party leaders that Harding, the new McKinley, would have no difficulty in carrying pivotal Ohio. Daugherty consulted with almost all of the National Committeemen in an effort to secure Harding pledges.[26] While he generally failed to win first-choice support, Daugherty persistently requested their backing on a second-, third-, or fourth-choice basis. This approach put Harding in a favorable position as a possible compromise candidate.

Harding declared his candidacy in the midst of Daugherty's activity. On December 16, he stated that he could no longer ignore the endorsement of Ohio Republicans as their favorite son. In making his decision, Harding indicated that he would not run simply to prevent the Ohio Wood supporters from taking over the state organization. He intended to run hard. He was, however, still a candidate for the Senate where, as he confided, he still desired to remain.[27]

Daugherty now officially became Harding's manager, a role he had for weeks informally assumed. No evidence exists that Harding asked him to direct the campaign. Perhaps that was unnecessary. After all, Daugherty had so identified himself with Harding's political future that any other choice was improbable.

Meanwhile, the Procter-led forces in Ohio now offered not to challenge Harding in his own state if he would consent to the election of a delegation whose second choice was for Wood. While Harding might have first considered the proposition, Daugherty was opposed. To Dan Hanna, he responded that he had no second choice until he lost his first choice. Daugherty believed that the Wood people would betray Harding after voting for him on the first ballot. Such an agreement would also alienate other candidates on whom Harding counted should their own candidacies collapsed. Daugherty pleaded with Harding not to consent to compromises that meant his destruction.[28] Harding agreed and was content to see Daugherty fight out the proposition. Although the Daugherty relationship sometimes embarrassed him, Harding thus benefited from his manager's gut fighting. Daugherty best expressed their association:

> I am far more comfortable as to your ability to cope with great public
> questions and public appearances, positions and utterances, than I am for

you to deal with those who are engaged in intrigue. I will take care of the latter and together we will make a fair combination in this great enterprise.[29]

Daugherty ran Harding's interference while the latter either apologized for Daugherty or attempted to cater to the anti-Daugherty opposition to offset the imbalance. Daugherty's aggressiveness obviously did not always work to Harding's disadvantage.

Differences in the Ohio Republican party intensified in the months after Harding announced his candidacy. The pro-Wood element considered poaching on Harding's domain by entering the April primaries. They also continued to flay Daugherty. It did not seem to matter that Daugherty held a Washington dinner for Ohio members of Congress in January, at which he explained that he had no selfish or personal interests in backing Harding.[30] Rumors still circulated that Daugherty intended to select the Ohio district delegates to the Republican national convention. One former Progressive claimed that behind Daugherty's support was a desire for a Senate seat or a cabinet position. Hard also told Harding that Daugherty and George Clark were suspicious of one another, as each wanted the limelight. Calling them two prima donnas, Hard suggested that Harding bring olive branches and an axe when he returned to Ohio.[31]

The most heated issue was Daugherty's decision to become a candidate for delegate-at-large to the Republican national convention. His decision to run, made as early as October, was unpopular, and it created further disunity within the Ohio party.[32] Harding could not help losing backers as the result of Daugherty's intentions. He nevertheless thought it expedient to permit his manager to make the race. But if voters opposed, he would "accept the result without a murmur." To Jennings, he wrote that the Daugherty situation has "given me infinite anxiety and annoyance."[33]

By mid-January, Harding had yet to commit himself publicly to Daugherty's candidacy. Clark of the advisory committee advised him of the bleak alternatives: if he spoke out for Daugherty, his presidential aspirations would suffer; if he did not, Daugherty would surely lose, again weakening Harding. To bolster Daugherty's chances, he recommended that Harding approve of his candidacy as quickly as possible. Harding eventually did, even asserting that Daugherty entered the race because he (Harding) insisted upon it.[34] Of the four Harding candidates for delegates-at-large, Daugherty was easily the most unpopular.

Daugherty refused to permit the opposition to bother him. Believing Harding to be the vehicle for his own political fortunes, he jealously guarded his commitment. And no one worked harder. Indeed, in December he labored eighteen hours a day. In a way very reminiscent of the 1912 Taft campaign, he encouraged supporters to "work; write letters; drive." He also took the time to write Harding facetiously that "you are nothing but a candidate and have no particular rights." He added, "Good Lord, let's kid a little—this is pretty serious. You may be nominated for the Presidency."[35] By the end of the month he assumed responsibility for running Harding's national campaign as well as supervising the Ohio operation. In January, Daugherty moved to Washington, D.C., where he opened the Harding headquarters at the shabby New Ebbitt Hotel. Jesse Smith of Washington Court House, a close admirer of Daugherty, became his secretary. Howard Mannington was also there. Robert Armstrong, a Washington correspondent for the *Los Angeles Times*, later joined the headquarters to handle publicity. The new letterhead contained two slogans that symbolized Harding in 1920: "Think of America First" and "Harding and Back to Normal."[36] From Washington, Daugherty directed the Ohio campaign through William Halley, Hoke Donithen, Hard, Clark, and other supporters. Daugherty was more effective in cultivating Harding nationally because he did not provoke the antagonisms that were associated with him in Ohio.

Of the leading Republican candidates, (General Wood, Governor Frank Lowden of Illinois, and Senator Hiram Johnson of California), Harding was the most adept at not alienating others. Harding and Daugherty were always careful not to challenge a favorite son. Neither did they attempt to pressure Republican leaders. They instead carefully continued their strategy of obtaining second-, third-, and even fourth-choice support from prospective delegates who were already committed to the other leaders. Typical of this was Daugherty's soliciting of W.L. Cole, chairman of the Republican state organization in Missouri. When Cole responded that Harding had little chance in his state, Daugherty quickly explained: "We are going to do nothing in Missouri only through the organization: we are not going to come in here and try to perfect a Harding organization in any capacity at all: all the work that we do we will do through the local organization."

Daugherty pressed Cole for a statement concerning Missouri's attitude toward Harding in the event of a convention deadlock. He asked Cole whether Harding was Missouri's second, third, or fourth choice to supplant Lowden following a possible stalemate with Wood. After receiving no answer, Daugherty then said, "We would like to investigate and find out what the sentiment in the state in that respect may be." Cole immediately replied that he had no time to determine the state's feeling for Harding. But Daugherty still persisted, "We want you to do it; we feel that you are inclined to be friendly to the Senator, and we want you to try out the sentiment." Daugherty reiterated that he would pay Cole's expenses for making the survey. Finally Cole consented and offered to send a bill, but Daugherty quickly protested: "No we do not do it in that way, if we did that, we would have so many of these bills coming in when the thing was over that we would not know where we stood. We want to pay as we go along. I will hand you a check for that purpose now." Daugherty wrote a $1,250 check which Cole accepted. The latter promised that when he had completed the work he would submit a statement of his expenses and would then remit the excess. Cole visited fourteen of Missouri's sixteen districts during the next month.[37]

In almost the same manner, Daugherty contacted Republican leaders in other states. In the west he relied on E. Mont Reily, the vice president of the National Republican League, who became his western manager. Reily had influence in Kansas, Missouri, and Oklahoma, while Daugherty worked with his friend Rush Holland in Colorado and with J.B. Adams in Kansas. In Texas, Daugherty favored Harding's friend Ed Scobey and brother-in-law David Walker. To impress huge Jake Hamon, who supposedly controlled over fifty delegates from the southwest, Daugherty duplicated Hamon's breakfast order of three fried eggs and plenty of ham. Afterward, the Oklahoma oil man promised him second-choice support.[38] Similar connections existed in the East. In New York, for example, Charles D. Hilles, George Aldrich, and humorist Finley Peter Dunne were most helpful.[39]

Daugherty especially excelled as a publicist. For example, he asked Hoke Donithen to obtain the Marion Chamber of Commerce endorsement of Harding and have the Associated Press publish it. "Also," he continued, "see that copies are mailed to every member of the Chamber of Commerce in the United States; every Republican member of Congress; the chairman of the state central committee; and every member of the National Committee." Daugherty stressed Harding's business accomplishments because he believed that the country would demand a man who had been a part of the business structure.[40] He also effectively presented Harding as a solution to the discontent caused by the overextension of executive power that lingered into the postwar period. To Daugherty, Harding meant representative government and America First, rather than Wilsonian dictatorship and internationalism. Harding was a resurrected McKinley both in appearance and in personality. "Comparing Harding with McKinley has been on my lips and pen for three months," Daugherty related to Scobey on January 22; "I have written a thousand interviews about it."[41] He repeatedly suggested that since McKinley had presided over the Republican convention that preceded the one at which he was nominated, why should not Harding, who chaired the 1916 convention, follow in McKinley's footsteps in 1920?

Because of Florence Harding's reluctance to present her photograph, Daugherty delayed publishing a Harding biographical pamphlet publicizing Harding as another McKinley. This caused the alarmed Scobey to comment on the amount of literature that other candidates issued. He advised Daugherty to print the pamphlet without the photograph, but Daugherty delayed until Mrs. Harding finally consented. He remarked that the extensive Wood and Lowden publicity had been wasted because it developed too soon. The time for propaganda was after the selection of delegates. He intended to peak in March and April.[42] Daugherty had to operate in this way because of meager campaign contributions, a matter that continually concerned him. Compared to the other canvasses, Harding's was easily the least solvent, partly because he refused to accept funds from big contributors. He reminded that the Senate primary campaign of 1914 cost him only $4,000.[43] As it turned out, Harding's decision not to buy a primary victory proved wise, for the "big money" campaigns of Wood and Lowden eventually destroyed their nomination chances.

In other respects, this was not a one-man campaign, as Daugherty later claimed.[44] Harding worked closely with others to obtain commitments. Charles Forbes was very active in Washington and Oregon, working for him in the preconvention campaign. Harding was in close touch with Republican leaders in West Virginia. He also courted many senatorial friends, including Reed Smoot of Utah, New and Watson of Indiana, Curtis of Kansas, and William Calder and James Wadsworth of New York. Favorite sons such as Governor William Sproul of Pennsylvania were especially friendly. His own skillful handling of the Hiram Johnson candidacy in California won the second-choice support of that state's delegation. The Harding Papers and Randolph Downes's Harding biography reveal the numerous contacts which Harding energetically pursued. In the final analysis, however, what insured Harding's nomination was his availability. That had first developed in 1916 when, as temporary and permanent chairman at the Republican national convention, he had made a favorable impression on the delegates as a parliamentarian and harmonizer. Many of those same delegates were reelected in 1920.[45] Daugherty, to be sure, was persistent, astute, and energetic, but he overstated his importance. Although a good national manager, he alone did not make Harding's nomination possible and, in fact, impeded it in the Ohio primary campaign.

By February, Daugherty began to concentrate on the primaries. While he had felt that a convention deadlock might lead to Harding's nomination, Daugherty thought it essential that Harding do well in the primaries. He personally put considerable importance on the Indiana contest, where he felt confident that Harding would defeat Lowden, Wood, and Johnson. He explained to Scobey that Indiana's two senators and thirteen congressman were inclined to favor Harding. A victory there, Daugherty believed, would enable Harding to "grab Pennsylvania, snatch Kentucky, and . . . take West Virginia."[46] One month later, however, Scobey wrote that Senator William A. Smith of Michigan had stated that Harding was out of the running in Indiana. "There must be something wrong about this," Scobey added, "or have you got a deal?" Calling the Smith statement a fake, the Daugherty headquarters countered that Harding was gaining in both Indiana and Ohio.[47]

But one month prior to the April primary, the Ohio situation was far from promising. The Wood people elected to oppose Harding and prepared to enter their own slate of delegates. Again, a major reason for their opposition was Daugherty. Harding had managed to regain the support of Brown and Hynicka. But Wolfe and Edward Turner, who had opposed Daugherty in 1913, were just two of several Republican leaders who refused to favor Harding because of his manager. Daugherty made matters worse in mid-February when he stated in an interview that fifteen men in a smoke-filled room would eventually nominate Harding at 2:11 A.M.[48] The publicity given to the interview embarrassed Harding and undoubtedly weakened his position. To inquiring constituents he considered the incident an unfortunate slip that no one regretted more than he. Jennings confided that Daugherty had little descretion when he talked to reporters because "he craves seeing his name in the headlines."[49]

The Wood forces directed much of their attack upon Daugherty, a candidate for delegate-at-large. Daugherty, fearing defeat, reminded that Harding supporters could not afford to neglect any part of the ticket. Harding received an anonymous letter, probably either from Daugherty or one of his close friends, asking that he more openly back his manager:

> He [Daugherty] is certainly working faithfully and effectively for you, and he has many friends here who are aware of the real situation and the sacrifice which he is making. These friends, who are none the less your friends, think it would be to your advantage if the real state of affairs could be laid before the people. You know and I know that the opposition to Mr. Daugherty is in reality opposition to you, and as it might make matters worse and would be rather embarrassing for Mr. Daugherty to combat this opposition himself, I think that it would be well for you to let it be known that Mr. Daugherty is unselfishly interested in your cause and is conscientiously bending every effort in behalf of the Republican party.[50]

While campaigning in Ohio to save his own political neck, Harding defended Daugherty. His efforts were undercut when stories circulated that Daugherty was instructing his friends to knife Herrick, another Harding candidate for delegate-at-large.[51] The situation became more acute when the Harding campaign ran out of money in Ohio. When Scobey partially blamed Daugherty for the problem, the latter complained that he had personally "gone down in my pocket away beyond the stopping point . . ." to make up for the deficit. Conversely, the Wood organization spent freely; in a single district alone, they spent close to $100,000.[52]

The April 27 primary results were far from encouraging to Harding. Despite extensive campaigning, he managed to win only thirty-nine delegates out of forty-eight. There were doubts that some of this support would hold steadfast after the first ballot. Herrick, Willis, and John Galvin were elected as delegates-at-large, but Daugherty went down to defeat to a Wood man.[53] Daugherty, with some justification, accused Hynicka and his friends of instructing Hamilton County Republicans to scratch him for either Turner or William Boyd. Herrick, who gathered the most votes, meanwhile, told Republican National Committee Chairman Will Hays that Daugherty had been successful in doing what he "had done before—messing up the Republican party." He hoped that Daugherty's defeat would eliminate him from the campaign.[54]

On top of the Ohio debacle, Harding ran behind Wood, Lowden, and Johnson in the May 5 Indiana race. Wood's primary success placed him in a leading position, followed by Johnson and Lowden. According to one account, Harding was on the verge of withdrawing after Indiana. Mrs. Harding, who had objected to his candidacy, now opposed his quitting. In her characteristic rasping voice, she reminded Harding of his obligations to friends in Ohio.[55] Harding reluctantly decided to continue. Even Daugherty was momentarily discouraged by the outcome. He told Scobey that he was not going to deceive anyone about Harding's position. He believed that it was now Wood against the field and that the senator's only chance lay in an understanding with Wood's opponents. If that occurred, Daugherty might be able to cash in on the second- or third- choice support. Since many delegates were either uninstructed or uncommitted, there was also a possibility that they would favor a compromise selection. Then again, Daugherty conceded that understandings failed at the 1916 convention, when Hughes survived an unfriendly consolidation.[56]

The situation remained grim in Ohio. Harding found it exceedingly difficult to prevent another conflict from erupting. Daugherty's desire to punish Hynicka and others for his defeat contributed to the trying circumstances. On May 8, he recommended that Harding aid in removing Hynicka as a member of the Republican National Committee for Paul Howland of Cleveland. "If we acquiesce in Hynicka's election," Daugherty stated, "we acquiesce in everything that has been done to you, and that would never do." Daugherty was also disinclined to trust Walter Brown. The Toledo boss had suggested that he could coax Hynicka to persuade the Wood men in Ohio to support Harding. Daugherty dismissed this as an impossibility.[57] If Daugherty had had his way, he would have purged Hynicka, Brown, and other laggers who were now in the Harding camp— all this to Harding's disadvantage, for Harding needed support, not reprisals. On May 20, a trace of vindictiveness appeared in Daugherty's letter to Harding:

The one thing that you must consider is, what will the loyal, faithful
Republicans of Ohio think of it if Hamilton County, under Hynicka and
after his treachery to you, is to take over the political affairs of the state?
This enthusiastic interest in the party's welfare on the part of Hynicka and
others at this time falls fruitless before a man like me who, in season and
out of season, for more years probably than any other man living, in defeat
and personal humiliation and disappointment, has always stood for the
party's welfare and for party success, and against the men who were cutting
the party's throat.[58]

Harding refused to accept Daugherty's solution. On May 15, Walter
Brown had advised Harding that he must not punish Hynicka for his
personal opposition to Daugherty. Harding agreed that nothing could be
accomplished through vindictiveness. He instead worked toward a conference with Hynicka and Procter. Harding believed that Hynicka was
willing to commit himself to a program that would further Harding's
presidential ambitions. He related his plans to Daugherty, remarking that
"I know you will receive this with a smile."[59] He nevertheless felt that he
must go as far as he could to harmonize party differences. But with
Daugherty anxious to get even, the truce between Harding and Hynicka
was an uneasy one. In mid-May, Harding's fortunes reached their lowest
ebb. As a consequence of the primaries, he was weakened nationally and
faced with a divided delegation at home.

The Making of the President
1920

IN one important respect, the making of the president in 1920 was no different from the making of presidents in our own day. The initial objective is still delegate support at the national nominating convention. The primaries provide only a measure of the total number of delegate votes needed. Sometimes, too, the psychological impact of primary successes is surprisingly small, especially if such victories are shared with other candidates, or if other events diminish their import.

In the spring of 1920, political writers overestimated the importance of the Republican primaries, in which Wood gained 124 delegates, Johnson 112, Lowden 72, and Harding only 39. This accounts for their low estimate of Harding's chances on the eve of the national convention.[1] Despite having some doubts himself immediately after the Indiana primary, Daugherty quickly regained a fighting spirit. Even though his wife and daughter were seriously ill, he continued to work relentlessly. On May 15, he wrote Reily that "the fight is by rounds and every participant receives his set-backs as round after round takes place in the great arena. The geography of the situation has not changed; Harding's availability has not changed; Harding can carry Ohio, and I do not know of anybody else who can."[2]

Wood's setbacks, indeed, had already begun. With Senator Johnson's encouragement, Borah of Idaho had introduced on May 6 a resolution calling for an investigation of all preconvention expenditures. Countless complaints that the Wood managers had spent enormously in the primaries created enough senatorial opposition that an investigatory committee under the chairmanship of William S. Kenyon of Iowa went into action. No one motive inspired the investigation. Many Republicans were genuinely concerned that if tainted, Wood, as the nominee, would hurt the party that fall. Republicans who backed other candidates wished to see Wood embarrassed.

As soon as Daugherty heard of the investigation, he wired Kenyon that he was willing on telegraphic notice to respond to any request for information regarding Harding's campaign expenditures.[3] By the end of May, despite being bedridden for a week, he appeared before the Kenyon Committee, where he effectively presented the modest figures of the Harding operation. The total receipts, according to Daugherty, were $113,109 which included a $14,500 contribution of his own, $13,950 from Carmi Thompson, an old Taft war horse, and $30,000 from the Citizens of Marion. Harding contributed a modest $1,000 and Colonel James G. Darden, later involved in Teapot Dome, donated $6,000. When asked whether the $113,109 represented the entire amount, Daugherty reported that because of token funds Harding was able to enter only the Ohio and Indiana primaries. He further aided the Harding cause when he tactfully refused to speculate on the enormous spending of the Wood campaign. He told Senator Pomerene of Ohio, a member of the Kenyon Committee: "It is not at all to my liking to criticize an opponent in a contest, or his friends, . . . and I do not like to speculate on rumors."[4] Daugherty suggested that if the committee wanted information on Wood, its members should ask his managers.

While Daugherty managed to show that the Harding campaign operated on a shoestring, the Wood organization could not. The Kenyon investigation listed Wood's official expenditure as $1,773,000, and indications were that it was several million more. His millionaire contributors included not only Procter, but also steelman and banker Dan Hanna and copper magnate William Boyce Thompson. The allegation that the Wood men attempted to purchase the nomination appeared to be true. Although Lowden's disbursement was only $414,984, he was also tainted. The committee proved that his Missouri manager paid two state delegates $2,500 each for switching their pledges from Wood to Lowden.[5] One week prior to the convention, the Kenyon revelations damaged the positions of the two front-runners. As a result, Harding seemed the most elevated because he was more moderate and less divisive than the progressive Hiram Johnson. Harding also managed to retain friendly relations with all of the candidates and had spent the least amount of money of the contenders.

Daugherty was confident that the investigation had aided Harding, but there was no way to determine the extent until the convention balloting. Meanwhile, he began to prepare for Chicago. His major problem was lack of funds, since only $5,000 remained from campaign receipts. He turned to friends like Finley Peter Dunne, who arranged an interview with oil magnates Harry Sinclair and Harry Whitney. Although supporting Wood, they agreed to lend Daugherty $15,000 to enable him to set up headquarters.[6]

In Chicago, Daugherty planned a well-organized operation. He sent Howard Mannington and William Miller there almost three weeks prior to the convention to make preliminary arrangements. Daugherty himself selected the accommodations. He rented the Florentine Room, the largest at the Congress Hotel, which served as the main headquarters at a cost of $750 per day. In addition, he secured about forty rooms at the Congress for delegates, friends, and part of the organization. He also obtained for his staff over twenty-five rooms at the Morrison and other hotels. When Harding came to Chicago, his entourage selected suites at the La Salle Hotel, a considerable distance from the Congress. Daugherty consequently asked his friend Ed Creager, a Texas delegate, to surrender to Harding the parlor and bedroom at the Auditorium Hotel, since an underground passage joined it to the adjacent Congress.[7]

Daugherty also gave considerable attention to the organization of his convention staff. Originally comprising five-hundred workers, the contingent expanded into a two-thousand-member volunteer force at the time of the nomination. Their tasks involved meeting every train that came into the "Windy City," greeting incoming delegates, and making engagements to see them. Harding lookouts were placed in every hotel in town. Daugherty's show of hospitality even included the employment of the seventy-five-member glee club of Columbus to serenade the delegates and candidates at their hotels.[8] The Daugherty-Harding strategy still involved obtaining delegate commitments on a second-, third-, or fourth-choice basis, assuming that a probable convention deadlock among the front-runners would bring on Harding's nomination. Daugherty kept a detailed record of the delegates' pledges, which he often referred to during the convention.

Maintaining friendly relations with the Lowden organization was part of the plan. The understanding not to compete in each other's territory had furthered that relationship. There is no evidence, however, that Daugherty agreed, as he later claimed, to lend delegates to Lowden until the latter passed Wood in the balloting.[9] Expecting Lowden to deadlock with Wood, Daugherty simply hoped for eventual delegate support. As he earlier explained, "When both realize they can't win, when they're tired and hot and sweaty and discouraged, both the armies will remember me and this little headquarters. They'll be like soldiers after a battle, who recall a shady spring along a country road, where they got a drink as they marched to the front. When they remember me that way, maybe both sides will turn to Harding—I don't know—it's just a chance."[10] Harding, meanwhile, continued to make contacts. He hoped to capitalize on his availability, a McKinley image, and a feeling that his nomination would not only insure a Republican victory in pivotal Ohio but national success as well. Certainly, he was in a better position than such dark horses as Herbert Hoover, Nicholas Murray Butler, Charles Evans Hughes, and Senator Philander Knox and Governor William Sproul, the latter two of Pennsylvania.

On Tuesday morning, June 8, in the flag-draped Coliseum, the smiling Republican National Chairman Will Hays announced that the Republican National Convention of 1920 was in session. Already the temperature inside was ninety degrees, and it would be even higher in the afternoons of convention week. The delegates began to remove their coats and loosen their collars. Many of them even pinned their "Wood" red and green feather emblems or various candidate buttons on their shirts rather than on their coats.

After the initial formalities, Hays introduced Senator Henry Cabot Lodge as the temporary chairman. The gray-bearded Brahmin's keynote address was mainly an hour-and-twenty-minute denunciation of Woodrow Wilson and the League of Nations. Nevertheless, Republican leaders, conscious of the divisive forces in the party that might produce a bolt, were able to resolve the League issue to the satisfaction of both isolationists and internationalists. They also produced the most conservative Republican platform in twenty years, which one reporter labeled as dull as the Chicago sky. Its conservatism enhanced Harding's availability, while it weakened that of the progressive Johnson.

Nominating speeches began on Friday, June 11. Lodge undermined the drama of the Wood nomination by mentioning Wood's name as he introduced the general's nominator, Governor Henry Allen of Kansas. Nevertheless, Allen's halting and cliché-filled address was followed by a forty-two minute demonstration, including the floating of red and green feathers released from the rafters by Wood men. The succeeding nominating speeches for Lowden, Johnson, and the others varied greatly in effectiveness, but all of them were lengthy. By the time the affable and bull-voiced Willis prepared to nominate Harding, the delegates were bored. But, as Daugherty later wrote, Willis, in a wisely brief speech, "lifted the tired delegates out of their seats." He caught their attention by describing all of the nominees as "great men" and then leaned his massive frame over the rail of the platform to say in an intimate tone, "say boys— and girls, too, why not nominate Warren Harding?" This evoked spontaneous laughter and applause from the delegates "who rose and cheered and began to march in the aisles, saying 'that's right we are all boys and girls, the girls are in politics now, too.'" In summarizing Harding's qualities, Willis focused on a persistent Daugherty theme:

> What we want is not brilliant maneuvers but safe and sane seamanship by a captain who knows the way, by a captain who as he walks the deck working with the officers and men in these troubling times can say, "Steady boys, steady." That is the type of man Ohio is presenting today. McKinley was a great President because he understood Congress, and could cooperate with it. This man understands the viewpoint of Congress and can cooperate with it.

My friends, in the name of the Republicans of Ohio I present for your deliberate consideration this great stalwart American-thinking Republican; not a professing progressive but a performing progressive. He delivers the goods. He is a man of sane statesmanship with eyes fixed on the future, a great typical American citizen.[11]

While the demonstration that followed lasted only ten minutes, it was "of considerable volume."

But the first ballot went almost as expected. Wood and Lowden were in the lead with 287½ and 211½ votes, respectively. Harding received sixty-five votes, which placed him in sixth place behind Wood, Lowden, Johnson, Sproul, and Butler. The succeeding three ballots were a close repetition of the first with Lowden and Wood increasing their leads. The fourth ballot concluded the voting for the day, leaving Harding in fifth place with 61½ votes. Wood had 314½, followed by Lowden with 289½, Johnson with 140½, and Sproul, 79½. Adjournment came after a consultation between Chairman Lodge and Senator Reed Smoot of Utah. A motion to adjourn until Saturday morning was then made and apparently not carried, but Lodge declared otherwise.[12] The party elders saw no solution in continuing the Wood-Lowden deadlock in an unorganized manner. There was also the possibility that Borah and other former Progressives would bolt if the financially exposed Wood or Lowden were selected as the party's choice. This threat, if fulfilled, would divide the party and again cost the Republicans an election.

There have been many accounts of how the "Senate Oligarchy" selected Harding during a Friday night conference and then imposed its will on the convention the following day.[13] Available evidence does not support this theory, nor did Daugherty's recollections.[14] It is true that there were conferences during the adjournment. This is a natural occurrence at any national convention, especially one that is in deadlock. The most publicized of these meetings was the one held on the thirteenth floor of the Blackstone Hotel in a suite rented by Will Hays, the Republican National Chairman, and George Harvey, editor of the *North American Review*. The original participants were Lodge, Harvey, and Senator Frank Brandegee of Connecticut, all of whom went to the Hays suite immediately following dinner. There was a constant flow of visitors throughout the evening; only Harvey and Brandegee remained the entire time. Senators James Wadsworth and W.M. Calder of New York, Medill McCormick of Illinois, and Smoot were among the men who were in and out. Noticeably missing was Penrose, one of the most influential Republican senators of his time. He was seriously ill, but maintained telephone contact with the Pennsylvania headquarters from his bedside.

Lodge and the rest of the group realized the hazard of having the evenly matched Wood and Lowden fighting it out the next day. Opinions were expressed concerning their chances, and such alternate choices as Hughes, Knox, Hays, Hoover, Sproul, and Harding were discussed. Harding's name was most frequently mentioned, but it was not always discussed in a positive manner. A few of his colleagues, who stopped by the Hays suite, did not think him a suitable choice. Others expressed their concern for party unity, making Harding a logical selection. Smoot was continually "talking up" Harding to those who came and went. A *New York Telegram* reporter, who met Smoot in the elevator during the early hours of the morning, asked whether the upstairs conference came to any decision. Smoot supposedly replied: "Yes, we decided on Harding, and he will be nominated this afternoon after we have balloted long enough to give Lowden a run for the money." This widely-quoted exchange contributed to the legend of the "Smoke-filled Room." But Smoot's own enthusiasm and his desire to promote Harding made him a subjective witness. Besides, he said no more than he had prior to the conference.[15]

Nevertheless, an apparent conflict of evidence exists. Delegate Joseph R. Grundy of Pennsylvania later wrote how Lodge opened the conference by alluding to Harding's "outstanding" availability. Those present agreed and "heartily joined in the movement to bring about the nomination of Harding."[16] Wadsworth, however, later related how he had met Harding in one of the corridors of the Blackstone about one o'clock Saturday morning and was told that there were no developments. Wadsworth stated unequivocally that he did not see Senator Harding again that night, and that at none of the several times he was in the suite was there anything even approaching a decision, an understanding, or a plan: "The crowd in Harvey's room were like a lot of chickens with their heads off." Other conferees later agreed.[17]

Harvey told two *Kansas City* [Mo.] *Star* reporters a completely different story around one o'clock Saturday morning. He said that the senators had agreed upon Harding and that the delegates would follow their instructions that day. Then, according to his secretary's subsequent account, Harding was brought to Harvey two hours later. He asked Harding to take an oath that nothing precluded him from accepting the nomination that might later embarrass the party or make it inexpedient for him to run for the presidency. Harding allegedly took ten minutes alone to decide before giving Harvey a favorable reply.[18]

Not being a delegate, Harvey's position in Republican inner circles came by self-appointment. He was a man of great intelligence, but there was no one with more vanity and ambition. Also, his secretary's account conflicts with later evidence, and neither Lodge nor Brandegee, who were with Harvey throughout most of the evening, ever confirmed it.[19] It seems evident that the men who attended the conference did no more than recognize a deadlocked situation, which they had not brought about and which they were powerless to change. Their performance on the following day supported this conclusion. The "fifteen men in a smoke-filled room" prophesy, conceived by Daugherty in a half-serious manner months before the convention, became enshrined after the Friday night recess by those who found the Harvey version more exciting.

Daugherty did not attend the conference in Hays's suite. He was probably not welcome, as senators like Wadsworth and Calder did not think highly of him. He later claimed that he held meetings of his own until two o'clock that morning to call in pledged support.[20] Harding had also gone that evening to an earlier conference which turned out to be more important than the Blackstone one. Hearing rumors that Rud Hynicka and other Ohio delegates planned to defect to Wood once the convention reconvened, he called a midnight caucus of the Ohio delegation to plead for continued support. There, delegate-at-large John Galvin, Mayor of Cincinnati, pledged that he would favor Harding for six or sixty ballots. Willis thereupon hugged him, but Galvin's statement did not prevent Hynicka and three other Hamilton County delegates from bolting momentarily to Wood on the sixth and seventh ballot later that day. Hynicka claimed afterward that loyalty to Harding dictated his actions. He switched to Wood only to stop the Lowden drive.[21]

The convention reconvened Saturday morning at ten o'clock. At the end of the fifth ballot, Lowden moved ahead of Wood, 303 to 299. Harding, meanwhile, had only seventy-eight votes. On the next three ballots the deadlock continued as Daugherty began to request the promised second- and third-choice votes from individual delegates. At the close of the eighth ballot, Harding had jumped to 133 1/2. To stem the Harding boom, Alvin Hert of Kentucky, a leader of the Lowden forces, presented a motion to recess until later in the afternoon. It was then seconded by a New York delegate. Daugherty was so perturbed about the possibility of an adjournment until Monday that he charged to the front of the stage, yelling at Lodge, "you cannot defeat this man in this way."[22] Lodge then wrongly suggested to Herrick, chairman of the Ohio delegation, that the recess might be beneficial to Harding.

There was much activity during the three-hour delay. Wood and Lowden, who disliked each other immensely, tried futilely to form a coalition. There was also an attempt by the Senate leaders to organize around Will Hays to stop the Harding drive. Their actions further disprove the assertion that Harding owed his nomination to a smoke-filled room. Most of the senators who had previously favored Harding at the Blackstone conference now backed Hays. Senator James E. Watson of Indiana later stated that because of the adverse press reaction to Daugherty's "2:11 A.M." prediction, other senators, even though not against Harding, were reluctant to vote for him.[23] This second conference proved as well that the

Republican leaders had no powerful hold upon the delegates. Senator Brandegee, for example, instructed his state's delegation to shift from Lowden to Hays. Chairman J. Henry Roraback told him that the delegation now elected to back Harding. Brandegee was powerless to alter the decision. Similarly, Lodge could impose no control upon the Massachusetts delegation, which favored Coolidge. The Hays push consequently collapsed from senatorial impotence.[24]

During this second recess, Daugherty visited delegations, pleading for additional second-, third-, and fourth-choice pledges. He later said that he also paid a visit to the headquarters of the Pennsylvania delegation where, in a room alone with an operator, he used a special telegraph wire to get in touch with the ailing Penrose. He asked him what support could be given Harding, who was to be nominated that afternoon. Penrose allegedly promised him the Pennsylvania delegation and stated that he would issue a statement publicly to that effect. Daugherty thereupon requested that he not publicize it because, as he later explained, "it was my idea not to have it said that Harding was nominated by the bosses and on that account I did not want Penrose to deliver the Pennsylvania vote until the last."[25] But Daugherty claimed he also sent a messenger to Governor Sproul, chairman of the Pennsylvania delegation, requesting support prior to the final ballot. He then arranged a meeting between Harding and Lowden at the Lowden headquarters. By the time he and Harding arrived, however, Lowden had departed for the convention.[26]

The ninth ballot finally began after the four o'clock recess was extended for another forty-five minutes. Lowden's failure to get Wood to concede in exchange for the vice-presidential nomination caused Lowden to release his delegates. Many now switched to Harding. The Harding-Daugherty strategy of securing second- and third-choice support, their early efforts to cater to Lowden men, and their friendly attitude to other candidates paid off.[27] The Lowden swing to Harding also caused defections from the Wood ranks. The break began when Connecticut switched from Lowden to Harding. Other defections followed. Then Kansas shifted from Wood, due in part to the plea of Senator Curtis who saw an emerging bandwagon. Led by Lowden manager Hert, the Kentucky delegation also cast its votes to Harding, and the Lowden delegates from Missouri, New York, North Carolina, Oklahoma, South Carolina, Texas, and Virginia did likewise. At the end of the voting, Harding had 347 1/2, Wood 249, Lowden 121 1/2, Johnson 82.

By then, Daugherty had joined Mrs. Harding in her box for Harding's expected nomination on the tenth ballot. She tensely removed her hat and, in her right hand, clutched two enormous hat pins. When Daugherty informed her that Harding would be nominated on the approaching ballot, she turned sharply, causing the pins to penetrate deeply into Daugherty's side. Daugherty thought he felt blood running from his side down his leg. Saying nothing to disturb her, he sat there, thinking that the pins had pierced a lung. He then felt a "queer swish" of blood in his shoe as he unsteadily left the box as the tenth ballot began. Only after Harding's nomination did he find out that his lung was not pierced and that his shoe was full of perspiration, not blood. Harding, meanwhile, was sitting with Nicholas Murray Butler of New York and Lowden in one of the small rooms behind the platform. Suddenly the door burst open and Charles B. Warren of Michigan lunged into the room shouting, "Pennsylvania has voted for you, Harding, and you are nominated!" Harding rose, grabbing both Butler's and Lowden's hands and said: "If the great honor of the Presidency is to come to me, I shall need all the help that you two friends can give me." Daugherty then entered and quickly took him back to the Auditorium Hotel.[28] Senator Harry S. New of Indiana later remarked of Harding's nomination: "In the contemplation of all that I have seen, I do not hesitate to say that I never saw a nomination come about more naturally— I had almost said inevitably—than the nomination of Harding in 1920." Daugherty stood in full accord with New's conclusions.[29]

An analysis of the balloting is revealing as far as the senatorial delegates are concerned. There were only sixteen, and only two of them voted for Harding on the first ballot. The number of states having a senator on their delegations was eleven, and from those states (excluding Ohio) Harding received just nine of their delegate votes on the first ballot: five from Missouri, two from New York, one from Colorado, and one from Utah. The senatorial performance is even more surprising after the Friday night recess, which followed the fourth ballot. Wadsworth of New York gave his support to Lowden until the eighth ballot; Calder of New York to Butler initially, then to Lowden following the fourth; Watson of Indiana to Wood on every ballot; New of Indiana to Wood until the eighth, then to Harding; Lodge of Massachusetts to Harding on the ninth ballot; Frelinghuysen and Walter E. Edge both of New Jersey to Wood until the end; L. Heisler Ball of Delaware to T. Coleman Dupont; Sherman of Illinois to Lowden until the tenth; Selden P. Spencer of Missouri to Lowden until released after the eighth ballot; Medill McCormick of Illinois to Lowden throughout; and Brandegee's Connecticut delegation to Lowden up to the ninth. Penrose did not release the Pennsylvania delegation to Harding until the final ballot. Only Smoot of Utah and Lawrence C. Phipps of Colorado voted for Harding on every turn.[30]

The lack of senatorial power was again exhibited in the vice-presidential nomination. The old guard's and Harding's choice was the progressive Senator Irvine Lenroot of Wisconsin, who would balance the ticket. Daugherty later wrote that the senators consulted him about the feasibility of choosing Lenroot. He replied that Lenroot was geographically right and had numerous friends.[31] The delegates, however, foiled the party leaders' feeble attempt to put Lenroot across. Calvin Coolidge of the Boston Police Strike fame was more to their liking in a period when strikes were associated with Bolshevism. The Governor of Massachusetts was quickly nominated.

The day after the convention Daugherty returned to Columbus, where he ordered a taxicab operator to drive him by the offices of newspaper publisher Robert Wolfe. Daugherty then leaned out of the taxicab window to hurl a "jeering" shout and gesture at the *Ohio State Journal* cartoonist, William Ireland, who worked near an open window. When Daugherty returned to his office, he asked his secretary, Katherine Carroll, to purchase a small alarm clock, to set the hands at 2:11, and to deliver it to Ireland at exactly that time. Afterward, he called several mutual friends of his and Ireland's, telling them to telephone Ireland immediately after 2:11. It was Ireland who had cartooned Daugherty holding a clock with its hands set at the appropriate moment. In a half-joking way Daugherty got back at an occasional golf partner.[32]

Still to come was the famous front-porch campaign in Marion where the personable Harding, in his familiar white coat and blue trousers, greeted the visiting delegations that came from all over the country. The press was there to publicize his well-prepared and soothing speeches on Americanism, Republican prosperity, and constitutional government. Governor James M. Cox of Ohio, the Democratic nominee, burdened by an unequivocal commitment to the League of Nations and by a backlash against Wilson, was not nearly as effective in his aggressive and strenuous campaign.

Daugherty's part in that contest originated one week after the national convention. On June 18, he traveled to Harding's Wyoming Avenue home in Washington, D.C., where other Republican leaders, including Hoover, Coolidge, Lodge, Hilles, and Hays, were also to confer. There Harding agreed that Hays should continue to serve as national chairman, despite the custom of replacing the incumbent after the national convention. Hays, known as "Telephone Bill" for his frequent use of that device, was a strong promoter of Republican unity and an excellent publicist, and so was much in harmony with Harding's conciliatory views. As chairman, he now became Harding's campaign manager.

Daugherty was clearly dissatisfied with the arrangement. He was suspicious of Hays. The previous winter he had had a disagreement with him, which remained unresolved as a result of Hays's alleged presidential ambitions. More importantly, Daugherty resisted any relinquishment of power. Despite Daugherty's later claim that the national chairmanship was his for the asking, the truth was that nobody made the offer. Concerned lest he be cut out altogether, he demanded a responsible role.[33] At Harding's request, Hays promptly appointed him to the executive committee of the national Republican organization. In time, a steering subcommittee of Daugherty, Hilles, Hert, former Senator John W. Weeks of Massachusetts, and ex-Progressive Raymond Robins evolved. It was to advise the Republican national headquarters in New York and in Chicago, the Harding staff in Marion, and Harding himself. Although some steering subcommittee members felt that Hays ignored their advice, Daugherty cooperated fully with him.[34] Despite the illness of his wife and his sister-in-law, he traveled extensively from headquarters to headquarters, either representing Harding or promoting organizational work. He did the latter especially well, but it was Hays who ran the campaign—not Daugherty.

One of the campaign's important features was the further reunification of the Republican party. Both Harding and Hays saw the need for it. No one was more suited than Harding to promote it. As a result former Bull Moosers like Hiram Johnson, James R. Garfield, and Robins played active roles. On the national level, Daugherty encouraged their participation. He advised Harding to write Johnson: "You know how to pump him, a letter that he will show his wife and then she will help. Say to Johnson by all means he must make two or three speeches in Ohio."[35]

In Ohio, however, where his personal power was involved and where festering animosities existed, Daugherty was less cooperative. At the Republican state convention in Columbus on June 29, he appealed for harmony and appeared on stage with William H. Boyd, who had defeated him in the April delegate-at-large race. But he remained vindictive toward Hynicka and critical of Wolfe, Brown, Hanna, and Clark.[36] When Harding decided to favor Brown for his Senate seat, Daugherty backed Willis. Willis had visited Daugherty at his Columbus residence to inform him of Harding's position. The response was that Harding had no business favoring Brown, despite Brown's active support since December.[37] Daugherty's opposition to Harding's unity efforts caused the latter to question his "unworthy motives." Nothing more depressed Daugherty. After Harding quickly forgave him, Daugherty then denied that any disagreement existed. On July 1, he wrote Harding that he had

> only one desire and one ambition—your success now and in the great days to come. We have gone this journey too far and too long together for misunderstandings. Whatever I do or refrain from doing is for you and your interests. No one else, much less men with selfish motives, can do more. I am not infallible, and while I have endured much, I have never for one moment lost sight of the great cause in which we are embarked together.[38]

Nevertheless, he continued to support Willis, who opposed Harding's request that he withdraw. Supported by the Anti-Saloon League and more known to voters, Willis then defeated Brown in the primaries. Such conflicts left the Ohio Republican party a potential powder keg throughout Harding's presidential years.

As the national campaign moved into final swing, Daugherty better served the Harding cause. It was because of his and publicist Judson C. Welliver's suggestions that a staff of experts existed at Marion to plan and to write Harding's speeches. The two agreed that former Senator George Sutherland of Utah should assist in the speech writing. Daugherty then suggested such "must" topics for speeches as the high cost of living, the tariff, the agricultural program, and the opening of foreign markets.[39] To offset the opposition of labor leaders like Samuel Gompers, Daugherty advised Harding that Republican Congressman William J. Burke of Pittsburgh, a labor man, visit Marion shortly after Gompers's Labor Day address. In the interests of the "practical" conservationists of the West, the unpopular Gifford Pinchot, Daugherty recommended, should be kept away and kept still. He also suggested that some Republicans believed that George Harvey was too much in the limelight in Marion. Harding generally followed Daugherty's suggestions.[40] To others elsewhere, Daugherty wrote letters offering advice, encouragement, or admonitions.

By mid-August, Daugherty, among others, thought that Harding should leave the front porch for periodic campaign tours.[41] The pressure to do so was especially great among local Republican managers and candidates who wanted him to help the ticket. As Cox's campaign intensified, Harding departed in late September for Pennsylvania and Maryland. Then in early October he campaigned in Omaha, Des Moines, Kansas City, and Oklahoma City. That same month he also spoke in Indiana, Kentucky, and Tennessee. His final trip was to Buffalo and Rochester. In the privacy of a personal train car, Daugherty generally accompanied the entourage.

He also advised Harding on some of his speeches. He reminded him to refer to women because they were to vote in a presidential election for the first time. He asked that Harding stick to the America-First theme, which would never lose him votes. To confront the pro-Leaguers at Buffalo and Rochester, Daugherty recommended the social justice speech, which expressed an appreciation of our obligations to the rest of the world. In no way, however, was Daugherty Harding's major speech adviser.[42] His suggestions were always informal and brief.

On election morning, November 2, Daugherty and Harding drove to Columbus for a round of golf at the Scioto Country Club. Afterward, they returned to Marion where they awaited the returns. Harding's victory was overwhelming. He won 60.2% of the popular vote, while Cox captured only 34.4 % and the imprisoned Eugene Debs, a surprising 5.4 %. Harding's win was not only a reaction to Wilsonianism, but also a tribute to his personal popularity and to a well-managed campaign. Daugherty played only a modest role in that victory, but he had contributed significantly to his nomination. After years of political frustration, he appeared to have reached the apex of a stormy career.

The Formation of the Harding Cabinet

DAUGHERTY's 1932 apologia maintained that he had desired no responsibility in the new administration. Mortally tired of politics, he intended to retire immediately to a profitable law practice. But the necessity of assisting the Republican National Committee in balancing its financial accounts detained him. Subsequently, hordes of officeseekers and "axe grinders," thinking Daugherty a cog in the new administration, besieged him in Columbus. Finally, Daugherty insisted, Harding himself refused to accept his recommendation that George Sutherland of Utah become Attorney General. The President-elect also chose to ignore the opposition of the press and of leading Republicans in making the Daugherty appointment. Under these circumstances, Daugherty wrote, he unwillingly accepted the attorney generalship, thereby committing "the tragic blunder of my life."[1]

Hindsight partially affected Daugherty's memory. Immediately after the November election, the Associated Press, in fact, speculated that the legally respected Sutherland was under consideration for Attorney General.[2] By early December, however, when Harding first gave serious attention to cabinet selections, he was not regarded as a contender. On December 10, Harding adviser Judson Welliver informed Sutherland that he would be Harding's first appointee to the Supreme Court. Daugherty also arranged a meeting with him to relate the same information.[3] There is no evidence that Daugherty ever recommended Sutherland for the attorney generalship.

Harding apparently considered Daugherty his choice from the outset. To protesting Senators Wadsworth and New in December, he indicated that Daugherty could have any cabinet position aside from Secretary of State, which he planned to offer to Charles Evans Hughes. He said that Daugherty had informed him he wanted to be Attorney General, "and by God he will be Attorney General." To former Senator Weeks of Massachusetts, he replied that the attorney generalship was all that Daugherty wanted and would take.[4] Gratitude caused Harding to accede to Daugherty's request. He explained to one dissenter: "I would not want the country to think me so much an ingrate that I would ignore a man of Mr. Daugherty's devotion to the party and to me as an aspirant and a candidate."[5] Harding could not easily forget that the often maligned Daugherty had invested considerable time and money in the vital preconvention fight. He undoubtedly also wanted Daugherty satisfied enough to handle effectively some of the grueling matters of patronage.

Daugherty had his own way of handling such opposition. An example occurred after he had asked an old friend, J.O.A. Preus, to persuade Senator Knute Nelson of Minnesota to support his probable nomination. Preus spoke frankly:

> You're not qualified, Harry, to be Attorney General. You ought to know it and I think I know it, and I have the courage to tell you that I don't think you'd do Harding any good and I don't think you'd do yourself any good. You've been a lobbying lawyer here in Washington and you're known as such in Ohio. And if I were you I wouldn't take it.

Daugherty looked at Preus for a moment and then said, "the President insists on it." Preus replied, "all right, that's a different proposition," and he then related Daugherty's response to Senator Nelson. According to Preus, Nelson said that the President "is entitled to his own cabinet and I'll vote for Dougherty [sic]. But I agree with you that he should not accept it."[6]

Daugherty did not seek the attorney generalship for financial gain. He could easily have enhanced his income by returning to private practice, as the campaign publicity had further enhanced his image with corporation magnates. Harding's presidency would have made Daugherty one of the busiest lobbyists in the country, for businessmen, involved in litigation with the government, would have readily pursued him. More than even a desire for power and prestige and an ultrapatriotic sense of serving country and party, he sought the office to vindicate a past which was constantly under suspicion. His character and legal ability were still suspect, even though he had recently achieved recognition as a skillful politician. Daugherty clearly could not be satisfied with anything less than becoming the nation's leading law officer. To appoint him elsewhere would have been an admission that he was neither qualified nor capable of performing as Attorney General. Consequently, his vindication would have been incomplete. As one contemporary writer astutely observed, the appointment would give him a certain respectability in legal circles that he had never had. He could then leave office with a title, ready for life upon a new level. In Daugherty's own words, he wanted it so that he could tell archcritic Robert Wolfe "to go to hell."[7]

Throughout December, Harding continued to express to Republican leaders who traveled to Marion his desire to appoint Daugherty. Charles Dawes, under consideration as Secretary of the Treasury, and Herrick, again to become Ambassador to France, both warned Harding not to select Daugherty. Others voiced similar objections.[8] Only William Howard Taft recorded a favorable, but qualified, response. Harding remarked to Taft, who breakfasted with the Hardings in December, that he "could see through Harry when Harry did not suspect it" but added that Daugherty was loyal and a good lawyer. Taft conceded that Harding was entitled to have such a friend in the cabinet.[9]

By the end of January, Harding departed from his "great listening post" at Marion for an extended vacation in Florida, where he combined cabinet making and relaxation. With him went an entourage of friends, including Daugherty. Throughout the sojourn the press continued to speculate on cabinet selections. The *New York Times*'s assumption that Daugherty's ambitions would be fulfilled only increased opposition to his appointment.[10] On February 6, Jennings wrote Harding that for the past few days staff men had visited Columbus from the New York *World*, the *New York Times*, and other newspapers, investigating "past history and interviewing men to gather stories which may lead to later investigations of [Daugherty's] legal and business operations." He stated that Wolfe was also making "war medicine" against Daugherty.[11] The *Chicago Tribune* had earlier put together some twenty potential charges, ranging from misappropriation of trust funds to confiscation of campaign monies. These accusations had allegedly been presented to Daugherty, who had made a three-hour explanation.[12]

The most comprehensive denunciation came from the Democratic New York *World*. Its somewhat exaggerated exposé, delving deeply into Daugherty's past, was serialized for five consecutive days beginning on February 17. Following each publication, the *World* sent the article to Daugherty, who was with Harding at St. Augustine. The hope was that Daugherty might use its columns either to deny or to explain the charges. He instead replied: "You cannot quote me by as much as one word."[13]

The *World* elaborated on several of Daugherty's earlier indiscretions, including his changed vote in the 1892 Sherman-Foraker contest, his "holding up" of Hanna in 1898, his involvement in the Morse case in 1911, and his role in the Columbus Savings and Trust debacle of 1913. It portrayed Daugherty as an accomplished lobbyist whose clients included the Ohio subsidiaries of the American Gas and Electric Company, the Western Union Telegraph Company, and the Ohio State Telephone Company. Daugherty frequently had represented these corporations before the Ohio Public Utilities Commission, where he succeeded in obtaining a sizable increase in Ohio telephone rates in 1919. His firm also made appearances before the Ohio Tax Commission in several tax reduction cases involving the above clients. Additionally, the *World* accurately depicted Daugherty's influence on the recent Ohio General Assembly, where crafty William Halley held sway as senate clerk, where the floor leader was an ally, and where the house clerk was also a Daugherty appointee. The newspaper also secured numerous statements from unnamed Ohio attorneys and judges that Daugherty had not appeared in an Ohio common pleas or state supreme court in recent years.[14] Overall, it characterized Daugherty as an unscrupulous lawyer-politician who would be dangerously out of character as Attorney General. The *World* endorsed Sutherland.

Even the independent *New York Times* pointed out that a "third-class lawyer" would be ill-equipped to handle the extensive war-claims cases, the difficult interpretations of the law in recent labor and railroad disputes, and the increasing number of other federal cases. Having no objection to Harding's rewarding Daugherty, it insisted that the reward be commensurate with his abilities.[15] Such staid Republican papers as the *New York Tribune* and the *Boston Evening Transcript* concurred. The *Tribune* concluded that Daugherty "doesn't measure up to the standards" established for the office.[16]

The press correctly assumed that a lobbyist would make an inadequate Attorney General. Even ignoring the question of qualifications, such an appointment would attract former associates to Washington to seek favors. They would attempt to influence Daugherty as he had sought to influence Taft, Wickersham, and others. An Attorney General with Daugherty's background would be more willing to ignore their indiscretions and to concede to their questionable requests than one more disciplined in the law. Interestingly, the press hardly touched on the potential conflicts of interest that can occur when a campaign manager assumes the attorney generalship.

But the aggressive press attacks against Daugherty in February did not go unchallenged in Ohio. Senator Willis publicly defended Daugherty, as did a number of Ohio attorneys and judges.[17] Many were long-standing friends like judges John E. Sater and E.B. Kinkaid. Even former Democratic state attorney general Timothy Hogan, who had attempted to curb Daugherty's lobbying activities, now stated that Daugherty was "a man of good sense, an excellent lawyer, and with a courage that welds his friends to him like steel to steel."[18] Hogan and others undoubtedly defended their fellow Ohioan because of the unmerciful criticism. Some, like Taft, implied that Daugherty's lobbying experience need not be a handicap. Taft reasoned that while an Attorney General has no time to prepare and argue cases, he must be persistent, a good organizer, and know how to deal with men. He predicted that Daugherty "would surprise a good many people with the efficiency of his views."[19]

Despite the strong sentiment against Daugherty, Harding followed his own inclinations. On February 21, two days after he declared Hughes his Secretary of State, he announced the Daugherty appointment. His announcement came at a St. Augustine press conference attended by two of Daugherty's chief critics—Louis Seibold of the New York *World* and Mark Sullivan of the *New York Evening Post*. Sullivan later made much of the fact that Seibold's presence so angered Harding that he snapped: "I am ready today to invite Mr. Daugherty into the cabinet as my Attorney-General; when he is ready there will be an announcement, if he can persuade himself to make the sacrifice; . . . and if I can persuade him to accept the position."[20] Harding's anger, however, did not cause him to act either rashly or hastily. Although criticism strengthened his resolve, he had promised Daugherty the position as early as November and had consistently intended to honor his commitment. A few minutes after the conference, Daugherty ran into Sullivan. When the latter remarked, "Well, you're going to be Attorney-General," Daugherty good-naturedly retorted: "Yes, no thanks to you, Goddam you." Later that day the prospective Attorney General proclaimed that "no man could refuse to serve a friend and his country under the circumstances. I am appreciative of both the honor and the responsibilities."[21]

Harding was almost as strong willed about his other cabinet appointments. He consulted the "best minds" of the country, but he made his own decisions. Daugherty, the senators, and the press were hard put to move Harding once he had decided.[22] In choosing his cabinet he relied on three criteria: a man's qualification for public service, which he considered to be the most important; the attitude of the public toward the man under consideration; and political considerations. He had varying degrees of success in following his own guidelines. Hughes, whom he highly respected, was his first and only choice for Secretary of State, even though the old guard favored Knox or Root. Harding judged the liberal Henry C. Wallace the best man for Secretary of Agriculture and again secured this selection despite the opposition of the packers and food-processing industries. His decision to appoint Herbert Hoover, however, caused tremendous opposition among Republican leaders. The old guard found Hoover, who had served so capably as Wilson's Food Administrator, too progressive, international-minded, ambitious, and politically undeserving. Daugherty claimed that former Progressives also objected to him, probably for the latter three reasons.[23]

Harding had to use considerable ingenuity to secure Hoover's nomination. He won the old guard only through political blackmail. Despite initially favoring Charles Dawes for Secretary of the Treasury, he turned to Pittsburgh multimillionaire Andrew Mellon as a quid pro quo. In early February, he sent Daugherty to Washington to talk to Mellon's two staunchest backers in the Senate, Penrose and Knox of Pennsylvania. Daugherty, acting under Harding's instructions, frankly told them that Harding would not appoint Mellon unless they agreed upon Hoover as Commerce Secretary. Penrose, Daugherty later remarked, "rose to heights of profanity I have never heard equaled. He swore in every mood and tense."[24] The two senators, nonetheless, reluctantly agreed to favor Hoover in order to save Mellon, who met Harding's anti-"Wall Street" criteria: He was neither a New Englander nor a New Yorker.

The President-elect's move was the more remarkable because Daugherty strongly advised against appointing the independent Hoover. Knowing Harding's determination in this matter, he warned Harding not to ignore the opposition. "There is very little support in Congress," Daugherty wrote, and "the Hearst's newspaper opposition" is very intense against this party." Harding promptly replied that the more he considered Hoover the more he thought well of him. "Of course," Harding added, "I have no quarrel with those who do not think as I do, but inasmuch as I have the responsibility to assume I think my judgment must be trusted in the matter."[25]

Harding bowed more to political exigencies in selecting the rest of his cabinet. Daugherty later said that Will Hays would not have been appointed Postmaster General had he (Daugherty) not insisted upon it while with Harding in Florida. He claimed that he had advised Harding that he must show the country that the President-elect "was loyal to friends he was under obligation to." The truth was that Harding had already offered him the position several days before their Florida departure in late January 1921.[26] There was never any hesitation on Harding's part in offering the efficient Hays the post that has customarily doubled as the patronage office. The hesitation came from Hays, who preferred to be Commerce Secretary.

Friendship and admiration as well as politics prompted Harding to select Senator Albert Fall of New Mexico as Secretary of the Interior. The President-elect had sat next to Fall in the Senate, where he had come to like this frontier baron with the handle-bar mustache, black cape, and broad-rimmed Stetson. Both enjoyed poker and a good story. Harding also respected Fall, whom he considered an expert on western and Latin American affairs. His senatorial colleagues were so agreeable that they cheerfully approved of his appointment. Indeed, only the conservationists were strongly opposed to Fall, whose senatorial record indicated an anticonservation bias and whose subsurface holdings appeared to spell trouble.[27] Daugherty, who disliked Fall because of his past progressivism, did not voice any objection to his selection. Moreover, later assertions that Fall's selection was related to a deal with the oil interests at the 1920

Republican convention run counter to prevailing evidence. As Daugherty accurately pointed out, the big oil operators had backed Wood. The fourteen leading oil states had given Harding only eighty out of 403 delegates prior to the ninth ballot. Of the eighty votes, thirty-nine had come from Ohio.[28] A recent historian on the 1920s rightly called the alleged deal "complete nonsense."[29] Fall's later unethical actions came as a shock to those who knew him well.

Harding rounded out his cabinet by appointing John W. Weeks as Secretary of War; Edwin Denby, Secretary of the Navy; and James J. Davis, Secretary of Labor. The capable Weeks, a former member of the Senate Military Affairs Committee, had surprisingly lost his Senate seat in 1918. Like Mellon, he was a chief financial contributor in the 1920 campaign. Denby came almost as an afterthought when Lowden declined the Navy post. Nevertheless, Denby appeared to be an excellent choice since he had an exceptional service record and had spent six years in Congress, where he had served on the House Naval Affairs Committee. Davis represented a political compromise. Although not associated with the Gompers faction, he had been an iron puddler and an active union member. A strong Harding supporter in 1920 and the Director General of the Loyal Order of the Moose, Davis quickly developed into Harding's top choice for the Labor assignment.

On March 4, immediately following the inauguration, President Harding visited the Senate, where he read out the names of his cabinet selections and then asked for their speedy approval. No President since Jefferson had followed this procedure, which Senator Henry Cabot Lodge had privately suggested to Harding. Probably the intent was to block possible senatorial opposition, for rumors had circulated that Hoover's appointment would be opposed. After Harding's short address, the Senate then went into executive session, where the various committees to which the nominees were referred quickly reported in favor of confirmation after they had been previously polled. The Senate Judiciary Committee, under the chairmanship of Senator Nelson, approved of Daugherty. Within less than ten minutes, the Senate had confirmed the entire cabinet.[30]

Of the ten members, Daugherty, at sixty-one, was the second oldest and one of the least solvent financially. He was the only Methodist and Harding's one selection from Ohio. He also represented Harding's greatest accommodation to personal rather than to public considerations. Though the press made favorable comment on the cabinet as a whole, almost universal opposition was reserved for Daugherty. The *New York Times* remarked that "from Hughes to Daugherty is a pretty long step."[31] In Ohio the Wolfe-owned *Ohio State Journal* labeled Daugherty as the one weak appointment. Privately, however, friends and foes alike congratulated him in his moment of personal triumph.

Old Friends and New Responsibilities

ATTORNEY General Daugherty began his tenure with a party. After taking the oath of office, he held a formal reception that lasted for an hour. Both personal friends and political leaders attended. His offices were filled with huge bouquets and potted plants. Among the guests were retired actress Lillian Russell, escorted by her wealthy husband Alex P. Moore, the Pittsburgh publisher, who had contributed so handsomely to the 1920 Republican campaign. She highlighted the ceremony by planting a kiss on Daugherty immediately after he had been formally inducted into office.

Daugherty also attended parties at places like "Friendship," the palatial estate of the Ned McLeans, multimillionaire owners of the *Washington Post* and *Cincinnati Enquirer*. Important people deferred to him. At age sixty-one he had reached the pinnacle of his career. Contemporary writers described Daugherty at this time as burly and thicknecked, usually wearing a derby hat, light-colored suits, and a diamond stickpin, with a pipe or a Wheeling stogy in hand. His eyes were "unsteady," one was imperfect and the other, according to Mark Sullivan, "seemed to circle round a man," as if Daugherty "was getting his impression, not from the physical man, but from psychic aura about him." His face was florid and alternately jovial and menacing.[1]

The new Attorney General soon found that his job necessitated a tremendous effort. Of all the executive branches in the Wilson administration, the Department of Justice had been one of the most inept. Attorney General A. Mitchell Palmer had neglected it in his two years in office to avert an imaginary Bolshevik revolution and to seek the presidential nomination. As a result, the Department had slowly degenerated. Corruption was now suspected, especially in connection with the unprosecuted war-fraud cases, in which the government stood to gain $192,000,000 from defrauding industries. Because of prohibition, the increase in mail fraud, violations of the Mann Act, and various wartime cases, the undermanned federal courts were faced with crammed dockets.[2] Not only did the court system need revamping, but the Department required a reorganization to include an influx of competent attorneys to tackle the backlog of cases. It was also essential that the new Attorney General formulate clear-cut policies to meet the Department's postwar responsibilities.

In the ensuing weeks Daugherty began to outline the priorities of his administration. High on the list was recommended legislation to expand the federal judiciary, enforcement of the antitrust laws, investigation of war frauds and high retail prices, and reorganization of the Bureau of Investigation. In his first public speech as Attorney General, at the American Bar Association convention in Cincinnati that August, he set down the basic theme of his attorney generalship. It was to be one of law and order. He emphasized that personal liberty can never come at the expense of duly enacted laws, nor could corporations and labor expect to violate the law. He reserved his greatest criticism for those dignifying the crimes and urging the release of the imprisoned "radicals" who had obstructed or hindered the government in the prosecution of the war. "Those who do not believe in our Government and the enforcement of our laws should go to a country which gives them their peculiar liberty," he declared. Conversely, foreigners should stay away unless they "intend to observe our laws."[3]

To accomplish his objectives, Daugherty promised to create a staff of top Republican lawyers. As a spoilsman, however, he hired too often on the basis of political and personal considerations. William Howard Taft later remarked that poor assistants had contributed to Daugherty's troubles.[4] Not all of his selections were ill-fated, but enough were to undermine the capabilities of the Department. To head his immediate staff, he selected Guy Goff, a stout man with "bulging cheeks of carmine," the son of a Republican West Virginia senator and later senator himself. Goff had been District Attorney in Milwaukee during the Taft administration, and a recess appointee to the Shipping Board in Wilson's presidency. But, as Goff's record soon revealed, he was mediocre. By 1922, Taft was especially critical of Goff's performance.[5] Yet Daugherty quickly placed additional responsibilities upon Goff aside from his general supervisory role as the Assistant to the Attorney General, his direct supervision of the Antitrust Division, and his review of Alien Property matters. This occurred after the much respected Henry L. Stimson, Taft's former Secretary of War, declined to take charge of the war-fraud investigations. Daugherty subsequently informed Stimson that next to him Goff was "the best man" for the job. In late July 1921, he made the assignment.[6]

By early 1922, members of Congress began to criticize the Department for failure to prosecute war-fraud cases. Daugherty argued that because appropriations from Congress were $3,000,000 less than the departmental estimate for 1922, he lacked the necessary funds. More disconcerting were accusations that Thomas B. Felder and other lobbyists influenced the postponement of specific investigations.[7] In May 1922, Congress appropriated $500,000 to expedite the prosecutions, and Daugherty, under pressure to complete the task, created a War Transactions Section to devote full time to the work. Later that same year Goff retired for a political career. The more able A.T. Seymour of Columbus, Ohio, a law partner of Arthur Vorys, replaced him. Daugherty and the Congress were probably more responsible than Goff for the early failures of the war-fraud investigation. That no cases were settled at the time of his resignation, however, was a commentary on Goff's ineffectiveness as well.

In contrast, the Goff-directed Antitrust Division served more actively. Surprisingly, it was mildly anti-big-business. Daugherty set the pace in mid-April 1921 when he warned that certain industries allied with the building trades were violating the antitrust laws. By July, the government instituted antitrust litigation against several cement manufacturers.[8] Other actions soon followed. More surprising was the Justice Department's critical attitude toward trade associations, which were viewed as instruments of price-fixing rather than tools to promote efficiency and stability. This attitude placed Daugherty in opposition to Secretary of Commerce Hoover's policy of encouraging such organizations. In a series of communiques with Hoover beginning in early 1922, Daugherty, even though eventually giving ground, was critical of association practices and conservative on what the law permitted. In this he had the backing of the Federal Trade Commission.[9]

In 1921, because of the high cost of living, the Antitrust Division additionally embarked on an investigation of retail establishments. As Goff explained, there was "too wide a [price] margin between producer and consumer." The Division sent questionnaires to some of the principal dealers in each city to enable them to justify the prices that they charged and to explain their side of the case. If such explanations were unsatisfactory, the government would undertake prosecution.[10] A representative response came from Fred Lazarus, Jr., the owner of a large department store in Columbus, Ohio: "Present high prices are due to high wages, high taxes, and expensive overheads caused largely by war conditions." Complaints from businessmen and politicians concerning the investigation contributed to its discontinuation in early 1922.[11] Whether it served as an effective moral force is doubtful. Nevertheless, prices had dropped, largely because of the continuing depression of 1921.

That Daugherty should be even mildly anti-big-business, given his legal background, needs some explanation. Public pressure played its part. In the inflationary postwar era of 1919-1920, some hostility existed toward big business, especially as a result of federal and state profiteering investigations.[12] More importantly, Daugherty also responded to the intense criticism generated at the time of his appointment that he would serve corporate interests. When such criticism persisted in 1921 and 1922, he adopted an even more critical view toward suspected corporate violations.[13] The Federal Trade Commission's rather aggressive antibusiness stance undoubtedly reinforced his attitude, as did some favorable court decisions. In the same vein, the administration's cost of living investigation was largely motivated by political considerations. This was frankly admitted by Special Assistant Attorney General G.E. Strong, who was in charge of the probe. Likewise, political backlash later brought it to an end.[14]

To help handle the Justice Department's other responsibilities, Daugherty selected six Assistant Attorneys General of varying caliber. Rush Holland, in charge of personnel, was a notorious example of a misguided political appointment. He had formerly run a weekly newspaper in Zanesville, Ohio, which had consistently favored Daugherty for the governorship. Holland later departed for Colorado, where he operated as a lobbyist. He crossed paths with Daugherty again while a delegate at the 1920 Republican national convention. There, he assisted in swinging the Colorado delegation to Harding on the last ballot. Mabel Willebrandt, an able Assistant Attorney General in charge of prohibition and taxation, contemptuously stamped Holland "a politician pure and simple." She and others blamed much of the Department's difficulties on him.[15]

Willebrandt was one of the few nonpolitical appointments. A Los Angeles public defender of women, she was highly recommended and reflected Daugherty's view that women in the Department would have a "wholesome effect."[16] Along with Assistant Attorney General John W.H. Crim, Criminal Division head and a long-time Justice employee, she served conscientiously and loyally. As head of the Land Division, Assistant Attorney General William D. Riter of Utah, a former law partner of Senator Sutherland, was a more respectable political appointee. So too was Albert Ottinger, chief of Admiralty Litigation, who would serve two terms as New York attorney general in the mid-1920s and would lose the gubernatorial election of 1928 to Franklin Roosevelt by less than 25,000 votes. Assistant Attorney General Robert Lovett, in charge of the Defense of Suits Against the United States Division, was formerly an Illinois judge and now a solid assistant. Additionally, Warren F. Martin, a former law partner of Philander Knox, ably and dedicatedly discharged his duties as Daugherty's Special Assistant, a position next to Goff's in authority.

Lower in the hierarchy were a number of Special Assistant Attorneys General who did their jobs without opprobrium. Hiram C. Todd of New York, who prosecuted several notorious lawbreakers, was truly outstanding. Obviously, the high echelons of the office of the Attorney General were not scandal ridden. To label Justice, as did one contemporary senator, the "Department of Easy Virtue" is to insult the vast majority who performed creditably.[17] Several of Daugherty's high appointees, in fact, served for several years after his resignation. The fact remains, however, that weaknesses existed. Because Daugherty lacked the temperament, experience, and ability of all other Attorneys General and was frequently away as a result of illness, shortcomings in personnel were magnified.[18]

Daugherty's other departmental appointments were again generally political or personal. By far they were his worst selections. The exception was the Solicitor Generalship, which he filled with archconservative James M. Beck, an eminent attorney who had served as Assistant Attorney General in the McKinley-Roosevelt administrations. Known as an eloquent speaker and as a devotee of Shakespeare, the slightly-built Beck also provided a measure of class. More typical was the appointment of J.E. Dyche as warden of the Atlanta Penitentiary. Dyche's qualifications were his intimate political association with Jake Hamon, a shady political boss from Oklahoma, who had delivered delegate support to Daugherty at the 1920 national convention and was later murdered that same year.[19] In 1922, Daugherty censured Dyche for permitting prisoners to have "undue liberties," such as conducting business affairs. The drug traffic among convicts remained unchecked, however, because Daugherty apparently feared unfavorable publicity.[20]

Unquestionably, William J. Burns of Columbus, Ohio, was Daugherty's most unfortunate selection. As Director of the Bureau of Investigation, he did more to discredit the Justice Department than any other appointee. A personal friend of Daugherty's for thirty years, they met while Daugherty was a member of the state legislature. By that time, Detective Burns had already made a name for himself by solving several local crimes in Columbus. He went on to become Chief of the United States Secret Service and in 1909 founded the Burns International Detective Agency. Sir Arthur Conan Doyle, the creator of Sherlock Holmes, once called him one of the world's greatest detectives.[21]

But Burns had several shortcomings. Labor despised him because his agency was often employed to spy on workers and to undercut union activity. Charges were also made that Burn's detectives, for their own reasons, occasionally fomented labor unrest.[22] There were several accusations that Burns had packed juries as well. In 1912, Taft's Attorney General George Wickersham had accused him of rigging a jury with "convictors." This report was later sent to Harding's secretary, who forwarded it to Daugherty, who had not yet appointed Burns. Also alarming was that Burns had been known to break into private offices for evidence and to employ disreputable people to do the "dirty work."[23] Such activities help to explain why the Burns agency generally got results.

Despite the opposition, rumors spread as early as April 1, 1921, of Burns's eventual appointment. He had already visited Daugherty in Washington on several occasions, during which they seemed to agree on a reorganization whereby all investigatory agents would be under the headship of the Bureau of Investigation. Meanwhile, the existing Bureau Chief, William J. Flynn, a Wilson appointee, operated out of headquarters in New York, where he was leading an inquiry into the Wall Street bombing episode of September 1920. On March 31, Daugherty tartly said to a reporter that he had yet to hear from Flynn.[24] Nevertheless, it was August 18 before Daugherty telegramed him that he was being replaced. On that same day he notified Burns, who immediately replied: "I cannot find words to fully express my appreciation of the confidence reposed in me by you in this appointment." Daugherty also informed the press that Burns would embark on a "housecleaning," and that it would be Burns's desire to stop the arrest of innocent persons that had occurred as the result of the Palmer raids of 1919-1920.[25]

The shake-up included the transferring on August 22 of the twenty-six-year-old J. Edgar Hoover from his position as Special Assistant to the Attorney General to that of Assistant Director of the Bureau of Investigation. Why Daugherty made this change is unclear, since Hoover, as the head of the Alien Radical Division, had been the red-baiting Palmer's top lieutenant. Perhaps it was his concern about possible radical activities that caused him to promote the nonpolitical Hoover, who had already impressed some officials with his anti-Communist zeal.[26] Shortly afterward, Daugherty established a New York training school for government detectives, which was to stress such topics as the laws of arrest, the rudiments of evidence, and the rights of United States residents.[27] This practically concluded the reorganization efforts, for an enlarged Bureau, which Burns and Daugherty had earlier envisioned, was not to be. Most likely, opposition from other affected agencies squelched that plan.

The short and plump Burns, wearing the checked frock coat of an earlier day, also instituted changes. He replaced agents with some of his former employees and with political appointees. Daugherty had already begun the latter in April 1921, when he made the owner of the *Washington Post*, Ned McLean, a special agent of the Bureau with compensation of $1.00 per day. McLean was not only a personal friend, but he later used the press to defend the Attorney General. Daugherty's alcoholic son, Draper, was also given a badge.[28] As it turned out, the most controversial appointment was Burns's former employee Gaston B. Means, a rotund extrovert, who had been indicted in 1917 for the first-degree murder of a rich widow. Embezzlement had been an alleged motive, as he had in fact forged her will. Because of insufficient evidence, however, the court had ruled the death accidental.[29] As a Bureau agent, Means was presently involved with Felder in several illicit operations, including the marketing of confiscated alcohol and the offering of protection to bootleggers at a price.[30] Even so, Burns permitted him to conduct important investigations. Daugherty first heard of Means following a complaint that he had used indecent and threatening language over the telephone to a New York attorney. Burns, who was to call a Brooklyn newspaper editor a "God d— liar" and a "damn big stiff," defended Means to Holland as "an excellent man and one of the best investigators in the Department." Nevertheless, subsequent complaints caused Daugherty to suspend him in February 1922.[31] But Means never left his office, nor was he removed from the payroll. Burns instead put him on special assignment. On a salary of $7 a day, he managed to retain house servants and a chauffeur-driven Cadillac, undoubtedly because of his thinly concealed influence-peddling, bootlegging, and other moonlighting operations. Later Daugherty permitted his "reinstatement" after Burns and Crim had convinced him that he was essential in the Bosch Magneto war-fraud case. In October 1923, Daugherty finally had Means indicted for over one-hundred violations of the Volstead Act.[32] Conviction was secured the following year, but by then the "spectacular rogue" had already embarrassed Daugherty and the Department.

In a way unequaled until the capers of the Richard M. Nixon administration, Burns also misused his power by harassing prominent Congressmen and public officials who questioned Daugherty's official policies or who found Burns's actions intolerable. Senators Caraway, La Follette, and Representative Roy O. Woodruff of Michigan were among those who had their offices ransacked.[33] Other public officials were trailed and put on a "suspect" list. In 1924, Secretary of Commerce Herbert Hoover complained to Daugherty of an agent following him. The Attorney General replied that a mistake had been made.[34]

On another occasion, Burns more understandably employed agents to suppress the publication of a book alleging that Harding was partly of Negro ancestry, an erroneous rumor hinted at ever since Harding's first political campaigns. With his genealogical circulars, Professor of Economics, Politics and Social Sciences William Estabrook Chancellor of Wooster College of Ohio had first attempted to besmirch Harding during the close of the 1920 campaign. Chancellor's activities concerned Daugherty and other Republican leaders, and angered Harding to the extent of wanting to thrash his accuser, but the material had no noticeable impact on the election.[35] Nevertheless, the racist Chancellor, whose activities had cost him his job, was now preparing a monograph expanding on his dubious genealogical findings. The planned publication of *The Illustrated Life of Warren G. Harding* was announced in February 1921. Daugherty consequently requested assistance from Attorney General Palmer, who ensured that Secret Service agents and a Post Office Inspector were sent to Chancellor's home, where he was forced to burn the manuscript.[36]

But Chancellor had another copy, which he boldly planned to publish in early 1922. Indeed, he and two compatriots hired a Dayton printer, and the newly-created Sentinal Press began to turn out copies of the libelous book, some of which even reached Washington. At that point, Daugherty ordered Burns to send his agents into Ohio to purchase or seize every copy they could get their hands on from book stores, libraries, and salesmen. They invaded the dingy Sentinal Press office in Dayton, where they confiscated the unsold copies and the plates. The latter were supposedly dumped into the Ohio River.[37] Chancellor, meanwhile, had quickly fled to Maine. Still unclear is how much Daugherty knew of the Bureau's myriad activities, but there is no question that when congressional investigations threatened his position, he was willing to use that power in retaliation.[38]

On the favorable side, Daugherty was instrumental in the appointment of Taft as Chief Justice of the United States Supreme Court. When the incumbent Edward White died in May 1921, Daugherty persistently suggested Taft to Harding, who thought he should consider other candidates before reaching a decision. Daugherty argued that the appointment must come immediately because of the congested courts, the inadequate number of judges, and a need for judicial reform. He said that he needed Taft to advise and guide him.[39] On July 30, 1921, the President made the appointment.

No one had a greater positive influence on the Attorney General than Taft. Because of his guiding hand, Daugherty was generally successful in recommending well-qualified judges to the federal courts. Even before Taft became Chief Justice, he wrote Daugherty: "If you don't mind it, my interests in the Federal Judiciary, where I know something of the situation, makes me anxious to give you the benefit of what I have learned from considerable experience."[40] Taft, in effect, had a veto over Daugherty's selections, for the latter continually acceded to him. Taft's disavowal of political exigencies influenced Daugherty so strongly that he advised Harding "that Senators and Representatives and political influences generally should be given to understand that they must not expect, as a matter of patronage, to dominate or dictate these appointments."[41] On one occasion, it was Harding who swayed Daugherty to uncharacteristically recommend a weak judicial candidate to satisfy a pleading senator. "He almost wept during our interview," Harding said of the senator, "and I am frank to say I am exceedingly reluctant to disappoint him."[42]

Daugherty also worked closely with Taft to expand the number of judges in the congested federal districts. After introducing himself as one "less experienced in the office than any of my predecessors," he informed the Senate Judiciary Committee of his expansion plans and proceeded to create a special committee of five federal judges and U.S. attorneys to iron out the specifics. Taft then took command by writing the tentative bill, cajoling indifferent legislators, and persuading Daugherty to help increase the number of new judges from eighteen to twenty-four.[43] By September 1922, the judicial expansion bill passed Congress. In the months prior to its passage, Taft felt that he and Daugherty were working for the same things. He sincerely advised his long-time associate: "My dear Harry, you want to refute your enemies, and you are going to do it, but one of the chief opportunities is through the selection of the highest standard of men for these . . . additional judges. I hope you will appoint some Democrats, in spite of the partisan bitterness of the attacks on you."[44] None of Daugherty's appointments, which included Democrats, was refused Senate confirmation.

Taft showed his gratitude by defending Daugherty in the months that followed. But because of the Attorney General's extensively criticized injunction against the striking railroad workers in September 1922, even the *Cincinnati Times-Star* became mildly critical. The *Star*'s criticism hurt Daugherty deeply: He told Taft that it was "the most hurtful and humiliating thing that could have happened to me."[45] The Chief Justice wrote owner Charles Taft that "there is nothing as aggravating to a man, when he is in the situation Harry has been in, as a slurring of him by those whom he expects to be his friends, and it was unfortunate that Hulbert or whoever wrote the article, should think it necessary to make concessions, at Harry's expense, in an article which he wished to be in Harry's favor." Meanwhile, Daugherty continued to express his hurt feelings to Taft, indicating that "I would give anything in the world if I could get over this insult but it does not seem possible for me to do so."[46]

Daugherty undoubtedly believed that the Tafts were obligated to him for his efforts in their behalf in 1912. Taft, indeed, had always felt indebted to Daugherty. One Taft, however, reminded the Chief Justice that the family had already repaid its obligation. In a revealing letter, nephew Hulbert reviewed the family's past association with Daugherty:

> My feelings toward Harry Daugherty are mixed. For ten years—since 1912—Uncle Charlie, the *Times-Star* and I have been his outspoken friends in Cincinnati. Because I mix around more and because people have not hesitated to attack one of our friends in my presence as they would when Uncle Charlie was around, I have felt the rub of it more than he has. We have a hundred editorials altogether in his favor. He asked our support for the Senate and we did everything we could in the face of the outspoken opposition of the organization and the sneering hostility of the intellectuals and the 'reform' crowd. And now the Attorney General, in the executive offices of the White House and before witnesses shouts out—'I deserve well of the Taft family. I have served them without thought of expense or of consequences. To this day I am pursued by the enemies in their cause.' It appears to me that this is ungracious and one-sided in failing to recognize that the Taft family, by your attitude in the Morse case and by our general support out here has not been neglectful of its obligations.[47]

Still, the elder Taft felt that Daugherty "has always been most friendly to us" and now "has consulted me a great deal about judicial appointments." For these reasons, he hoped that the family would be "scrupulous to avoid any reflection on him, or any comparison, to his disadvantage, with other Attorneys-General." After all, "Harry is an honest man and a courageous man," Taft asserted, "and he has had against him some of the greatest pretenders and frauds . . . that this country affords. When one, therefore, finds a friend slurring one with contemptuous reference, it cuts most deeply and makes one review his entire relations, and gives one the impression that the particular former friend is going with the yellowing pack."[48] Despite some realization of Daugherty's inadequecies, Taft rejected most of the criticism.

There was more behind Daugherty's difficulties than a few bad appointments and an incompetence for the office. His friends used the Justice Department as the vehicle for their own profit. The "ring leader" of the mythical "Ohio gang" was a Washington Court House dry goods merchant, Jesse (Jess) Smith, a long-time companion of Daugherty's. Mark Sullivan colorfully but accurately described him when he appeared in Washington in the spring of 1921:

> Smith was a large loose-framed, rather stout man in his late thirties or early forties, with pink, loose-hanging cheeks, a black mustache and large brown eyes. He was naive, crude, and friendly, quite unread except as to newspapers, and in them, only as to the political and sports news, perhaps also the 'funnies'—a country come-to-town.[49]

Smith was born and reared in Washington Court House. In high school he was known as a snappy dresser and was popular with his classmates, but he was also effeminate and timid, having a dislike of athletics and firearms. He also feared being alone. When excited, he had a habit of expectorating, which made him the butt of some cruel jokes. After graduating in 1890, he went to Bristol, Tennessee, where for seven years he studied the retail business under the tutelage of his uncle, F.G. Pitzer, one of the leading merchants of the South. Upon returning home, his mother (his father was deceased) purchased for him a half-interest in the T.R. Rapp department store. In 1903, Jess became the sole owner of what was then one of the leading emporiums in the county. That same year he was elected to the Board of Public Service, probably the only public office he ever sought.[50]

Smith became the town's Beau Brummell. No social event was complete without his swaggering presence. Women particularly enjoyed him because he eagerly chattered about the latest fashions and gossip. A local reporter later recalled that on the hot afternoons of summer, women frequently sought shelter in his store, where he entertained them with the latest rumors. Whenever a newly-married couple had their first baby, he led the others in counting fingers.[51]

He surprised the community by eventually falling in love. The girl, Roxie Stinson, was an attractive and stylish redhead who with her mother had only recently come to Washington Court House and had rented the second floor above Smith's emporium, where they established a conservatory of music. Because Smith persistently sought her daughter, Mrs. Stinson, believing Roxie too good for him, sent her to Europe to study music. Upon returning, she was even more beautiful, and far more independent. She and the thirty-six-year-old Smith were married in November 1908. The marriage lasted one and a half years before Roxie sued for divorce. The main problem was Smith's overly possessive mother, who constantly interfered. After the divorce, and after Smith moved his mother from the Cherry Hotel back into his house, he and Roxie resumed their friendship. Surprisingly, they became better friends than ever.

By then, World War I and the attendant farm prosperity enabled Smith's store to flourish. To show his gratitude and his patriotism, he delivered Liberty Bond speeches and sold savings bonds. He also became the head of the Elks in Ohio. After the armistice, he was a leading advocate of a memorial arch for the courthouse lawn and a homecoming day in honor of the returning soldiers. The celebration in May 1919 featured Smith, stiffly mounted on a horse leading the parade. Perspiring and red-faced, he barely managed to remain on the prancing mount as the band began to play.[52]

The Daugherty-Smith relationship is a curious but understandable one. It began when Daugherty first handled Smith's legal affairs in the late 1890s. Smith idolized the outwardly self-assured Daugherty, who was twelve years his senior. Having a layman's interest in politics and desiring to be around important people, he eagerly attached himself to Daugherty. Daugherty, troubled by family problems, likewise depended on Smith's companionship. When legal or political activity took him away from home, Smith usually made arrangements to accompany him. While Daugherty carried on his business, Smith spent time in hotel lobbies chatting with acquaintances or swaying in a rocker, smoking a cigar. At night Daugherty, an occasional insomniac, never liked to sleep unless the door to Smith's room remained opened.[53]

In the midst of political campaigns, Smith became more active. He made travel arrangements, acted as a secretary, and handled other Daugherty-assigned tasks. He was especially helpful in the senatorial primary campaign of 1916 and the 1920 presidential contest. Whenever such activity subsided, Harry and Mal Daugherty, Smith, and their guests relaxed at "The Shack," a $27,000 lodge they had built on Sweetbriar Ridge high above Deer Creek in neighboring Pickaway County. In the

Harding administration, it continued as a retreat for Daugherty, who invited countless high officials and celebrities.

Smith remained Daugherty's shadow after the Attorney General appointment. Opposition prevented Daugherty from securing him the post of Commissioner of Indian Affairs or Treasurer of the United States.[54] Consequently, Smith came to Washington as Daugherty's right-hand man. He handled the job seekers who sought Daugherty after Harding's inauguration. He continued to act as a valet and a close companion who accompanied him at social functions. The President was one of many who found the genial Smith a delightful acquaintance.

Daugherty and Smith initially resided in a little house on H Street, which they rented from the Ned McLeans. The latter sent a servant and cook, and Armour and Company donated its specialties. Conveniently located between the Justice Department and the White House, it provided private quarters on the second floor and an office and dining room downstairs where they conversed with visitors who came because of patronage or other governmental matters. Smith handled most of the minor problems and arranged for Daugherty to deal with the rest. Occasionally, Daugherty had dinner parties there. The Hardings, the McLeans, and top governmental officials like Will Hays were among the guests.[55]

In October 1921, they moved to a $7,600 a year sixth-floor suite at the Wardman Park Hotel. The rheumatically crippled Mrs. Daugherty now joined them from Columbus. Previously, she had undergone treatment at Johns Hopkins Hospital in Baltimore. Daugherty brought her to Washington primarily to insure that she received more extensive medical attention. Much of her time would be spent at Johns Hopkins. Whenever she returned, Smith helped care for her.

Smith also had a sixth-floor office near Daugherty's in the Department of Justice. Having no official capacity, he nevertheless had access to secretarial assistance and Justice files. Like McLean, he also carried a Bureau of Investigation badge and sometimes assisted Burns and consorted with Means.[56] His status created some confusion among the employees. Mrs. W.O. Duckstein, a confidential secretary, considered him "second in authority" to the Attorney General; on the other hand, Miss Mary Yeager, a stenographer, said he was little more than a public relations man. L.J. Bailey, of the Bureau of Investigation, thought him important because Daugherty referred him to Smith in matters on which the Attorney General was too busy to act.[57]

In reality, Smith acted as Daugherty's aide. He paid his personal bills and kept his house accounts. As he did at the H Street house, he conducted interviews for minor political appointments, performed liaison work, and assisted E.S. Rochester, the public relations officer for the

Department of Justice, and Burns. Some of his routine correspondence
with Fall, Forbes, and Rochester still exists. While he used Departmental
stationery, no title appeared beneath his signature. Smith also spent
considerable time taking stock-market reports over Daugherty's private
wire. He reportedly lost considerably more than he gained.[58]

His closeness to Daugherty made him a target for an assortment of
lobbyists and grafters, who desired accommodations with the government.
Finley Peter Dunne recalled Smith sitting behind his large desk, smoking
a dark cigar. He thought it curious that Thomas Felder should be sitting
opposite him with his feet on the desk and his hat on the back of his
head.[59] Lobbyists like Felder easily persuaded the unstable and insecure
Smith to misuse his influence. Perhaps recent stock losses also affected
him. In any case, Smith had little trouble obtaining from the Treasury
Department's corrupt Prohibition Bureau permits to withdraw liquor out
of bonded government warehouses. To those who sought such favors in
Ohio, Smith relied on the cooperation of J.E. Russell, the lax state
Prohibition director, and William Halley, Daugherty's Ohio party boss.[60]
He was even more successful in using his influence in the Justice Department. Assuming that he acted in Daugherty's behalf, unsuspecting employees released confidential information to him on the progress of cases
and pardon recommendations, and he occasionally secured immunities
from prosecution. He also received $224,000 for his part in the American
Metal case, which was in the custody of the Alien Property Custodian's
office.[61]

Smith often promised more than he could deliver. George L. Remus, a
Cincinnati bootlegger, supposedly paid him more than $250,000 for im-
munity from prosecution. But Smith failed, and the angry Remus underwent confinement at the Atlanta Penitentiary.[62] Smith tried in vain for a
commutation of the sentence. By late 1922, he had made so many similar
mistakes that he lived in fear of retaliation from disappointed favor
seekers.

But Smith had not acted alone. The headquarters of corruption centered at 1625 K Street, where Howard Mannington and his cronies
resided. Aside from Smith, Mannington was by far the closest person to
Daugherty. Their friendship had begun in the early 1890s. After managing
Harding's front-porch campaign, Mannington eventually departed for
Washington, D.C., at Daugherty's request to help review applications for
minor appointments. He found his work extremely profitable. By July
1921, Malcolm Jennings reported to Harding that he had heard that
"Mannington has some sort of a government brokerage office . . . and that
people desiring government favors have to apply through him. Of course
this is silly," Jennings qualified, "but I have heard it very frequently."[63]
Apparently Harding did nothing, for Mannington continued his activi-

ties. He, M.P. Kraffmiller from Illinois, whom Mannington had met at the 1920 Republican convention, and Fred A. Caskey from Marietta, Ohio, also worked with Smith in obtaining liquor withdrawal permits from the Prohibition Bureau. Indeed, Smith was a frequent visitor to the house, where he consulted with Mannington about various illegal activities, most of which were in New York. In 1924, Kraffmiller admitted that Mannington obtained two manufacturing and one wholesale liquor permits for J.B. Scheuer and Co. in exchange for a $25,000 fee. Kraffmiller also related that he, Mannington, and Caskey divided $20,000 after delivering wholesale permits to the General Drug Co. of Chicago.[64] Mannington later fled to Paris when it appeared that he was to be indicted in New York.

Other Ohioans came to Washington representing clients who sought favorable governmental action. Daugherty's former law partner, John E. Todd, found himself so much in demand that he opened a law office there. Another attorney, Wade Ellis, once Ohio attorney general and a Taft political leader, pushed so hard in one client's behalf that Alien Property Custodian Thomas Miller complained to Harding.[65]

Nevertheless, the "Ohio gang" label, used so often in the mid-1920s to characterize the grafters, is an oversimplification. No gang-like organization existed. Furthermore, many who undermined the administration were not from Ohio. Felder was a Georgian operating out of New York. Bill Orr came from New York and Fred Urion from Chicago.

In addition to their other illegal activities, Orr and Urion disregarded the 1910 Rodenberry Act, which prohibited the interstate transportation of prize-fight films. The bill's origin was admittedly racist, for it had been enacted after white pugilist Jim Jefferies had lost a championship fight to Negro Jack Johnson. The Wilson administration, nonetheless, had clamped down on profiteers in enforcing the measure. The situation changed in the succeeding administration when Orr, Urion, and others collaborated with Smith to assure F.C. Quimby, who shared the rights to the Jack Dempsey-Georges Carpentier fight of July 1921, that a safe and profitable venture was at hand. For almost half of the profits, the New York film entrepreneur permitted Smith and his friends to market his films in more than twenty states with nothing to fear but a small fine.[66] Soon the Jack Dempsey-Jess Willard 1920 fight films went into circulation despite complaints. Daugherty made no conscientious attempt to enforce the law until March 1924, even though he must have realized that Urion, Orr, and the rest were capitalizing on his friendship.[67]

What stands out so clearly about the Justice-related corruption is that those involved were friendly to Daugherty or his intimate friends. Undoubtedly, Daugherty was aware of some of the activities of Smith, Mannington, and other close acquaintances. He not only lived with Smith, but Mannington was a frequent visitor at the H Street residence.[68] He also entertained Felder during the latter's many lobbying trips to Washington. Even if one accepts the argument that he knew nothing of Felder's illicit activities, their continued association indicated Daugherty's inability or unwillingness to break with the past. As late as 1922, he considered Felder "a distinguished and prominent" lawyer.[69] Neither is there any evidence that he ever censored the misdeeds of his friends. On the contrary, he seemed to ignore their activities and, in effect, use his office to protect them. Bernard Baruch later described an incident from this period that casts further suspicion on Daugherty's sense of public service. Somewhat in his cups, Daugherty approached him at a party at Ned McLeans' country home and mockingly referred to Baruch's wartime service in Washington by saying, "Baruch, you're an honest so-and-so."[70]

Subsequent investigations circumstantially but rather convincingly revealed that Daugherty himself profited financially from the American Metal case (see Chapter XIII). But the evidence elsewhere is either flimsy, inconclusive, or, in some instances, in Daugherty's favor. The same is true regarding the allegation that he succumbed to pressures from friends who sought privileged information. For example, on May 5, 1922, Mannington wrote Daugherty that he wished to speak with him about a pending suit involving several tobacco companies. Daugherty in turn wrote Assistant Attorney General Lovett that since he knew nothing of these cases, he desired a memorandum. He also indicated that "this is the only matter in the Department of Justice" that Mannington, a "life-long acquaintance," had ever brought to his attention.[71] Lovett requested United States District Attorney Colonel William Hayward, who was in charge of the litigation, to write him on the disposition of the cases. After receiving Hayward's informative letter of July 6, Daugherty replied: "I note your reference to my personal interest in the matter. I have no more personal interest in this case than I have in any other case before the Department and only asked for information at the instance of parties having a legitimate interest."[72] Although he provided Mannington with information, Daugherty had acted cautiously. There is no evidence that he behaved illegally or unethically. Curiously, he responded rather sensitively to Hayward's personal reference, indicating perhaps how concerned he was about possible public criticism.

Few other such requests exist in the Departmental files. It could be that records were culled or that little was put on paper. Equally likely, and as the evidence seems to reveal, such inquiries generally went to Jess Smith, who dealt with the pertinent division in the Department, or they went directly to the division involved where Smith or others attempted to influence favorable action. In some cases, Smith was unsuccessful because of the recalcitrance of Justice employees; in others, he had only to claim that the Attorney General wanted something done.[73] How much of a role Daugherty played, if any, may never be known because Smith destroyed his papers, and key participants of that era died without testifying.

Daugherty's unhappiness as Attorney General, however, seems evident. The social activity, which he enjoyed, and the status of the office failed to compensate for the enormous problems that remained unsolved. Additionally, by early 1922, not only did public criticism mount, but private disapproval also existed. In February 1922, Henry Stimson angrily wrote Daugherty for having advanced an agreed upon trial date without having informed him. "I am less accustomed to the rapier than to the club," Stimson commented.[74] In the Congress, committee members of his own party privately took him to task for appearing without having done his homework.[75]

Such criticism only increased Daugherty's insecurity, which his outgoing personality concealed. From Wolfe or Herrick, for example, he had learned to expect rebuke. But from those whose respect really mattered, the slightest rejection or criticism bothered him immensely. Unable to face reality, he blamed it on his role in the party war of 1912. In an extraordinary letter to Charles Hilles, Daugherty revealed the main sources of his insecurity: a strong need to be accepted, anxieties over status that caused him to look askance at the eastern establishment, and a growing awareness that the attorney generalship brought neither vindication nor peer respectability. To Hilles, he brooded about the supposed coolness of New Yorkers like former Attorney General Wickersham and Senators James Wadsworth, Jr., and William M. Calder. Perhaps they have "an estimate of me that is prevalent among certain people in New York who have hired me to do things in the last twenty-five years which they were not able to do themselves." But, he continued, they "would know a great deal more . . . if they only knew that people west of New Jersey could get along without them." Of Wadsworth, Daugherty acknowledged,

> I like [him] very much but he has a wrong measure of the Attorney General, taken from the New York *World* or conversations with people like the Roosevelts. It would be better for him to accept the estimate shown by the facts and records and accomplishments of the Department of Justice rather than the vaporings of people who insist upon considering a man's character and accomplishments from the viewpoint of the battle of 1912.

Daugherty wanted Wadsworth to understand him, although remarking sarcastically that he had

> seen men quite as big as Jim Wadsworth, but of course at a very great distance. I have been fair and generous . . . but I have never heard Jim Wadsworth or Calder stand up in the Senate and say that they knew the

Attorney General to be a man of forty years experience as a lawyer, a man of good character and a great deal of energy, though they pestered me to death and were always willing to give me plenty of advice. I will get along without them and they are privileged to continue to get their inspiration from the New York *World*, the *Tribune* and a few people who are still nervous over the fight of 1912 and insisting that that is the thing they must keep alive. As far as I am concerned they can all go to hell.[76]

Hilles was surprised. "Wadsworth," he wrote, "likes you as well as he does me" or "any member of the Cabinet." But Wadsworth was not demonstrative, Hilles explained.

I have never heard him give any defense or praise of anyone in public. I do not believe that he has . . . even commended the President in the Senate. In fact, as I drove away from your apartment the other night with the President, the President remarked to me that he did not know how Wadsworth felt about him, but that he had tremendous admiration for Wadsworth.[77]

Criticism aside, Daugherty's burdens were increased by his wife's worsening condition, the sickliness of his daughter, and the instability of his alcoholic son. His own health deteriorated under the strain of the pressures and the work load. As a result, rumors persisted in 1921 that Daugherty would resign.[78] Instead, with his constant companion Jess Smith, he often sought solace at the Ned McLeans, who were a "wonderful comfort" and whose estate was "a place of protection." On one occasion they lunched there even though the McLeans were not at home. "We didn't have time to darn any socks or re-arrange the furniture," Daugherty explained, "but we sat down in the library after luncheon and enjoyed ourselves as a couple of kings would if they were entitled to it."[79]

Another diversion was Ohio politics. It remained an arena to satisfy his combative nature and something he felt he understood. By supervising the distribution of federal patronage, he attempted to strengthen his domination of the party organization. Nonetheless, opposition against him and his lieutenant, William Halley, existed. Only days after the inauguration, Daugherty involved himself in a patronage fight with Walter Brown over the internal revenue collectorship at Toledo. He and Senator Willis opposed Brown's candidate despite the President's wish that Brown name the appointment. It was not until June that Harding recommended Brown's choice. Harding then had to confront Willis's objection to a Senate confirmation. In October the former won out, but only after the intraparty bickering had embarrassed the administration.[80]

Through Halley, the Attorney General also attempted to crush Hynicka as a political force.[81] Such exclusive policies contributed to the weakened state of the Ohio Republican party, which lost the governorship in 1922. One loyal Harding supporter, Mary Lee, complained bitterly in 1922 that

despite "the hurrah and shouting about Daugherty's fine political sagac-
ity [,] . . . he has lost everytime he has been a candidate; . . . he came
blamed near losing Ohio [for] Harding and . . . he has lost control of the
State Central Committee." She concluded that it was Daugherty's "satellites that brought trouble from Washington to Columbus and his satellites
that gave us the disgrace of 'we boys' and he himself is not entirely free
from the suspicion down here." In another letter she reminded Harding
that a number of Republicans "don't like Daugherty."[82] Jennings also
informed the President that there was a feeling of opposition to any party
dominance on Daugherty's part.[83]

While he deprecated the intraparty bickering, Harding discreetly refused to criticize his Attorney General. He, in fact, retorted to Jennings
that nobody could have been more considerate than Daugherty in the
distribution of patronage in Ohio. He said this with the full realization
that Daugherty had intended to divert patronage from the Brown-
Hynicka group.[84] Harding assured a doubting Walter Brown that "the
Attorney General has a very exalted conception of his official obligation."
He promised Brown that Daugherty, at least, would not interfere with
Brown's senatorial candidacy in 1922. Yet, to his last days in Washington,
Daugherty continued a personal vendetta against Brown, Hynicka, and
Wolfe.[85]

In the first year of the administration, Daugherty and Harding remained good friends. Perhaps the dissatisfaction they felt about the
confining nature of their jobs even drew them closer. Both loved poker,
and this, in itself, brought the two together socially for one or two
evenings per week. While the President found that he could relax better
with cronies like Daugherty than with Hughes or Hoover, the Attorney
General wielded no great influence on Harding. On one of the major
issues involving the Justice Department in 1921, Harding found himself in
disagreement with Daugherty. It was Daugherty who had to recast his
beliefs.

The question involved the imprisoned radicals who had opposed and
allegedly obstructed America's participation in the war. Many had been
prosecuted under the provisions of the Espionage and Sedition Acts
despite their often harmless offenses. The Wilson administration had
consistently refused to free the 197 political prisoners, including the
Socialist Eugene Debs and a large number of IWW revolutionaries. By
1921, liberal and reform groups clamored for their release. Opposing a
general amnesty, Harding instructed Daugherty to review their records on
an individual basis. For political as well as humanitarian reasons, he
especially wanted to release Debs. Daugherty consequently asked that
Debs be transported from the Atlanta Penitentiary to his office for a
personal interview. He desired to show Debs and his followers "that our

system of govenment was fair enough and generous enough to permit any man to present his cause to the executive branch of the Government." Daugherty found that Debs not only had an excellent personal record, but was a man of much personal charm. "In the world he has undertaken," Daugherty warned, "these qualities make him a very dangerous man."[86]

After the interview, Jess Smith drove Debs to the train station where he would depart for Atlanta. During the drive Smith asked if there was anything he needed. Debs replied that he had never been able to obtain quill toothpicks since he left Atlanta. Smith asked the chauffeur to stop the car when he saw a store. Debs returned with a huge bundle of toothpicks.

Daugherty opposed Debs's release. He argued that clemency would place a premium on "disloyalty, lawlessness, and defiance of the authority of the government." That the war had ended, that his crime had been political, and that mercy should be extended did not alter the situation. Debs's offenses, according to Daugherty, "are crimes of far greater menaces to society and to the government at large than ordinary crimes, for they go to the life and strength of the nation."[87] He did, however, reluctantly accept Harding's decision to release Debs. In his December 23 brief to Harding, he alluded to Debs's advanced age, his poor health, and his martyred image in recommending that Harding commute his sentence on December 31, 1921. Even then, Daugherty advised Harding not to require Debs to take a loyalty oath. He asserted that "he is such an habitual violator of the laws of this country and has such a chronic disregard for his country and is so ignorant of his obligation to society that he might go upon his honor, if he has any."[88] Harding elected to give Debs his freedom on December 25, despite Daugherty's contention that such an act would only desecrate Christmas.[89]

On January 6, Harding wrote Jennings that Daugherty was not the only one advising against clemency. "The esteemed lady whom you delight to address as 'Duchess' was very much opposed to any clemency being shown to Debs," Harding claimed. In spite of his wife's beliefs, he was convinced that he had done the right thing. Harding went on to say that a half dozen members of the House and the Senate were as deserving of the penitentiary.[90]

The Attorney General was more strongly opposed to releasing the 150 to 160 IWWs. After examining their records for a four-day period, Daugherty preached that "we soon forget." He further affirmed that "the crimes of these men were more horrible than outright murder, and in many instances murder was part of their crimes." And their oath was the most "revolutionary, uncivil and wicked that could be taken with any sacredness."[91] Nevertheless, Harding requested releases periodically, although he was opposed to a general amnesty. Daugherty reluctantly agreed to commute the sentences of several aliens in the summer of 1921 on the stipulation that they return to Russia.[92] Harding ordered additional commutations in the next two years. By the time of his death, only twenty-one still remained confined.

The President found that he could not always rely upon Daugherty regarding more conventional pardons. In late August 1921, the Attorney General requested that Harding sign the pardon petition of Lee Gibson of Arkansas. Afterward Harding found that he had been misled. He had pardoned a man who had not served one day of his sentence. Harding thereupon wrote angrily that he wished Daugherty "would admonish those who make up reports on which the Executive must base his clemency that hereafter I must have full information in every case. I have been subjected to unfair criticism," he continued, "because I was not fully informed in this particular instance."[93] Daugherty declared that the trial judge and the prosecuting attorney had also recommended the pardon. He conceded, however, that it would have been better if the pardon attorney had wired for information on whether Gibson had been imprisoned.[94] There were other instances of such pardons. Although the evidence was thin, accusations persisted that by employing Jap Muma, a New York newspaper representative of McLean, or John E. Todd, Daugherty's former law partner, a few wealthy convicts were either pardoned or paroled. Muma was never indicted for his other illegal activities, thereby encouraging the belief that friends of the Attorney General enjoyed special license.[95]

Harding learned to be more cautious of Daugherty's official recommendations. On October 18, 1921, the Attorney General advised that an executive proclamation was not necessary to terminate the state of war with the Central Powers, since Congress had already enacted two joint resolutions providing for cessation. But Hughes had earlier felt that such a proclamation was legally essential. Harding also remained unconvinced as to Daugherty's correctness, even though a peace treaty had been signed with Germany in August 1921. To provide "full understanding all around," the President decided to seek the advice of the State Department, which recommended executive action.[96]

Neither did Daugherty receive a free hand in patronage recommendations. After Daugherty had suggested a candidate for the postmastership of Columbus, Harding quickly asked Jennings to "write me in confidence whether this is the appointment to make." His friend replied that this man was a "rough neck" who had been accused of shady dealings.[97] In the process of investigating another Daugherty selection, Harding surprisingly learned that the candidate desired the position in order to get even with Hynicka and the Hamilton County organization. He promptly told Daugherty that public office ought not to be used for that purpose.

Equally shocking to Harding was hearing that Daugherty appointed railway officials as U.S. marshals in the face of a threatening railroad strike. He again told Daugherty to alter "this colossal error."[98] No wonder, Daugherty exaggerated to his friend Finley Peter Dunne in April 1922, that Harding

> never took any advice from me about anything; he never listens to me, never pays any attention to me, doubts my loyalty to him, he doesn't see how I am serving him or the government and on the whole considers me of very little good. I guess he is right. Nobody at the White House cares for me but Mrs. Harding, and she takes a delight in rubbing me the wrong way 'good-naturedly' every time I see her. I can't quarrel with a woman so I take it out on the dog.[99]

Harding's feelings did not prevent Daugherty from imposing on him in this period. Daugherty had committed himself to speak before the National Electric Light Association's annual meeting on May 18, 1922. Since the NELA had been a former client, he did not wish to disappoint the organization. But one day prior to his scheduled speech he decided that he had too much work and asked Harding to send him a note, requesting that he remain in Washington the following day to work on a very important matter. "I don't want you to lie for me as I would be delighted to lie for you," Daugherty stated, "but you can do this in a second and I will forgive you what you owe me on account of the bet you made Saturday morning."[100]

Harding defended Daugherty publicly no matter how he felt privately about his performance. By spring 1922, criticism against the Attorney General swelled to serious proportions. In April, Congressmen Ray O. Woodruff of Michigan and Royal C. Johnson of South Dakota began to accuse Daugherty of failure to prosecute the war-fraud cases and demanded an investigation of the Department of Justice.[101] In May, Senator Caraway obtained additional evidence on Daugherty's involvement in the Morse case. He not only denounced the Attorney General in the Senate, but he also asked that he resign. Other attacks were directed against his official policies. Yet Harding stood up strongly for his Attorney General. He advised one inquisitive constituent that he "felt quite sure about the high purpose and the thoroughly justified course" that the Attorney General was taking. "Mr. Daugherty," he related to James T. Williams, Jr., of the *Boston Evening Transcript*, "is really giving us a fine administration of a very difficult and important office." Harding concluded that he "should be the last man to shield or defend anyone whom I believed guilty of a betrayal of a public trust."[102] Of course, there was little else the President could say to allay attacks which indirectly discredited him and which, he probably believed, were politically motivated. A sense of gratitude and attachment also dictated his course. Ironically, even though he relied on Daugherty less in his last year, he became more sympathetic toward him as the criticism grew worse.

Daugherty and Harding: The Final Year

CRITICISM of Daugherty was heightened by his actions in the railroad strike of 1922. To liberals, labor union members, and the majority of the press, Daugherty came out as a strong-arm reactionary who violated civil liberties and sought the destruction of effective unionism. His sweeping injunction against the railworkers aroused the anger even of cabinet members. The reaction put Daugherty on the defensive for the remainder of the Harding administration. All of this contributed to the troubles of Harding's nightmarish final year.

The railroad strike began on July 1, 1922, when 400,000 members of the A. F. of L. shopmen's unions, under the leadership of Bert M. Jewell, walked out. This followed a major coal strike, which had begun that spring and still remained unsettled. One of the reasons for the two walkouts was wage reductions. In the shop'men's case, the National Railroad Labor Board's order decreeing a 13% wage cut to aid the staggering railroads was only an immediate issue. The shopmen found the Railroad Labor Board, created by the Esch-Cummins Act of 1920, a poor substitute for the Railroad Administration of the Wilsonian period, which had enforced collective bargaining and had provided for national arbitration. In contrast, the nine-member Railroad Labor Board, representing the government, the carriers, and the unions, proved ineffective in handling the shopmen's problems. Workers now faced the threat of the company union, which General W. W. Atterbury had already put into effect on the Pennsylvania. A growing movement for the open shop permeated the other roads.[1] The carriers also hindered collective bargaining by refusing to agree upon national adjustment boards that were to be implemented in accordance with the Esch-Cummins Act. The unions were especially dissatisfied with Railroad Labor Board chairman Ben Hooper, whom they thought promanagement. On the eve of the walkout, he issued a proclamation outlawing the actions of the strikers and their organizations. Three days afterward, Hooper announced that men taking the strikers' jobs would be performing an "indispensable service" and therefore "entitled to the protection of the government."[2]

After failing to mediate a settlement in the coal strike, Harding, in late July, turned to the railroad crisis. He suggested mediation based on the workers' going back to their jobs in return for the retention of their seniority rights. The railroad executives refused to approve the latter, even though the strikers had agreed to the wage reductions. On the other hand, Harding's proposition of August 7 was unsuitable to labor because it called for the Railroad Labor Board adjudicating the issue of seniority rights, a question that it had already decided upon. As in the coal strike, Harding's objective posture brought no results.[3] Relying on the moderate advice of Secretaries Hoover and Davis, which had reinforced his own inclination to compromise and "harmonize," he had shunned the advocates of arbitrary governmental action. In the next few weeks, however, Harding frustratedly moved in that direction after Congress had failed to provide a solution, public opinion had grown more vocal against the strikers, and scattered incidents of labor violence and vandalism had occurred.[4]

By mid-August, labor violence was not uncommon as shootings, rock-throwing, and acts of sabotage took place. Crews abandoned several passenger trains, including both passengers and cargoes, in the Arizona desert, at Needles (California), Ogden (Utah), and elsewhere. At Needles some stranded passengers collapsed in the 113 degree heat. As one union president told union attorney Donald Richberg: "A strike ain't no pink tea." Nevertheless, the press exaggerated the number of such incidents, as did Daugherty. Often, his reports to Harding involved attempts to dynamite shops, trains, or bridges rather than actual acts of destruction. When Daugherty learned that the Interstate Commerce Commission had reported that one-half of the locomotives inspected were defective, he, without evidence, concluded that "something aside from wear and tear had happened to the locomotives."[5] More significantly, on August 15 he accused the IWW of attempting to take over the railroads and the local governments in the West. One week later he blamed the IWW for "fanning the flames" of the railroad strike at Shawnee, Oklahoma. There is no mistaking his efforts to link the strike to a red conspiracy, an approach that no other cabinet member adopted. Daugherty would later blame the "red borers" inside the shopmen's unions for the strike itself.[6]

As a former corporation lawyer, Daugherty was never sympathetic to organized labor. Certainly, his appointment of Burns as Bureau Director reflected that viewpoint. But he was on record since 1921 as not opposing the right to strike and as favoring an impartial governmental inquiry to resolve labor disputes without obligating labor or management to accept its findings. During the outset of the coal strike he even conceded that "the operators made a mistake when they did not at least meet with the miners."[7] In June, however, when a railroad strike threatened, he considered issuing a temporary restraining order against the railroad and mine workers on the grounds that a conspiracy to interfere with interstate commerce existed. By preventing the production of coal for transportation, he argued, the coal miners alone were obstructing transportation, consequently violating the law, which made an injunction and criminal proceedings possible.[8] Even though Harding opposed an injunction at this time, Daugherty gradually became more outspoken in his hard-line approach.

Why Daugherty now took this position is not entirely clear. Apart from his antilabor attitude, it could be that, as a practical politician, he responded to an antilabor public that wanted an end to the strike. He might have reacted to the frequent accusations that he failed to act against war grafters and certain antitrust violators. By responding quickly and courageously in a national emergency, he could deflate criticism in other areas. Moreover, later reports of violence no doubt encouraged him to act, and convinced him that revolutionaries were behind the outbreaks. That the public itself feared radicalism unquestionably caused him to emphasize it more. The concern, nevertheless, was real. Burns and Hoover of the Bureau of Investigation, who both exaggerated the conspiratorial activities of the Communist International in the United States, had warned him of the danger.[9] As often happened, Daugherty overreacted.

Exactly when Harding accepted Daugherty's advice is not known. It was probably on a three-day Potomac cruise aboard the *Mayflower* beginning on August 26. Hoover, Fall, Lasker, and several from Capitol Hill also went, but Harding and Daugherty had opportunities to be alone. In any case, by August 28 a restraining order was prepared, with Daugherty still undecided on the district in which to file it.[10] The next day he settled on the Northern Illinois District Court at Chicago where Judge James H. Wilkerson, appointed by Daugherty two weeks earlier, would hear the case.

On Friday afternoon, September 1, a day before the coal strike was settled without direct governmental involvement, Daugherty personally presented the bill to Wilkerson, who granted a temporary restraining order against the strikers. No discussion had taken place in the cabinet, where earlier suggestions of such a policy had been opposed. Daugherty kept Harding informed on the progress of the hearings in Chicago, but even the President did not know the exact nature of the order.[11] Harding's total dependence on his Attorney General in this period was ill-advised, given what he knew about his earlier performances. But Harding was frustrated, almost desperate, over his failure to end the strikes. Moreover, Daugherty persuaded him that a restraining order would work. He allayed Harding's doubts by arguing that Departmental lawyers had approved the order. He justified its necessity in the same manner that President Grover Cleveland's advisers had defended it in the 1894 Pullman strike. Daugherty eventually presented Harding with a copy of the 1895 Debs case, in which the Supreme Court had sanctioned an injunction to insure the freedom of interstate commerce and the transportation of the mails. "The chief difference," Daugherty explained, "lies in the fact that the unions are much better organized, new plans for interference have been adopted, [and] the acts of strikers are more widespread and more modern." He consequently sought a stronger court order.[12]

Indeed, what resulted was the most comprehensive injunction ever imposed on American labor. It forbade almost all action that contributed to the furtherance of the strike. Workers could no longer tamper with the operations of the railroads, nor could they or union officials interfere with those still employed. The temporary restraining order also enjoined peaceful picketing, newspaper interviews, meetings, addresses, and other forms of communications. It restrained the use of labor-employment funds, and even declared the strike an unlawful act because the strikers refused to comply with the decision of the Railroad Labor Board, although the law did not compel them to do so.[13] The shop crafts had followed the law by having brought their case before the board.

But Daugherty saw a national emergency that threatened the very fabric of government. He alluded to thousands of violent acts allegedly Communist inspired. By interfering with the mails and disrupting transportation, the strikers, he felt, had further relinquished their rights. Not taking any chances, he approved the shadowing of such "suspects" as attorney Clarence Darrow and Bert Jewell.[14]

Although the restraining order was clearly Daugherty's idea, the evidence is less clear on how much of it he had drafted himself. Among those who advised him was George Rothwell Brown, political and labor writer and friend of Ned McLean, who was "loaned" to him during the strike crisis. Brown, supposedly an expert on past strikes, spent much time with Daugherty in this period. Daugherty claimed that he "is the best and most reliable man I know."[15] Former Ohioan Blackburn Esterline, the Assistant to the Solicitor General, also assisted him and handled much of the court work. Assistant to the Attorney General Goff played an important advisory role. After favorably briefing Daugherty's subsequent restraining order, which differed little from the first, he added a scrawled postscript: "I have read and studied this order with great care, and [see] nothing offensive in it." Solicitor General James Beck also wrote: "I never was so proud to be a member of the Department of Justice as today when it is doing such great work . . . for the maintenance of our form of government."[16] If there were any objections to the injunction within the Department, they have never been recorded.

By the time of the initial court order, however, reports indicated that strikers were returning to work. Daniel Willard of the B & O had already opened his doors to negotiate a settlement that would consider the workers' seniority rights. Jewell had agreed to begin discussions.[17] The weakened unions had run out of funds and had been badgered enough by the state injunctions and the militias.

That the federal restraining order came when the strike was on its last legs was damning in itself. It needlessly punished the strikers and restricted their efforts to obtain an honorable settlement. As a result, many shopmen had to accept the loss of their seniority rights in order to return to their jobs. Almost 35% did not go back because of unsatisfactory agreements. A fair number of the carriers took advantage of the situation to institute the open shop and the company union.[18] Daugherty indicated that this was one of his objectives. In presenting his argument before the court, he stated that he would use his power to prevent "the unions of the country from destroying the open shop."[19] He arbitrarily attempted to settle a question that, at the least, should have been decided in a fair struggle between capital and labor.

Daugherty's actions shocked many senators and representatives from his own party, particularly progressives like Borah.[20] Even though conservative newspapers, such as the *Boston Transcript,* the *New York Herald Tribune,* and the *Philadelphia Inquirer,* favored the injunction, the press was generally also astonished. The *New York Times,* previously opposed to the strikers, now severely criticized Daugherty for issuing a restraining order "apparently not warranted by federal law," while the New York *World* considered Daugherty's conduct plausible ground for impeachment. The *New York Evening ·Post* and the *Newark News,* meanwhile, labeled his action a "blow below the belt" and a "gag law," respectively. The liberal *New Republic* asserted that the injunction "abandons all pretense of government impartiality." It too asked Daugherty to resign.[21]

Cabinet members were also startled by Daugherty's restraining order. Herbert Hoover later recalled his reaction:

> The morning papers brought me the news. I was outraged by its obvious transgression of the most rudimentary rights of men. Walking over to the Cabinet meeting that morning, I met Secretary Hughes. He said that it was outrageous in law as well as morals. I suggested that he raise the question in Cabinet. He replied that it scarcely came within his functions as Secretary of State to challenge the actions of the Attorney General, and suggested that as Secretary of Commerce interested in the economic consequences, I had the right to do so.

Hoover said that he and Hughes protested to Harding, who demanded from Daugherty an explanation of the illegal passages. Daugherty, according to Hoover, "could only mumble that the objectionable passages were approved" by Departmental lawyers. Harding then abruptly instructed him to withdraw the disputed sections of his restraining order.[22] Daugherty later admitted that his action was criticized by cabinet members, but denied that censure came from Hoover or Hughes. He claimed that neither Hoover nor Hughes raised a voice when Interior Secretary Fall and Assistant Secretary of the Navy Theodore Roosevelt, Jr., (sitting in for Denby) strongly objected to the injunction. "The President stopped it all," Daugherty said, "by saying that it was my responsibility, that he had been consulted and he approved what was done and he didn't want to hear any more discussion about it in the cabinet or on the outside."[23]

No matter how much he might have objected initially to specific features of the court order, in the ensuing weeks Harding consistently supported Daugherty's action. He found solace in the position that action was necessary and that the maintenance of national transportation was more important than any other issue involved.[24] In a time of personal tragedy in which his wife was near death because of the recurrence of an old kidney ailment, Harding also felt closer to Daugherty, who often expressed his concern and sorrow. On one particularly critical evening, he sat with Harding until dawn.

On September 11, Daugherty extended the restraining order for ten days, this at a time when the strike was over in all but a few areas. A week and a half later he secured another extended injunction from Wilkerson that differed little from the original order. A few of the disputed clauses were removed, but the injunction was nearly as firm and as comprehensive. The shop crafts did not passively accept this action.[25] To them, the crucial issue involved was labor's right to strike. Their attorneys, led by Donald Richberg, challenged the injunction in the courts, and the legal battle continued into the summer of the following year. Daugherty and his legal counsel did not give an inch. They sought a permanent injunction that would conform as nearly as possible to the exact phraseology of the preliminary injunction order. As Daugherty confided, "if it could be said that the final order was not as drastic as the temporary order, it might be interpreted as a reversal of the court's judgment [and a defeat for the government]. I hope the court will recognize the importance of this phase of the matter. We are entitled to the full fruits of victory."[26] On September 23, 1923, Wilkerson sustained the final decree in its entirety. Although a Supreme Court decision in another case upheld the railway unions' right to strike, the fact is that railway labor lost much and gained little. For this they never forgave Daugherty, who in later years not only saw more red in the shop crafts' strike, but had also convinced himself that the injunction was the outstanding event of his career.[27]

Attorney General Daugherty was rarely on labor's side. In late December 1922, however, he revealed that the Builders' Exchange of San Francisco violated the conspiracy clause of the Clayton Antitrust Act in enforcing an open-shop labor policy. After the federal government had won its case, the San Francisco Labor Council forwarded a copy of the resolutions in praise of the Department of Justice and other individuals who contributed to the victory. It did not mention Daugherty. He angrily wrote: "why omit my name in resolutions whereas I heard, directed and ordered it all."[28]

By now Daugherty faced an even greater crisis than the railway strike. The House Committee on the Judiciary was considering specifications calling for his impeachment. The impeachment drive, which had begun shortly after the September 1st restraining order, was organized labor's first and main response to the injunction. Favored by Samuel Gompers of the AFL, labor had the legal assistance of several prominent prolabor lawyers, including New Yorker Samuel Untermyer who also opposed Daugherty for his refusal to act on war-fraud cases and antitrust violators in the building trades which the New York Lockwood Committee exposed.[29] Also assisting was Congressman Oscar E. Keller, a single taxer and an independent Republican from Minnesota, and Senator Caraway of Arkansas.

On September 10, Keller formally introduced an impeachment resolution in Congress, requesting that it be referred to the House Committee on the Judiciary. It was not until December that Keller submitted specifications to the committee to substantiate the resolution. Among his fourteen charges, he stated that Daugherty had appointed the unscrupulous Burns as Director of the Bureau of Investigation; neglected to enforce the railway appliance law; accorded special favors to individuals and corporations affiliated with J. P. Morgan; refused to prosecute the warfraud cases; failed to enforce the Antitrust and Federal Trade Commission Acts; allowed Thomas Felder to pervert Justice Department operations; and instituted the injunction against the striking shopmen. Keller offered testimony on only two charges. The evidence he offered on the alleged failure of the Attorney General to enforce the railway safety appliance law was so flimsy that his own attorney admitted that it did not sustain the charges.[30] His material on Burns was not incriminating enough and certainly not grounds for impeachment. The nervous and unstable Keller was so unsuccessful in presenting these two specifications that he refused to proceed. Since he previously claimed that he had evidence to support his other charges, the committee secured a subpoena requiring Keller to testify. He failed to obey the order. The Committee on the Judiciary then ended the hearing by disapproving all fourteen specifications. The House of Representatives approved the report by a 204 to 77 vote. Neither organized labor nor Keller had distinguished themselves.

Daugherty was not inactive during the inquiry. Even though he had once considered resigning, recent charges made him put such inclinations aside and instead triggered a fighting instinct that had few equals in public life. On October 21, he defended his injunction in a speech at a Republican rally in Canton, Ohio. When the local county committee and congressman had protested strongly against his coming, he had become all the more insistent. Theodore Roosevelt, Jr., claimed that the state organization had not been able to find any other city that wanted him. At Canton, Daugherty justified the injunction by stating that the labor leaders had mutinied against the government, which "they mocked and pillored [sic] in scorn." The injunction, according to Daugherty, had prevented a civil war.[31] While lecturing to the audience, he later wrote that he had smelled a strange pungent odor that came from an enormous bouquet of flowers that stood beside the speakers' rostrum. Daugherty thought that the enemy had slipped a deadly gas trap into the floral arrangement.[32]

The Attorney General also utilized his power against Keller. Burns's agents investigated him and searched his office for incriminatory material.[33] In more formal fashion, the staff of the Department of Justice helped Daugherty publish a detailed reply in pamphlet form which was distributed among congressmen and government leaders. In it Daugherty not only challenged each specification, but he also lashed out at his critics. He labeled them as grafters, profiteers, war defaulters, and radicals, who had attempted to intimidate him because he had chosen to enforce the laws. "Getting a man's goat is a great game," Daugherty later stated, but "I never had a goat farm and they could not get a goat where there was none."[34]

Daugherty's critics remained unconvinced. They argued that congressmen and newspapers did not criticize him for a failure to act, but for neglecting to perform positively or judiciously. Months before the September injunction and Keller's impeachment resolution, Daugherty had faced this sort of stricture. Although Keller was now viewed as a tool of labor, Daugherty's opposition felt that the House Committee on the Judiciary should have investigated the other twelve specifications. Questions relating to Burns's misuse of the Bureau remained unanswered, as well as Daugherty's failure to take action against the whiskey ring. The influence of Felder and other lobbyists required explanation. They wondered too why Daugherty still lagged on the war-fraud cases.[35] There was also dissatisfaction with the manner in which some cases failed in court because of poorly prepared briefs. That Daugherty often appointed nondepartmental counsel contributed to the poor performances, since such counsel were selected on a political basis. In contrast, Daugherty's successor, Harlan F. Stone, used departmental personnel and often argued important cases personally—something Daugherty almost never did.[36]

Likewise, Daugherty's claim of commencing as many antitrust actions as his predecessors did not prevent the opposition from charging that favoritism and ineptitude had characterized the work. Particularly did they emphasize his failure to investigate suspected violations concerning, among others, the J. P. Morgan interests, the American Tobacco Company, and the building trades in New York state and the District of Columbia. A frequent charge was that he tackled the small combinations rather than the giants.[37]

The United Gas Improvement Company antitrust case of early 1922 especially weakened Daugherty's position. It was then that Congressman Keller became such a strong critic. On March 6, 1922, under the direction of Special Assistant to the Attorney General R. Colton Lewis, a New York grand jury indicted the company and some of its officers for Sherman Act violations. At the same time, Lewis instituted a civil suit to dissolve the company. On May 4, however, Daugherty requested that criminal and civil proceedings be suspended because of insufficient evidence and the general weakness of the indictment. Critics claimed that political considerations had influenced him. United Gas Improvement Company officials, including President Samuel Bodine, indeed had visited with Daugherty and Goff and had employed, as attorney, New Yorker Francis S. Hutchins, a close friend of Daugherty's. There were several "Dear Harry" letters in which Hutchins clearly sought to influence the Attorney General. As it turned out, Bodine and his associates had also contributed to the Harding campaign of 1920. Lewis later claimed that a Justice official close to Daugherty told him: "Put yourself in the Attorney General's position. He has indicted these people and he finds now that they were friends and contributed to the campaign [in] which he had charge." And after the alleged influence on Daugherty had occurred, Daugherty replaced Lewis with a friend, Harry F. West of Columbus, who was to "reinvestigate" the charges and indictments. Soon afterward Daugherty dropped the indictment.[38]

Still, some of the criticism was unfair and politically inspired. Charges of not prosecuting certain trusts had been made against every president or attorney general since the Sherman Antitrust Act, but never so strongly before and never with an accompanying effort at impeachment. Too often, evidence of other alleged wrongdoing was insufficient or unconvincing. In Congress, accusations often became *ad hominem* harangues. Daugherty obviously became a lightning rod for those who wished to attack the administration.

But to say that about all of Daugherty's critics or all of the criticism would be equally unfair. In the spring of 1922, Republican Congressman Ray Woodruff of Michigan raised specific and fair-minded questions about certain alleged shortcomings of the Department of Justice. He also inserted a letter into the *Congressional Record* from H.F. Scaife, who recently had resigned as an investigator of the Department. Scaife had written Daugherty on May 3, asking pertinent questions that were related to the reasons he left: Why were specific war-graft cases, which he mentioned by name, put aside once they reached a certain point in the investigation and why was the Bureau of Investigation used to spy on several members of Congress?[39]

Also, in May, Senator Tom Watson of Georgia, an avowed Democratic partisan, raised pointed questions about Felder.[40] There were others who asked similar questions. Daugherty chose to ignore most of them. He also became inaccessible to reporters or to members of Congress. In the few instances that he did respond, he was often misleading and belligerent. On at least one occasion, he suggested that there were sinister forces behind the movement to discredit him.[41] While it is true that Senator Caraway was unduly partisan in the Morse case discussion that May, Daugherty wrongly assumed that all inquiries were designed to discredit him. His overly suspicious nature, cultivated by forty years of Ohio political infighting and past charges of wrongdoing, and his own negligence caused him to mishandle the criticism. As a result, a snowballing of opinion against him occurred, especially after the 1922 injunction, leaving him with little congressional support a year later.

The crises of 1922 affected Daugherty's health; overwork and mental strain taxed his nervous system and weakened him to the point that he could no longer perform his job. In early January 1923, along with Jess Smith and brother Mal, he went to French Lick Springs, Indiana for a rest. There he drank the waters, was bathed and rubbed, and played golf. He returned to Washington later that month, still not well. Then one morning at his Wardman Park Hotel suite, he complained to assistant Warren Martin, who stayed with him when Smith was in Ohio, that he felt dizzy. The doctors admitted him into the Navy Hospital, where he underwent tests. They found him on the verge of a nervous breakdown and suffering from high blood pressure. They took blood from him to relieve the pressure, put him on a stringent diet, and urged him to remain in bed for two weeks without transacting business or seeing anyone. Otherwise, Martin was told, it was only a matter of time before he would have a stroke.[42] For the following month Daugherty remained under the care of a private nurse. On February 28, he wrote Harding that he felt better. Even then, he said that he was unable to talk much because it "makes me a little nervous." Daugherty's nurse later claimed that Harding visited him at his apartment sometime in February. From another room, she heard the two argue, with Daugherty responding "I cannot agree with you Mr. President" and "we could not permit anything like that to happen."[43]

The nature of that conversation is unknown. The nurse recalled, however, that Jess Smith's visits to the Attorney General's room left Daugherty in an "agitated frame of mind." Perhaps Harding had already received some inkling of Smith's activities and had brought it to Daugherty's attention. By this time, Washington reeked of such suspicion. Another possibility concerned Harding's Veteran's Bureau Chief Charles Forbes. That February, the President became aware that Forbes, among other things, was selling for personal consideration governmental supplies to private contractors at cut-rate prices. Disenchanted and worried, Harding could have rebuked his Attorney General for not having investigated Forbes. Daugherty stated in his 1932 apologia that he and Dr. Charles Sawyer, White House physician and a personal friend of Harding, had, in fact, revealed Forbes's shady activities to the President. No evidence exists, however, that Daugherty had played such a role.[44] Because of his protracted illness, it is unlikely that he could have.

In any case, Harding and Daugherty were still friendly afterward. In March, Daugherty departed for Florida along with Harding and a presidential party that included Jess Smith. Sawyer, who was treating Daugherty, left instructions at the Department of Justice that no mail or business be brought to the Attorney General's attention. Nonetheless, Daugherty's health was not improving. Harding felt sorry about Daugherty's condition and did everything that he could to aid his recovery. He encouraged him to take as much time as necessary to recuperate. After Harding returned to Washington, Daugherty left for an extended rest at Asheville, North Carolina, where he began to improve. He wrote Taft that he did not know it was possible to have been so sick. He added that he could now be up for an hour in the morning and an hour and a half in the afternoon, but he was hardly strong enough to resume his position.[45]

Jennings thought Daugherty would never get back to par. Although he sincerely hoped for improvement, he informed Harding that Robert Wolfe of the *Ohio State Journal* would support the President's reelection, provided that Daugherty would not interfere in Ohio matters. Harding confessed that Daugherty had "spread some irritation in some quarters." He depreciated Daugherty's future political involvements, however, because of his serious illness.[46]

Daugherty could not accept political retirement. To bolster his sagging public image as Harding's political adviser, Daugherty announced to Florida newspapermen on March 17 that Harding would seek renomination. Daugherty wrote Harding that he hoped that he had not embarrassed him. He said that he had never previously spoken for him without explicit authority. "Just what happened," Daugherty explained, "was that newspapermen had importuned me to give them a visit." He asserted unconvincingly that he had not acted with any expectation of exploitation. He simply had given his personal opinion, although he acknowledged that he had stated that there would be a more concrete revelation of Harding's convention plans that summer or fall. The newspapers logically believed that Daugherty had spoken for the President.[47]

The Attorney General did embarrass Harding, who planned a summer western trip as a nonpolitical "voyage of understanding" in which he would communicate to the people the aims and goals of his presidency. Harding felt that Daugherty's interview had created the impression that he would travel across the country as a candidate for renomination.[48] Of course the President had this in his mind. To portray that aim, however, could only jeopardize his desire to crystalize popular support for himself as well as his programs. Not wishing to hurt the stricken Attorney General, Harding said little to Daugherty about the faux pas.

Daugherty never depended more on the President. Throughout April he eagerly awaited Harding's letters, which helped to ease his depression. Although claiming that he was homesick for the Hardings and restless to return to work, he conveyed a reluctance to go back to Washington.[49] Daugherty had lost confidence in his abilities to administer a job that was often too big for him. He perhaps feared possible disclosures in his own department that would necessitate an explanation. These factors might even have prolonged his illness. Harding, however, continued to remain sympathetic to Daugherty. He explained that while he was anxious to have him return, he thought that he should remain as long as he continued to benefit from the stay in Asheville. "The main thing," Harding explained, "is for you to get well—back to normalcy." Harding thoughtfully added that "everybody in public service inquires about you every day so that I spend about as much time telling people how I think you are as I do in carrying on the affairs of the state."[50]

Always the political animal, Daugherty, upon learning that Harding was concentrating on plans for the western trip, notified Harding on April 24 that he was coming back to Washington. That Walter Brown was handling the preparations must have irked Daugherty. Not wanting to be left out, he desired to discuss the speaking sites and to offer a few suggestions. Knowing that Harding contemplated joining the World Court, Daugherty advised him not to commit the country to the tribunal without safeguards. He suggested that a specific congressional declaration precede any Court jurisdiction in American disputes. He apologized for offering unsolicited advice, but he thought the subject too critical not to.

Daugherty spoke in vain. Harding was now listening to Hughes and Hoover, who were more internationally-minded. Daugherty had less to say about his own departmental duties. He promised, however, that he would be capable of doing a vast amount of work that summer, provided it was done in his own way.[51]

Daugherty stayed only a short period in Washington. He conferred with Harding, who presented him with evidence of Smith's illegal escapades. Daugherty professed to be stunned. He subsequently told Smith that the President did not want him on the western trip and desired him out of Washington. Daugherty also attended a couple of cabinet meetings and visited his office. He then departed with Smith for Columbus where he conducted his official duties for two hours each morning at his Federal Building office. He rested at the "Shack," where Smith remained with him.

Smith's last day there (May 25) was traumatic. According to Roxie Stinson, a visitor from Columbus arrived in the afternoon, and was so persistent in wanting to see Daugherty that Smith reluctantly woke him from his nap. Daugherty was enraged. He swore at Smith repeatedly for having disturbed him, quickly got dressed, and then threatened to leave without him. Eventually, he cooled off enough to have his nephew, H. Ellis Daugherty, drive Smith to Washington Court House. Ellis later claimed that Smith mumbled to himself and tried to jump out of the automobile as they returned to Washington Court House. Smith then went to a hardware store and, despite his fear of firearms, purchased a revolver.[52]

Daugherty's rebuff, if we can believe Roxie Stinson's story, contributed to Smith's suicide. For weeks the threat of exposure and arrest had also weighed upon him. In his last days, according to Roxie, Smith lived in mortal fear. He became suspicious of strangers, refused to go out at night or sleep alone, and needed constant reassurance.[53] His declining health added to his volatile and depressed state. In May 1922, he had entered Mt. Carmel Hospital in Columbus, suffering from acute appendicitis complicated by diabetes. He was in a semiconscious state for several days before and after the operation. Discharged one month later, he was forced to wear a trusslike belt because the incision had never healed.

On Sunday, May 27, Daugherty permitted Smith to return with him to Washington. But he was to remain only until he saw a few friends and put his affairs in order. When they arrived, Daugherty went to the White House, where he had arranged to stay for a couple of days. Because of Smith's "queer" behavior, he asked Martin to stay with him at the Wardman Park suite. On May 29, Smith played golf at McLean's estate with Martin, Dr. Joel Boone, and Major Peyton Gordon, the federal attorney of the District of Columbia. Smith, who Boone thought behaved pensively, did not join in the drinks after the round. He instead went to his

Justice Department office to clean out his papers and destroyed them before his death the next day.[54]

Early on May 30, Martin was aroused from his sleep by a noise from Smith's room. He found Smith, in his pajamas and robe, on the floor with his bloodied head in a wastebasket and with a revolver in his hand. Martin quickly called Burns, who occupied an apartment below. Dr. Boone was also summoned and after examining the body, told the press that Smith had been seriously ill for a year and had despondently taken his life. At the White House that evening, Smith's death preoccupied the small group of dinner guests. After dinner, they viewed a movie in the upstairs hall, where Daugherty broke the silence with an occasional "O-o-o-o-o-o-o."

Still disturbing about Smith's death was the fact that no autopsy was performed, and that Burns had misplaced the revolver shortly after he entered Smith's room. Too, as others have suggested, Smith had conveniently removed himself and his personal papers at a time when embarrassing scandals were about to unfold.[55] Circumstantial evidence, however, strongly indicates that Smith took his own life. On his desk was an unwitnessed and revised will, in his own handwriting, in which he divided equally his $200,000 estate among the two Daugherty's, Stinson, and two cousins. Judged invalid, this will was never probated. His 1922 will left the Daughertys and Stinson each with $25,000, with the rest parceled among relatives, friends, and charities. His funeral was in Washington Court House. Unable to stand the strain, Daugherty did not attend. Accompanying the body was Assistant Attorney General Holland who, on arrival, allegedly presented Mally Daugherty with a sealed package. He, after breaking the seal, quickly burned the contents in his bank's furnace.[56]

Harry Daugherty blamed Smith's suicide upon his acute diabetes. "Poor old Jess—," Daugherty wrote Ned McLean, "he was a great friend of yours. I know the whole story now and some day I will tell you enough of it to convince you that he did not commit an act of cowardice; what he did is traceable to sickness. Everything will be all right and his soul is safe, because he was the soul of honor and integrity." To Mrs. McLean, he added, "it is a sad story but nothing in it to reflect upon his good character."[57] After wrongdoing was proved, Daugherty blamed Smith's misbehavior on, again, declining health. Sometime in 1922, he wrote a decade later, Smith's diabetic condition contributed to a personality change. Subtlely, a genial, kind, and honest man ceased to be.[58]

Shortly after Smith's death, Harding completed plans for his western trip. Daugherty appeared to have little to do with it. He later wrote that he had advised Harding to reduce his planned speaking engagements after noting his wearied appearance. He might, indeed, have cautioned him.

Their last correspondence, however, does not reflect his concern. His only comment came on April 24, when he had remarked that while the tour would be a strain, he knew that Harding was an expert in handling himself under the circumstances.[59] The overworked and overly worried Harding, suffering from the aftereffects of influenza and from a weak heart, high blood pressure, and probable Bright's disease, denied himself the rest that he so kindly conceded to his subordinates.

The progress of the war-fraud cases was the subject of one of Daugherty's last letters to Harding. Obviously the problem concerned the President, since reports continued to circulate that the Department was not obtaining sufficient results. Daugherty admitted that it would take a long time to complete the work because of the large number of cases and the crowded court dockets. He claimed that hundreds of cases were under investigation aside from the $3,000,000 that had already been collected from successful court actions. His statistics were not impressive, however, when compared to the estimated $192,000,000 total of possible collections. By February 1924, the money recovered amounted to only a little over $4,500,000.[60]

Daugherty might have feared that additional questions would follow on specific cases in which the Department had allegedly delayed prosecution due to outside influences. On July 12, he asked Assistant Attorney General John Crim to forward a memorandum on the controversial Bosch Magneto case, which involved a defrauding corporation that had employed Felder to safeguard its interests.[61] After hearing that Crim was no longer investigating the matter, he contacted Assistant Attorney General Seymour to relate that while the case had been "side-tracked," he now desired that the investigation "be pushed as rapidly as possible, for we are losing valuable time." Similarly, Daugherty finally requested that the Department aggressively handle the equally controversial and long-delayed New York City war-fraud cases, which critics claimed that Felder had delayed.[62]

Although Daugherty had sometimes disappointed and embarrassed Harding, their last correspondence indicated that there was no personal estrangement.[63] The estrangement instead developed over official matters, in which the President learned to rely upon the advice of more competent cabinet members. One exception was the shopmen's strike of 1922, in which Harding himself had leaned toward a tougher approach. The President had less control over or knowledge of departmental concerns. By 1923, he might have suspected that his Attorney General was involved in an unseemly or corrupt way. But it was still Daugherty's word against that of his critics. Wanting to think well of Daugherty, and desiring that no party embarrassment occur, he defended him from what he chose to consider unfair criticism. Ultimately, he probably shifted the blame upon himself for appointing a political intimate who lacked the character and training to be Attorney General. This perhaps explains why Harding continued to act kindly toward him.

Daugherty saw the President for the last time in mid-June, a few days before the latter embarked on his western trip. Not feeling able to accompany him for the entire sojourn, he planned to be in Los Angeles in late July, where he would join the presidential cruise to Panama. That meeting never occurred, for the strain of delivering eighty-five speeches in six weeks prevented Harding from reaching Los Angeles.

Additional revelations of scandals in the administration had also unnerved Harding. Near Hutchinson, Kansas, he related to William Allen White, the influential publisher of the Emporia *Gazette,* that "I have no trouble with my enemies. I can take care of them. It is my friends that are giving me my trouble." White recorded that he had also visited Harding in a Kansas City hotel on the previous evening. There, Mrs. Albert Fall later appeared unexpectedly to consult with Harding in an adjoining room. While White had left before they reappeared, he claimed that Senator Arthur Capper of Kansas, another guest, told him the following day that Harding came out of the meeting frustrated, worried, and excited.[64]

In his *Memoirs,* Herbert Hoover later remembered a similar incident. On July 3, he and his wife joined the presidential party at Tacoma, Washington, for the Alaskan excursion. Harding asked Hoover to come to his cabin during the voyage. There the President supposedly questioned him: "If you knew of a great scandal in our administration, would you for the good of the country and the party expose it publicly or would you bury it?" Hoover's reply was to publish it in order to get credit for integrity. Harding retorted that this method might be dangerous politically. His Commerce Secretary then asked for the specifics. Hoover later recalled Harding's reply: "He said that he had received some rumors of irregularities, centering around Smith, in connection with cases in the Department of Justice." Hoover asked if Daugherty was in any way involved. Harding, according to Hoover, "abruptly dried up and never raised the question again."[65]

Harding suffered a heart attack on his return from Alaska. Dr. Sawyer, erroneously attributing the collapse to ptomaine poisoning, had the remainder of Harding's engagements cancelled.[66] The presidential train sped for San Francisco, where Harding was to recuperate. He was put to bed at the Palace Hotel. There he contracted pneumonia, which often follows some heart disorders. His condition was grave.

George Christian notified Daugherty, who came directly to San Francisco. Although the President rallied from pneumonia by August 1, Daugherty did not visit him. He later said that there were too many people at the hotel for him to add to the confusion. Daugherty told Mrs.

Harding that he would see the President in a couple of days. On August 2, he held a reception for a few West Coast judges and lawyers at his hotel. That evening Dr. Boone and a nurse walked softly into his room to inform him that Harding had succumbed to a probable cerebral hemorrage. Daugherty could scarcely say a word. "I had received the hardest blow of my life," he later wrote, for "I had felt the foundations of the world sink."67 He managed to wire Vice President Calvin Coolidge immediately, suggesting that he take the oath of office at once.

Daugherty returned to the "Shack" after Harding's funeral. He wrote Finley Peter Dunne that he was still crushed over Harding's death and wanted to be alone. He confessed that his heart was not in Washington and that he would be happier if he were out of public life. Retirement was, nevertheless, unthinkable. "I am going to stay in the Cabinet," he asserted, "because the President desires me, and many want me to stay and many enemies don't want me to." To another friend he reiterated that he would leave public service if he felt he were no longer useful. He added that the nation was fortunate to have a man like President Coolidge who was safe, sincere, and capable. "I will give him as much help as I can," he promised.68 In the face of all his difficulties, Daugherty tenaciously held on, still hoping to vindicate himself.

Coolidge, Wheeler, and Resignation

THE outset of the Coolidge administration must have been an unhappy period for Daugherty. Harding's death remained on his mind, and he also worried about his wife Lucy's deteriorating condition. The doctors had attempted to correct her arthritic limbs by breaking the leg joints, but she collapsed after the first operation and had to wear heavy casts on her legs. It was hoped that leg movement could be restored through the gradual adjustment of the casts; she did not, however, respond to treatment. At times she was unable even to lift her head from her pillow. The concerned Daugherty took her to Atlantic City for two weeks in mid-September in the hope that she would improve.[1] Lucy would, however, die of pneumonia on November 23, 1924.

Draper also troubled him, for the war had left him in even more unhappy circumstances. In March, he had been peripherally linked to the Dorothy King murder case. An attractive model who preferred wealthy, married men, she was mysteriously chloroformed in her New York apartment. Draper, who was an intimate friend, made the newspapers after claiming that the victim's brother attempted to blackmail him. The brother promised not to reveal Draper's association with Dorothy in return for a job in the Justice Department. To Draper's credit, he went to the police.[2]

When the authorities failed to determine the assailant, Draper left for Mexico. Shortly after returning, his wife and Uncle Mal, with his father's approval, committed him for alcoholism to the Stamford Hall Sanitarium in Connecticut. Draper admitted to the examining physicians that while drinking he frequently wrote checks larger than his resources. He was considerably in debt and on the verge of a nervous breakdown. In June, however, he escaped and fled to Chicago, where he secretly obtained employment with the Wade Coal Company. He was finally discovered in late July and returned to New York City.[3]

As Thomas Felder now informed the Attorney General in September, he had loaned Draper over $4,000 and had found him a position with the New York Life Insurance Company. Within three weeks Draper wrote

$200,000 in insurance. For a brief period he stayed sober and repaid his debts. Then he again fell into the wrong crowd, subsequently overdrew his bank account, and went into debt. Without thought of reward, Felder wrote Daugherty, he paid off the bills and provided Draper with letters of introduction. But it was obvious that Felder was using Draper to protect himself.

By September, Felder was apprehensive. He was about to be indicted for his connection in the Glass Casket mail fraud. The promoters of the glass burial casket had so misrepresented their company that they paid Felder, Gaston Means, and a certain Elmer Jarnecke $65,000 after the three had persuaded the Glass Casket people that they could squelch the Justice Department investigation. Hiram Todd, the Department's independent special assistant, moved relentlessly after discovering the arrangement, causing Felder to write Daugherty. It was on September 7 that he told Daugherty of his assistance to Draper. Yet, he wrote, he was accused of evil and of "capitalizing" on the son of the Attorney General. "I have reached the point in regard to these infamous rumors," he continued, "that with me, 'patience has almost ceased to be a virtue.'" He intimated that Daugherty should intercede.[4]

There was no way that Daugherty could help him. To do so would only invite overwhelming criticism and further weaken his attorney generalship. And unlike Harding, Coolidge was under no obligation to protect him. Even after Felder seemed to threaten Daugherty in November, Daugherty refused to impede the Department investigation, which eventually led to Felder's 1925 conviction.[5] His friend's recent betrayal and collapse only added to Daugherty's sadness.

But Daugherty was determined to win the confidence of Coolidge, a cautious, shy, and taciturn man. He attempted to convince him that he was, indeed, an active and valuable Attorney General. After submitting a progress report on the war-fraud cases that fall, Daugherty remarked that as soon as he had assumed the office he had quietly begun this vigorous investigation. He added that the extent of this work would soon astonish the nation. In December, he further informed the President that he had recently prepared bills for Congress, proposing a separate federal prison for women, a program for employing young attorneys in the Justice Department, a division of criminal investigation, and additional federal district judges.[6] He even sent Coolidge replies from friends who had commented favorably upon specific cases handled by the Department. Admitting that he was sending an unusual number of letters, Daugherty added that "I do not send you one out of a hundred [that] I should like to have you see." On another occasion he reiterated that there were so many things for him to discuss that he was sometimes ashamed to impose upon Coolidge and purposely overlooked some matters.[7] Always he took advantage of the opportunity to renew his "assurances of high esteem and cordial regard."

Daugherty obviously did not feel secure in the new administration from its inception. Although Coolidge did not wish to disturb his predecessor's cabinet for the remainder of the term, he would have no obligations upon reelection, as Daugherty realized. As early as the fall of 1923, Daugherty tried to tighten his hold on the attorney generalship by telling the new President that he would swing the Ohio delegation to the President in 1924. On October 23, he wrote Charles Hard that he must insist on becoming a delegate-at-large to the 1924 Republican national convention. This, of course, meant fighting Hynicka, Brown, Wolfe, and the rest of the anti-Daugherty crowd. Daugherty was not unwilling to do this. Claiming that he believed in frank politics, he accused them of conspiring against him, "slipping around on gum shoes, and operating after methods which I do not hold." Daugherty consequently opposed Hynicka's remaining a member of the National Committee. While Harding had chosen to ignore Hynicka's actions, Daugherty reminded Hard that he was different. Such betrayal "is not good for the discipline of the party," he added, "and it is not fair to President Harding's memory." Daugherty eliminated Walter Brown by stating that he was "late getting into the wagon" in 1920 and "did not do much anyway."[8]

Even the *Cincinnati Times-Star* did not share Daugherty's views. It reported that Coolidge would not risk alienating any faction within the Ohio party. This caused Daugherty to send the article to Taft, complaining that the *Times-Star* was trying to embarrass him and was attempting to put "Hynicka and Robert Wolfe in the White House."[9] Taft did not agree with Daugherty. He believed that Coolidge should be willing to establish friendly relations with Brown, Hynicka, and Wolfe. Although conceding that he did not like that association any better than Daugherty, he thought that a united party behind Coolidge was certainly a desirable goal:

> Of course you are too old in politics to need any suggestions from me, but I think you are a bit too sensitive in respect to such a matter as this. I know what a strain you have been under and how justified you are in your feeling of contempt and disgust toward your unscrupulous opponents . . . but I depreciate it, and I think as the situation wears on you will agree with me that you borrow trouble by worrying over such an incident.

Daugherty retorted that Taft failed to see the entire picture.[10] Coolidge's decision to cooperate with the anti-Daugherty faction did undercut Daugherty's political ambitions in his own state, as well as damage his political influence in the new administration.

Far more disturbing to Daugherty that fall was the investigation of the naval-oil-reserve leases. On October 22, Senator Reed Smoot of Utah convened the Senate's Public Lands Committee. By January, the austere Senator Thomas Walsh of Montana, the Committee's informal leader, already had enough circumstantial evidence to indicate that in April and July 1922, Secretary of the Interior Albert Fall had, without competitive bidding, leased naval oil reserves at Teapot Dome, Wyoming, and Elk Hills, California, to private concerns in return for personal remuneration. As the investigation progressed, attention gradually shifted to Daugherty. After all, Fall must have sought the Attorney General's judgment prior to leasing the reserves.

Actually, no written opinion existed to implicate Daugherty. He later testified that Fall had never come to him for an opinion, nor had the matter been discussed in the cabinet. He further denied that he had given an oral judgment. Probably no Attorney General, he asserted, ever offered unwritten opinions.[11] It is, nevertheless, unlikely that Harding failed to consult Daugherty before acceding to Fall's lease of Teapot Dome to Harry Sinclair and the Elk Hills reserve to Edward Doheny. Moreover, Sinclair had been a major contributor to the 1920 campaign. He was also a good friend of Daugherty.

Daugherty and Harding, in fact, helped Fall enforce the lease at Teapot Dome. One month after Fall had turned over the Wyoming reserve to Sinclair, Harding learned from Fall that his friend James Darden, who had contributed $6,000 to Harding's campaign, continued to drill on his small claim in the Teapot Dome reserve despite Fall's orders to get out. Darden thought that he had a legal right to the small portion of the reserve and decided to take his case into court. Fall, fearing publicity over his own leasing, convinced Harding that Darden must be quickly removed. On July 24, Harding wrote Daugherty that the Darden friendship did not justify the defiance of government authority. "If you have had the interview and he has declined to comply," he stated, "please advise me and I will then be justified in ordering a naval contingent to put an end to the activities of his company." Daugherty replied that he knew absolutely nothing about the matter aside from Darden's belief that he had a claim to the property. Harding, in any event, hoped that Daugherty would expedite the interview with Darden. "I have a very pressing letter from Secretary Fall," he persisted, indicating that "our position will be more difficult if we proceed with a suit at law and believes that forceful action should be taken."[12] A small contingent of marines finally succeeded in removing the unfortunate Darden from Teapot Dome.

Both Harding and Daugherty undoubtedly acted out of the conviction that Fall had leased the reserves out of national interest. Little did they know that he had received over $400,000 in bribes. It was probably not

until the western trip that Harding first learned that Fall had betrayed
him. By that time Fall was no longer Interior Secretary. He had resigned
on March 4, 1923, to take a lucrative position with the Sinclair oil
interests. Whether Daugherty knew prior to the investigation that Sinclair
and Doheny had bribed Fall is unlikely. There exists in the Fall Papers,
however, an intriguing letter from Daugherty, who wrote Fall two weeks
after Harding's death, about two months prior to the convening of the
Senate investigation. Although Daugherty later asserted that he had never
been close to Fall, his letter began on a note of intimacy:

> My Dear Friend Albert:
> I tried to see you before I came away but it was impossible as I was fussed
> around with and had so many things to do. I don't think there was anything
> special that I wanted to talk with you about but wanted to have another
> little visit with you before we separated. There is a matter I will write you
> about when I have confirmation of a report I received recently.[13]

Aware of the approaching investigation, Daugherty might have wanted to
discuss the leases to insure that Fall would not implicate him in any way.
That he had been Attorney General at the time of the leasing was enough
to involve him indirectly.

By January 1924, the Senate investigation increased Daugherty's political liability. Having sat in the Harding cabinet, where critics insisted that
the leases had been discussed, he was hardly in a favorable position to
prosecute the alleged offenders. Coolidge at first appeared to ignore such
a concern. On January 24, he reminded Daugherty to have a competent
member of his staff attend the Senate hearings so that the Department
might take any necessary steps to protect the financial interests of the
United States. In addition, he directed him to examine all evidence disclosed at the hearings and to make any independent investigation that
the Attorney General thought essential. Coolidge intimated that Daugherty would supervise the subsequent prosecution. Daugherty replied that
Rush Holland was attending all the meetings. "All phases of this matter
are under observation, investigation, and consideration by the Department," Daugherty assured, "and I can, with great pleasure assure you that
your instructions and desires meet with my hearty and cordial support."[14]

On January 26, Coolidge wavered when he heard that Walsh and other
Democrats were preparing a resolution that would authorize Coolidge to
bring suit to annul the leases, to prevent further extraction of oil, and to
appoint special counsel to prosecute the guilty parties. That evening he
seized the initiative by stating that he intended to employ special counsel
drawn from both political parties to handle the oil-lease litigation. Claiming that possible guilt tainted both parties, Coolidge promised that any
wrongdoing would be punished, any civil liability would be enforced, and

any illegal contract would be cancelled. Every right of the people and the government, he affirmed, would be protected.[15]

Daugherty, resting with his wife in Florida, heard about Coolidge's proposed statement a few hours prior to its release. He responded to the oblique slap shortly before it was made public by boldly wiring Coolidge to appoint special counsel. He did not want to avoid responsibility, he wrote, but nonetheless, since he had served in the cabinet with Fall, Coolidge's approach was in the best interests of all involved. Two days later Daugherty publicly released his telegram. On January 31, he congratulated Coolidge on the two men he had appointed to investigate the leases. He assured the President that the Department would be ready to furnish all needed assistance.[16]

On February 8, Daugherty returned from Florida. By this time he, too, was under a barrage of criticism from the opposition in Congress, which doubled its efforts to link him to the oil scandals. The issue clearly had political overtones. The Democrats, led by Senators J. Thomas Heflin of Alabama, Kenneth D. McKellar of Tennessee, and Caraway, concentrated on the vulnerable Daugherty to discredit the administration further in an election year. Fall had already been dishonored. Secretary of the Navy Edwin Denby was also under fire for having permitted Fall to transfer the oil reserves from the Navy to the Interior Department. On February 18, he tendered his resignation to Coolidge. After the *Literary Digest* stated that Coolidge had lost confidence in his Attorney General, Daugherty wrote one of its executives that if he thought this were true, "my resignation will be placed in your hands to carry to him." But Daugherty was not about to run away because "some irresponsible scalawag and gossip scavenger . . . makes an attack on me."[17]

Considerable speculation existed over how long Coolidge could retain Daugherty. This was especially true after February 19, when Democratic Senator Burton K. Wheeler introduced a resolution asking for an investigation of the Department of Justice. Opposed to Daugherty's politics and attorney generalship, and anxious to duplicate the successes of his fellow Montanian, Wheeler, with much less restraint and patience than Walsh, demanded an inquiry on the grounds that Daugherty had failed to arrest and prosecute Fall, Doheny, Sinclair, Forbes, and other conspirators who had defrauded the government. He also revived charges that Keller had made in December 1922. He presented his case in a rather injudicious fashion, intimating that he intended a freewheeling investigation. Wheeler informed the Senate:

> Recently when the oil scandal first developed it appears that the Attorney General's name was mixed in it. It appeared, if you please, that he was a friend of Ned McLean. Everybody knows that he was the friend of Doheny. Everybody knows that these three men met in the apartment of the Attor-

ney General from time to time. Everybody knows that Jess Smith, who was brought from the State of Ohio and had an office in the Department of Justice, and who was not on the payroll, was accepting cases that arose in the Department of Justice.[18]

The charge that "everybody" knew Daugherty's culpability threw the Republican senatorial leadership into a state of confusion. After the embarrassing disclosures regarding Forbes and Fall, they panicked at the thought of another Democratic-inspired investigation, especially one involving Daugherty. Knowing that Daugherty would never resign voluntarily, progressive Senator William Borah, the most outspoken and important Republican critic, told Coolidge at the White House on the evening of February 18 that the President must ask for Daugherty's resignation. While Borah was stating his reasons, Daugherty joined them in the study. Coolidge had cagily arranged a meeting between the two antagonists, obviously hoping to learn from the confrontation.[19] When the Idahoan momentarily hesitated, Daugherty sarcastically remarked: "Well don't let my presence embarrass you." Borah, recovering his poise, shot back: "I think I should be the least embarrassed person here." He then told Daugherty that he should quit because he no longer commanded the respect of the country. The Attorney General retorted that the matter was not one for the senator or the Senate to decide. He reportedly added: "I don't know why you want me to resign. I have never had to turn you down. You never asked me for anything." They continued their heated discussion for about an hour as the silent Coolidge listened intently while twirling his horn-rimmed glasses. According to a White House secretary, Daugherty finally left "white with rage."[20] On the following day Republican Senator George W. Pepper of Pennsylvania asked Daugherty to resign at a Daugherty-arranged conference in the Attorney General's Wardman Park suite. This only angered Daugherty, who later charged that Pepper had resented not being named Solicitor General.[21]

In the next few days, Coolidge received Lodge, Borah, Pepper, Hughes, and Hoover. All asked for Daugherty's dismissal. Hughes even offered to arrange to have all members of the cabinet place their resignations in Coolidge's hand so that the latter could then reappoint whomever he wished. "No, don't do that," Coolidge supposedly warned, "it might leave me alone with Daugherty."[22] Finally Taft, at Coolidge's suggestion, advised Daugherty to resign. But the President also heard from Republicans who wanted Daugherty retained. Republican National Chairman John T. Adams and a number of old-guard national committeemen did not want him to yield to the Democratic "gang." Senators Willis and Fess of Ohio argued that Daugherty's dismissal would split Ohio and give it to the Democrats.[23] Coolidge simplified the issue when he told former Progressive Raymond Robins that "it is a sound rule that when the President dies in office it is the duty of his successor for the remainder of that term to maintain the counsellors and policies of the deceased President."[24]

Daugherty, meanwhile, refused to sacrifice himself for the party, accusing Republicans who favored his dismissal of cowardice. On February 21, he issued an open letter to Senator Pepper in which he indicated that he did not object to an impartial investigation, but asserted that the charges made against him in the Senate were unfounded and malicious. Daugherty warned that he would carry the issue to the country and, in public addresses, denounce the actions of the administration if he were removed from office pending investigation.[25] On February 27, upon hearing that Coolidge intended to ask for his resignation, he again declared that he did not propose to resign. On the following day he pleaded with Coolidge that he had "as much at stake as you have and you must do me the justice of assuring yourself on that point." He then pathetically scrawled:

> All things will come out all right. You will not be injured but helped. I see the way. No straight path. If they could get you to doubt me and [if] they could have you say . . . [that] I would soon quit, or resign then they could say they were right and justified in what they have done. I haven't told you how secure I am.[26]

Unknown to Daugherty and to most Republican leaders, Coolidge had already made his decision. Perhaps recent testimony in the naval-oil-reserve-hearings that Daugherty owned Sinclair oil stock, or Borah's threats to initiate impeachment proceedings against Daugherty were the last straws.[27] By the end of February, Coolidge asked his old friend, Harlan Fiske Stone, a former dean of the Columbia Law School, to come to Washington to discuss Daugherty's replacement. Taft was also busily helping Coolidge find a new Attorney General. On March 6, he related to brother Horace that despite the "reckless charges," the President could not politically afford to carry Daugherty any longer and "Harry ought not to ask it." The Chief Justice recommended Judge George Carpenter of Chicago, who owed his federal judgeship to Taft.[28] In mid-March Coolidge settled on Stone. Even then the President continued to delay his announcement.

The select Senate committee's investigation of the Attorney General convened on March 13, after Wheeler and his colleages had raked Daugherty in the Senate for the preceding two weeks and the Senate had adopted the investigating resolution by a 66 to 1 vote. The committee included the forty-two-year-old Wheeler, who acted as counselor and dominated the proceedings, Democrat Henry Ashurst of Arizona, and three Republicans: Chairman Smith W. Brookhart of Iowa, Wesley L. Jones of Washington, and George H. Moses of New Hampshire. Of the three Republicans, the square-jawed, muscular Brookhart was easily the most critical of Daugherty. Having supported the Progressive party in 1912, he was aligned with the Republican progressive wing that found the Attorney General both politically and ethically objectionable.

Meanwhile, the Attorney General countered with an investigation of Wheeler, including the ransacking of his office by Burns's agents. Daugherty later had Wheeler, whom he labeled the "leader of the IWW," indicted in Montana on a bribery charge. (He was finally acquitted in April 1925.)[29] The atmosphere was extremely emotional, and certainly unconducive to an impartial inquiry.

Wheeler initially based his case on evidence presented by such questionable personalities as Gaston Means, the former Bureau investigator, and Roxie Stinson, the ex-wife of Jess Smith. Eventually ex-convicts, grafters, and bootleggers also testified. Wheeler justified such reliance by stating that Daugherty did not associate with preachers.[30] The cherubic and cocky Means, under federal indictment in New York for accepting bribes to obtain whiskey withdrawal permits, testified after Daugherty refused to succumb to his threats of exposure.[31] In order to punish Daugherty, and hoping to avert prosecution, he sometimes fabricated incidents of bribery, extortion, and corruption by persons close to the Attorney General. Without evidence, he also enmeshed Daugherty in the K Street activities. On one occasion he accused Jess Smith of collecting $100,000 from a corporation that he said faced prosecution by the department. Subsequent investigation proved that the department never had the case to prosecute.[32] Wheeler managed to corroborate some of Means's accusations, but came under press criticism when he permitted his star witness to ramble from one undocumented episode to another. Furthermore, the documents Means promised to present were suddenly "stolen."[33]

Roxie Stinson more directly implicated Daugherty. The still attractive redhead recalled her ex-husband's role in the Dempsey-Carpentier fight-film transactions:

> *Miss Stinson.* He [Smith] declared that 'we' had a big thing if this could be put over a concession—I mean the rights to display it, that it meant a lot of money; he even mentioned a sum of money.
> *Senator Wheeler.* When he said it was for 'we,' you understood it to mean that it was for Harry Daugherty?
> *Miss Stinson.* There might have been others in it, but whenever he discussed anything of that sort, it referred to Mr. Daugherty.[34]

She testified, but again was unable to prove, that Daugherty was also involved in the whiskey permit operations. Her admission that Harry and Mal Daugherty had allegedly cheated her out of $11,000 of the Smith estate weakened her credibility. She introduced many letters from her ex-husband as evidence, but these established no direct link between Daugherty and the corruption.[35] To discredit Roxie, Daugherty circulated "evidence" of her promiscuity. Actually, however, Roxie was framed. A. L. Fink, a past friend, had recently asked her to meet with him at the Hotel Hollenden in Cleveland on the pretext of discussing a business deal. Fink, apparently in the employ of the Daughertys, signed the hotel registry as if they were man and wife and sleeping in the same room. This was done to persuade Roxie to withhold her testimony from the committee.[36]

After testifying, Roxie soon receded from the spotlight. Eventually she remarried, and spent most of her remaining years in Washington Court House with her husband. To historians and reporters alike who visited her home on Mulberry Street, she refused to talk about the past, although she occasionally hinted to townsmen that she knew more about the Harding administration than she revealed. For years, Harding scholars believed that she had a cache of papers in an unnamed bank in Washington Court House that would with certainty implicate Daugherty with Jess Smith in all manner of dire things. After her death of congestive heart failure on January 1, 1973, no such evidence was revealed. But the more-than-ninety-year-old Roxie Stinson Brast left a net estate of over $190,000.[37]

The investigation meanwhile had dragged on for three months after Stinson's revelations, mired in politics and characterized by innuendo and vituperation. One witness was interrogated as follows:

> *Mr. Miller.* About a year ago Mr. Traylor made a trip to New Mexico.
> *Senator Wheeler.* For you?
> *Mr. Miller.* For the Marland Oil Co. and me together.
> *Senator Wheeler.* And who is the Mellon Oil Co.?
> *Mr. Miller.* The Marland, M-A-R-L-A-N-D. . . .[38]

The following exchange occurred when Roxie Stinson was testifying:

> *Senator Wheeler.* Mr. Smith was one of Mr. Daugherty's partners was he not?
> *Senator Moses.* (interposing) Oh no.
> *Senator Wheeler.* I say, he was one of Mr. Daugherty's partners was he not?
> *Miss Stinson.* In law?
> *Senator Wheeler.* No, in crime. . . .[39]

By March 27, 1924, Wheeler, nonetheless, managed to disclose enough about Daugherty and his Department to allow Coolidge to ask for Daugherty's resignation. Coolidge's decision to delay his announcement until then minimized charges that he was acting hastily. To delay longer would have incited further criticism that Coolidge had bowed to the "old reactionary crooked crowd."[40] Daugherty's refusal to allow the committee access to certain files in the Justice Department gave the President the needed justification. He stated that while Daugherty was correct in not releasing information or documents that would be detrimental to the public interests, he would be able to form an independent judgment of Daugherty only after an impartial Attorney General presented the facts. Not intending to prejudge, Coolidge continued:

> I am not questioning your fairness or integrity. I am merely reciting the fact that you are placed in two positions, one your personal interest, the other your office of Attorney General, which may be in conflict. How can I satisfy a request for action in matters of this nature on the grounds that you, as Attorney General, advise against it, when you as the individual against whom the inquiry is directed necessarily have a personal interest in it?[41]

That Coolidge based his request on a technicality brought some criticism even from administration friends. Chief Justice Taft called it the letter of a lawyer. Inferring that Hughes had written the communication, Taft told his son, Bob, that the request might have stated a much stronger case.[42] In any case, the letter provided Daugherty with an opportunity to reply forcefully. On March 28, he complied with the President's request to resign, but pointed to the dangers of forcing a man from office for the reasons stated in the letter:

> Your suggestion that an attack upon a cabinet officer disqualifies him from further official service is a dangerous doctrine. Mr. President, all the pretended charges against me are false. But, whether true or false, if a member of the Cabinet is to be incapacitated or disqualified by the preferment of charges against him, no matter how malicious and groundless, and he is compelled to give up his responsible position and sacrifice his honor for the time being because of such attacks, no man in any official position is safe, and the most honorable, upright and efficient public servants could be swept from office and stable government by clamor.[43]

The leading newspapers, nevertheless, approved the President's action. Republican papers like the *New York Herald Tribune,* the *Boston Herald,* and the Philadelphia *Public Ledger* all supported the forced resignation. The independent *New York Evening Post* wrote that Daugherty "went not one day too soon." The *Detroit Free Press,* another independent, stated that "nearly everything that he did while in office tended to increase the impression that he was a mistake." Too, the *New York Times* reminded readers that "from the first day" Daugherty was "a gross misfit" as Attorney General. While some newspapers thought that Coolidge should have asked for Daugherty's resignation earlier, a few others felt that Coolidge had succumbed to political exigencies. Still the Republican *St. Louis Globe-Democrat* reluctantly approved: "It is with regret and relief that we view the resignation—regret that it was forced by unfair and outrageous methods; relief that the government has been relieved of an embarrassment that was a great burden." The Democratic New York *World* and the liberal *Nation* magazine more strongly criticized Coolidge. Such critics argued that the President had been entirely satisfied with Daugherty; by asking for his resignation now, he was denying Daugherty the opportunity to defend himself in the face of overwhelming—and sometimes unfair—criticism. Coolidge was, some asserted, also inviting further resignation demands on other cabinet members such as Mellon, whom some Democrats especially wished to investigate.[44]

Immediately after the resignation, Daugherty quickly left the Department in disgust, asking his secretary to gather his pipes and his other personal possessions. He then went by train to Atlantic City to rest and to visit his daughter, who was in the hospital. He unwound by strolling along the boardwalk with his son-in-law and by joking with reporters. To photographers, he mockingly warned: "Don't come too close boys, you'll be contaminated." Despite the banter, Daugherty gave the impression of being deeply wounded. "Sometimes," according to one reporter, "his smile would die away rather pathetically, as if he obtained only momentary relief from jestering."[45] He withheld any further public comment about his resignation; he would tell the "big story" in his own time and in his own way.

Daugherty privately contended that if the President had "kept his feet" twenty-four hours longer he would have had the "wolves about licked."[46] He continued to maintain that his official household and private life had always been pure, that he had never violated his oath of office, and that only in the "hellhole" of Washington could such injustice occur. He blamed Coolidge's timidity for his discharge, for it took a strong man to withstand a storm that had swept from the Justice Department to the White House. Even though he had suffered, he would do everything he could to reduce his personal resentment in order to prevent harm to the party, the country, or the President. "I can stand anything," Daugherty wrote Postmaster General Harry New, "and thrive on it."[47]

It was only a matter of time before Daugherty resumed his defense by linking the Wheeler Committee to a Communist conspiracy. On April 23, at a testimonial dinner held in Columbus, he stated that he resigned so as not to surrender to Wheeler and Brookhart the Department files, containing "abundant proof of the plans, purposes, and hellish designs of the Communist International." The two senators, "who spent last summer in Russia with their Soviet friends," were part of an effort to "capture, by deceit and design, as many members of the Senate . . . as possible and to spread throughout Washington City and in the cloakrooms of Congress a poison gas as deadly as that which sapped and destroyed brave soldiers in the late war. The enemy is at the gate," continued Daugherty; "he aims at nothing short of the overthrow of the institutions which are your protection and mine against tyranny." He had evidence to prove his assertions. All would be revealed when the country was "willing to hear and in condition to comprehend it," but "for protection of innocent persons much of it must now be withheld."[48]

Daugherty's overreaction was entirely in character. His conservative Ohio background and conspiratorial personality made him react strongly to radicalism, but his current focus on a Communist conspiracy appeared to be nothing more than political reprisal. Just as he had attempted to discredit Roxie Stinson, he now sought to do the same with the Wheeler Committee. In his correspondence with Solicitor General James Beck, however, he never mentioned the Communist threat. He instead referred to Wheeler and other opponents as "crooks" and "demagogues."[49]

Daugherty, in his Columbus address, also alluded to the Wheeler Committee's reliance on liars and criminals as witnesses. He accused it of nefarious activities, including the deploying of spies and the burglarizing of his Columbus home. Consequently he denied the authority of such an "unlawful inquisition" against a private American citizen. Despite having clamored for a hearing since the committee's inception, he now implied that he would have little to say. Throughout the speech, Daugherty's friends frequently applauded his criticism of the investigation and his extensive defense of his attorney generalship (before his resignation, according to Daugherty, the Department functioned more efficiently "than at anytime in the history of the government"). A telegram from Mrs. Harding was then read, reminding guests of Daugherty's loyal friendship for the Hardings.[50]

Four days later, six former departmental associates released a joint communication expressing admiration of Daugherty's courage, industry, and integrity in matters which came under their personal observation. They also complimented him on his kindness, courtesy, and cooperation. That such former colleagues as Beck, Mabel Willebrandt, A. T. Seymour, and Rush Holland would still publicly support him deeply touched Daugherty.[51]

On June 5, he finally announced that he would neither testify nor allow counsel to represent him before the committee. He justified this decision on three grounds: The committee had ample opportunity to learn about his official acts through assistants in the Department; asserting that no one had introduced any incriminating testimony "except by way of the grave," he declared the committee existed solely to blacken his reputation by depending upon unreliable witnesses instead of pursuing a fair and impartial inquiry into his official conduct as Attorney General; finally, he stated that the powers of the committee were "absolutely void and without constitutional authority."[52]

The basis for Daugherty's final assertion developed after his brother Mal had prevented John L. Phelon, a Senate committee accountant, from finishing his investigation of Daugherty's accounts at the Midland National Bank in Washington Court House. Cited for contempt of the Senate, Mal appealed to the courts and obtained from an obliging federal judge, A. M. J. Cochran of Kentucky, an opinion that the committee had exceeded its powers by compelling the testimony of outsiders. In June 1924, because of Daugherty's failure to testify and the action of the court, the Senate investigation came to an end. On June 5, by a 70 to 2 vote, the Senate voted to condemn the court ruling. Only Willis and Fess defended Judge Cochran, whose decision, they argued, was a matter which should be left to the courts.[53]

The investigation, although partly political, revealed that the Department of Justice had been an ineffective operation under Daugherty. The more than 3,000 pages of testimony did not fundamentally alter earlier criticism. In war-fraud and in other cases, unexplained delays, favoritism, and ineptness too often characterized the Department's performance. The investigation confirmed, however, that conditions had improved somewhat in Daugherty's last fifteen months in office. How much this had been due to his efforts is unknown. He had been ill for much of this period. Moreover, the investigation failed to implicate Daugherty in the oil and Veterans' Bureau scandals.

But the committee succeeded in disclosing that a criminal organization, of which Jess Smith was most prominent, existed in the household of the Attorney General. Likewise, it revealed that Daugherty and Burns abused their power by investigating and spying on opponents of the Department of Justice. Recent revelations, embarrassing to Daugherty, also remained unexplained. Phelon's incomplete inquiry at Washington Court House divulged at least $75,000 in uncancelled certificates of deposit bearing the name of H. M. Daugherty. Four other certificates of $5,000 each were endorsed by him. The sum was not huge, but in relation to his Ohio tax returns for 1920 and 1921, it required explanation. In 1920, Daugherty's liabilities were $27,000 and his assets $22,730, including 500 shares of Wright-Martin aircraft stock. (All of his assets were not calculated, since the tax exempted certain Ohio bonds and stocks, for example.) In 1921, he erased his entire indebtedness, increased his holdings in Wright-Martin fivefold, and showed assets of $12,445.[54] Daugherty's annual salary was now $12,000, but he and Smith shared expenses amounting to $50,000 per year.

In the midst of increasing questioning over Daugherty's integrity, the Republican national convention met in Cleveland, Ohio, on June 10. By then Coolidge's nomination was assured. He had overcome the progressive and old-guard opposition. Among the Ohio delegates pledged to his nomination was Daugherty. The former Attorney General had originally planned to play a major role in Coolidge's presidential campaign. After the March resignation, rumor persisted that he sought a seat in the Senate.[55] Partly to bolster his political position, he ran as a Coolidge-pledged delegate-at-large in the Ohio primary on April 29. Many of his Ohio friends and supporters voted only for Daugherty in order to assure him of an imposing vote. Daugherty still ran last among the seven elected Coolidge delegates-at-large.[56]

At the Republican convention, Daugherty was powerless and inconspicuous. Whenever not attending convention proceedings, he remained in his suite at the Hotel Winton, where the Ohio delegation established headquarters. To the press, he had nothing to say. On the evening of June 9, he did attend the caucus of the Ohio delegation. As he entered the headquarters, delegates applauded. It was obvious, however, that despite the efforts of friends, he lacked the votes to be selected chairman of the delegation. He took himself out of the contest and acceded to a harmony program in which Senator Willis was elected chairman and Fess was selected to the committee on resolutions. No agreement existed for the national committeeman election. Daugherty's and Willis's candidate, Louis H. Brush, the part owner of the Marion *Star,* lost by a 27 to 24 vote to Maurice Maschke, who was backed by Fess and Rud Hynicka, the retiring committeeman.[57] Clearly, Daugherty's political position in Ohio had lessened.

Meanwhile, the twenty-eight member Wisconsin delegation, following Senator Robert LaFollette's leadership, unsuccessfully sought a vote of condemnation against Daugherty and Albert Fall that would have excommunicated them from party councils and any position of party trust. That Daugherty even served as a delegate appalled Republican progressive Senator George W. Norris of Nebraska.[58] Daugherty's reply was a breakfast address to the Republican women of Ohio, in which he condemned the LaFollette, Norris, and Brookhart progressive Republicanism as being Communist-oriented. "The party will never be LaFolletteized," Daugherty asserted, "and this country will never be Russianized with the good women of the land taking their part, as they will."[59]

Afterward Daugherty viewed the presidential campaign as an opportunity to further refute his critics and vindicate his attorney generalship. In mid-August, he asked Solicitor General Beck to deliver speeches defending him and the Department of Justice. Beck replied that he was hesitant to comply because the Republican National Committee had not yet invited him to participate. More importantly, such a defensive posture would conflict with Coolidge's intent to focus on positive features of the administration, such as prosperity and stability. Besides, Coolidge's presidential opponents, John W. Davis of the Democratic party and LaFollette of the newly created Progressive party, in criticizing the Teapot Dome scandal, had made no specific accusations against the Department of Justice. Neither did Beck think it wise to respond to the Wheeler Committee investigation since it was "old" news, and a presidential race was a poor time to invoke such a "considerate judgment of issues of fact. Men who are disposed to be fair at other times," according to Beck,"are not fair in a Presidential campaign."[60]

Daugherty acknowledged Beck's good sense. He conceded that he had been overly sensitive. Nevertheless, "the failure of those who should defend the Department of Justice, and even defend me, is extremely trying to say the least and looks foolish to a man like me who has established, I think, the fact that he always stands with the other eight players in the ball game." Also, he reminded Beck that Davis, in his acceptance speech, attacked him and chided him in a later address. Daugherty expected more of such criticism. Consequently, he was confident that Beck and former associates would speak out. They should do so, he advised, only after seeking the approval of Attorney General Stone, whom Daugherty thought a fine man.[61]

Despite Daugherty's encouragement, Beck continued to advocate a waiting policy. He played down the rather "vague statements" that Davis had made about the Department, and suggested that no response be given to Wheeler, LaFollette's running mate, because "thoughtful people . . . have taken his measure." By early September, however, as Daugherty indicated, Davis, Wheeler, and LaFollette were "whacking away at the Department and everybody in the administration." Such attacks got on his nerves, he wrote. He again advised Beck to answer the charges.[62] Beck finally conceded to discuss the matter with Stone, who would have no personal objections to Beck's defending Daugherty's attorney generalship. But the present Attorney General agreed with Beck's assessment: it would be neither helpful to Daugherty nor to the Department (and Coolidge) to make such suggested speeches. There is no evidence that Beck ever did.[63] But he managed to retain Daugherty's friendship by his considerate and sympathetic expressions.

Because Coolidge spokesmen opposed a defensive campaign, Daugherty decided to conduct his own defense. There was, however, little that he could do. The few speeches he delivered received little newspaper attention. On September 19, he wrote Davis a public letter, asserting that "imperfect" newspaper reports had influenced the Democratic nominee's anti-Daugherty comments. He also claimed that witnesses who had testified against him had repudiated their testimony. He was primarily referring to Means, who was attempting to curry favor with the administration in the face of a recent conviction for liquor violations and a probable conviction for his role in the Glass Casket case. Daugherty, moreover, justified not appearing before the Senate investigation because of its irresponsible effort "to get Daugherty." He advised Davis that the real test was not political affiliation, but whether we are real Americans who oppose the overthrow of our government by leaders "fresh from a baptism of Bolshevism in lurid and suffering Russia."[64]

As it turned out, Daugherty in no way influenced the 1924 presidential election. Despite the Harding scandals, Coolidge won handily. He won because he convinced voters that he was personally honest and responsible for the emerging prosperity and for the restoration of integrity in the national government. Whatever edge the Democrats might have had regarding Republican corruption soon receded when it was determined that oil money had reached former Secretary of the Treasury William Gibbs McAdoo, the leading contender for the Democratic presidential nomination, in 1923. McAdoo had been an attorney for Edward Doheny who, it was revealed, had employed as counsel another former Wilson cabinet member, Secretary of the Interior Franklin K. Lane.[65]

After the election, Daugherty continually sought vindication. In late 1924 and early 1925, the Gaston Means and Thomas Felder Glass Casket trial became the vehicle. Daugherty wanted to testify not because he had information that could lead to their conviction, but because the trial would provide him with a podium on which he could relate his own story to the press. He testified that the defendants had never spoken to him about the Glass Casket matter and that he had talked with Means on only one occasion. Clearly he had little to add to the case. But he had much he wished to say about conditions in Washington, where "certain people were Hellbound and on the other side spellbound. It is time that the truth about some things ought to be told," he continued.[66] The trial judge informed him that the courtroom was not the proper place to tell his story.

Means's conviction on January 29, 1925, undoubtedly brought Daugherty some satisfaction. Next to Roxie, it was Means who most implicated Daugherty during the Wheeler Committee hearings. But because of his recent conviction and the Republican victory of 1924, Means obviously thought even more that he had backed the wrong horse. Less than three weeks following the trial, Means wrote Daugherty that he wished to meet in order to rectify the wrongs he had committed against him. He hinted that he could expose the sinister purposes of the Wheeler Committee.[67]

So anxious was Daugherty to vindicate himself that he wanted to see Means. He asked Special Assistant Attorney General Hiram Todd, who prosecuted Means, for advice. Todd advised Daugherty that because "Means is such an infernal liar it is well to have plenty of witnesses on hand when he talks—particularly when he carries on an interview which he has solicited."[68] Means and Daugherty met in New York. There, Means dictated an extended apologia for his life since the fall of 1921. He confessed to only one misdeed—he had injured Daugherty, for which he blamed Senator Wheeler. The latter, according to Means, had planned to frame Daugherty in order to create a political issue on which Senator LaFollette could emerge as the Republican nominee for president in 1924. If that failed, LaFollette would become a candidate on the Progressive ticket. The story seemed plausible in light of recent events. According to Means's biographer, Edwin Hoyt, Means had used one of his standard antics: He had twisted recent facts to play on the emotions of his intended victim.[69]

In his statement, Means also conceded that Roxie Stinson's testimony was prepared in advance. It was designed to smear the Harding administration, the judiciary system of the United States, and Calvin Coolidge. In short, it represented Wheeler's and Brookhart's efforts "to destroy, if possible, the government."[70] Daugherty accepted Means's statements, despite the latter's refusal to sign his name to them. He also attempted to persuade Todd to use the "evidence" in yet another trial against Means, this time for Means's forgery of Senator Brookhart's name.[71] The approaching trial might serve as a vehicle to expose the Wheeler-Brookhart Committee as well as a defense of Daugherty.

Todd, although sympathetic, resisted Daugherty's recommendations. Meanwhile he had begun an investigation of the Alien Property Custodian's activities in the Harding administration, which eventually implicated Daugherty, Jess Smith, and Alien Property Custodian Thomas Miller in the American Metal Company case. Ironically, part of the evidence had come out of the Means investigations and testimony at the Wheeler Committee hearings. As a result, Daugherty's efforts to vindicate his attorney generalship suffered a major reverse.

On Trial

THE American Metal Company case, in two grueling trials in 1926 and 1927, led to the near conviction of Harry Daugherty and the imprisonment of Alien Property Custodian Colonel Thomas W. Miller. Only the favorable vote of one juror kept Daugherty from becoming the first cabinet member to be imprisoned for maladministration. Such exposure profoundly embarrassed Daugherty and further convinced public opinion that he had been unethical, if not criminal. Daugherty's image rests as much on the American Metal Company related trials of 1926-1927 as on the earlier Wheeler investigation.

The United States government had become involved with the American Metal Company in 1918, when the Alien Property Custodian's Office seized as enemy property 49% of the company's stock owned by Metallgesellschaft and Metallbank of Germany.[1] One year later the stock was auctioned to American citizens. But then in March 1921, Richard Merton, a former captain in the German Army, president of Metallgesellschaft, and chairman of Metallbank, came to the United States, claiming $6,500,000 as compensation for the confiscation. Merton contended that the American seizure was illegal, since the stock in question had been transferred to a Swiss holding company, the *Société Suisse pour Valours de Metaux,* one month prior to the American declaration of war. In reality, the Merton family assigned its holdings in the American Metal stock to the Swiss holding company one year after the war had ended.

In 1920, the Mertons began legal action to obtain compensation from the United States government. John Foster Dulles of Sullivan and Cromwell, employed to look into the possibilities, quickly discerned that since the transfer to the Swiss concern occurred in 1919, the Mertons' legal position was shaky. His opinion was reinforced by Miller's first assistant, George N. Williams, whom Dulles had consulted.

Consequently, Merton searched for other help shortly after his arrival. He was introduced to John T. King, a Republican National Committeeman from Connecticut, General Leonard Wood's first 1920 preconvention manager, and a Daugherty colleague during the subsequent presidential campaign. In fact, Daugherty had informed Harding that "John . . . as you know [is] a good deal like me. He has his friends and his enemies."[2] Like Daugherty, King was forceful and aggressive—one who worried little about the legal niceties of a problem. No lawyer himself, he in fact advised Merton to rid himself of lawyers. The matter could best be handled by practical men. In April 1921, King introduced Merton to Jess Smith, who had just joined Attorney General Daugherty in Washington, D. C. He also arranged several meetings with Miller, a former congressman from Delaware and war hero, who now, as Alien Property Custodian, was friendly with Smith; and with subordinates from the Office of the Alien Property Custodian and the Department of Justice, which had responsibility for a claim's final approval. There was one session in New York at which Daugherty was probably present.[3]

After Miller's assistant, Williams, had advised Merton how to best prepare his claim, Merton returned to Europe in May to alter the documentation so that it appeared that the stock had been indeed transferred to a Swiss company just prior to the United States' entry into the war. The record now showed an oral transfer for 1917, which was confirmed in a November 1919 agreement. Once Merton had strengthened his claim, he came back to the United States in July, when he again met with King. They agreed to an arrangement whereby King would receive a $50,000 retainer as compensation for his continued service and a commission of 5% of whatever money he recovered in behalf of the Merton interests.

In the summer of 1921, the American Metal Company case received a favorable review from the Alien Property Custodian office despite some obvious discrepancies in its records. The claim was brought to the Justice Department late in July, where Henry Foster of the Alien Property Division was assigned to review it. Foster later testified that both Smith and King asked him to expedite this "praiseworthy" case. Smith informed him that the Attorney General was interested. But Foster refused to allow the claim because it did not come within the law.[4] It was therefore removed from him and reviewed by Adna R. Johnson, Jr., an Ohio family friend of Daugherty, who was in charge of the Justice Department's Alien Property Division. After finding some obvious inconsistencies, Johnson postponed action on the case while Merton again departed for Europe to doctor the records. Three days after Merton's return, Johnson accepted the claim without going beyond Merton's questionable documentation.[5] Quite likely, Smith had influenced him to do so. On September 21, Miller formally approved of the release. Two days later, Assistant to the Attorney General Guy D. Goff, who signed most Alien Property claims, acted in behalf of Daugherty, who later declared he knew nothing of the case. On September 26, Merton received Treasury checks and Liberty Bonds from the United States Treasury for $6,500,000. At a champagne dinner in a private room at the Ritz Hotel in New York shortly afterward, he gave King, Miller, and Smith gold cigarette cases as souvenirs. The next day he gave King a $50,000 check and $391,000 in Liberty Bonds; King in turn paid Miller $50,000, Smith $224,000 and himself $112,000 in bonds. The prosecution contended that Daugherty's share came out of Smith's excessive fee.

The American Metal Company decision was first questioned in June 1922, when Charles Calvert, a disgruntled Alien Property Custodian employee, complained to Harding that Daugherty and Miller had allowed claims for reasons other than a fair consideration of the facts. Among the cases he listed was the American Metal Company. Harding asked the two principals for an explanation, even though "it was possible that these were mere vagrant rumors for which there is no foundation."[6] Daugherty submitted a letter from Goff, contending that the American Metal case contained "the best prepared proof submitted to the Department in any of the thousands of claims presented as yet." The President must not have been satisfied, because he then assumed personal supervision of all alien property claims that exceeded $10,000.[7]

As was mentioned earlier, it was not until the investigations of Gaston Means (in whom Jess Smith confided) and Daugherty that the American Metal case received an extensive review. Its irregularities intrigued Wheeler and eventually Attorney General Stone. The latter assigned Special Assistant Hiram Todd to investigate the transaction. Todd traced $50,000 of the Liberty Bonds to Thomas Miller, and also determined that Jess Smith deposited some of his bonds in Mal Daugherty's Midland National Bank in Washington Court House, Ohio. Todd subsequently subpoenaed Mal Daugherty during a grand jury investigation in October 1925. He was dismissed after only twenty minutes of questioning. Moreover, Todd neglected to scrutinize the bank records to determine more about the late Smith's involvement. This was a major failing in an otherwise impeccable performance as a Special Assistant to the Attorney General. It is impossible to determine whether an obligation to Harry Daugherty for his appointment might have made Todd reluctant to pursue the Washington Court House matter, which might have proved embarrassing to the Daughertys. In any case, Todd's evidence led to the October 3 indictment of Miller and Merton and his European associates for conspiracy to defraud the government of the United States. King was not indicted, according to Todd, because "he was such an important and necessary witness for the Government."[8]

On December 1, Todd resigned from the case because of the requirements of his private law practice. Emory Buckner, United States Attorney for the Sourthern District of New York, took over the matter. Buckner, son of a Methodist minister and for years one of the most distinguished attorneys of New York City, decided, against the wishes of the Coolidge administration that had appointed him, to reopen and expand the inquiry to include former Attorney General Daugherty. That the Todd indictment was now under attack on the grounds that a charge of defrauding the United States government was barred by the statute of limitations provided Buckner with added justification for the new investigation.

In December 1925, under Buckner's direction, the grand jury reconvened. King was subpoenaed to give further testimony. So was Mal Daugherty after Buckner determined that four of the $10,000 Liberty Bonds that Smith had obtained from Merton had been converted into certificates of deposit and placed in Harry Daugherty's account at Mal's Washington Court House bank. One day before that transaction, the Department of Justice had processed transportation requests from Harry Daugherty and Smith for travel from Washington, D. C., to Columbus, Ohio. Additionally, Buckner's investigations had revealed that a $22,000 cashier's check from John King, derived from the sale of Liberty Bonds, was cashed at Mal's bank on the day of Harry Daugherty's arrival.[9]

When Mal was asked to submit the bank records to the grand jury, he testified that he had turned them over to his brother early in 1925 and that the latter, he believed, had burned them. Harry Daugherty at first refused to respond to such questions. He instead filed with Judge Thomas Thacher a written statement:

Having been personal attorney for Warren G. Harding for a period of several years, and before he was Senator from Ohio and while he was Senator, and thereafter until his death,

—And for Mrs. Harding for a period of several years, and before her husband was elected President and after his death,

—And having been attorney for the Midland National Bank of Washington Court House, O., and for my brother, M. S. Daugherty,

—And having been Attorney-General of the United States during the time that President Harding served as President,

—And also for a time after President Harding's death under President Coolidge,

—And with all of those named, as attorney, personal friend, and Attorney-General, my relations were of the most confidential character as well as professional,

—I refuse to testify and answer questions put to me, because: The answer I might give or make and the testimony I might give might tend to incriminate me.[10]

As a result, on Buckner's advice, the grand jury cited Daugherty for contempt of court. Thacher then directed him to answer questions that were put to him. Daugherty thereupon revealed only that Mal gave him the ledgers, which he admitted destroying after Todd had indicated that he did not wish to see them.[11]

After additional investigation, Buckner asked for an indictment that included Daugherty and King as well as Miller. He also rescinded the Todd indictment against Merton and the other Europeans. In return he obtained Merton's cooperation. On May 7, 1926, the grand jury responded, charging Daugherty, Miller, and King with conspiracy to deprive the government of the honest services of Miller and Daugherty. A three-year statute of limitation prevented the charge of bribery. Under the new indictment, the government did not have to prove that the Merton claim was bad. It only had to show that it had not been properly considered. A similar indictment had been obtained in 1906, Buckner remembered, against government subordinates in the Department of Agriculture, who provided advance information on cotton crops for the purpose of permitting certain New York brokers to profit. "Embezzlement of loyalty" was how Buckner characterized such activity.[12]

Throughout the weeks preceding and following the indictment, Daugherty, of course, was very anxious and worried. To James Beck he confided that "this man Buckner has done a horrible thing." Initially he attempted to get Buckner to drop the investigation. In April, although aware of the delicacy of the matter, he asked Beck and John Crim of the Department of Justice to contact Henry Wise, former United States Attorney for the Southern District of New York, who "is about the only man that [sic] can talk to Mr. Buckner."[13] Daugherty also had his attorney, Hoke Donithen, inform Buckner that any investigation of Daugherty's financial affairs might unearth information detrimental to former President Harding that Daugherty was pledged to conceal. Buckner assured him that he had no interest in the former President, but as he proceeded with the indictment, the Daugherty people charged that Buckner was using the case to embarrass Harding and to advance his own political ambitions.[14] Daugherty finally employed Max Steuer of New York, one of the most sought-after trial lawyers in the country. For years, this slightly built man with gimlet eyes earned more than $1,000,000, defending such renowned people as promoter Tex Rickard and such rascals as Boo Boo Huff of the Philadelphia underworld.

But Steuer was no help in solving Daugherty's family problems, which were worsening. On September 24, 1925, he had his thirty-seven-year-old son committed to the Lima State Hospital for the Criminally Insane for "psychopathic constitution enhanced by a life of dissipation." This was apparently a result of Draper's recent heavy drinking and forging of several checks for over $1,000 each against the family accounts. Initially reluctant to visit or to write Draper, Daugherty continually advised the hospital to postpone his son's release.[15] Draper had caused him enough trouble and, in the most critical time of Daugherty's life, he wanted his son out of the way. Daugherty was especially concerned that Draper might again become a burden before the trial. Already, an actress sweetheart of Draper's, Pearl Baremore, was writing an embarrassing thirteen-day serial in the New York *Evening Graphic* of their lengthy and torrid love affair which, she charged, Daugherty was trying to dissolve by incarcerating Draper.[16]

Daugherty's letters to Dr. Charles H. Clark, Superintendent of Lima State Hospital, clearly reflected ambivalent feelings toward Draper—feelings of guilt and devotion as well as resentment, suspicion, and denial of responsibility. Daugherty frequently remarked of Draper's incarceration that he "did not put him there, nor did [he] contribute to the cause of his being there." Consequently, "there is no reason why this boy should have any feeling against me." He recalled that Draper contacted him only when he "wanted something," but "the poor boy never thought of me when he was going the pace and associating with people who were making him worse." On another occasion, when Draper requested additional clothing, Daugherty responded that he would not need "his dress suit, frock coat and his high hat and high flying clothes." Nevertheless, he wrote Clark, "my affection for him has never diminished, notwithstanding his shortcomings and mistakes. . . . I would do anything in the world to help him." And after reluctantly agreeing to Draper's probationary release in June 1926, he confided:

> Let us give this boy the fairest chance anyone ever had. Then our hands will be clean and tho our hearts will be broken if it does not turn out as we hope, the consciousness that we have done the fair thing by the boy will ultimately heal the wound, if we can live through it.

As the trial neared, Daugherty now believed that it might be to his advantage to have his son testify. Draper had assured him of his good intentions, but instead of taking a job in Detroit as he had promised, he went to New York City, where he joined Pearl Baremore. Daugherty was beside himself, suspecting that an intoxicated Draper might embarrass him during the trial. Any such behavior "will help to kill me," Daugherty wrote Clark.[18] In July, Daugherty visited Draper for three hours in New York, where the latter assured him that he was selling insurance and could have a successful business if his father provided financial assistance. This Daugherty characteristically was willing to do. "New York," Daugherty rationalized to Clark, "is as good a place as any, . . . for there are better opportunities there, . . . and . . . more people . . . who care nothing about what a man has done in the past, than anywhere else. In New York they only figure on what they can get off a man now." By the time of the trial, however, Draper was once again "hopelessly in debt."[19]

The trial began on September 7, 1926, in New York City. By then the third defendant, John T. King, had died after suffering a nervous breakdown and pneumonia undoubtedly brought on by the indictment. Buckner began his opening statement by stressing the weakness of the Merton claim and outlining the relationship of Merton with King, Miller, and—through Smith—Daugherty, which led to the speedy approval of the claim and the Liberty Bond payment. Then he traced some of the Liberty Bonds and their coupons through brokerage houses and banks. Among the witnesses he called were Merton, who described conferences with King, Miller, Smith, and various assistants; and Mal Daugherty who testified that his brother burned the bank records after having taken them to the "Shack" where he was unable to "make anything out of them."[20]

During the defense, Miller's attorney, Colonel William S. Rand, argued that Miller's assistant, Williams, had actually passed on the claim for the Office of Alien Property Custodian after barely consulting with Miller. Upon cross-examination, Williams admitted that he had never before approved a transaction based on an oral transfer, and also conceded that the claim was weak. Goff, who signed the claim for the Justice Department, testified that he had never discussed the matter with Daugherty. Unlike Williams, however, Goff, now a Republican senator from West Virginia, insisted that the claim was justifiable.

Of the two defendants, Miller's position seemed the weaker because of his more direct involvement and because Buckner was able to trace the Liberty Bonds directly to Miller's personal accounts. Given the collusion between Miller and King that Merton and others had revealed, Miller's defense that the Liberty Bonds could have come from another source was not too convincing. Conversely, after tracking Liberty Bonds and uncancelled checks from Smith and King to the Midland National Bank in Washington Court House, Buckner could not prove how much went into Harry Daugherty's account, because of the latter's destruction of the ledgers. In summation, Steuer contended that

> it was in some mad, lone moment that Harry Daugherty destroyed these sheets. They had been produced before the Todd grand jury in October. The prosecutor had said he didn't want to see them. They went back to Ohio. What happened? Harry Daugherty took them to that little shack of his and his brother's outside Washington Court House. Harry Daugherty, yesterday sought after by all the land, today hounded; a broken man; his life spent; his best friend, the President, dead; his close friend Jess Smith, gone, a suicide; his wife gone; his political career over. He went to the shack—and those whom the gods would destroy they first make mad. So this lonesome old man, alone with those records, destroyed them. He thought of the . . . barking dogs, the yelpers who wanted to know how the funds were used in the 1919-1920 campaign of President Harding. He said to himself: 'They

will never see them. They will never see them.' And he destroyed the sheets they wanted.[21]

That at least $40,000 of Smith's cancelled Liberty Bonds had found their way into Daugherty's account could not be denied. But Daugherty's attorneys and his brother explained that circumstance. They asserted that, as Daugherty's financial agent, Smith had owed $60,000 from money he had collected during the 1920 campaign. In order to make up some of the deficit, Smith gave Mal, just prior to Smith's suicide in May 1923, five $10,000 Liberty Bonds that were a part of the American Metal transaction. Not knowing that the bonds were derived from that source, Mal explained that in November 1923 he sold four of them. On December 21, he issued certificates of deposit for $49,165 to Harry Daugherty's personal account. According to Mal, Harry had never seen either the original bonds or the certificates and did not hear of the $49,000 transaction until June 1924. It was then that the defendant converted the certificates into cash.[22] But Mal neglected to explain why they had never turned over the money to the Republican national or state committees.

Like Miller, Daugherty did not take the stand in his own defense. Again, he intimated that in some dark way he would betray the confidence of the late President or Mrs. Harding by testifying. To some people Daugherty's argument seemed plausible. Too many rumors circulated about Harding's personal life, his part in scandals, and the nature of his death. In 1926, for example, Samuel Hopkins Adams's thinly disguised novel, *Revelry,* depicted the President as a degenerate who ended his life by his own hand. Taft, for one, felt that Daugherty's refusal to testify "was made rather to save Harding's memory than to save himself." Although he still thought Daugherty personally honest, Taft conceded that his destruction of evidence was damning.[23]

Moreover, even the jury was divided. For three days and three nights, Judge Julian Mack kept it in deliberation. But the deadlock was not resolved. As the final votes were announced, 10-2 for conviction of Miller and 7-5 for conviction of Daugherty, Daugherty nursed an inflamed eye with a handkerchief, as he had throughout most of the trial. But Mal Daugherty was unable to repress his happiness at the outcome. He shook hands with members of the jury, slapped reporters on the back, and attempted to dance the Charleston. Nonetheless, Harry Daugherty professed to be saddened for not being acquitted. Steuer conceded that Daugherty's failure to take the stand might have hurt him as did his destruction of evidence. But, he persisted, "if the jury knew the real reason for destroying the ledger sheets they would commend rather than condemn Mr. Daugherty."[24]

Later several jurors told Buckner's assistants that all of them would have been ready to find the defendants guilty of accepting bribes, but that some did not believe that the prosecution had met the standards of proof for such a highly technical indictment, made more so by Judge Mack's complicated rendition to the jury. Buckner later wrote that "we have had trouble before with jurymen in considering a charge of conspiracy. Conspiracy sounds like a horrible crime to them and they think of it in terms of a subterranean gunpowder plot."[25]

Nevertheless, after consulting with such legal associates as Felix Frankfurter, Buckner pressed for a new trial. The date was set for December 1926 and eventually rescheduled for February. The announcement of the retrial was especially disturbing to Daugherty, who was emotionally exhausted from the first ordeal. He wrote that the holidays were especially sad for him. He managed to travel to Washington Court House to see his ninety-year-old mother and visit the cemetery and then returned home where "a man and his wife . . . came to spend Christmas with me, and made the best of everything."[26] Shortly after the holidays he received another setback when the United States Supreme Court announced the reversal of the Cochran decision, which prevented the Senate from acting upon Mal Daugherty's refusal to testify before the Wheeler Committee in 1924. Daugherty now was concerned that the Senate could "yank [Mal] before it and give him some sort of punishment" or refer the matter to the United States Attorney for investigation. "This," he wrote Beck, "would break his heart, and mine, and be a terrible thing on the banks and on him." In another letter, he said: "I am just about at the end of my string." He asked Beck to act as his attorney. The latter declined because the case originated while he had been Solicitor General.[27]

Meanwhile, the second trial began on February 7. Because of Max Steuer's illness and other trial commitments, his long-time partner, Harold H. Corbin, now represented Daugherty. Miller too employed new counsel—the aggressive young Aaron Sapiro of Chicago. The trial judge was John C. Knox, a former New York assistant district attorney.

After reviewing the nature of the claim and the reasons the Alien Property Custodian and the Attorney General were involved, Buckner, in his opening statement, focused on the $391,000 in Liberty Bonds that Merton had paid King and his associates for their abbreviated service. In more considerable detail than the first trial, he traced the disbursement of these bonds. This approach, which the press characterized as "inferential," was more damaging to Daugherty because it tied him more closely to the payoff:

> $5,000 of the $391,000 we shall not be able to trace for you. That leaves $386,000. Thomas W. Miller . . . got $50,000, traced right either directly or through the proceeds, into his personal brokerage accounts in Wilmington and New York City. That leaves . . . 336.
>
> Divide 336 by three and we get 112—one-third. And $112,000 of these identical Liberty Bonds will be traced . . . by documents into John T. King's

possession. That leaves 224. And this [224] we will trace for you either by the bonds themselves or by coupons where the bonds cannot be found . . . to Harry Daugherty and the late Jess W. Smith.

[W]e will show by documents and records that four of these bonds, or $40,000, turn up in the Daugherty bank . . . put into certificates of deposit to Harry M. Daugherty himself.

We will show you that just a few days after Merton and King walked out of that office, . . . on [October 13, 1921] King sells $24,000 . . . and sends a check to the Daugherty Bank. [The individual ledger sheets for October 13 and 14, 1921, which possibly contained the entry in the account of Harry Daugherty, Buckner revealed, had mysteriously disappeared. Two Justice Department telephone operators also attested that Daugherty had been in telephone contact with King throughout this period.][28] That leaves $160,000. We will produce . . . out of Mal Daugherty's pocket . . . one ten-thousand bond. That leaves 150. We will show by bankers' and brokers' records in Washington, D.C., that Jess Smith, through his account . . . sold over the counter, for raising cash, $40,000. That leaves 110.

[W]e will show you that the interest on that $110,000 went to Jess Smith. The next coupon date, six months later . . . John T. King again deposited the interest coupons on one hundred thousand, without the ten . . . and he sent a check . . . [and] we find the interest on one hundred thousand dollars' worth of bonds credited to Harry Daugherty's special account. [W]e will show you that on those one hundred thousand dollar bonds . . . no coupons have been presented at all for something like three years . . . since the newspaper publicity, through the Wheeler Committee, concerning this case. [F]or the last three years, those bonds have been in hiding.[29]

Consequently, Daugherty's counsel decided to defend. Among the character witnesses Daugherty called upon were Beck and Assistant Attorney General Mabel Willebrandt, ironically now one of Buckner's bosses. Daugherty asked Willebrandt to attest that he had never instructed his assistants to render any decision that contradicted their judgment and that Jess Smith had never interfered with departmental business. "I hate to cause you any trouble," he continued, ". . . but this may be an important phase of the trial this time."[30] Beck "gladly" also testified. He not only believed in Daugherty's innocence, but claimed that he would "have felt small indeed if, having shared the honors of his administration, I had not been willing to help him in his hour of trial." Afterward Corbin wrote Beck that whenever Daugherty tried to talk of the loyalty and sacrifice of his former associates, his efforts ended in tears.[31]

Both Beck and Willebrandt had testified that Daugherty had permitted his assistants to run their own departments, implying that assistants had decided the American Metal Company case. More essential to Daugherty was that former Assistant to the Attorney General Goff reiterated how he had given the Department's final approval to the case. Goff, as in the first trial, explained that indeed he had done so after a careful examination of the papers. Unfortunately for Goff, Buckner now produced a copy of Goff's grand jury testimony, which he referred to in the cross-examination after he got Goff to agree that, in his official capacity as assistant, he had seen 50 to 75 visitors daily, signed some 100 to 150 letters a day, and approved close to 800 claims of the Alien Property Custodian from March 15, 1921, to September 23, 1921, the date the claim was allowed.[32]

Buckner questioned whether Goff had really examined the papers in the American Metal case. Goff responded that he had, but Buckner reminded that Goff had testified before the 1925 grand jury that only the facts were stated to him prior to his approval. Rather than examining the records, he had relied on the opinion of Adna Johnson of his department and a letter from the Alien Property Custodian. Goff, obviously flustered, tried to correct that testimony by stating that he had looked at some of the papers. But as Buckner persisted, Goff dug himself an even deeper hole.[33] Most likely the inconsistency in Goff's testimony was due to his recent status as United States senator. He did not want to admit in open court, as he had stated in the privacy of a grand jury hearing, that he had signed a claim without examining the records. To have said this during the September 1926 trial would have probably ensured his election defeat that November. For that reason, perhaps, the Republican Buckner did not pursue the issue.

Martin Mayer also suggests a less probable explanation for Goff's actions. At the time of the grand jury investigation, Goff was in danger of being linked to a conspiracy involving alleged fraud, provided that the government could first prove that he had looked at the questionable claim. It was in his interest then, to testify that he had not examined the papers. By September 1926, of course, he was in the clear and could say that he had scrutinized the record.[34]

Goff's testimony probably worked against Daugherty and Miller because Goff's credibility was now so much under attack. Nonetheless, neither defendant testified. In his summation, Corbin argued that Buckner had prosecuted Daugherty to further his own political ambitions—but he was not going to "make himself Governor over Harry Daugherty's grave," Corbin warned. Corbin also blamed Jess Smith for Daugherty's troubles. Smith's suicide, he maintained, resulted from a "voice of conscience crying in his heart." He concluded that Daugherty would never go to the penitentiary, for "a conviction would kill him on the spot."[35]

After Buckner's nine-and-one-half hour summation, in which he contended that Daugherty and Miller had defrauded the government of the honest, faithful, and impartial performance of their duties, the case went to the jury on March 1. For three days it disagreed. At 11:00 P.M. on the final day, Judge Knox received word that the jury wished to see him. He quickly returned to the courtroom area, where he saw Daugherty. "He was walking slowly" Knox later recalled, "with his head down. He did not even look up as I passed him, and I noticed how old he looked. One leg, too, was dragging. He would take one step, and then drag the other foot forward. Step. Drag. Step. Drag. And all the time his head was down— his eyes on the floor."[36]

The foreman of the jury informed the judge that the jury had convicted Miller in one hour on three ballots, but it could not reach agreement on Daugherty. The first vote against him was 7 to 5 and it went to 11 to 1 where it remained for 48 hours. Later it was revealed that the dissenting juror was a florist at the Hotel Astor who had insisted that he had not been convinced "beyond a reasonable doubt." In an autobiography, published in 1940, Judge Knox admitted that the evidence against Daugherty was "not conclusive."[37] Knox himself had persuaded Buckner to nol-pros the indictment.

Afterward Buckner contended that the role Smith had played was the most vital single point in his case. Buckner believed that the evidence, including Daugherty's written instructions to his accounting office, indicated that Smith was an extension of the Attorney General. The witness who disputed that interpretation was Mabel Willebrandt of whom Buckner was especially critical. "Perhaps you had assumed that she was only called as a 'character witness,'" he wrote Justice Harlan Stone.

> On the contrary, she sought vigorously to belittle the functions of the late Jess W. Smith, contrary to all the undisputed evidence. . . . The episode is so interesting and so shocking that I thought you might like to know the actual fact. Her appearance on the witness stand, without any communication with me, the tone of her testimony and attitude constitute an extraordinary performance.[38]

Upon hearing the verdict on March 4, Daugherty spoke for the first time in his own defense:

> May it please the court, perhaps I am taking a liberty few men could take. I am the only Attorney General, I believe, except one that has ever been tried for a felony. I am innocent of this charge. I am grateful to the court for its courteous consideration during the performance of its duty, which was not easy.

His brother then grasped his hand, and the two left the courtroom. In another room Daugherty broke down in tears. He said that he intended to return to Columbus to resume his law practice.[39] Miller, meanwhile, was sentenced to eighteen months in the Atlanta Penitentiary and fined $5,000.

For the most part, the press was critical of the Daugherty verdict. According to the *New York Evening Post,* "Before the bar of public opinion, Daugherty and Miller both stand condemned, whatever the legal verdict may be." Similar comment came from the *Cleveland Plain Dealer, Milwaukee Journal,* and a dozen other dailies. The *St. Louis Post-Dispatch,* meanwhile, commented that "vengeance upon Daugherty is of little importance, but the warning of what he suffered for his evil-doing has been made with an emphasis that nobody can mistake. The country has Mr. Buckner to thank for that." Expressing a minority view, the *Cincinnati Enquirer* contended that we too "falsely accuse public officials and drag their names through the mire of scandal and their persons through the courts."[40]

In retrospect, the decision of the court was not so unreasonable. While Daugherty was undoubtedly the knowing recipient of dishonest money, the evidence that he unlawfully, willfully and knowingly conspired to defraud the government of his services, as the indictment charged, was not proved beyond a reasonable doubt. He was not as directly linked with the conspiracy as Miller. Nor is it possible to prove that Jess Smith had acted as Daugherty's agent, or that Daugherty knew fully of his activity in 1921, despite all that we now know about their relationship.

Nonetheless, it is still difficult to ignore Daugherty's unwillingness to testify and his destruction of evidence. His use of Harding to justify the burning of the bank ledgers appears to have been an act of expediency and desperation at the former President's expense. At the worst, such records could have revealed nothing more than what Daugherty had already implied—that Harding was somehow involved in personal or political indiscretions which necessitated the use of political funds.[41] Surely, though, the records would have better revealed whether Daugherty had conspired with King and Smith. This was the only concern of Buckner, who expressed no desire to probe into a former President's conduct.

What was so significant about the Daugherty verdict was not that one juror had voted for acquittal but that eleven had favored conviction. Because vindication had been so overwhelmingly denied, Daugherty received an enormous psychological blow. For the rest of his life, he would seek almost obsessively to restore his damaged reputation.

[XV]

Retirement and Reputation

AFTER the trial, Daugherty returned to his large house on East Town Street in Columbus where, excluding his attorney generalship, he had lived since 1904. There he remained until the mid-1930s, when he moved to the Seneca Hotel. He resumed his law practice, which he continued until retirement in 1935. In Columbus, personal disaster quickly followed public misfortune. Within a five-year period, Daugherty's son, son-in-law, and mother died. Draper's sudden death in 1930 following an appendectomy was an especially severe blow. After his release from Lima State Hospital, Draper had divorced his estranged wife, Jean, and married Estelle Sturges, the former wife of Preston Sturges, a New York perfume manufacturer. Because of his apparent rehabilitation, Draper's last three years had provided a source of comfort to his father, making his death even more difficult to accept. Daugherty's only surviving child, Emily, verged on insanity and was an addict as a result of drugs she had taken for a female disorder.[1] Additionally, the depression and improper banking practices brought about the collapse of his brother's Ohio State Bank, a consolidation of his Midland and Commercial Banks with the Fayette Bank. Mal Daugherty was convicted in 1931 of misapplication of the bank's funds, false entries, concealment of loans, embezzlement, and deceiving the state examiners. A reversal on appeal saved him from imprisonment, but it could not protect him from the ostracism of the community, which had lost its savings. Mal was so despised that while walking along the streets of Washington Court House he looked into the store windows to keep from being pointedly ignored by people he had known well.[2]

Harry Daugherty's setbacks were intensified by the success of some of his opponents. In 1929, Herbert Hoover became President, and Walter Brown served as Postmaster General while also controlling the Republican party in Ohio. Adding to Daugherty's discomfort was the scathing picture writers painted of Harding and his official family. By 1930, Daugherty contemplated publishing his own account to counteract alleged misrepresentations, to "leave a good name," and to offset his trial expenses of the mid-1920s. The first two explanations seemed to represent the primary motivations. Unquestionably, he felt maligned by the press and other commentators, particularly regarding his role in the Teapot Dome scandal, to which he was still erroneously linked. The press "covered me with oil for so many years," Daugherty quipped, "that I had to quit smoking because I was afraid to light a match for fear of becoming ignited."[3] Also, the recent family tragedies might have made him more aware of impending death as he passed the age of seventy, making it more imperative that vindication not be deferred.

Still, not wanting to write about himself, he preferred that a respected and a friendly source undertake the task. He asked Harding's Solicitor General James Beck to write "a story about Harding some and me some and much about the Dept. [of Justice]."[4] After Beck declined and President Hoover delivered his long-delayed dedication address for the Harding Memorial at Marion on June 17, 1931, Daugherty decided to act. Daugherty was on the platform as a trustee of the Harding Memorial Association when Hoover declared to a silent crowd of 20,000:

> Here was a man whose soul was seared by a great disillusionment. We saw him gradually weaken, not only from physical exhaustion, but also from mental anxiety. Warren Harding had a dim realization that he had been betrayed by a few of the men whom he had believed were his devoted friends. It was later proved in the courts of the land that these men had betrayed not alone the friendship and trust of their staunch and loyal friend but they had betrayed their country. That was the tragedy of the life of Warren Harding.

Daugherty was so aroused that he immediately employed former novelist Thomas Dixon, the author of such racist works as *The Leopard's Spots, Birth of a Nation,* and the *Klansman,* to help refute such accusations. In the process, Daugherty characteristically overcompensated, as he not only challenged certain falsehoods but distorted certain truths as well. The book began with the admonition that Hoover's words did not apply to Daugherty because "no charge against me was ever proven in any court and Mr. Hoover knew this."[5]

The *Inside Story of the Harding Tragedy* was more an attempt to rehabilitate Daugherty than a truthful revelation of the Harding presidency—its stated objective. It revealed, as did Daugherty's correspondence, both an unconscious and a conscious concern that Daugherty be remembered as a man of importance and of integrity. In many instances, self-vindication came at the expense of veracity and of Harding, even though he defended Harding's personal integrity and his presidency. Daugherty was probably more responsible than any other person for creating the fictitious caricature of Harding as a negligible politician, a submissive personality, and one totally dependent upon Daugherty.[6] So persuasive was he in asserting that he had guided Harding from political oblivion that he influenced Charles Hard, a Harding lieutenant, who had best understood Daugherty's role prior to January 1919. In 1939, however, Hard remarked that in 1916 Daugherty had been the brains behind a movement to nominate Harding in 1920.[7] By 1939, the Daugherty myth had won acceptance.

Daugherty devoted a major portion of his book to justifying his service as Attorney General. No admissions of poor judgment or misguided acts marred his lofty self-appraisal. He denied knowledge of Jess Smith's illicit operations until just prior to his suicide, and made no explanation as to why Smith had an office in the Department.[8] Daugherty's analysis of his official acts was no more enlightening. He defended his 1922 railroad injunction, for example, on the grounds that it prevented a communist revolution and dismissed opponents as communists, self-seekers, or avengers.[9] Immediately prior to the book's publication, Daugherty wrote Hard that while Harding's administration had been a success, "I was right effective myself, when my work is examined."[10] He followed this premise unequivocally in the *Harding Tragedy*.

Despite mostly unfavorable reviews, Daugherty thought the book a colossal success in curbing the falsehood of the times. He claimed over 5,000 favorable letters and telegrams in addition to hundreds of splendid editorials. Daugherty took full credit for this literary achievement, confiding that he had destroyed Dixon's inaccurate and sensational first draft and had written the book himself. His secretary, Katherine Carroll, expressed his difference with Dixon in another way. Dixon, she wrote, "did not always recognize the importance of the political angle."[11]

Daugherty implied afterward that he had not dealt sufficiently with his enemies. In July 1933, he wrote Charles Hilles that he had "a few debts to settle which I always settle no matter what kind they are." He went on to say that he was not friendly to Hoover and Brown:

> Hoover does not know much that is worth anything to the country and he could never work with anyone but fellows like Walter Brown. Brown never got anywhere in this State until Hoover put him on the map. Both he and Hoover were disloyal to Coolidge and I know they were disloyal to Harding. I could say so for publication and prove it if necessary.[12]

Although he never published again, Daugherty influenced others who wrote on the Harding period. In 1932, former Postmaster General Harry New relied on Daugherty to help prepare an article for the *Saturday Evening Post* on the 1920 Republican National Convention. "The Senatorial Oligarchy" was one of the first refutations of the influence of the senatorial cabal at that convention. Much of the statistical material that New incorporated came from Daugherty. While the article was a fairly accurate analysis of the division and lack of influence among the senatorial delegates, it was not until 1955 that an historian first discounted the "Smoke-filled Room" theory.[13]

Much more important to Daugherty's reputation was journalist Mark Sullivan's contemplated sixth volume of *Our Times: The United States, 1900-1925.* By early 1935, Sullivan had already completed his account of the Harding era. In order to verify its accuracy, he sent galley proofs to several leading participants. Daugherty found much of the draft totally unacceptable. "He said some terrible things about Harding," Daugherty later wrote, "and he drew a most unpleasant picture of me."[14] Daugherty contended that Sullivan had obtained his information from people who either depended on their imagination or their prejudice. Sullivan's errors were compounded by the fact that he "was a Progressive and never got over it."[15]

Sullivan wanted to visit Daugherty in Florida to discuss the critique. Unable to see him there, he came to Columbus upon Daugherty's return. In June 1935, Sullivan spent several days with Daugherty, whom he found "still salient, self-reliant, [and] defiant of any standards except his own." During the visit, he acceded to many of Daugherty's recommendations. Although Sullivan refused to change some portions of his text, Daugherty was satisfied because "what he finally wrote about Harding was not one-one-hundredth part as bad as his first draft."[16] Moreover, Daugherty insured that Sullivan made him the master of Harding's fortunes. Sullivan's final interpretation of that relationship was most flattering to Daugherty. He credited him with having directed Harding's political destiny from the first moment that Harding entered the political arena, and with having almost single-handedly pushed Harding into the White House. Always, Daugherty dominated their association.[17] Sullivan was also charitable in assessing his years as Attorney General. He reasserted Daugherty's claim that he had unwillingly accepted the cabinet post to protect Harding from the crooks. Conceding that Daugherty had been unable to protect his own Department, Sullivan, after study of the Daugherty investigations, could not believe that any dishonest money had ever reached him.[18]

Daugherty likewise attempted to sway would-be biographers of Harding. Early in 1932, Allan Nevins published a critical article on Harding for the *Dictionary of American Biography.*[19] The essay incensed Daugherty, who must have thought of Nevins in his Columbus Kiwanis Club address of November 2, 1932 when he said: "Men's tongues wag too freely in spreading false gossip about public officials."[20] Nevins's essay also angered Ray Baker Harris, a Library of Congress employee, who believed that historians had unfairly abused Harding.[21] He vowed to write an impartial biography based on existing source materials and the testimony of Harding's contemporaries. Harris consequently sought Daugherty's recollections, and so did Cyril Clemens, Mark Twain's nephew, who desired to compose a sympathetic account of Harding's life.

Neither Harris nor Clemens succeeded. Clemens failed to publish because his manuscript was too eulogistic, and death eventually overtook the meticulous Harris after thirty years of awaiting access to the Harding correspondence from the Harding Memorial Association at Marion.[22] What makes both Harris and Clemens significant is their extensive correspondence with Daugherty, which is presently available to researchers. In supplying them with information, Daugherty continued to exaggerate his influence. Harding, he wrote Harris, "appealed to me for advice more than to any or all other men put together in the more than twenty years of our intimate acquaintance and association." After Harris suggested that he intended to visit Marion, Daugherty recommended that he see him first, since "there are certain things that no one else can tell you and I want to help keep you straight on some matters." Daugherty also wished to read his manuscript "so that any mistakes that might have crept in may be corrected."[23] Obviously, Daugherty was deeply concerned about his role in history.

By the end of 1938, with the assistance of Harris, Daugherty decided to write his memoirs because:

> When the world is through with me there will be dug up and hashed up a lot of stuff that will be mostly unreliable, and it might afford my friends some comfort and do justice to what small family I have left, if I were to leave a record of many things that no one else knows about.

But Harris, Daugherty added, must first study the story and become familiar "with my theory of it." Daugherty became more determined to publish after reading William Allen White's *Puritan in Babylon,* a Coolidge biography that treated Daugherty in critical fashion.[24] In April 1939, Daugherty was so shocked to hear that former muckraker Samuel Hopkins Adams was also writing a book on the Harding period that he asked Harris to request that Adams's publisher, Houghton Mifflin, suspend publication. Daugherty acknowledged that Adams had a good reputation, but he argued that Adams was trying to rehabilitate himself for his mediocre novel of 1926, *Revelry,* which critically portrayed a thinly-disguised President Harding. In any case, he felt that Adams would not write a favorable account.[25]

Daugherty's last years were not always consumed with the past. Even though he tried to suggest otherwise, he was a man of some wealth. On his return to Columbus in 1924, he retained both his secretary and his chauffeur. In 1928, he toured England and Ireland. In the winters he departed for Sarasota, Florida, where he rested at the scenic Gulf Inn and the Hotel El Vernona. There, he enjoyed a circle of friends, including the famous defense attorney Clarence Darrow, newspaper publisher and a former political enemy Charles Knight, and former president of the United Press Karl Bickel. In the summers Daugherty often rested at the Grand Hotel on Mackinac Island in the Straits of Mackinac. In the months that he stayed in the Columbus area, he frequently resided at the "Shack" on weekends, where he cultivated a garden and relaxed. Yet occasional loneliness and dissatisfaction persisted. To his friend Harry New, he confessed that living without the companionship of a good woman was a hard life. He admitted that he should have remarried. But "having one who never had a fault," he "was afraid of the chance after she was called." Besides, he added, "I can't recommend myself."[26]

While his political withdrawal preceded his legal retirement by more than ten years, Daugherty retained an interest in politics. In the 1930s, he remained a staunch Republican, even though he complained to former Democratic senator Atlee Pomerene of Ohio of past Republican mistreatment: "I would have to say that my party was about the worst— except the Progressives—and . . . I can say the Democrats treated me with more respect and consideration . . . , but I only knew the best among the Democrats, and I was compelled at times to come in contact with the worst among Republicans."[27] He privately criticized President Franklin D. Roosevelt's experimentation in unsound theories and dismissed the New Deal as a "quagmire of socialism." He had characterized Hoover's defeat in 1932 as the destruction of Republican progressivism and the return of the party to real Republicanism.[28] In 1936, Daugherty saw salvation in Alf Landon of Kansas, who "is safe and has his feet on the ground." He also predicted a possible Republican landslide that November because of the opposition of Al Smith and several other leading Democrats to Roosevelt as well as Landon's "considerable" appeal. In 1940, his choice for the Republican nomination was Senator Robert Taft of Ohio. Daugherty reminded newspapermen that he had always espoused conservative Republicanism because he had never been "nervous enough" to become a progressive.[29] This was Daugherty's final public expression of his political creed.

Never in good health in the 1930s, Daugherty was hospitalized for shingles in November 1938. Upon his release five months later, he moved to the Broadwin Hotel, where he spent his last two years. There he worked on his memoirs, answered correspondence, read newspapers, and listened to the radio. His spirit and wit still remained. He confided that he committed no crimes lately because so few enemies survived. And in this time of "confusion and confiscation, I keep as happy and philosophical as possible."[30] On January 26, 1940, in honor of his eightieth birthday, Daugherty permitted a rare interview in which he announced that "given the same circumstances I would not change an official or personal act of mine while I was Attorney General. That's a clear conscience for you."[31] In June of the following year, a heart attack further weakened him. He remained in bed throughout the summer. That September he suffered a second seizure, and his condition gradually worsened until he went into a state of semiconsciousness a couple of days before his death. On October 13, 1941, his brother, daughter, and secretary sadly witnessed Daugherty's death. His body was returned to Washington Court House to be entombed in the family mausoleum.

Daugherty did not die impoverished. The gross value of his estate exceeded $372,000 and included a sizable amount of real estate in the Washington Court House area. He had inherited some property from his mother and had received a modest return from his book and his infrequent law practice after 1924. Even so, he did remarkably well after having suffered an alleged financial deficit in 1920 and considerable trial expenses in the mid-1920s. The subsequent depression appeared to have affected him little. Enough remained to take care of his diminished family and employees in fine fashion.[32] Missing from Daugherty's estate were his papers. Although he willed them to his daughter Emily, he undoubtedly changed his mind and destroyed them prior to his death.[33]

Epilog

DAUGHERTY once wrote that he had learned his politics from Matthew Quay, the notorious political boss of Pennsylvania, whom he had met at the 1892 Republican National Convention.[1] He admired the old-guard politicians like Quay, Boies Penrose, Marcus Hanna, and Tom Platt of New York, and tried to emulate them. Once, when James R. Garfield neglected to honor one of Platt's endorsements, Daugherty responded characteristically: "If I was to receive such a letter . . . [,] I would break my neck to secure a position for such a man, or if I could not secure it, I would break somebody else's neck."[2]

Like Quay, and like the old-guard leadership generally, Daugherty sought to rule the state Republican organization and thus to elevate himself to high political office. He was not a champion of the people, being too much a believer in the machine and the political convention. Had he achieved his ultimate ambition—a seat in the United States Senate—he most likely would have aligned himself with the senatorial old guard. His ambition was thwarted, however, partly because of the relative weakness of his political base in Fayette County, and partly because of his scheming and intriguing personality, which brought him into conflict with the reigning powers in the Ohio Republican party.

The explanation for much of his behavior undoubtedly lies in the circumstances and events of his early years. Those who have previously written about Daugherty have stressed his confident manner, without realizing that it masked an underlying anxiety and insecurity, feelings that arose from the early loss of his father and the subsequent deprivations and hardships that marked his childhood, instilling in him an urgent desire to achieve success quickly. His ambition, coupled with his competitive spirit, spurred him to aggressiveness and, occasionally, impulsiveness.

Repeated frustrations in political life served to intensify his ambition and combativeness, and led him into sometimes bitter personal conflict with those who opposed him. His vendetta against the renegade progressives during and after the 1912 campaign is but the most extreme example of the nature of his vindictiveness.

He was not, however, without his good qualities. He was outgoing and friendly, and critics and opponents often found him witty and congenial. Even his most bitter adversaries could not deny his faithfulness and devotion to his wife Lucy, who spent much time in hospitals and medical centers. To the best of his recollection, he never charged female clients for his legal services, and he appointed women to responsible government positions at a time when it was not fashionable to do so. He was always thoughtful and considerate of those who worked for him, and they in turn spoke well of him when he was being investigated. He also had personal courage. Few men of his time would have dared challenge the entrenched power of Foraker, Hanna, and Dick at state political conventions. His dedication to candidates whose cause he supported was fiercely loyal, and his steadfast refusal to resign the attorney generalship in the face of overwhelming political pressure drew the grudging admiration of his opponents.

Most important, he was also a skillful manager and organizer, and he provided considerable assistance to the presidential candidacies of Republicans from McKinley to Harding. In the latter's 1920 campaign, Daugherty, even though his role has been overrated, was especially useful in developing nomination strategy and in lining up support from national committeemen and delegates.

But his energies and abilities were devoted almost exclusively to party interests and personal advancement. He was a doer rather than a thinker, and his political views were narrow. Daugherty sought to perpetuate a brand of Republicanism typical of the McKinley era, representing the well-to-do, preaching the status quo, and supporting corporate interests, but offering few solutions to the problems confronting a modern urban industrial society.

When he finally did achieve power, he did not use it wisely. He failed to give the Justice Department adequate direction, and his record as a prosecutor of war-fraud cases and antitrust suits was uneven. His abilities as a presidential adviser were unsatisfactory; Harding came to rely on him less and less, and Coolidge not at all. Much more damning were the nefarious activities of the Bureau of Investigation and the chicanery associated with the Department during his tenure. He permitted lobbyists like King and Felder to undermine his authority, and friends like Mannington and Smith to further their illegal schemes. Daugherty himself was probably illicitly involved in the American Metal case, and hurt his own cause by destroying important testimony and refusing to testify.

History will always judge him harshly for his performance as Attorney General, but given what we know of his personality and background, some of his actions and beliefs are at least understandable, if not always justifiable. His antipathy toward organized labor, progressivism, and the League of Nations typified his narrow political creed, and his attitude toward dissenters and postwar radicals reflected his rural conservative upbringing. Perhaps to an even greater degree than did Harding, Daugherty represented the spirit of provincial small town America. Although a part of Daugherty will always remain hidden in the correspondence he most probably destroyed, the man as he is known to history belongs to that large and growing number of American leaders who, in sacrificing principle to personal gain, have failed the American people.

Notes

ABBREVIATIONS

HMD   Harry M. Daugherty
WGH   Warren G. Harding
HP   Warren G. Harding Papers
RBHP   Ray Baker Harris Papers
TPS 2   Presidential Series 2, William Howard Taft Papers
TPS 3   Presidential Series 3, Taft Papers
TS 3   Series 3, Taft Papers
TL   Letterbook, Series 8, Taft Papers
DJF   National Archives, Department of Justice File

PREFACE

1. HMD to Cyril Clemens, June 16, 1939, Cyril Clemens Papers, Box 1/13, Ohio Historical Society.

CHAPTER I

1. For population and election statistics regarding Fayette County and Washington Court House, see Ohio, *Annual Report of the Secretary of State* for the appropriate years.

2. *Fayette Republican,* January 26, 1881; *Cyclone and Fayette Republican,* July 17, October 30, and December 11, 1889.

3. Although not always accurate, Daugherty's genealogy can be found in the following Fayette histories: Frank M. Allen (ed.), *History of Fayette County Ohio: Her People, Industries, and Institutions* (Indianapolis, 1914); R. S. Dills, *History of Fayette County* (Dayton, 1891); Chapman Brothers, *Portrait and Biographical Record of Fayette, Pickaway and Madison Counties, Ohio* (Chicago, 1892). See also James N. Giglio, "Daugherty, Harry Micajah," *Dictionary of American Biography,* ed. by Edward T. James, Supplement 3 (New York, 1973), pp. 213-14.

4. John H.'s and Micajah's estate data is found in Probate Court Records, Washington Court House, Ohio. George Robinson, Jr., of Washington Court House, a distant relative of Daugherty by marriage and an officer of the Fayette County Historical Society, furnished the information about Micajah's meager support (February 11, 1974).

5. Robert S. Harper, "Before Revelry," *Plain Talk,* III (July 1928), 44-51.

6. For the Tocqueville observation, see John Braeman, *Albert J. Beveridge, American Nationalist* (Chicago, 1971), p. 8. HMD to Ray Baker Harris, June 7, 1938, RBHP, Box 9/3, Ohio Historical Society.

7. HMD to Harris, June 7, 1938, *ibid.: Columbus Citizen,* January 29, 1939; *New York Times,* October 13, 1941.

8. R. M. McFarland to Calvin Coolidge, March 31, 1924, Calvin Coolidge Papers, Box 28, Library of Congress; James M. Cox, *Journey Through My Years* (New York, 1946), p. 302.

9. The Fayette situation is discernible from a perusal of the county newspapers of the 1880s and 1890s, which clearly showed almost every attorney active politically.

10. "How Daugherty Helped Harding Into the White House," *Literary Digest* LXIX (April 9, 1921), 42.

11. HMD to Harris, June 7, 1938, RBHP, Box 9/3.

12. *Ibid.*

13. The best description of the Sherman-Foraker comparison is in Randolph C. Downes, *The Rise of Warren Gamaliel Harding, 1865-1920* (Columbus, 1970), pp. 96-101. See also Francis Russell, *The Shadow of Blooming Grove: Warren G. Harding in His Times* (New York, 1968), pp. 115-16. Russell suggests that there were also strong ideological differences separating the two eventual antagonists.

14. *Fayette Republican,* August 13, 1886, *Fayette County Record,* June 18, 1903 for the Daughertys' newspaper investments.

15. *Cyclone and Fayette Republican,* August 7, 1889.

16. HMD to Charles L. Kurtz, October 30, 1889, uncataloged Charles L. Kurtz Papers, Ohio Historical Society.

17. *Cyclone and Fayette Republican,* April 30 and July 30, 1890. In July, the *Cyclone* reprinted an editorial from the *Chillicothe Gazette* on Daugherty.

18. *Ibid.,* February 12 and April 2, 1890; Ohio, *Journal of the House of Representatives,* 68th General Assembly, 1890, LXXXVI, 245.

19. *Ibid.,* April 30, 1891. The *Cyclone* cited other newspaper sources that wrote favorably of Daugherty.

CHAPTER II

1. Everett Walters, *Joseph Benson Foraker: An Uncompromising Republican* (Columbus, 1948), pp. 99-100.

2. *Cincinnati Enquirer,* August 1, 1891.

3. Joseph Benson Foraker to HMD, August 1, 1891, Copy, Joseph Benson Foraker Papers, Box 27, Cincinnati Historical Society.

4. HMD to Foraker, August 3, 1891, Foraker Papers, Box 32/D.

5. *Cyclone and Fayette Republican,* August 20, 1891; Cox, *Journey,* 304. Daugherty told a local political leader that he would not only support Sherman's reelection in the General Assembly but would also back his renomination in the party caucus. Mills Gardner to John Sherman, December 15, 1891, John Sherman Papers, Vol. 561, Library of Congress.

6. Foraker to Kurtz, November 1, 1891, uncataloged Kurtz Papers.

7. Walters, *Foraker,* p. 101.

8. *Cyclone and Fayette Republican,* November 12, 1891; *Cincinnati Enquirer,* November 14, 1891.

9. *Ibid.,* December 24, 1891.

10. Gardner to Sherman, January 19, 1892, Sherman Papers, Vol. 568.

11. Foraker to Kurtz, December 4, 1891, uncataloged Kurtz Papers.

12. William Hahn to Sherman, December 11, 1891, Vol. 560; *ibid.,* December 15, 1891, Vol. 561, Sherman Papers.

13. Daugherty showed Foraker the pledge statement on December 29. Although he did not indicate when he had signed it, his mid-December meetings with Hahn and Sherman seemed the logical time. Foraker to HMD, January 18, 1892, Copy, Foraker Papers, Box 27.

14. *Ibid.*

15. *Cyclone and Fayette Republican,* January 7, 1892.

16. Herbert Croly, *Marcus Alonzo Hanna: His Life and Work* (New York, 1912), p. 163.

17. Ohio General Assembly, *House Journal, 1892,* Appendix, "In the Matter of the Investigation of the Charges Published in the *Columbus Post* vs. Hon. H. M. Daugherty, in the Recent Senatorial Contest," pp. 30, 39. Cited hereinafter as "Senatorial Investigation."

18. Foraker to Kurtz, January 14, 1892, uncataloged Kurtz Papers.

19. *Cincinnati Enquirer,* January 27, 1892.

20. Daugherty wrote freely and extensively to Sherman in this period. His response to Sherman's letter exonerating him especially revealed his gratitude: "I will long preserve the letter and hand it down to those I love. I would rather have that letter Senator than the $3,500 I have been charged as having received for voting for you." HMD to Sherman, January 19, 1892, Sherman Papers, Vol. 573.

21. "Senatorial Investigation," pp. 47, 63.

22. *Ibid.,* pp. 64, 68.

23. *Cyclone and Fayette Republican,* April 7, 1892; HMD to Sherman, May 6, 1892, Sherman Papers, Vol. 579.

24. Harper, "Before Revelry," p. 47.

25. *Cincinnati Enquirer,* January 13, 1892; HMD to Harris, June 7, 1938, RBHP, Box 9/3.

26. Cox, *Journey,* p. 304.

27. New York *World,* February 17, 1921.

28. HMD to Harris, June 7, 1938, RBHP, Box 9/3.

29. *House Journal, 1893,* p. 169.

30. *Ohio State Journal,* January 5, 1892.

31. *Ibid.,* February 10, 1892; *Columbus Dispatch,* January 26, 1892.

32. *Ibid.,* March 23, 1892.

33. *Ibid.,* June 7, 1893.

34. *Ibid.,* April 22, 1893; *Cyclone and Fayette Republican,* April 27, 1893; HMD to Harris, June 7, 1938, RBHP, Box 9/3.

35. *Cyclone and Fayette Republican,* June 16, 1892.

36. *Ibid.,* June 30, 1892.

37. HMD to Sherman, August 21, 1892, Sherman Papers, Letterbook 586. Daugherty wanted to wait until he completed his final term in the legislature. By then the present district attorney's reelection would ensure Daugherty a four-year appointment. There is no indication that Sherman offered it to him again.

38. HMD to Foraker, November 11, 1893, Foraker Papers, Box 32/D.

39. *Cyclone and Fayette Republican,* March 29, 1894, August 16, 1894 (which cited a *Columbus Dispatch* article).

40. *Ibid.,* August 31, 1893.

41. Circleville *Democrat and Watchman,* October 19, 1894.

42. *Cincinnati Enquirer,* September 7, 1894. The *Enquirer* dismissed the charges against Daugherty as "malignant and devilish" after its own informal inquiry; *Cyclone and Fayette Republican,* October 4, November 1, 1894.

43. Circleville *Democrat and Watchman,* October 19, 1894.

44. HMD to Harris, June 7, 1938, RBHP, Box 9/3.

45. *Cincinnati Enquirer,* May 19, 1895.

46. *Ibid.,* May 19, 1895.

47. Walters, *Foraker,* p. 109.

48. *Cincinnati Enquirer,* May 30, 1895.

49. *Ohio State Journal,* May 30, 1895; *Cincinnati Enquirer,* May 30, 1895.

50. *Cyclone and Fayette Republican,* May 30, 1895.

51. *Ibid.,* February 20, 1896.

52. HMD to Harris, June 7, 1938, RBHP, Box 9/3.

53. *Cyclone and Fayette Republican,* March 5, 12, 19; April 3, 1896.

54. *Cincinnati Enquirer,* May 21, 1899.

55. *Ohio State Journal,* March 11, 1896.

56. *Cyclone and Fayette Republican,* September 17, October 8, 1896.

57. *Ohio State Journal,* June 23, 1897.

58. Croly, *Hanna,* pp. 250-60.

59. According to Huling, Judge George K. Nash advised Dick to employ counsel. Nash most likely suggested both Daugherty and Huling. *Cincinnati Enquirer,* May 12, 1899.

60. HMD to Mark Hanna, May 16, 1898, Charles Dick Papers, Box 1/5, Ohio Historical Society; George A. Myers to James Ford Rhodes, April 30, 1920, cited in John Garraty, ed., *The Barber and the Historian: The Correspondence of George A. Myers and James Ford Rhodes, 1910-1923* (Columbus, 1956), pp. 106-07.

61. Dick to HMD, May 19, 1898, Dick Papers, Box 1/5.

62. HMD, Cyrus H. Huling, and G.L. Marble to Dick, May 27, 1898, *ibid.*

63. *Cincinnati Enquirer,* May 10, 1899; Myers to Rhodes, May 22, 1922, *Barber and the Historian,* p. 145.

64. *Ohio State Journal,* June 23, November 10, 1898.

65. Kurtz to Foraker, June 3, 1898, Foraker Papers, Box 36.

66. *Cincinnati Enquirer,* January 6, 1899.

67. *Ohio State Journal,* January 23, 1899; *Cincinnati Enquirer,* May 15, 1899.

68. *Cincinnati Enquirer,* May 10, 11, 12, 1899.

69. *Ibid.,* May 12, 17, June 3, 1899.

70. *Ohio State Journal,* May 28, 1899; *Cincinnati Enquirer,* May 29, June 4, 1899.

71. *Cincinnati Enquirer,* June 1, 1899.

72. *Ibid.,* June 3, 1899; *Toledo Blade,* May 31, 1899; *Columbus Dispatch,* May 23, 1899.

73. *Ohio State Journal,* June 3, 1899.

74. *Cincinnati Enquirer,* June 2, 3, 1899.

75. See, for example, William H. Phipps to HMD, May 22, 1899, William H. Phipps Papers, Box 1/5, Ohio State Historical Society.

76. The *Cincinnati Enquirer* published several articles on Daugherty's proposed punishment in the weeks following the election; for example, June 3, 6, 1899.

CHAPTER III

1. *Columbus Evening Dispatch,* January 1, 1900; Ralph W. Tyler to George A. Myers, March 8, 1900, George A. Myers Papers, Box 8/1, Ohio Historical Society; Walters, *Foraker,* p. 180.

2. Tyler to Myers, May 25, 1900, Myers Papers, Box 8/3; *ibid.,* March 8, 1900, Box 8/1.

3. *Cincinnati Enquirer,* April 22, 1900; *Columbus Evening Dispatch,* April 23, 1900.

4. *Cincinnati Enquirer,* June 20, 23, 1901; *Ohio State Journal,* June 22, 1901.

5. *Ohio State Journal,* June 23, 25, 1901; Thomas W. Marchant to WGH, June 15, 1901, HP, Box 708/7, Ohio Historical Society.

6. *Fayette County Record,* October 23, 1902; HMD to Foraker, November 4, 1901, Foraker Papers, Box 32/D.

7. HMD to Dick, January 12, 1906, Dick Papers, Box 7/4.

8. *Ibid.,* February 22, 1905, Box 6/4; HMD to Foraker, December 19, 1905, Foraker Papers, Box 42/D; C. C. Firestone to Foraker, December 21, 1905, Box 42/F, *ibid.*

9. Foraker to Firestone, December 23, 1905, Copy, Foraker Papers, Box 42/F; HMD to Dick, January 13, 1906, Dick Papers, Box 7/4.

10. Phipps to HMD, January 1, 1900, Phipps Papers, Box 1/6.

11. See Mark Sullivan, *Our Times, 1900-1925,* VI, *The Twenties* (New York, 1935), 35-36 n. 14.

12. For example, see *Fayette County Record,* January 2, 9, 1902.

13. Myers to HMD, February 17, 1902, Copy, Myers Papers, Box 11/1; HMD to Myers, February 19, 1902, *ibid.*

14. *Fayette County Record,* January 2, 16, 23, 30, 1902.

15. *Cincinnati Enquirer,* May 27, 1902.

16. *Fayette County Record,* March 5, 1903; *Cincinnati Enquirer,* June 4, 1903.

17. *Fayette County Record,* April 14, May 19, 1904; *Cleveland Leader,* June 16, 1912.

18. *Ohio State Journal,* January 14, 1927.

19. HMD to Arthur Garford, November 11, 1905, Arthur Garford Papers, Box 16/6, Ohio Historical Society.

20. See Braeman, *Beveridge,* p. 1, for a recent discussion of this point of view.

21. I interchangeably refer to Daugherty as an "insurgent," "progressive," and "reformer" because he briefly and in a narrow way acted as a political progressive.

22. Forrest Crissey's *Theodore Burton: American Statesman* (Cleveland and New York, 1956) is the only major work on Burton. It completely ignores his transition from insurgent reformer in 1906 to a defender of conservatism in 1912.

23. HMD to Garford, November 11, 1905, Garford Papers, Box 16/6.

24. *Toledo Blade,* March 31, 1906. Foraker believed that the ICC lacked the constitutional power to set railroad rates which, in his view, came under the sole jurisdiction of the courts.

25. Garford to HMD, August 17, 1906, Garford Papers, Box 18/2; *Cincinnati Enquirer,* August 17, 1906.

26. *Cleveland Plain Dealer,* August 26, 1906.

27. Garford to HMD, August 17, 1906, Garford Papers, Box 18/2; *Cincinnati Enquirer,* September 10, 1906.

28. *Ohio State Journal,* September 4, 9, 1906.

29. *Ibid.,* September 12, 1906.

30. *Ibid.,;* *Cincinnati Enquirer,* September 12, 1906.

31. *Cincinnati Enquirer,* September 13, 1906; *Ohio State Journal,* September 13, 1906.

32. Russell, *Blooming Grove,* p. 178.

33. *Ohio State Journal,* September 13, 1906; *Cincinnati Enquirer,* September 13, 1906.

34. *Ohio State Journal,* May 23, 1905; HMD to William Howard Taft, May 29, 1905, TPS 2, Box 103/5, Library of Congress.

35. E. N. Huggins to James R. Garfield, January 14, 1907, James R. Garfield Papers, Box 124/11, Library of Congress; for Daugherty's speech, see *Cleveland Leader,* March 8, 1907.

36. *Ohio State Journal,* March 4, 1908; *Cleveland Leader,* March 4, 1908.

37. *Philadelphia Record,* December 17, 1908, clipping in Theodore Burton Papers, Box 67/4, Western Reserve Historical Society.

38. *Cleveland Leader,* June 14, 1908.

39. HMD to Garford, November 9, 1908, Garford Papers, Box 22/2; Garford to HMD, November 10, *ibid.*

40. James H. Cassidy to Burton, December 2, 1908, Copy, Burton Papers, Box 12/1.

41. Crissey, *Burton,* p. 75.

42. *Ohio State Journal,* January 11, 1911. Daugherty received almost twice as many votes as his nearest rival, Senator Charles Dick.

CHAPTER IV

1. H. Ellis Daugherty to the author, telephone conversation, December 12, 1977; George Robinson, Jr., to the author, January 28, 1974; WGH to Charles E. Sawyer, March 23, 1917, Charles E. Sawyer Papers, Box 1, Ohio Historical Society; Russell, *Blooming Grove,* p. 304.

2. Information on Draper's early life comes from H. Ellis Daugherty to the author and the Draper Daugherty medical file #1713 of Lima State Hospital (Ohio). The file contains personal material on Draper and the family including correspondence between Harry Daugherty and the hospital superintendent. For Daugherty's early concern about Draper, see Arthur Vorys to Charles D. Hilles, October 26, 1912, TP 3, Folder 227; for Draper's fall see also the *New York Times,* July 13, 1928.

3. Draper Daugherty medical file 1713, especially Daugherty to Dr. Charles H. Clark, October 20, 1926.

4. Daugherty later said of his earlier legal career: "There was never a murder case while I lived in the county [Fayette] that I was not employed in to defend and not a man I defended was ever convicted of murder in the first degree." HMD to Harris, June 7, 1938, RBHP, Box 9/7.

5. Jacob Meckstroth to the author, Interview, September 13, 1967; New York *World,* February 17, 1921.

6. W. A. Ireland, *Club Men of Columbus in Caricature* (Columbus, 1911), p. 421.

7. HMD to Harris, June 7, 1938, RBHP, Box 9/3.

8. Hoyt Landon Warner, *Progressivism in Ohio, 1897-1917* (Columbus, 1964), pp. 279-280.

9. Cox, *Journey,* p. 304.

10. *Columbus Dispatch,* January 1, 1900.

11. Cox, *Journey,* p. 303.

12. Warner, *Progressivism,* pp. 200-01; Russell, *Blooming Grove,* p. 200.

13. Meckstroth to the author, November 22, 1974. Meckstroth was a reporter for the *Ohio State Journal* in 1913. In later years, he reinvestigated the Columbus Savings and Trust affair but could not determine to what degree Daugherty was involved; Cox, *Journey,* pp. 304-05. See also Warner, *Progressivism,* pp. 224, 242 n. 36.

14. See, for example, New York *World,* February 17, 20, 1921.

15. *Ibid.,* February 17, 1921; Warner, *Progressivism,* p. 389.

16. HMD to James M. Cox, April 8, 16, 1913, Governor James M. Cox Papers, Box 3/1&2, Ohio Historical Society.

17. *Cleveland Leader,* August 10, 18, 1912; *Ohio State Journal,* October 26, 1912; Taft to Helen Taft, July 9, 1912, TPS 2, Box 49; HMD to Taft, November 17, 1915, TPS 3, Box 327/7.

18. *Congressional Record,* 59th Cong., 1st Sess., 6374.

19. HMD to Dick, February 15, 1906, Dick Papers, Box 7/4.

20. HMD to Foraker, February 19, May 9, 1906, Foraker Papers, Box 48/D: *Congressional Record,* 59th Cong., 1st Sess., 6373-74.

21. *Congressional Record,* 59th Cong., 1st Sess., 6374.

22. HMD to Foraker, May 9, 1906, Foraker Papers, Box 48/D.

23. The best published account of Morse's escapades is found in Henry F. Pringle, *The Life and Times of William Howard Taft* (New York, 1939), II, 627-37; *New York Times,* July 25, 1926; Frederic L. Thompson, "Morse, Charles Wyman," *Dictionary of American Biography (DAB)* ed. by Dumas Malone, XIII (New York, 1934) 239-41; Frederick Lewis Allen, *The Lords of Creation* (Chicago, 1966), pp. 116-17.

24. *DAB,* XIII, 239-40; *New York Times,* July 25, 1926; Henry L. Stimson to George Wickersham, December 17, 1910, Pardon Case File 204-43-407, National Records Service (NRS), Suitland, Maryland.

25. White House Memorandum, undated, TPS 2, Folder 1189; James M. Beck to Taft, March 14, 1911, *ibid.* See also Pringle, *Taft,* II, 629. The various requests and petitions are contained in Pardon Case File 204-43-407, NRS.

26. Stimson to Wickersham, December 17, 1910, Pardon Case File 204-43-407, NRS; see also James A. Finch to Wickersham, January 15, 1912, *ibid.*

27. Daugherty to Taft, November 17, 1915, TS 3, Box 327/7; *Congressional Record,* 67th Cong., 2nd Sess., 7378. See also *New York Times,* January 19, 1912; Harry M. Daugherty and Thomas Dixon, *The Inside Story of the Harding Tragedy* (New York, 1932), p. 114.

28. Robert LaDow to William Moyer, July 25, 1911, DJF 60-120197, National Archives; Moyer to LaDow, July 27, 1911, Telegram, *ibid.*

29. HMD to Hilles, July 28, 1911, Telegram, TPS 2, Folder 1189; *ibid.,* August 2, 1911, Charles D. Hilles Papers, Box 48, Yale University Library; *ibid.,* August 29, 1911, TPS 2, Folder 1189.

30. Dr. Alfred L. Fowler to Whom It May Concern, August 28, 1911, Pardon Case File 204-43-407, NRS; HMD to Hilles, August 29, 1911, TPS 2, Folder 1189.

31. Rudolph Forster to Hilles, September 23, 1911, Memorandum, TPS 2, Folder 1189; HMD to Theodore Roosevelt, September 16, 1911, Theodore Roosevelt Papers, Box 175/7, Library of Congress; *ibid.,* September 21, 1911, Box 175/12; HMD to Hilles, September 11, 1911, TPS 2, Folder 3257; HMD to Forster, September 19, 1911, Folder 1189, *ibid.*

32. HMD and Thomas Felder to Hilles, November 21, 1911, Telegram, TPS 2, Folder 1189. Hilles scrawled that they could see Taft on Saturday at 11:40 A.M.

33. Wickersham to Taft, November 22, 1911, *ibid.* Two civilian physicians also independently examined Morse in this period. One detected no organic abnormalities whatsoever; the other concluded that a previous rheumatic condition had "crippled his heart" and his urine indicated probable Bright's disease. The latter physician argued, however, that if Morse were allowed to remain "perfectly quiet and at ease, he could live as well in prison as well as on the outside." See Dr. William Simpson Elkin to Walter H. Johnson, November 1, 1911 and Dr. E. C. Davis to Johnson, November 1, 1911, Pardon Case File 204-43-407, NRS.

34. HMD to Hilles, November 22, 1911, Telegram, TPS 2, Folder 3527.

35. White House Memorandum, November 24, 1911, Folder 1189, *ibid.; Congressional Record,* 67th Cong., 2nd Sess., 7317, 7378; *New York Times,* May 21, 1922.

36. HMD to Hilles, November 25, 1911, TPS 2, Folder 3527; *ibid.,* December 8, 1911, Folder 1189.

37. J. A. Fowler to Taft, December 21, 1911, Folder 1189, *ibid.;* Taft to Wickersham, December 24, 1911, *ibid.*

38. HMD to Hilles, December 17, 1911, *ibid.;* HMD to Wickersham, December 17, 1911, Pardon Case File 204-43-407, NRS; HMD to J. A. Fowler, December 21, 1911, *ibid.*

39. Felder to Hilles, December 26, 1911, TPS 2, Folder 1189; Felder to Taft, December 26, 1911, Pardon Case File 204-43-407, NRS; White House Memorandum, December 29, 1911, TPS 2, Folder 1189.

40. George Torney to the Adjutant General of the Army, December 30, 1911, TPS 2, Folder 1189; HMD and Felder to Taft, January 9, 1912, *ibid.;* Wickersham to Taft, January 12, 17, 1912, *ibid.*

41. *Congressional Record,* 67th Cong., 2nd Sess., 7378. See also Sullivan, *The Twenties,* p. 21 n. Pringle is in error in stating that no parole system then existed. According to the Criminal Parole Act, effective 1910, Morse would have had to serve five years, however, to be eligible for parole. Pringle, *Taft,* II, 637; Henry Wise to Wickersham, December 23, 1910, Pardon Case File 204-43-407, NRS.

42. See, for example, James C. German, Jr., "The Taft Administration and the Sherman Antitrust Act," *Mid-America,* LIV. (July 1972), 172-86. German points out that Taft did not hesitate to take action against corporations directed by his personal friends.

43. Pringle, *Taft,* II, 626.

44. Finch to Wickersham, January 15, 1912, Pardon Case File 204-43-407, NRS; see also *New York Times,* August 5, 1917.

45. Charles Hough to Finch, January 17, 1912, Pardon Case File 204-43-407, NRS.

46. Archie Butt, *Taft and Roosevelt, The Intimate Letters of Archie Butt, Military Aide* (New York, 1930), II, 591.

47. *New York Times,* January 11, March 17, November 16, 1913; January 11, 1916. In early 1916, Taft also delivered a similar speech at Bangor, Maine, causing Morse to threaten the ex-President with legal action. Taft replied: "For you to say that you will hold me responsible for true statements I have made or shall make, is an exhibition of the most unlimited audacity in history. The sooner you begin the suit the better." Charles W. Morse to Taft, February 14, 1916, Copy, Henry Stimson Papers, Box 47, Yale University Library; Taft to Morse, February 15, 1916, Copy, *ibid.*

48. HMD to Wickersham, February 11, 1913, DJF 60-151887; Wickersham to HMD, February 13, 1913, Telegram, *ibid.*

49. HMD to Taft, November 17, 1915, TS 2, Box 327/7.

50. Taft to HMD, November 22, 1915, Copy, TS 3, Letterbook 38, P370A; *New York Times,* May 24, 1922.

51. *New York Times,* July 25, 1926, January 13, 1933; *New York Herald,* February 28, 1922; *DAB,* XIII, 241.

52. *Congressional Record,* 67th Cong., 2nd Sess., 6175, 7317. See also *New York Times,* August 5, 1917. Caraway referred to Felder's recent contacts with Daugherty regarding the Bosch Magneto Company, which Felder represented to curtail a Justice Department war-fraud investigation. *Congressional Record,* 67th Cong., 2nd Sess., 7317-18.

53. *Congressional Record,* 67th Cong., 2nd Sess., 7378-79.

54. *Ibid.,* 7318, 7374, 7379. While Taft was aware of the possible deception surrounding Morse's release, he refused to believe that Daugherty had been involved. He wrote Daugherty a sympathetic letter after Caraway's attack. Taft to HMD, May 21, 1922, Copy, TS 3, Box 516/6. The author failed to locate in the National Archives or elsewhere the "damaging evidence" Felder alluded to. There is, however, a 1917 letter from Henry Stimson's former assistant attorney, who now asserted that Morse was guilty of gross fraud in obtaining his release. See Henry Wise to Francis Caffey, November 12, 1917, Pardon Case File 204-43-407, NRS.

55. *Congressional Record,* 67th Cong., 2nd Sess., 7317; *New York Times,* May 21, 1922.

56. "The Case of Attorney General Daugherty," *Outlook,* LXXXI (June 7, 1922), 247; *Congressional Record,* 67th Cong., 2nd Sess., 6175.

57. Report of the Board of Medical Officers, December 1911, Pardon Case File 204-43-407; Major General Leonard Wood to Wickersham, December 18, 1911, *ibid.;* Felder to Taft, December 26, 1911, *ibid.* The possibility exists, however, that all sources which had information on Morse's medical history received it from Morse.

58. Benjamin F. Miller, M.D., *The Complete Medical Guide* (New York, 1967), pp. 411-12; conversations with urologists Ross Dees Blades, October 10, 1972, and Warren Warres, November 6, 1972, Springfield, Missouri. Dr. Arthur Knabb, a retired physician who began his practice in the second decade of the twentieth century, contended that physicians had treated acute nephritis by prescribing a proper diet, plenty of rest, and nursing care, which Morse managed to receive while in Europe. Interview, October 21, 1972, Springfield, Missouri.

59. Morse to Taft, February 14, 1916, Copy, Stimson Papers, Box 47.

60. See pp. 164-65, 140-41.

61. Anonymous physician, United States Penitentiary to Bert M. Fernald, Copy, January 21, 1922, Pardon Case File 204-32-115, NRS.

62. Dr. Fowler to HMD and Felder, December 23, 1911, Copy, Pardon Case File 204-43-407, NRS; HMD and Felder to Taft, January 16, 1912, *ibid.*

63. *Congressional Record,* 67th Cong., 2nd Sess., 7378; R. K. Heston to the author,

October 25, 1972. Heston is Chief of the Civilian Management and Technical Staff of the National Personnel Records Center, St. Louis, Missouri, where Dr. Fowler's sketchy personnel folder as prison physician is now housed.

64. *Congressional Record,* 67th Cong., 2nd Sess., 7318-20; *New York Times,* March 13, 1926.

65. *DAB,* XIII, 241; *New York Times,* July 16, 1926, January 13, 1933.

66. Daugherty's first expression of concern to the administration about Morse's health came on August 29, 1911. See HMD to Hilles, August 29, 1911, TPS 2, Folder 1189.

CHAPTER V

1. George E. Mowry, *Theodore Roosevelt and the Progressive Movement* (Madison, 1947), p. 203; Warner, *Progressivism,* p. 357. Warner indicated that Roosevelt's colorful personality and his "safe" approach toward business also attracted Hanna.

2. For Roosevelt's conflict with Hanna, see Walters, *Foraker,* pp. 201-03.

3. For example, HMD to Harris, January 29, 1938, RBHP, Box 9/3.

4. *Cleveland Leader,* June 17, 1912; *Ohio State Journal,* August 7, 1912.

5. Charles J. Thompson to Lewis Laylin, April 25, 1912, TPS 2, Folder 22 A. This folder contained several other letters of complaint regarding Hitchcock.

6. Taft to HMD, March 12, 1912, Folder 335, *ibid.*

7. HMD to William B. McKinley, April 16, 1912, Hilles Papers, Box 95.

8. HMD to Hilles, May 9, 1912, Box 100, *ibid.*

9. Pringle, *Taft,* II, 785-86.

10. *Ohio State Journal,* May 7, 9, 1912.

11. *Washington Court House Herald,* May 19, 1912. Clipping in RBHP, Box 4/6; HMD to Harris, May 4, 1937, *ibid.*

12. HMD to Hilles, May 23, 1912, Hilles Papers, Box 102.

13. HMD to Harris, May 4, 1937, RBHP, Box 9/4.

14. Downes, *Harding,* p. 179.

15. HMD to Hilles, March 24, 1912, Hilles Papers, Box 89.

16. *Cleveland Leader,* June 16, 1912.

17. HMD to Taft, June 24, 1912, Hilles Papers, Box 107.

18. Taft to HMD, June 26, 1912, *ibid.*

19. Warner, *Progressivism,* p. 371.

20. HMD to Hilles, June 30, 1912. Hilles Papers, Box 108.

21. Elihu Root to Taft, July 1, 1912, TPS 2, Folder 3527; Edmund B. Dillon to Arthur Vorys, July 7, 1912, Telegram, Folder 335, *ibid.; Ohio State Journal,* July 8, 1912.

22. Taft to Helen H. Taft, July 9, 1912, TPS 2, Box 49. There is some irony that Dausherty strongly backed Vorys for the chairmanship in 1908 only to see him rejected. Daugherty to Taft, June 2, 1908, TPS 3, Box 169/2.

23. Taft to HMD, July 17, 1912, TL, Letterbook 40. Although Taft referred to Daugherty's complaining letters, they appear to have vanished, for they are neither in the Taft nor the Hilles collections.

24. HMD to Taft, July 23, 1912, TPS 2, Folder 3527; HMD to Harris, January 9, 1940, RBHP, Box 9/5; HMD to Cyril Clemens, June 16, 1939, Cyril Clemens Papers, Box 1/13, Ohio Historical Society.

25. *Ohio State Journal,* July 19, 1912.

26. *Cleveland Leader,* August 5, 1912; *Cincinnati Enquirer,* August 6, 1912.

27. *Ohio State Journal,* August 8, 1912.

28. *Ibid.,* August 11, 1912; *Cleveland Leader,* August 13, 1912.

29. *Ohio State Journal,* August 11, 1912.

30. Brown also officially resigned as chairman of the Republican state central committee and as national committeeman. W. L. Parmenter of Lima eventually became the new central committee chairman.

31. *Ohio State Journal,* August 12, 1912; *Cleveland Leader,* August 10, 1912.

32. *Cincinnati Enquirer,* August 15, 1912; Taft to Myron T. Herrick, September 17, 1912, Copy, TPS 2, Folder 218.

33. HMD to Edward H. Cooper, October 21, 1912, Phipps Papers, Box 127; Newton Fairbanks to Herrick, February 8, 1916, Newton Fairbanks Papers, Box 1/1, Ohio Historical Society.

34. HMD to County Chairmen, November 7, 1912, Phipps Papers, Box 128.

35. `Ohio State Journal,* August 18, 25, September 1, 1912.

36. *Ibid.,* October 1, September 25, 1912.

37. HMD to Ralph W. Tyler, September 15, 1912, Copy, Hilles Papers, Box 116.

38. HMD to Carmi Thompson, August 27, 1912, TPS 2, Folder 3527.

39. *Ibid.,* September 16, 1912, Hilles Papers, Box 116; Thompson to HMD, September 13, 1912, Letterbook 26, *ibid.*

40. HMD to Thompson, August 28, 1912, TPS 2, Folder 22 A; Gus Karger to Thompson, September 18, 1912, Folder 162, *ibid.*

41. All citations are in TPS 2: John E. Todd to Thompson, September 5, 1912, Folder 3416; HMD to Thompson, September 9, August 26, 1912, Folder 3416; *ibid.,* August 28, 1912, Folder 22 A. Also HMD to Taft, October 2, 1912, TPS 3, Folder 366.

42. HMD to Thompson, September 11, 1912, TPS 2, Folder 3527; Taft to Hitchcock, September 13, 1912, Copy, Folder 3416, *ibid.*

43. HMD to Taft, October 2, 1912, TPS 3, Folder 366.

44. Taft to HMD, October 6, 1912, Copy, TPS 2, Folder 162; HMD to Thompson, October 13, 1912, Telegram, *ibid.*

45. HMD to Taft, October 24, 1912, Folder 1775, *ibid.;* HMD to Hilles, November 25, 1912, *ibid.*

46. HMD to County Chairmen, undated, Hilles Papers, Box 116.

47. HMD to Thompson, August 21, 1912, Box 114, *ibid.*

48. HMD to Hilles, October 11, 12, 1912, Box 120, *ibid.;* Thompson to HMD, October 3, 1912, Letterbook 26, *ibid.*

49. HMD to Hilles, October 17, September 28, 1912, *ibid.*

50. Vorys to Hilles, October 26, 1912, TPS 2, Folder 227; HMD to Hilles, October 27, 1912, Hilles Papers, Box 122.

51. HMD to Thompson, August 28, 1912, TPS 2, Folder 22 A.

52. Root to Taft, September 4, 1912, Folder 152, *ibid.*; HMD to Taft, September 21, 1912, Copy, Folder 3527, *ibid.;* HMD to Foraker, September 19, 1912, Foraker Papers, Box 103/D.

53. HMD to Taft, September 27, 1912, Hilles Papers, Box 118; Taft to Herrick, September 17, 1912, Copy, TPS 3, Folder 218.

54. *Ohio State Journal,* October 16, 1912; B. B. Buckley to Thompson, November 11, 1912, TPS 2, Folder 2340; HMD to Thompson, September 25, 1912, *ibid.;* Thompson to HMD, October 22, 1912, Hilles Papers, Letterbook 26; HMD to Foraker, October 18, 1912, Foraker Papers, Box 103/D.

55. For example, see HMD to Foraker, October 5, 1912, Foraker Papers, Box 103/D; HMD to Taft, October 7, 1912, TPS 3, Folder 366.

56. *Ohio State Journal,* October 30, November 4, 1912.

57. HMD to WGH, January 13, 1913, HP, Box 725/5; HMD to County Chairmen, November 7, 1912, Phipps Papers, Box 128.

58. Frank B. Willis and Simeon Fess are two examples. Out of political expediency, Willis had continually advocated a reunion of the Progressives and Republicans in his 1912 congressional campaign. He eventually endorsed a number of Progressive planks in the postelection period. Fess was sympathetic to Roosevelt's progressivism. In his congressional campaign, he successfully straddled the two platforms and was certainly an advocate of reconciliation afterward. Gerald E. Ridinger, "The Political Career of Frank B. Willis" (unpublished Ph. D. dissertation, Department of History, The Ohio State University, 1957), p. 44; Simeon Fess to HMD, December 23, 1915, Copy, TS 3, Box 334/1; John Nethers, *Simeon Fess, Educator and Politician* (New York, 1973), p. 114.

59. HMD to WGH, November 16, 1912, HP, Box 725/3.

CHAPTER VI

1. HMD to Taft, April 17, 1913, TS 3, Box 254/2. Daugherty referred to the ultraliberal Scripps-McRae newspapers.

2. *Ibid.; Dayton Journal,* August 19, 1915. Clipping in Burton Papers, Box 73/3.

3. HMD to Taft, April 17, 1913, *ibid.;* HMD to Mary E. Lee, May 20, 1913, Mary E. Lee Papers, Box 1/4, Ohio Historical Society.

4. *Ohio State Journal,* February 13, 15, 1914; *Cincinnati Enquirer,* April 9, 1914.

5. *Cincinnati Enquirer,* November 5, 6, 11, 12, 1913.

6. Malcolm Jennings to WGH, January 2, 1914, HP, Box 726/1; *Cleveland Leader,* February 26, 1914; *Ohio State Journal,* February 13, 1914.

7. *Ohio State Journal,* February 13, 15, 26, 1914.

8. HMD to Foraker, February 21, 1914, Foraker Papers, Box 110/D.

9. *Ohio State Journal,* February 27, 1914.

10. Crissey, *Burton,* pp. 224-36.

11. *Cleveland Leader,* June 17, 1912; *Ohio State Journal,* August 7, 1912; *Cleveland Plain Dealer* to Foraker, June 29, 1914, Foraker Papers, Box 110/C; Foraker to *Cleveland Plain Dealer,* June 29, 1914, Telegram, *ibid.* Daugherty, Vorys, Parmenter, Harding, and Samuel Granger of Zanesville were among the Republicans who attended the meeting.

12. Crissey, *Burton,* pp. 237-38.

13. J. S. Hampton to WGH, April 10, 1914, HP. Box 726/2; *Cincinnati Enquirer,* April 9, 1914; *Cleveland Plain Dealer,* April 9, 1914.

14. HMD to Foraker, February 21, 1914, Foraker Papers, Box 110/D.

15. "Memoirs of Maurice Maschke," *Cleveland Plain Dealer,* August 14, 1934. Beginning on August 1, it was published on a daily basis for about a month; Crissey, *Burton,* p. 238; Downes, *Harding,* p. 199.

16. Mark Sullivan, *Twenties,* pp. 28, 30. The statement referred to 1920, but Daugherty's description of Harding for 1914 is similar even though less colorful.

17. *Cleveland Plain Dealer,* July 12, 1914.

18. See the Frank B. Willis Papers, Ohio Historical Society: Frank Parrett to H. L. Eliot, April 14, 1914, Box 1/49; Claude C. Waltermire to F. F. Tipton, June 27, 1914, Box 2/54; H. C. Thompson to Homer J. Ward, April 3, 1914, Box 1/35; C. A. Jones to C. O. Redinbo, April 4, 1914, Box 1/36.

19. HMD to Thompson, April 3, 1914, Box 1/35, *ibid.;* F. M. Hopkins to Tipton, June 27, 1914, Box 2/54, *ibid.*

20. All are in the Willis Papers: Bert B. Buckley to Frank B. Willis, August 12, 1914, Box 5/2; Clarence Middleswart to Willis, August 13, 1914, Box 5/5; Charles E. Wood to Willis, August 14, 1914, Box 5/7.

21. *Springfield News,* August 22, 1914, clipping in Burton Papers, Box 68; *Columbus Evening Dispatch,* September 4, 1914, clipping in Garfield Papers, Box 159/2.

22. *The Week* (Ohio Republican weekly), December 19, 1914, January 2, 1915; HMD to Fairbanks, November 19, 1914, Fairbanks Papers, Box 1/1.

23. HMD to WGH, October 19, 1914, HP, Box 728/3.

24. *Ohio State Journal,* September 18, 1915; *Mansfield Shield,* November 8, 1915, clipping in Burton Papers, Box 73/2; *Steubenville Star,* November 9, 1915, clipping in Burton Papers.

25. HMD to Taft, September 22, 1915, TS 3, Box 322/2.

26. Taft to HMD, October 6, 1915, Copy, Box 327/8, *ibid.*

27. Fairbanks to Herrick, February 8, 1916, Fairbanks Papers, Box 1/1.

28. Fess to HMD, December 23, 1915, Copy, TP 3, Box 334/1. Gus Karger of the *Cincinnati Times-Star's* Washington Bureau sent Taft a copy of the letters "between the good Dr. Fuss and Harry Mayhem Daugherty." Karger to Taft, January 12, 1916, *ibid.*

29. HMD to Fess, December 25, 1915, Copy, *ibid.*

30. HMD to F. E. Scobey, January 17, 1916, F. E. Scobey Papers, Box 1/3, Ohio Historical Society; *Ohio State Journal,* August 29, 1915.

31. HMD to Harris, June 7, 1938, RBHP, Box 9/3; HMD to Scobey, January 17, 1916, Scobey Papers, Box 1/3.

32. See, for example, HMD to Scobey, January 17, 1916, Scobey Papers, Box 1/3.

33. *Cincinnati Times-Star,* January 17, March 7, 1916.

34. WGH to Jennings, January 28, 1916, Malcolm Jennings Papers, Box 1/1, Ohio Historical Society.

35. HMD to Scobey, January 17, 1916, Scobey Papers, Box 1/3.

36. *Columbus Evening Dispatch,* May 7, 1916.

37. WGH to Dick, May 15, 1916, Dick Papers, Box 43/3; WGH to Jennings, July 29, 1916, Jennings Papers, Box 1/1.

38. *Cleveland Plain Dealer,* June 9, 1916; *Cincinnati Enquirer,* June 9, 1916.

39. Lee to WGH, February 23, 1916, Lee Papers, Box 9/1. Lee thought Willis's support the "kiss of death."

40. *Cincinnati Enquirer,* July 29, 1916; *Ohio State Journal,* August 7, 1916.

41. Lee to Reuben Rankin, May 29, 1916, Lee Papers, Box 1/7; *Cincinnati Enquirer,* July 19, 30, 1916; *Cleveland Leader,* July 22, 1916.

42. Tyler to Myers, May 1, 1916, Myers Papers, Box 17/2; Foraker to Herrick, July 19, 1916, Foraker Papers, Box 113/H; WGH to Jennings, July 29, 1916, Jennings Papers, Box 1/1.

43. *Cincinnati Enquirer,* August 3, 1916; HMD to Harris, June 7, 1938, RBHP, Box 9/3.

44. *Cincinnati Times-Star,* July 24, 26, 1916; *Cincinnati Enquirer,* July 27, August 11, 1916. To keep the Anti-Saloon League neutral, however, Herrick pledged to support a national prohibition amendment.

45. *Cincinnati Enquirer,* August 6, 1916.

46. Ohio, *Annual Report of the Secretary of State, Election Statistics for 1916* (Springfield, Ohio), pp. 558-59. Daugherty won in Adams, Brown, Clermont, Clinton, Fayette, and Highland Counties.

47. HMD to Taft, August 18, 1916, TS 3, Box 354/3.

48. *Dayton Journal,* August 19, 1915, clipping in Burton Papers, Box 73/3; *Cincinnati Enquirer,* July 29, 1916.

49. Kurtz to Foraker, June 6, 1916, Foraker Papers, Box 113/K; Foraker to Kurtz, June 7, 1916, *ibid.*

50. WGH to Jennings, August 26, 1916, Jennings Papers, Box 1/1.

51. HMD to Taft, August 18, 1916, TS 3, Box 354/3.

52. *Ibid.*

53. *Cincinnati Enquirer,* August 3, 1916.

54. Herrick to WGH, January 9, 1920, HP, Box 688/5; Hoke Donithen to WGH, December 30, 1919, Box 686/3, *ibid.*

55. WGH to Scobey, December 4, 1916, Scobey Papers, Box 1/3.

CHAPTER VII

1. WGH to Scobey, May 7 and October 6, 1917, Scobey Papers, Box 1/4; Downes, *Harding,* pp. 283-85.

2. HMD to Harris, June 7, 1938, RBHP, Box 9/3; *ibid.,* September 13, 1939, Box 9/5; George W. Worden to WGH, November 11, 1899, HP, Box 705/8.

3. HMD to WGH, November 22, 1899, HP, Box 705/9; HMD to Harris, May 24, 1934, RBHP, Box 9/3.

4. Marchant to WGH, June 15, 1901, HP, Box 708/7.

5. *Cleveland Plain Dealer,* August 26, 1906; Scobey to WGH, August 25, 1906, HP, Box 719/4.

6. *Ohio State Journal,* July 28, 1910.

7. HMD to WGH, January 13, 1913, HP, Box 725/5; *ibid.,* November 16, 1912, Box 725/3.

8. Daugherty asked Marionite Hoke Donithen: "Is Harding identified with any business enterprise in Marion?" HMD to Donithen, December 19, 1919, Copy, Hoke Donithen Papers, Box 1/2, Ohio Historical Society; WGH to Jennings, January 20, 1920, Jennings Papers, Box 1/5. Formerly of Piqua, Ohio, F. E. Scobey was clerk of the Ohio Senate when Harding was a member. He eventually moved to San Antonio for his health.

9. Daugherty and Dixon, *Harding Tragedy,* for example, Chapter 2.

10. HMD to WGH, March 7, 1913, HP, Box 725/6.

11. Hard to WGH, December 15, 1918, Box 464/3, *ibid.*

12. HMD to Fairbanks, February 6, 1918, Fairbanks Papers, Box 1/2.

13. HMD to WGH, May 31, 23, 1918, HP, Box 685/2.

14. William Wood to WGH, February 3, 1918, George Christian, Jr., Papers, Box 738/2, Ohio Historical Society.

15. · See, for example, HMD to Willis, February 13, 1918, Willis Papers, Box 13/87.

16. HMD to Willis, January 24, 1918, Willis Papers, Box 13/87; Rudolph K. Hynicka to Willis, February 15, 1918, Willis Papers, Box 5.

17. WGH to HMD, March 30, 1918, Copy, HP, Box 681/1; HMD to WGH, February 14, 1918, *ibid.*

18. HMD to Willis, April 4, 1918, Willis Papers, Box 13/87.

19. WGH to HMD, May 25, 1918, HP, Box 685/2; HMD to WGH, May 31, 1918, *ibid.*

20. HMD to WGH, June 3, July 23, 1918, *ibid.* The two Willis opponents were Edwin Jones of Springfield and John H. Arnold of Columbus.

21. *Cleveland Plain Dealer,* August 20, 1918.

22. Downes, *Harding,* pp. 289-90; HMD to WGH, June 8, 1918, HP, Box 685/2.

23. Ridinger, "Willis," p. 141. Sole blame cannot be placed on Hamilton County. The attacks on Willis's patriotism and his poor showing as governor from 1914 to 1916 lost him a number of votes throughout the state.

24. HMD to WGH, November 18, 1918, Box 686/2.

25. WGH to HMD, November 23, 1918, *ibid.*

26. WGH to Charles E. Hard, November 27, 1918, Charles E. Hard Papers, Box 1/5; WGH to Fairbanks, December 12, 1918, Fairbanks Papers, Box 1/2.

27. WGH to Jennings, November 30, 1918, Jennings Papers, Box 1/3; WGH to Fairbanks, December 12, 1918, Fairbanks Papers, Box 1/2.

28. HMD to WGH, November 26, 1918, HP, Box 686/2; *ibid.,* June 3, 1918, Box 685/2.

29. *Ibid.,* December 17, 1918, Copy, Fairbanks Papers, Box 1/2.

30. WGH to HMD, November 27, 1918, Copy, HP, Box 686/2.

31. WGH to Jennings, November 27, 1918, Jennings Papers, Box 1/3; WGH to Hard, November 14, 1918, Hard Papers, Box 1/5.

32. WGH to Hard, December 7, 12, 1918, Hard Papers, Box 1/5.

33. Hard to WGH, December 1, 1918, HP, Box 464/3.

34. Hard to WGH, December 15, 1918, HP, Box 464/3; HMD to WGH, December 7, 1918, Box 686/2, *ibid.;* WGH to Hard, December 12, 1918, Hard Papers, Box 1/5.

35. WGH to Hard, December 12, 1918, Hard Papers, Box 1/5; Hard to WGH, December 15, 1918, HP, Box 464/3. Hard astutely wrote that Daugherty would forget the "heinous crimes of Cincinnati in just one half second" if it were in his interest.

36. WGH to HMD, December 20, 1918, Copy, HP, Box 686/2.

37. *Ibid.*

38. HMD to WGH, December 30, 1918, *ibid.*

39. *Ibid.* Such a ticket was not unlikely. See Downes, *Harding,* 291.

40 Hard to WGH, January 7, 1919, HP, Box 464/3.

41. HMD to WGH, January 9, 1919, Box 686/2, *ibid.*

42. WGH to HMD, January 11, 1919, Copy, *ibid.*

CHAPTER VIII

1. Mark Sullivan was the first to exaggerate Daugherty's wisdom. See Sullivan, *The Twenties,* pp. 22-23, 34.

2. Christian, Sr., to Scobey, May 15, 1915, Scobey Papers, Box 1/2; Scobey to WGH, March 30, 1915, *ibid.*

3. Harry S. Byrne to HMD, January 30, 1919, HP, Box 686/2; HMD to Byrne, February 4, 1919, *ibid.*

4. HMD to WGH, January 31, 1919, *ibid.;* Daugherty's suggestion to Christian is scrawled on Byrne to HMD, February 7, 1919, *ibid.*

5. Henry Jackson to HMD, February 19, 1919, Copy, *ibid.;* HMD to WGH, February 24, 1919, *ibid.*

6. HMD to WGH, February 17, 1919, *ibid.;* WGH to HMD, February 19, 1919, Telegram, *ibid.*

7. Downes, *Harding,* pp. 305-06.

8. HMD to WGH, July 3, 19, 1919, HP, Box 681/1; WGH to HMD, July 11, 1919, Copy, *ibid.*

9. WGH to HMD, July 30, 1919, Copy, HP, Box 686/1; HMD to WGH, July 25, 1919, *ibid.;* WGH to Clark, June 13, 1919, Copy, Christian, Jr., Papers, Box 782/1.

10. HMD to Fairbanks, October 15, 1918, Fairbanks Papers, Box 1/2; HMD to WGH, April 17, 1918, HP, Box 686/1.

11. HMD to WGH, March 22, April 2, 1919, HP, Box 686/2; *New York Times,* February 13, 1930; WGH to HMD, April 4, 1919, *ibid.,* HMD to WGH, August 20, 1919, Box 685/2, *ibid.*

12. HMD to WGH, September 6, 1919, Box 686/1, *ibid.;* Hard to WGH, September 5, 1919, Hard Papers, Box 1/7; Downes, *Harding,* pp. 333-34.

13. HMD to WGH, October 21, 1919, HP, Box 686/1; *ibid.,* October 11, 1919, Box 686/2; WGH to HMD, October 15, 1919, *ibid.*

14. HMD to WGH, October 24, 1919, Box 685/2, *ibid.*

15. *Ibid.;* Downes, *Harding,* pp. 311-12; WGH to Hard, October 25, 1919, Hard Papers, Box 1/8.

16. HMD to WGH, October 31, 1919, HP, Box 685/2; *Columbus Citizen,* November 4, 1919.

17. WGH to Hard, November 3, 1919, Hard Papers, Box 1/8.

18. Robert F. Wolfe to WGH, December 19, 1919, Christian, Jr., Papers, Box 783/3. That Daugherty opposed Wolfe's appointment to the state advisory's finance committee in February did not improve his relationship with Wolfe. Brown to WGH, February 11, 1920, HP, Box 684/2.

19. J. W. McConkie to Hynicka, January 14, 1920, Copy, uncataloged Preston Wolfe Papers, Ohio Historical Society; Herrick to WGH, January 9, 1920, HP, Box 688/5; Phipps

to WGH, January 31, 1920, Box 689/5, *ibid.;* Unpublished Manuscript of George Christian, Sr., pp. 81-85, in George B. Christian, Sr., Papers, Box 892, Ohio Historical Society; Scobey to WGH, December 24, 1919, Scobey Papers, Box 2/5; Jennings to Scobey, March 22, 1920, Box 2/7, *ibid.*

20. WGH to Scobey, January 20, 1920, Scobey Papers, Box 2/6; *ibid.,* December 16, 1919, Box 2/5.

21. WGH to Jennings, February 4, 1920, Jennings Papers, Box 1/5; Downes, *Harding,* pp. 347-50.

22. WGH to Scobey, January 20, 1920, Scobey Papers, Box 2/6.

23. HMD to Christian, Jr., November 2, 1919, HP, Box 685/2.

24. HMD to Scobey, December 4, 1919, Scobey Papers, Box 2/5; HMD to E. Mont Reily, December 3, 1919, Daugherty Letters, VFM 1581, Ohio Historical Society; WGH to Scobey, November 22, 1919, Scobey Papers, Box 2/4.

25. *Ohio State Journal,* November 23, 1919.

26. HMD to I. R. Foster, December 4, 1919, Copy, HP, Box 685/2; "How Daugherty Helped Harding Into the White House," 40.

27. See, for example, WGH to H. M. Sewall, December 16, 1919, HP, Box 690/1.

28. HMD to WGH, December 16, 1919, Box 685/1, *ibid.; ibid.,* December 23, 1919, Box 685/2; Downes, *Harding,* pp. 381-82.

29. HMD to WGH, December 26, 1919, HP, Box 685/1.

30. A. E. B. Stephens to Hynicka, January 17, 1920, Copy, uncataloged Wolfe Papers.

31. Clark to WGH, January 14, 1920, Christian, Jr., Papers, Box 782/1.

32. HMD to WGH, October 24, 1919, HP, Box 685/2; Donithen to Christian, Jr., December 30, 1919, Box 686/3, *ibid.*

33. WGH to Jennings, January 20, 1920, Jennings Papers, Box 1/5.

34. Clark to WGH, January 14, 1920, Christian Jr., Papers, Box 782/1; WGH to Herrick, March 16, 1920, Copy, HP, Box 688/5.

35. HMD to Reily, December 24, 1919, Daugherty Letters, VFM 1581, HMD to Scobey, January 19, 1920, Scobey Papers, Box 2/6; HMD to WGH, December 19, 1919, HP, Box 685/2.

36. HMD to Reily, January 26, 29, 1920, Daugherty Letters, VFM 1581.

37. H.F. Alderfer, "The Personality and Politics of Warren G. Harding"(unpublished Ph. D. dissertation, School of Citizenship and Public Affairs, Syracuse University, 1928), p. 17.

38. HMD to Reily, December 24, 1919, Daugherty letters, VFM 1581; *ibid.,* January 26, 1920; Reily to WGH, December 31, 1919, HP, Box 690/1; HMD to Scobey, January 19, 1920, Scobey Papers, Box 2/6; Downes, *Harding,* p. 424; Sullivan, *The Twenties,* p. 23.

39. Downes, *Harding,* p. 421; HMD to Finley Peter Dunne, April 10, 22, 1920, Finley Peter Dunne Papers, Box 6325/D, Library of Congress.

40. HMD to Donithen, December 19, 1919, Copy, Donithen Papers, Box 1/2.

41. HMD to Scobey, January 22, 1920, Scobey Papers, Box 2/6.

42. Scobey to HMD, January 22, 1920, Copy, Scobey Papers, Box 2/6; HMD to Scobey, January 27, 1920, *ibid.*

43. Downes, *Harding,* pp. 379-80.

44. HMD to Harris, June 29, 1938, RBHP, Box 9/3.

45. Downes, *Harding,* pp. 361-70.

46. HMD to Scobey, February 1, 1920, Scobey Papers, Box 2/7; HMD to Charles Forbes, February 16, 1920, Daugherty Letters, VFM 1869.

47. Scobey to HMD, March 18, 1920, Scobey Papers, Box 2/7; Mannington to Scobey, March 22, 1920, *ibid.*

48. Charles Hilles later explained Daugherty's account to Mark Sullivan: Daugherty was hastily packing his bag in a New York hotel room when two reporters called. Daugherty expressed regret that he had no time for an interview. One reporter followed Daugherty, trying to provoke him to reiterate how he expected to put Harding across when an authentic

table of the delegates did not support his boast. The reporter, answering his own question, said that he (Daugherty) must expect to win by manipulation, probably in some back room of a hotel with a small group of political managers and party leaders. The reporter went on to say that he presumed they would surrender at 2:00 A.M. in a smoke-filled room. Unaffected by the taunt, Daugherty replied carelessly, "make it 2:11." Sullivan, *The Twenties,* p. 37n.; Press Release from Allan B. Jaynes, June 18, 1920, uncataloged Will Hays Papers, The Indiana State Library.

49. WGH to Birch Helme, March 22, 1920, Copy, HP, Box 688/5; Jennings to Scobey, March 22, 1920, Scobey Papers, Box 2/7.

50. HMD to Donithen, March 27, 1920, Copy, Donithen Papers, Box 1/2; Anonymous to Harding, March 30, 1920, HP, Box 685/1. As a similarity in style exists, Daugherty may have composed the letter.

51. E. G. Burkham to WGH, April 14, 1920, HP, Box 684/6.

52. Scobey to Robert Armstrong, April 19, 1920, Copy, Scobey Papers, Box 2/8; HMD to Reily, April 23, 1920, Daugherty Letters VFM 1581.

53. Of the six delegate-at-large candidates, four were selected. Herrick led with 131,190 votes, followed by Willis with 121,942 and Galvin, 118,197. The Wood candidate, Boyd, won the final spot, gathering 107,449 votes. Daugherty finished in fifth position with 106,490, barely ahead of Turner, 105,945. Secretary of State, *Election Statistics for 1920,* p. 634.

54. HMD to Reily, May 15, 1920, Daugherty Letters VFM 1581; Charles Dean to Christian, Jr., March 22, 1920, HP, Box 686/3; Herrick to Hays, May 5, 1920, uncataloged Hays Papers.

55. Sinclair, *Available Man,* p. 132.

56. HMD to Scobey, May 7, 8, 1920, Scobey Papers, Box 2/8.

57. HMD to WGH, May 8, 14, 1920, HP, Box 685/1.

58. HMD to WGH, May 20, 1920, *ibid.*

59. Brown to WGH, May 15, 1920, HP, Box 684/8; WGH to Brown, May 17, 1920, Walter Brown Papers, Box 1/2, Ohio Historical Society; WGH to HMD, May 17, 1920, HP, Box 685/1.

CHAPTER IX

1. Wesley M. Bagby, *The Road to Normalcy: The Presidential Campaign and Election of 1920* (Baltimore, 1968), pp. 36, 52.

2. HMD to Reily, May 15, 1920, Daugherty Letters, VFM 1581.

3. HMD to William S. Kenyon, May 22, 1920, Telegram, Copy, HP, Box 685/1.

4. U. S. Congress, Senate, Subcommittee of the Committee on Privileges and Elections, *Presidential Campaign Expenses,* 66th Cong., 2nd Sess., 1920, I, 267-68.

5. *Ibid.,* 172-202, 285-306, 590-618, 631-50.

6. HMD to Dunne, May 13, 1920, Dunne Papers, 6325/D; Finley Peter Dunne, "A Look at Harding from the Sidelines," *Saturday Evening Post,* CCIX (September 12, 1936), 25.

7. HMD to Harris, June 29, 1938, RBHP, Box 9/3.

8. Daugherty and Dixon, *Harding Tragedy,* pp. 37, 43.

9. William T. Hutchinson, *Lowden of Illinois,* II (Chicago, 1957), 423, Frank Lowden to Harris, August 8, 1938, RBHP, Box 2/6. Lowden denied the understanding with Daugherty. For Daugherty's account, see Daugherty and Dixon, *Harding Tragedy,* p. 36.

10. Sullivan, *The Twenties,* pp. 35-36.

11. *Ibid.,* p. 52. Russell, *Blooming Grove,* p. 375.

12. *Official Report of the Proceedings of the Seventeenth Republican National Convention* (New York, 1920), p. 195.

13. For two examples, see William Allen White, *A Puritan in Babylon: The Story of Calvin Coolidge* (New York, 1959), pp. 228-29 and Adams, *Incredible Era,* pp. 149-58.

14. HMD to Harry S. New, March 4, 1932, Harry S. New Papers, Box 1/4, Indiana State Library.

15. Ray Baker Harris, "Warren G. Harding: An Account of His Nomination for the Presidency by the Republican Convention of 1920" (Washington, D. C., 1957), pp. 9-11, RBHP, Box 3/1. Harris, an amateur historian, wrote an excellent account of Harding's nomination. For later versions, see Bagby, *Road to Normalcy,* pp. 85-100 and Robert K. Murray, *The Harding Era: Warren G. Harding and His Administration* (Minneapolis, 1969), pp. 32-42; Reed Smoot to Harris, August 11, 1939, RBHP, Box 2/6.

16. Joseph Grundy to Harris, June 20, 1938, RBHP, Box 2/6.

17. James Wadsworth to Harris, October 8, 1932, *ibid.;* Wadsworth to Mark Sullivan, March 5, 1935, Copy, Wadsworth Family Papers, Box 17/12, Library of Congress. Ex-Senator John W. Week's testimony, for example, supports Wadsworth's account. See Joe Martin, *My First Fifty Years in Politics* (New York, 1960), pp. 141-42.

18. Bagby, *Road to Normalcy,* p. 89. According to Bagby, two senators were present at the interview; Daugherty later claimed that the oath-taking story was a fabrication of Harvey's former secretary, Willis Fletcher Johnson, who first mentioned it in a *Saturday Evening Post* article of August 31, 1929. HMD to Clemens, July 3, 1939, Clemens Papers, Box 1/13.

19. Harris, "1920 Republican Convention," p. 20; Hilles to Sullivan, March 2, 1935, Copy, Wadsworth Family Papers, Box 17/12; Nicholas Murray Butler to Sullivan, March 22, 1935, Copy, *ibid.*

20. Daugherty later admitted that Wadsworth was not "warmed up to me" and " a lot of people who I liked didn't like me so much." HMD to New, March 13, 1932, New Papers, Box 1/4; William Calder to Harris, August 2, 1933, RBHP, Box 2/6; HMD to Clemens, July 3, 1939, Clemens Papers, Box 1/3.

21. Downes, *Harding,* pp. 419-22. At least one Harding friend implied that Hynicka's actions were the result of his determination to beat Daugherty. Lee to Mrs. Florence Kling Harding, February 23, 1922, Lee Papers, Box 9/3.

22. HMD to Harris, June 29, 1938, RBHP, Box 9/3.

23. Bagby, *Road to Normalcy,* p. 94; James E. Watson, *As I Knew Them: Memoirs of James E. Watson* (Indianapolis and New York, 1936), p. 220.

24. Bagby, *Road to Normalcy,* p. 94; White, *Puritan in Babylon,* 210.

25. HMD to Harris, May 24, 1934, RBHP, Box 9/4; James Davis to Harris, May 22, 1934, Box 2/6, *ibid.* In another letter Daugherty admitted that Penrose had only controlled part of the delegation. HMD to Harris, November 30, 1937, Box 9/4, *ibid.* In his often unreliable *Harding Tragedy,* Daugherty claimed that Penrose had instead telephoned him! pp. 48-49.

26. HMD to Harris, October 6, 1939, RBHP, Box 9/5; Bagby, *Road to Normalcy,* p. 95.

27. For Lowden's withdrawal, see Hilles to Wadsworth, March 9, 1935, Wadsworth Family Papers, Box 17/12; Bagby, *Road to Normalcy,* p. 95.

28. Daugherty and Dixon, *Harding Tragedy,* pp. 53-55; Butler to Sullivan, March 22, 1935, Copy, Wadsworth Family Papers, Box 17/12.

29. Harry S. New, "The Senatorial Oligarchy," *Saturday Evening Post,* CCIV (May 28, 1932), 84; HMD to New, March 4, 1932, New Papers, Box 1/4.

30. New, "Senatorial Oligarchy," 21, 84; Daugherty Inclosure, March 3, 1932, New Papers, Box 1/4; Harris, "1920 Republican Convention," p. 19.

31. HMD to Harris, October 9, 1939, RBHP, Box 9/5; Downes, *Harding,* p. 425.

32. Sullivan, *The Twenties,* p. 67n.; Jaynes Press Release, June 18, 1920, uncataloged Hays Papers.

33. HMD to Harris, June 29, 1938, RBHP, Box 9/3; HMD to Reily, August 16, 1920, Daugherty Letters, VFM 1581; *New York Times,* June 20, 21, 1920.

34. *New York Times,* June 23, 1920; *St. Louis Daily Globe-Democrat,* August 30, 1920,

clipping in uncataloged Hays Papers; HMD to Reily, August 16, 1920, Daugherty Letters, VFM 1581.

35. HMD to WGH, July 19, 1920, HP, Box 763/2.

36. *New York Times,* June 30, 1920; *Ohio State Journal,* June 30, 1920; all are in the Harding Papers: HMD to WGH, June 25, 1920, Box 763/4; *ibid.,* August 23, 1920, Box 763/3; *ibid.,* August 15, July 15, 1920, Box 763/4; Hanna to WGH, July 3, 1920, Box 594/4.

37. Charles A. Jones, interview, April 2, 1967; Ridinger, "Willis," p. 153.

38. HMD to WGH, July 1, 1920, HP, Box 763/4; Harding wrote Jennings that, as far as Daugherty was concerned, he (Harding) was "not wholly to blame for some of the manifestations which are lacking in good taste." WGH to Jennings, June 24, 1920, Jennings Papers, Box 1/5.

39. Judson C. Welliver to Scott C. Bone, August 3, 1920, uncataloged Hays Papers.

40. HMD to WGH, August 29, September 5, 1920, HP, Box 763/3.

41. Bagby, *Road to Normalcy,* p. 124.

42. HMD to WGH, October 17, 18, 1920, HP, Box 656/2. For the most comprehensive account of the 1920 campaign, see Downes, *Harding,* pp. 427-640.

CHAPTER X

1. Daugherty and Dixon, *Harding Tragedy,* pp. 68-91.

2. Lindsay Rogers to George Sutherland, November 9, 1920, George Sutherland Papers, Box 3/35, Library of Congress; Frank T. Hines to Sutherland, November 11, 1920, *ibid.*

3. Welliver to Sutherland, December 10, 1920, Box 3/36, *ibid.;* HMD to Sutherland, December 9, 1920, *ibid.*

4. Wadsworth to Harris, June 20, 1938, RBHP, Box 2/6; J. T. Williams Transcript, 556, Columbia Oral History Center of New York.

5. WGH to Bishop F. Anderson, February 20, 1921, HP, Box 655/1.

6. J. O. A. Preus Transcript, pp. 101-02, Minnesota Historical Society Oral History Collection.

7. Clinton Wallace Gilbert, *Behind the Mirrors: The Psychology of Disintegration at Washington* (New York and London, 1922), p. 316; Sullivan, *The Twenties,* p. 149. Several of Daugherty's Ohio friends later repeated his remarks to Sullivan.

8. Bascom N. Timmons, *Charles Dawes: Portrait of An American* (New York, 1953), p. 203; Colonel T. Bentley Mott, *Myron T. Herrick: Friend of France, An Autobiographical Biography* (Garden City, New York, 1929), p. 256; for example, Calder to Harris, August 2, 1933, RBHP, Box 2/6.

9. Taft to Helen H. Taft, December 26, 1920, cited in Pringle, *Taft,* p. 955.

10. *New York Times,* January 14, 1921.

11. Jennings to WGH, February 6, 1921, Copy, Jennings Papers, Box 1/6.

12. J. Reuben Clark, Jr., to Philander Knox, April 9, 1921, Philander Knox Papers, Volume 23, Library of Congress.

13. *New York World,* February 17, 1921. The exposé was exaggerated in that Daugherty was linked to *some* incidents where wrongdoing was by no means proved. The *World* also neglected to name most of its informants.

14. *Ibid.,* February 17-21, 1921.

15. *New York Times,* February 11, 1921.

16. The reaction of the *Tribune* and other leading newspapers is in the *St. Louis Post-Dispatch,* February 23, 1921.

17. For Willis's defense, see the *New York Times,* February 22, 1921.

18. Willis to Managing Editor, *New York Tribune,* March 1, 1921, Copy, Willis Papers, Box 13/87. Willis cited a number of Daugherty defenders in his letter.

19. Taft to Karger, February 14, 1921, Copy, TL, Letterbook 98. One current historian also felt that Daugherty's understanding of lobbying tactics could have been beneficial for

the protection of the common good. But Daugherty was not often motivated by such altruism. See Murray, *Harding Era,* pp. 107-08.

20. Sullivan, *The Twenties,* p. 151; *New York Times,* February 20, 1921. Sullivan's account does not square fully with that of the *Times.*

21. Sullivan, *The Twenties,* p. 152; *New York Times,* February 22, 1921.

22. Murray convincingly portrayed Harding as acting independently and conscientiously in selecting his cabinet. Murray, *Harding Era,* pp. 93-109. For a more traditional view, see Sinclair, *Available Man,* pp. 181-97.

23. *New York Times,* February 22, January 14, 1921; HMD to WGH, February 6, 1921, HP, Box 363/5.

24. HMD to WGH, February 6, 1921, Telegram, Copy, HP, Box 695/1; Daugherty and Dixon, *Harding Tragedy,* p. 99. Daugherty also stated, "I had 'cussed' a little at times when unduly provoked. But I listened in awe to my master's voice."

25. HMD to WGH, February 6, 1921, Copy, HP, Box 695/1; WGH to HMD, February 9, 1921, Copy, *ibid.*

26. HMD to New, May 26, 1936, New Papers, Box 1/5; Hays to L. W. Henley, February 4, 1921, Copy, uncataloged Hays Papers. In his book, Daugherty stated that he made only two cabinet recommendations: Mellon and Sutherland. Daugherty and Dixon, *Harding Tragedy,* p. 98.

27. Burl Noggle, *Teapot Dome: Oil and Politics in the 1920's* (Baton Rouge, 1962), p. 13.

28. Daugherty and Dixon, *Harding Tragedy,* pp. 77-78; Daugherty inclosure to New, March 3, 1932, New Papers, Box 1/4.

29. Murray, *Harding Era,* p. 106.

30. *New York Times,* March 5, 1921; *Washington Post,* March 5, 1921.

31. "Strength and Weakness of the Cabinet," *Literary Digest,* LXVIII (March 12, 1921), 7-9; *New York Times,* February 22, 1921; *Ohio State Journal,* February 23, 1921.

CHAPTER XI

1. Sullivan, *The Twenties,* pp. 22-23; Gilbert, *Behind the Mirrors,* p. 138.

2. "Bad News for War Grafters," *Literary Digest,* LXXIII (May 27, 1922), 14; *Investigation of the Honorable Harry M. Daugherty,* U. S. Senate Select Committee, 68th Cong., 1st Sess. (Washington, D.C., 1924), 3185-86. Cited hereafter as *Daugherty Investigation.*

3. *New York Times,* September 1, 1921.

4. Taft to A. I. Vorys, November 13, 1922, Copy, TS 3, Box 527/13.

5. *Ibid.*

6. HMD to Stimson, July 30, 1921. Stimson Papers, Box 204; *New York Times,* July 29, 1921.

7. Gilbert, *Behind the Mirrors,* p. 137.

8. *New York Times,* April 13, 1921; Guy Goff to Charles Polleser, July 21, 1921, Copy, DJF 60-10-0-6.

9. The Daugherty-Hoover correspondence in the Herbert Hoover Papers, Herbert Hoover Presidential Library, clearly reveals their differences. For example, HMD to Hoover, February 8, 1922, Hoover Papers, 1-1/179; see also Robert F. Himmelberg, "Relaxation of the Federal Anti-Trust Policy as a Goal of the Business Community During the Period 1918-1933," unpublished Ph. D. dissertation (Pennsylvania State University, 1963), pp. 96-107.

10. Goff to J. E. Stuckey, December 28, 1921, DJF 60-0-16; Himmelberg, "Anti-Trust Policy," p. 99.

11. Fred Lazarus, Jr., to HMD, January 6, 1922, DJF 215000-9; Himmelberg, "Anti-Trust Policy," p. 99; Jennings to WGH, January 6, 1922, Copy, Jennings Papers, Box 1/8.

12. Himmelberg, "Anti-Trust Policy," p. 92.

13. *Ibid.*, pp. 105-07.

14. *Ibid.*, pp. 97-99.

15. Alpheus Thomas Mason, *Harlan Fiske Stone: Pillar of the Law* (New York, 1956), p. 165; Charles L. Lobingier to Thomas Walsh, January 29, 1925, Thomas Walsh Papers, Box 278/1, Library of Congress.

16. *New York Times,* March 11, 1921.

17. Adams, *Incredible Era,* p. 332. Senator Henry Ashurst of Arizona first coined that term.

18. What also hurt was the 1922 death of Will Herron, Taft's brother-in-law, who was one of the best lawyers in the Department. *Daugherty Investigation,* p. 2575.

19. HMD to WGH, May 3, 1921, HP, Box 219/2; *New York Times,* May 13, 1921.

20. HMD to J. E. Dyche, November 3, 1922, DJF 4-1-4-61-2; A. T. Seymour to Dyche, July 11, 1923, 4-1-4-61-5, *ibid.; Daugherty Investigation,* pp. 977-78.

21. *New York Times,* August 19, 1921.

22. Fred J. Cook, *The FBI Nobody Knows* (New York, 1964), p. 118.

23. Russell, *Blooming Grove,* p. 516.

24. *New York Times,* April 1, 1921.

25. Don Whitehead, *The FBI Story: A Report to the People* (New York, 1956), p. 56; *New York Times,* August 19, 1921.

26. Murray, *Harding Era,* p. 297; Cook, *FBI,* p. 118.

27. *New York Times,* September 11, 1921.

28. HMD to Edward B. McLean, April 5, 1921, RBHP, Box 4/6; *Daugherty Investigation,* p. 2453.

29. Rush Holland to HMD, January 12, 1922, DJF 191307-8.

30. Edwin P. Hoyt, *Spectacular Rogue: Gaston B. Means* (Indianapolis, 1963), p. 147.

31. Holland to HMD, January 12, 1922, DJF 191307-8; Joseph J. Early to George Christian, Jr., February 24, 1923, HP, Box 28/2; Edward Swann, District Attorney of New York City, to HMD, January 27, 1922, DJF 191307-9.

32. HMD to Seymour, April 27, 1923, Telegram, DJF 191307-12X; Hoyt, *Spectacular Rogue,* Chapter XI.

33. *Congressional Record,* 67th Cong., 2nd Sess., 6364-65, 7772-73; *Daugherty Investigation,* p. 2543; Cook, *FBI,* pp. 130-31; Max Lowenthal, *The Federal Bureau of Investigation* (Westport, 1971), pp. 290-93.

34. Hoover to HMD, February 26, 1924, Copy, Hoover Papers, 1-J/20.

35. Russell, *Blooming Grove,* pp. 403-04, 413-15; Clark to Hard, October 13, 1920, Hard Papers, Box 2/11.

36. Russell, *Blooming Grove,* pp. 431-32. Sometime after Russell used the Chancellor file at the U.S. Secret Service branch office in Boston, the Secret Service destroyed it. John W. Warner, Jr., Assistant to the Director, to the author, February 7, 1975.

37. Russell, *Blooming Grove,* pp. 528-31. A couple of copies of the Chancellor book still exist, one of which is in the Ohio Historical Society Library.

38. See, for example, Cook, *FBI,* pp. 133-35; *Daugherty Investigation,* p. 2543.

39. Pringle, *Taft,* II, 959; Alpheus Thomas Mason, *William Howard Taft: Chief Justice* (New York, 1964), pp. 78-79.

40. Taft to HMD, May 2, 1921, Copy, TS 3, Box 487/2.

41. HMD to WGH, April 8, 1922, HP, Box 29/4.

42. WGH to HMD, February 28, 1923, Copy, Box 195/1, *ibid.*

43. HMD to A. J. Volstead, August 18, 1921, Copy, TS 3, Box 498/12; Mason, *Taft,* pp. 98, 122.

44. Taft to HMD, June 5, 1922, Copy, TS 3, Box 517/5.

45. HMD to Taft, January 3, 1923, Box 531/3, *ibid.* The strike is covered in Chapter XII.

46. Taft to Charley Taft, January 3, 1923, Copy, *ibid.;* HMD to Taft, January 4, 1923, *ibid.*

47. Hulbert Taft to Taft, January 6, 1923, Box 531/6, *ibid.*

48. Taft to Hulbert Taft, January 7, 1923, Copy, Box 531/7, *ibid.*

49. Sullivan, *The Twenties,* p. 24.

50. *Fayette County Record,* March 26, 1903.

51. Harper, "Plain Talk," p. 46.

52. *Ibid.,* p. 50.

53. Sullivan, *The Twenties,* p. 25; *Daugherty Investigation,* p. 531.

54. *Cincinnati Times-Star,* May 11, 1921.

55. For the H Street activities, see *Daugherty Investigation,* pp. 684-723.

56. *Ibid.,* pp. 2473-74; evidence exists that Smith and Means participated in the Bureau investigation of Chancellor. *Ibid.,* pp. 2532-33.

57. *Ibid.,* pp. 2536, 2217, 2456.

58. *Ibid.,* p. 31.

59. Dunne, "Look at Harding," p. 79.

60. *Daugherty Investigation,* pp. 1451-52, 1457, 1479, 2181. Although Russell's appointment was backed by Daugherty, it was opposed by Senator Willis and the Ohio Anti-Saloon League. Ridinger, "Willis," p. 222.

61. See Chapter XIII.

62. *Daugherty Investigation,* pp. 2405-14.

63. Jennings to Harding, July 12, 1921, Jennings Papers, Box 1/7.

64. *Daugherty Investigation,* pp. 2171-78, 448.

65. *Ibid.,* pp. 2363-64.

66. *Ibid.,* 130, 157.

67. DJF 81-203014, and *passim.*

68. *Daugherty Investigation,* p. 690.

69. HMD to Herrick, June 27, 1922, Copy, DJF 215000-10.

70. Bernard Baruch, *Baruch: The Public Years* (New York, 1960), 188-89.

71. Howard D. Mannington to HMD, May 5, 1922, DJF 184753; HMD to Robert Lovett, May 25, 1922, *ibid.*

72. HMD to William Hayward, July 11, 1922, *ibid.;* Mannington to HMD. July 18, 1922, *ibid.*

73. For an example of employee recalcitrance, see *Daugherty Investigation,* p. 3235. See also pp. 2361-62.

74. Stimson to HMD, February 16, 1922, Stimson Papers, Box 204.

75. Marvin Jones Transcript, Columbia Oral History Project, 276.

76. HMD to Hilles, March 2, 1923, Hilles Papers, Box 189.

77. Hilles to HMD, March 5, 1923, Hilles Papers, *ibid.*

78. *New York Times,* September 12, 1921.

79. HMD to Mrs. Ned McLean, December 26, 1921, February 1, 1922, McLean Family Papers, Box 5/D, Library of Congress.

80. *Toledo Times,* March 18, 1921; *Cleveland Leader,* March 13, 1921; *Toledo News-Bee,* May 6, 1921; and *Toledo Blade,* August 18, 1921. Clippings in Willis Papers, Box 10/5; Newt Miller to Willis, May 11, 1921, Willis Papers, Box 10/3.

81. Lee to Mrs. Harding, February 23, 1922, Copy, Lee Papers, Box 9/3.

82. Lee to Charles E. Sawyer, February 15, 1922, Copy, Box 2/5, *ibid.;* Lee to WGH, February 15, 1922, Copy, *ibid.;* Lee to Mrs. Harding, February 16, 1922, Copy, *ibid.*

83. Jennings to WGH, August 15, 1921, Copy, Jennings Papers, Box 1/7.

84. WGH to Jennings, August 13, 1921, *ibid.;* HMD to WGH, June 9, 1921, HP, Box 248/7.

85. WGH to Brown, April 14, 1922, Brown Papers, Box 1/B; Taft to HMD, November 16, 1923, Copy, TS 3, Box 547/11; HMD to Hard, October 20, 1923, Hard Papers, Box 2/2.

86. HMD to WGH, December 23, 1921, DJF 35-386-3336.

87. *Ibid.*

88. *Ibid.,* December 17, 1921, HP, Box 154/5.

89. *Ibid.* In retrospect, Daugherty wrote admiringly of Debs. Daugherty and Dixon, *Harding Tragedy,* pp. 116-21.

90. WGH to Jennings, January 6, 1922, Jennings Papers, Box 1/8.

91. HMD to WGH, December 17, 1921, HP, Box 154/5.

92. HMD to Harry Weinberger, October 12, March 18, 1921, Harry Weinberger Papers, Box 50, Yale University Library.

93. WGH to HMD, September 2, 1921, Copy, HP, Box 363/4.

94. HMD to WGH, September 7, 1921, *ibid.*

95. *Daugherty Investigation,* pp. 1874-75, 2225, 1486-87, 1449.

96. HMD to WGH, October 18, 1921, Department of State File, 711-62119-96; Charles Evans Hughes to HMD, July 6, 1921, 62119-98A, *ibid.;* WGH to HMD, October 24, 1921, DJF 198333-46X.

97. WGH to Jennings, November 15, 1921, Jennings Papers, Box 1/7; Jennings to WGH, November 20, 1921, Copy, *ibid.*

98. WGH to HMD, April 17, 1922, Copy, HP, Box 29/4; July 19, 1921, Box 695/1, *ibid.*

99. HMD to Dunne, April 8, 1922, Dunne Papers, Box 6325/D.

100. HMD to WGH, May 17, 1922, Copy, HP, Box 695/2; WGH to HMD, May 18, 1922, *ibid.*

101. *Daugherty Investigation,* p. 783; *Congressional Record,* 67th Cong., 4th Sess., 2427; *New York Times,* March 2, 1924.

102. WGH to Osborne Mitchell, May 25, 1922, Copy, HP, Box 28/3; WGH to James T. Williams, Jr., June 13, 1922, *ibid.*

CHAPTER XII

1. William E. Hooper, "General Atterbury's Attitude toward Labor," *World's Work,* XLIV (September 1922), 507; Bert M. Jewell, "The Railroad Strike: Striker's Viewpoint," *Current History,* XVII (November 1922), 207; Allen M. Wakstein, "The Origins of the Open-Shop Movement," *Journal of American History,* LI (December 1964), 470.

2. Budd L. McKillips, "Company Unions on the Railroads," *Nation,* CXLII (January 8, 1936), 48.

3. Edward Berman, *Labor Disputes and the President of the United States* (New York, 1924), pp. 231-34.

4. Murray, *Harding Era,* p. 253; Robert H. Zieger, *Republicans and Labor, 1919-1929* (Lexington, 1969), pp. 129-33.

5. Donald Richberg, *My Hero: The Indiscreet Memoirs of an Eventful but Unheroic Life* (New York, 1954), p. 116; HMD to WGH, August 16, 1922, HP, Box 62/1; *New York Times,* August 30, 1922.

6. *New York Times,* August 16, 23, 1922; Daugherty and Dixon, *Harding Tragedy,* p. 127.

7. *New York Times,* September 1, 1921; HMD to S. Pemberton Hutchinson, April 1, 1922, DJF 16-155-17X.

8. HMD to Will Herron, June 24, 1922, Memorandum, DJF 16-150-100-1.

9. See, for example, Lowenthal, *F.B.I.,* pp. 271-72.

10. Murray, *Harding Era,* p. 254; HMD to Blackburn Esterline, August 28, 1922, DJF 16-150-100-1.

11. Murray, *Harding Era,* pp. 254-55; WGH to HMD, September 2, 1922, Copy, HP, Box 62/1; Zieger, *Republicans and Labor,* p. 140.

12. HMD to WGH, September 14, 1922, HP, Box 30/3.

13. *New York Times,* September 2, 1922.

14. Holland to HMD, September 7, 1922, Telegram, DJF 16-150-100-1.

15. HMD to Mrs. McLean, July 20, 1922, McLean Family Papers, Box 5/D; Martin to George Rothwell Brown, DJF 218896-48-57X.

16. Goff to HMD, September 8, 1922, Memorandum, 160-150-100, *ibid.;* Beck to HMD, September 14, 1922, 16-15-100-4, *ibid.*

17. Richberg, *My Hero,* pp. 116-17; Zieger, *Republicans and Labor,* p. 139.

18. Harry D. Wolfe, *The Railroad Labor Board* (Chicago, 1927), pp. 265-66; Richard Waterman, "Shopmen's Strike—Who Won It?" *Nation's Business,* X (November 1922), 25.

19. *New York Times,* September 2, 1922.

20. *Ibid.,* September 4, 1922; William Borah to Roy N. Castle, September 14, 1922, William Borah Papers, Box 214/4, Library of Congress.

21. "Smothering A Strike By Injunction," *Literary Digest,* LXXIV (September 16, 1922), 7-9; "Labor Injunction Must Go," *New Republic,* XXXII (September 27, 1922), 109; "Daugherty Declares War," (September 13, 1922), 58, *ibid.*

22. Herbert Hoover, *The Memoirs of Herbert Hoover: The Cabinet and the Presidency, 1920-1933* (New York, 1952), pp. 47-48.

23. HMD to Harris, September 19, 1936, RBHP, Box 9/4.

24. Murray, *Harding Era,* p. 258.

25. *New York Times,* September 12, 22, 24, 1922.

26. HMD to J. M. Dickinson, June 12, 1923, Copy, DJF 160-150-100; Esterline to HMD, June 22, 1923, 16-150-100-200X, *ibid.*

27. *Ohio State Journal,* October 13, 1941. In the long run, labor profited some from both the strike and injunction. The former led to the defeat of the Railroad Labor Board and to the eventual creation of the more liberal 1926 Railroad Labor Act. The latter in part inspired the Norris-LaGuardia Act of 1932. See Zieger, *Republicans and Labor,* pp. 141-42.

28. HMD to John T. Williams, December 28, 1922, DJF 60-12-4-23X; clipping of Resolution in 60-12-4-4, *ibid.;* Homer Cummings and Carl McFarland, *Federal Justice: Chapters in the History of Justice and the Federal Executive* (New York, 1937), 459-60.

29. *New York Times,* September 18, 19, 1922.

30. "Uncle Sam's Prosecutor Prosecuted," *Literary Digest,* LXXV (December 16, 1922 11; *Congressional Record.* 67th Cong., 4th Sess., 2413.

31. Theodore Roosevelt, Jr., to Edwin Denby, October 16, 1922, uncataloged Edwin Denby Papers, Burton Historical Collection, Detroit Public Library; *Cincinnati Enquirer,* October 22, 1922.

32. Daugherty and Dixon, *Harding Tragedy,* p. 152.

33. *Daugherty Investigation,* p. 2543.

34. *Reply by the Attorney General of the United States, Hon. Harry M. Daugherty, to Charges Filed with the Committee on the Judiciary of the House of Representatives, December 1, 1922, by Hon. Oscar E. Keller, Representative from Minnesota* (Washington, D.C., December 1, 1922), pp. 45-56, HP, Box 30/4; HMD to Harris, November 18, 1932, RBHP, Box 9/3.

35. *Congressional Record,* 67th Cong., 4th Sess., 2428-29; "Mr. Daugherty Comes Clear," *Literary Digest* LXXVI (February 10, 1923), 16.

36. Mason, *Stone,* pp. 166-67; "The Attack on Daugherty," *Literary Digest,* LXXVII (February 16, 1924), 16.

37. In thirty-six months as Attorney General, Daugherty commenced fifty-two antitrust actions to forty-four for his successors, Harlan F. Stone and John G. Sargent, over a comparable period. See *The Federal Antitrust Laws: With Summary of Cases Instituted by the United States* (New York, 1949), pp. 121-45. The Taft administration had set the pace with eighty-one in four years.

38. *Daugherty Investigation,* pp. 2673-796, especially pp. 2753-57; Daugherty to J. A. Fowler, April 1, 1922 and Ragland Momand to Harlan Fiske Stone, June 28, 1924, DJF 60-156-6-87 and 141X.

39. *Congressional Record,* 67th Cong., 2nd Sess., 6364-65.

40. *Ibid.,* pp. 7625-26.

41. *Ibid.,* pp. 6364- 65; Adams, *Incredible Era,* pp. 314-15.

42. Martin to Mrs. McLean, January 26, 1923, McLean Family Papers, Box 5/D.

43. Memorandum of Special Agent Shine's interview with Mrs. E. C. Kidd, February 1, 1927, DJF 22830; HMD to Mrs. Harding, February 28, 1923, Florence Kling Harding Papers, Box 789/5. According to Daugherty, Harding had visited him that day.

44. Memorandum of Kidd interview, February 1, 1927, DJF 22830, Daugherty and Dixon, *Harding Tragedy,* pp. 181-82.

45. HMD to Taft, April 4, 1923, TS 3, Box 536/4.

46. Jennings to WGH, April 13, 1923, Copy, Jennings Papers, Box 1/10; WGH to Jennings, April 16, 1923, *ibid.*

47. HMD to WGH, April 16, 1923, Copy, HP, Box 695/3; New York *World,* March 18, 19, 1923; HMD to Clemens, August 15, 1939, Clemens Papers, Box 1/13.

48. WGH to Jennings, April 16, 1923, Jennings Papers, Box 1/10.

49. HMD to WGH, April 16, 1923, Copy, HP, Box 695/3.

50. WGH to HMD, April 19, 1923, *ibid.*

51. HMD to WGH, April 24, 1923, Box 360/4, *ibid.*

52. *Daugherty Investigation,* p. 544. Telephone conversation, H. Ellis Daugherty with author, December 12, 1977.

53. *Ibid.,* pp. 538-43.

54. Daugherty and Dixon, *Harding Tragedy,* p. 249; *New York Times,* May 31, 1923.

55. Daugherty and Dixon, *Harding Tragedy,* p. 363; Russell, *Blooming Grove,* p. 570.

56. Russell, *Blooming Grove,* p. 570.

57. HMD to McLean, June 4, 1923, McLean Family Papers, Box 5/D; HMD to Mrs. McLean, June 17, 1923, *ibid.*

58. Daugherty and Dixon, *Harding Tragedy,* p. 248.

59. *Ibid.,* p. 268; HMD to WGH, April 24, 1923, HP, Box 360/4.

60. HMD to WGH, May 22, 1923, HP, Box 30/2; "Bad News," p. 14; Coolidge to HMD, February 14, 1924, Copy, Coolidge Papers, Box 26/10.

61. HMD to John Crim, July 12, 1923, Copy, DJF 70-337-191677-71X.

62. HMD to Seymour, July 22, 1923, Copy, 70-337-191677X-72X, *ibid.*; HMD to Crim, July 16, 1923, Telegram, 36-1456, *ibid.*

63. See, for example, WGH to HMD, May 21, 1923, HP, Box 367/3. Harding was polite and understanding when Daugherty desired to delay his return in order to attend the Shriners' convention.

64. William Allen White, *The Autobiography of William Allen White* (New York, 1946), pp. 623-24. Senator Capper later contended, however, that Harding was not nervous after the visit with Mrs. Fall. Murray, *Harding Era,* p. 442.

65. Hoover, *Memoirs,* II, 49.

66. For an accurate and detailed account of Harding's illness and subsequent death, see Murray, *Harding Era,* pp. 448-51.

67. Daugherty and Dixon, *Harding Tragedy,* pp. 269-71.

68. HMD to Dunne, August 22, 1923, Dunne Papers, Box 6325/D; HMD to Fred Seely, August 26, 1923, RBHP, Box 9/3.

CHAPTER XIII

1. HMD to Mrs. Harding, September 13, 1923, Florence Kling Harding Papers, Box 789/5; HMD to William Jennings Bryan, January 5, 1923, William Jennings Bryan Papers, Box 36, Library of Congress; HMD to Mrs. McLean, June 17, 1923, McLean Family Papers, Box 5/D.

2. *New York Times,* March 16, 21, 28, 29, 1923; R. F. Rarey to Smith, March 27, 1923, Telegram, cited in *Daugherty Investigation,* p. 599.

3. *New York Times,* April 27, July 20, 1923.

4. Felder to HMD, September 7, 1923, cited in Hoyt, *Spectacular Rogue,* pp. 227 (see also pp. 201-09). The Daugherty-Felder correspondence, which Hiram Todd made available to Hoyt, was apparently destroyed after Todd's death. Edward Maguire, Jr., to the author, February 19, 1975. Maguire is Todd's grandson.

5. Hoyt, *Spectacular Rogue,* p. 227.

6. HMD to Coolidge, October 1, December 31, 1923, Coolidge Papers, Box 26/10.

7. *Ibid.,* December 15, 1923, January 5, 1924.

8. HMD to Hard, October 20, 1923, Hard Papers, Box 2/2.

9. HMD to Taft, November 14, 1923, TS 3, Box 547/9. See also *Cincinnati Times-Star,* November 7, 1923.

10. Taft to HMD, November 16, 1923, Copy, Box 547/11, *ibid.;* HMD to Taft, December 4, 1923, Box 548/11, *ibid.*

11. HMD to Clemens, September 24, 1938, Clemens Papers, Box 1/12; Atlee Pomerene to Paul Howland, July 22, 1931, quoted in Daugherty and Dixon, *Harding Tragedy,* pp. 307-11.

12. WGH to HMD, July 24, 27, 1922, Copies, HP, Box 695/2.

13. HMD to Albert Fall, August 20, 1923, Albert Fall Papers, Box 1, University of New Mexico Library. Despite Fall's outburst against the 1922 railroad injunction, it is untrue, as Robert Murray contends, that Daugherty and Fall were unfriendly or rarely conferred with one another in the mid-1920s. Only *after* Daugherty failed to testify favorably at the 1931 Fall trial regarding the oil leases did antagonism develop. Murray, *Harding Era,* p. 474. See also HMD to McLean, January 2, 1924, McLean Family Papers, Box 5/D; *Daugherty Investigation,* p. 693.

14. Coolidge to HMD, January 24, 1924, DJF 22016X; HMD to Coolidge, January 24, 1924, Copy, *ibid.*

15. Noggle, *Teapot Dome,* pp. 91-92.

16. HMD to Coolidge, January 26, 31, 1924, Coolidge Papers, Box 26/10. On January 29, Coolidge had nominated Republican Silas H. Strawn of Chicago and Democrat Thomas W. Gregory of New York as special counsel. By February, however, they were no longer acceptable, and Democrat Atlee Pomerene of Ohio and Republican Owen J. Roberts of Pennsylvania became Coolidge's final choices. Noggle, *Teapot Dome,* pp. 98-114.

17. HMD to Robert J. Cuddiby, February 16, 1924, Copy, Coolidge Papers, Box 26/10; "Attack on Daugherty," p. 16.

18. *Congressional Record,* 68th Cong., 1st Sess., 2769.

19. Daugherty later wrote that he had requested the White House meeting with Borah. Daugherty and Dixon, *Harding Tragedy,* p. 287. But see also *New York Times,* February 19, 1924 and Donald R. McCoy, *Calvin Coolidge, The Quiet President* (New York, 1967), p. 212.

20. The basis for this story came from White House secretary Mary Randolph, an eyewitness, and was retold in White, *Puritan in Babylon,* pp. 268-69. For other variations of the same incident, see Marian C. McKenna, *Borah* (Ann Arbor, 1961), pp. 202-03 and McCoy, *Coolidge,* pp. 212-13. For Daugherty's account, see Daugherty and Dixon, *Harding Tragedy,* pp. 287-88. Daugherty later claimed that Borah had opposed him because he had held Daugherty responsible for the defeat of the resolution recognizing the Soviet Union. Daugherty to Harris, January 21, 1939, RBHP, Box 9/4.

21. George Pepper, *Philadelphia Lawyer: An Autobiography* (Philadelphia, 1944), pp. 198-99; *New York Times,* February 21, 1924; Daugherty and Dixon, *Harding Tragedy,* pp. 282-83.

22. Merlo J. Pusey, *Charles Evans Hughes,* Vol. II (New York, 1963), 565.

23. *Congressional Record,* 68th Cong., lst Sess., 2891-92; Noggle, *Teapot Dome,* pp. 118, 125. The Ohio Senators were Daugherty's only senatorial backers. On one occasion Willis, obviously carried away, characterized Daugherty as being "as clean as a hound's tooth." *Congressional Record,* 68th Cong., lst Sess., 3394.

24. McCoy, *Coolidge,* p. 214.

25. *Congressional Record,* 68th Cong., lst Sess., 2890.

26. HMD to Coolidge, February 28, 1924, Coolidge Papers, Box 26/10.

27. *New York Times,* February 27, 1924; *Congressional Record,* lst Sess., 2982. Although there is no evidence that it influenced Coolidge's decision, a New York federal court ruling on January 3 to dismiss the Justice Department's suit against the Chemical Foundation was both well publicized and damning to Daugherty. According to the *New York Times,* the government's conspiracy to defraud "had been so loosely framed . . . that several specifications were withdrawn in the course of the trial. The case goes on the list— already too long—of the court failures of the Department of Justice under the present Attorney General." *New York Times,* January 5, 1924. For another critical reference, see "Attack on Daugherty," p. 16.

28. Taft to Horace Taft, March 6, 1924, Copy, TS 3, Box 554/6.

29. Murray, *Harding Era,* pp. 478-79. For Daugherty's disparaging remark, see Daugherty and Dixon, *Harding Tragedy,* pp. 214, 198.

30. Burton K. Wheeler with Paul Healey, *Yankee from the West* (Garden City, New York, 1962), p. 234; Wheeler remained adamant in his views of Daugherty, Wheeler to the author, May 15, 1968.

31. HMD to Willis, January 10, 1924, Copy, DJF 36-1534.

32. Hiram C. Todd to HMD, March 11, 1924, DJF 191307-37X; Murray, *Harding Era,* p. 478; *Daugherty Investigation,* pp. 921-41.

33. *New York Times,* May 22, 1924.

34. *Daugherty Investigation,* p. 19.

35. *Ibid.,* pp. 566-601.

36. HMD to Hoover, September 8, 1924, Hoover Papers, Box 1-5/20; Wheeler and Healey, *Yankee from the West,* pp. 224-25.

37. Fayette County Probate Court case 73P-E9471.

38. *Daugherty Investigation,* p. 1199. George L. Miller was an Oklahoma rancher who became involved in an illegal transaction with the Otoe and Ponca Indians.

39. *Ibid.,* pp. 42-43.

40. Robert James Maddox, "Keeping Cool with Coolidge," *Journal of American History,* LIII (March 1967), 778. See also LeRoy Ashby, *The Spearless Leader: Senator Borah and the Progressive Movement in the 1920's* (Urbana, 1972), p. 149.

41. Coolidge to HMD, March 27, 1924, quoted in Daugherty and Dixon, *Harding Tragedy,* pp. 311-12.

42. Taft to Robert Taft, March 30, 1924, Copy, TS 3, Box 555/15.

43. HMD to Coolidge, March 28, 1924, quoted in Daugherty and Dixon, *Harding Tragedy,* pp. 313-17.

44. *New York Times,* March 29, 1924, contained editorial summaries of many of the leading newspapers; "Mr. Coolidge Dismisses Mr. Daugherty," *Nation,* CXVIII (April 9, 1924), 386.

45. *New York Times,* March 29, 30, 1924.

46. HMD to Fairbanks, April 3, 1924, Fairbanks Papers, Box 1/4.

47. HMD to New, April 1, 1924, New Papers, Box 1/3.

48. *New York Times,* April 24, 1924; *St. Louis Post-Dispatch,* April 24, 1924.

49. HMD to James M. Beck, August 26, 1924, uncataloged James M. Beck Papers, Princeton University Library.

50. *New York Times,* April 24, 1924. On April 8, Daugherty had announced that his unoccupied Columbus home had been forcibly entered and some of his private correspondence stolen. *Ibid.,* April 9, 1924.

51. *Ibid.,* April 28, 1924.

52. HMD to Smith W. Brookhart, June 4, 1924, DJF 226225-1.

53. *Daugherty Investigation,* pp. 1426-27; *New York Times,* June 1, 6, 1924. In 1927, the United States Supreme Court reversed Cochran's decision in McGrain v. Daugherty.

54. *Daugherty Investigation,* pp. 1424-25. Curious, too, was Daugherty's huge increase in Wright-Martin stock. The Department of Justice failed to prosecute that corporation for war fraud, a charge that had evolved in the Wilson administration.

55. *New York Times,* April 9, 1924; Daugherty and Dixon, *Harding Tragedy,* pp. 280-81.

56. *Washington Post,* April 30, 1924; *Columbus Dispatch,* April 31, 1924.

57. *New York Times,* June 10, 1924.

58. *Ibid.;* Richard Lowitt, *George W. Norris: The Persistence of a Progressive, 1913-1933* (Urbana, 1971), p. 238.

59. *New York Times,* June 10, 12, 1924.

60. HMD to Beck, August 17, 1924, uncataloged Beck Papers; Beck to HMD, August 21, 1924, Copy, *ibid.*

61. HMD to Beck, August 26, 1924, *ibid.*

62. Beck to HMD, August 30, 1924, Copy, *ibid.:* HMD to Beck, September 2, 1924, *ibid.*

63. Beck to HMD, September 5, 1924, *ibid.;* Harlan F. Stone to Beck, September 12, 1924, Memorandum, *ibid.*

64. HMD to Beck, September 2, 1924, *ibid.:* HMD to John W. Davis, September 19, 1924, Copy, Willis Papers, Box 13.

65. For the 1924 election, see Noggle, *Teapot Dome,* pp. 167-76, and J. Leonard Bates, "The Teapot Dome Scandal and the Election of 1924," *American Historical Review,* LX (January 1955), 303-22.

66. Hoyt, *Spectacular Rogue,* pp. 266-67.

67. *Ibid.,* pp. 271-72.

68. Todd to HMD, March 3, 1925, cited in *ibid.,* p. 272.

69. *Ibid.*

70. *Ibid.,* p. 273.

71. HMD to Todd, April 23, 1925, cited in *ibid.*

CHAPTER XIV

1. The best account of the American Metal Company litigation is Martin Mayer's *Emory Buckner* (New York, 1968). Unless otherwise cited, the background information comes from Mayer.

2. HMD to WGH, September 5, 1920, HP, Box 763/2.

3. *Daugherty Investigation,* pp. 699-700; according to government travel vouchers, Daugherty, Smith, and Miller were in New York City together on April 18 or 19, 1921. *New York Times,* September 18, 1926.

4. Special Agent Eddie Toland interview with Henry I. Foster, February 5, 1927, DJF 228730.

5. *Daugherty Investigation,* pp. 2983-3002.

6. WGH to Thomas Miller, June 30, 1922, Copy, HP, Box 124/1; Charles Calvert to Harding, January 22, 1923, *ibid.;* Miller to Christian, Jr., February 15, 1923, *ibid.*; Mayer, *Buckner,* p. 210. Calvert strangely dropped the charges in January 1923.

7. *New York Times,* October 5, 1926.

8. *Ibid.,* October 31, 1925.

9. Mayer, *Buckner,* p. 213; *New York Times,* September 9, 1926.

10. Mayer, *Buckner,* p. 215.

11. *New York Times,* January 23, 1926; unsigned Memorandum, January 25, 1926, DJF 228730-238.

12. Mayer, *Buckner,* p. 216.

13. HMD to Beck, July 26, April 15, 1926, uncataloged Beck Papers.

14. Emory R. Buckner to William J. Donovan, January 25, 1926, DJF 228730-239; *ibid.,* January 29, 1926, 228730-246.

15. Draper Daugherty medical file 1713; Daugherty to Clark, October 12, December 1, 1925, June 1, 1926, *ibid.* All of the subsequent Clark correspondence is in *ibid.*

16. Daugherty to Clark, June 1, 14, 1926; New York *Evening Graphic,* May 27-June 22, 1926. Clippings in *ibid.*

17. Daugherty to Clark, December 1, 1925, May 26, June 14, 18, 24, July 8, 1926. See also Daugherty to Clark, October 2, 1925, June 19, 1926.

18. Daugherty to Clark, June 16, 17, 1926; Katherine Carroll to Clark, July 7, 1926.

19. Daugherty to Clark, July 8, 17, 22, 1926; Draper Daugherty to Clark, July 25, 1926; Daugherty to Clark, October 20, 1926.

20. *New York Times,* October 6, 1926.

21. *Ibid.,* October 8, 1926.

22. *Ibid.,* October 6, September 28, 1926; Buckner to Donovan, January 25, 1926, DJF 228730-239. The evidence does not suggest, as Murray and others have contended, that the $40,000 was put into a political account, "Jess Smith Extra No. 3," managed by Smith. Murray, *Harding Era,* p. 480; Sullivan, *The Twenties,* pp. 352-53; Daugherty and Dixon, *Harding Tragedy,* p. 255. Undoubtedly, Daugherty originated the story.

23. Taft to Elihu Root, September 17, 1926, TS 3, Box 606/2.

24. *New York Times,* October 11, 12, 1926.

25. Mayer, *Buckner,* pp. 220-21.

26. HMD to Beck, December 27, 1926, uncataloged Beck Papers.

27. *Ibid.,* January 18, 21, 1927; Beck to HMD, January 19, 1927, Telegram, Copy, *ibid.*

28. *New York Times,* February 16, 1927; H. L. Shine to ? Cook, February 7, 1927, Memorandum, DJF 228730.

29. Mayer, *Buckner,* pp. 225-26. In focusing on the interest credited to Daugherty's account, Buckner most likely relied on a J. Edgar Hoover-directed Bureau of Investigation report which disclosed that several of the cancelled coupons from untraced Liberty Bonds were cashed at the American Security and Trust Company in Washington, D. C. Both Harry Daugherty and Smith had safety boxes there. At the time that the coupons were redeemed, February and April 1924, Smith was already in the grave. Moreover, a bank cashier, J. O. Gray, Jr., remembered having transactions with Daugherty. That same report also revealed that King converted cancelled Liberty Bond coupons, totaling $2,125, into a check on April 23, 1922, which was deposited by May 1, 1922 to Harry Daugherty's Midland Bank account. J. Edgar Hoover Memorandum, June 26, 1926, DJF (restricted) 228730-1.

30. HMD to Mabel Walker Willebrandt, January 31, 1927, DJF 228730-605.

31. Beck to Harold H. Corbin, February 21, 1927, Copy, uncataloged Beck Papers; Corbin to Beck, February 19, 1927, *ibid.*

32. *New York Times,* February 18, 1927; Mayer, *Buckner,* p. 229.

33. Mayer, *Buckner,* pp. 229-32.

34. *Ibid.,* p. 233.

35. *New York Times,* February 25, 1927.

36. John C. Knox, *A Judge Comes of Age* (New York, 1940), pp. 256-57.

37. *Ibid.,* p. 257.

38. Buckner to Harlan F. Stone, April 12, 1927, Harold F. Stone Papers, Box 7, Library of Congress.

39. *New York Times,* March 5, 1927.

40. "Miller Guilty; Daugherty Free," *Literary Digest,* XCII (March 19, 1927), 11. Neither the *New York Times* nor the *Washington Post* expressed an editorial opinion.

41. Late in 1927 Nan Britton published *The President's Daughter,* which described her lengthy and somewhat surreptitious love affair with Harding, which led to the birth of their alleged child in October 1919. The 1964 disclosure of love letters between Mrs. Carrie Phillips, the beautiful wife of a Marion, Ohio businessman, did the most to substantiate early rumors of Harding's extramarital activities. During the 1920 campaign Republican leaders may well have sent the Phillipses abroad to prevent possible embarrassment. Russell, *Blooming Grove,* p. 402.

CHAPTER XV

1. *New York Times,* September 30, 1925, July 13, 1928, February 13, 1930; George Robinson, Jr., to the author, January 28, 1974.

2. *Ohio State Journal,* March 5, 8, 19, 1931; *New York Times,* November 26, 1931; George Robinson, Jr., to the author, January 28, 1974.

3. HMD to E. S. Rochester, November 22, 1927, E. S. Rochester Letters, File 1, Ohio Historical Society.

4. HMD to Christian, Jr., May 20, 1929, Christian, Jr., Papers, Box 30/D; HMD to Beck, March 17, 1930, uncataloged Beck Papers.

5. Beck to HMD, March 24, 1930, Copy, uncataloged Beck Papers. Interestingly, in 1930, Gaston Means had employed Dixon's sister, May Dixon Thacher, to write the scurrilous *The Strange Death of President Warren G. Harding.* She later repudiated her own work when Means characteristically failed to provide the documentation. Thomas Dixon's biographer claimed that, because Dixon had admired Harding, he accepted Daugherty's employment in part "to set the record straight." Raymond Allen Cook, *Fire from the Flint: The Amazing Careers of Thomas Dixon* (Winston-Salem, 1968), p. 215; Daugherty and Dixon, *Harding Tragedy,* p. 3 which also contains the relevant portions of Hoover's speech.

6. Daugherty and Dixon, *Harding Tragedy,* especially chapters II and III.

7. Hard to Clemens, November 5, 1939, Clemens Papers, Box 2/9.

8. Daugherty and Dixon, *Harding Tragedy,* p. 252.

9. Daugherty appropriately entitled his chapter on the strike, "The Conspiracy of 1922;" *ibid.,* pp. 132-38, 161, 207, 214, 281-82.

10. HMD to Hard, January 12, 1932, Hard Papers, Box 2/4.

11. HMD to New, March 31, 1934, New Papers, Box 1/5; Carroll to New, March 3, 1932, *ibid.;* HMD to Maurice Maschke, January 6, 1932, Maurice Maschke Papers, in the possession of Maurice Maschke, Jr., Cleveland, Ohio.

12. HMD to Hilles, July 21, 1933, Hilles Papers, Box 214.

13. Carroll to New, March 3, 1932, New Papers, Box 1/4; Wesley Bagby, "The Smoke-Filled Room and the Nomination of Warren G. Harding," *Mississippi Valley Historical Review,* XLI (March 1955), 657-74.

14. HMD to Clemens, May 23, 1936, Clemens Papers, Box 1/2.

15. HMD to Harris, May 21, 1935, RBHP, Box 9/4; HMD to Maschke, July 15, 1935, unprocessed Maschke Papers.

16. HMD to Harris, September 19, 1936, RBHP, Box 9/4.

17. Sullivan, *The Twenties,* pp. 26-67.

18. *Ibid.,* pp. 149-50, 356.

19. Allan Nevins, "Harding, Warren Gamaliel," *DAB,* ed. by Dumas Malone, VIII (New York, 1932), 252-57.

20. Copy of Daugherty's Kiwanis-Club Speech in RBHP, Box 4/6. For Daugherty's reaction to Nevins's article, see Carroll to New, February 20, 1932, New Papers, Box 1/4.

21. Carroll to New, February 20, 1932, New Papers, Box 1/4.

22. David Muzzey to Clemens, September 18, 1939, Clemens Papers, Box 2/20; Harris to Carl W. Sawyer, and *passim,* RBHP, Box 9/6.

23. HMD to Harris, May 24, 1934, September 11, 1934, RBHP, Box 9/4.

24. *Ibid.,* January 3, 21, 1939.

25. *Ibid.,* May 19, 1939. Adams published the *Incredible Era: The Life and Times of Warren G. Harding* later that year.

26. HMD to New, March 31, 1934, New Papers, Box 1/5.

27. HMD to Atlee Pomerene, January 30, 1932, Atlee Pomerene Papers, Folder 48, Kent State University Library.

28. `HMD to Clemens, May 23, 1936, Clemens Papers, Box 1/12; HMD to Hilles, June 23, 1936, Hilles Papers, Box 223; HMD to Beck, November 15, 1932, uncataloged Beck Papers.

29. HMD to Hilles, June 23, 1926, Hilles Papers, Box 223; *ibid.,* July 16, 1936, Box 224; *Columbus Citizen,* January 26, 1940, clipping in Clemens Papers, Box 1/4.

30. HMD to Mrs. Ned McLean, October 12, 1939, McLean Family Papers, Box 5/D.

31. *Columbus Dispatch,* January 26, 1940.

32. Columbus Probate Court, File 94856, Harry M. Daugherty Estate.

33. In 1937, Daugherty had bequeathed his daughter his records, letters, copies of speeches, and statements. The Daugherty estate, however, did not list these as real property, although it included two empty file cabinets. A True Copy of the Will of Harry Daugherty, RBHP, Box 9/5. In my extensive search for Daugherty correspondence, I became convinced that no large collection exists. H. Ellis Daugherty, Harry's closest surviving relation, wrote to this writer in April 1967 that he knew nothing of his uncle's papers.

EPILOG

1. HMD to Harris, May 24, 1934, RBHP, Box 9/3.

2. HMD to William C. Beer, July 25, 1905, William C. Beer Papers, Yale University Library.

Bibliography

One would expect that detailed information on early twentieth-century public figures is easily accessible, but such is not always the case. Not only were Daugherty's papers nonexistent, several contemporaries who corresponded with him either destroyed their collections, or they or their descendants culled the files. By far the most profitable collections were the Warren G. Harding Papers, which were especially useful for 1918 to 1923, and the William Howard Taft Papers of 1908-1924.

It was my hope to augment existing manuscript and newspaper collections with genealogical studies and interviews with family members in order to learn more about Daugherty's background and personal life. I quickly discerned that no such genealogical study existed, and that Daugherty's family was diminished and not very helpful. His two children died childless. His brother's only child, Ellis, an octogenarian residing in Pompano Beach, Florida, has provided scant information. Ellis's daughter, Mrs. Charles Dunton, a flower girl at Jess Smith's funeral, has not responded to inquiries. Moreover, many of the older residents in Washington Court House and Columbus, Ohio, remember little. But the probate court records, the remembrances of a few old-timers, and the opportunity to visit Daugherty's community of thirty-four years made my two trips to Washington Court House at least a partial success.

Along with the United States *Congressional Record* and the testimony of the Senate Committee investigation on Attorney General Daugherty, the most important public documents were the Department of Justice records housed in the National Archives in Washington, D. C. The Archives staff was exceedingly helpful and a correspondence card file exists to help researchers, but the records are not well organized, nor is there a subject file of cases and other related departmental business. Despite denials from Justice officials, my impression is that not all of the relevant Justice material was sent to or retained in the Archives, and that some of Daugherty's Special Assistant Attorneys-General neglected to turn in several case files.

Because of the liberalization of the Freedom of Information Act, however, previously restricted Bureau of Investigation material in the National Archives or the Federal Bureau of Investigation headquarters is now more accessible to researchers. Nevertheless, the FBI Freedom of Information Act Unit moves very slowly in processing requests, and it does not permit researchers to peruse material before reproducing it at a cost. Only when all of the old Bureau files are turned over to the Archives without limitation can one effectively use these records. Indications are that this transfer will soon be accomplished.

Manuscript Collections in Ohio Historical Society, Columbus, Ohio

Walter Brown Papers
George Christian, Jr., Papers
George Christian, Sr., Papers
Cyril Clemens Papers
Harry M. Daugherty Letters
Charles Dick Papers
Hoke Donithen Papers
Newton Fairbanks Papers
Arthur Garford Papers
Governors' Papers: James M. Cox
Charles E. Hard Papers
Florence Kling Harding Papers
Warren G. Harding Papers
Ray Baker Harris Papers
Malcolm Jennings Papers
Charles Kurtz Papers
Mary Lee Papers
George A. Myers Papers
William H. Phipps Papers
E. S. Rochester Letters
Charles E. Sawyer Papers
F. E. Scobey Papers
Frank B. Willis Papers
Preston Wolfe Papers

Manuscript Collections in Library of Congress, Washington, D.C.

William Borah Papers
Calvin Coolidge Papers
Finley Peter Dunne Papers
James R. Garfield Papers

Charles E. Hughes Papers
Philander Knox Papers
William McKinley Papers
McLean Family Papers
Theodore Roosevelt Papers
John Sherman Papers
Harlan F. Stone Papers
George Sutherland Papers
William Howard Taft Papers
Wadsworth Family Papers
Thomas Walsh Papers

Other Manuscript Collections

James M. Beck Papers, Princeton University Library, Princeton, New Jersey
William C. Beer Papers, Yale University Library, New Haven, Connecticut
Theodore Burton Papers, Western Reserve Historical Society, Cleveland, Ohio
Edwin Denby Papers, Detroit Public Library, Detroit, Michigan
Albert Fall Papers, University of New Mexico Library, Albuquerque, New Mexico
Joseph B. Foraker Papers, Cincinnati Historical Society, Cincinnati, Ohio
Will Hays Papers, Indiana State Library, Indianapolis, Indiana
Charles Hilles Papers, Yale University Library, New Haven, Connecticut
Herbert Hoover Papers, Herbert Hoover Presidential Library, West Branch, Iowa
Maurice Maschke Papers, in possession of Maurice Maschke, Jr., Cleveland, Ohio
Harry New Papers, Indiana State Library, Indianapolis, Indiana
Atlee Pomerene Papers, Kent State University Library, Kent, Ohio
Raymond Robins Papers, The State Historical Society of Wisconsin, Madison, Wisconsin
Henry Stimson Papers, Yale University Library, New Haven, Connecticut
Harry Weinberger Papers, Yale University Library, New Haven, Connecticut

Public Documents

Columbus. Probate Court. *File 94856: Harry M. Daugherty Estate*
Fayette County. *Probate Court Records*
Ohio. General Assembly. *Journal of the House of Representatives*. Vols. LXXIX and LXXXVI

Ohio. Lima State Hospital. Draper Daugherty Medical File 1713

U.S. *Congressional Record.* Vols. XL and LXII-LXV

U.S. Department of Justice. *Annual Report of the Attorney General of the United States for the Fiscal Years, 1921-1925*

U.S. Department of Justice. *Appendix to the Annual Report of the Attorney General of the United States for the Fiscal Year of 1922*

U.S. Department of Justice. *Official Opinions of the Attorney General of the Unped States Advising the President and Heads of Departments in Relation to their Official Duties.* Vols. XXXII-XXXIV

U.S. Department of Justice. *Pardon Files, 1908-1923.* National Records Service, National Archives. Suitland, Maryland

U.S. Department of Justice. *Records, 1921-1927.* National Archives

U.S. Department of Justice. *Reply by the Attorney General of the United States, Hon. Harry M. Daugherty, to Charges Filed with the Judiciary of the House of Representatives, December 1, 1922 by Hon. Oscar E. Keller, Representative from Minnesota*

U. S. Department of State. *Records, 1921-1923.* National Archives

U.S. Senate, Select Senate Committee. *Hearings on the Investigation of the Attorney General.* 11 vols. 68th Cong., 1st Sess., 1924

U.S. Senate, Subcommittee of the Committee on Privileges and Elections. *Hearings on S. R. 357, Presidential Campaign Expenses.* 66th Cong., 2nd Sess., 1920

Newspapers

Cincinnati Enquirer
Cincinnati Times-Star
Circleville Democrat and Watchman
Cleveland Leader
Cleveland Plain Dealer
Columbus Citizen
Columbus Evening Dispatch
Cyclone and Fayette Republican
Fayette County Record
Fayette Republican
New York Daily News
New York Times
New York *World*
Ohio State Journal
St. Louis Post-Dispatch
The Week (Ohio Republican weekly)
Toledo Blade
Washington Court House Herald
Washington Post

Oral History

Transcripts

Marvin Jones, Columbia Oral History Center of New York
J. O. A. Preus, Minnesota Historical Society Oral History Collection
J. T. Williams, Columbia Oral History Center of New York

Interviews

Dr. Ross Dees Blades, October 10, 1972, Springfield, Missouri
Charles A. Jones, April 2, 1967 and February 20, 1968, Columbus, Ohio
Dr. Arthur Knabb, October 21, 1972, Springfield, Missouri
Jacob Meckstroth, September 13, 1967, Columbus, Ohio
Dr. Charles P. Pritchett, May 28, 1968, Columbus, Ohio
Dr. Warren Warres, November 6, 1972, Springfield, Missouri

Books

Adams, Samuel Hopkins. *Incredible Era: The Life and Times of Warren Gamaliel Harding.* Boston: Houghton Mifflin Company, 1939.

Allen Frank (ed.). *History of Fayette County Ohio: Her People, Industries and Institutions.* Indianapolis: B. F. Bowen & Company, 1914.

Allen, Frederick Lewis. *Only Yesterday.* New York: Harper and Brothers, 1931.

————— . *The Lords of Creation.* Chicago: Quandrangle, 1966.

Anderson, Donald F. *William Howard Taft: A Conservative's Conception of the Presidency.* Ithaca: Cornell University Press, 1973.

Ashby, LeRoy. *The Spearless Leader: Senator Borah and the Progressive Movement in the 1920's.* Urbana: University of Illinois Press, 1972.

Bagby, Wesley M. *The Road to Normalcy: The Presidential Campaign and Election of 1920.* Baltimore: The Johns Hopkins Press, 1962.

Baruch, Bernard. *Baruch: The Public Years.* New York: Holt, Rinehart and Winston, 1960.

Berman, Edward. *Labor Disputes and the President of the United States.* Vol. II: *Studies in History, Economics, and Public Law.* Edited by the Faculty of Political Science of Columbia. New York: Longmans, Green and Company, 1924.

Bowden, Robert D. *Boies Penrose, Symbol of an Era.* New York: Greenberg Press, 1937.

Boyer, Richard O. *Max Steuer: Magician of the Law.* New York: Greenberg, 1932.

Braeman, John. *Albert Beveridge, American Nationalist.* Chicago: University of Chicago Press, 1971.

Britton, Nan. *The President's Daughter.* New York: Elizabeth Ann Guild, Inc., 1927.

Butler, Nicholas Murray. *Across the Busy Years, Recollections and Reflections.* 2 vols. New York: Charles Scribner's Sons, 1939-1940.

Butt, Archie. *Taft and Roosevelt, The Intimate Letters of Archie Butt, Military Aide.* 2 vols. New York: Doubleday, Doran, and Company, 1930.

Chapman Brothers, *Portrait and Biographical Record of Fayette, Pickaway and Madison Counties, Ohio.* Chicago: Chapman Brothers, 1892.

Cook, Fred J. *The FBI Nobody Knows.* New York: MacMillan Company, 1964.

Cook, Raymond Allen. *Fire From the Flint: The Amazing Careers of Thomas Dixon.* Winston-Salem: John F. Blair, 1968.

Cox, James M. *Journey Through My Years.* New York: Simon and Schuster, 1946.

Crissey, Forrest. *Theodore E. Burton: American Statesman.* Cleveland and New York: The World Publishing Company, 1956.

Croly, Herbert David. *Marcus Alonzo Hanna: His Life and Work.* New York: MacMillan Company, 1912.

Cummings, Homer and McFarland, Carl. *Federal Justice: Chapters in the History of Justice.* New York: Macmillan Company, 1937.

Daugherty, Harry M. and Dixon, Thomas. *The Inside Story of the Harding Tragedy.* New York: Churchill Company, 1932.

De Chambrun, Clara Longworth. *The Making of Nicholas Longworth.* New York: Ray Long & Richard R. Smith, Inc., 1933.

DePew, Chauncey M. *My Memories of Eighty Years.* New York: Charles Scribner's Sons, 1922.

Dills, R.S. *History of Fayette County.* Dayton: Odell & Mayer Publishers, 1881.

Downes, Randolph C. *The Rise of Warren Gamaliel Harding, 1865-1920.* Columbus: Ohio State University Press, 1970.

Fausold, Martin L. *James W. Wadsworth, Jr., The Gentleman from New York.* Syracuse: Syracuse University Press, 1975.

Fenno, Richard F., Jr. *The President's Cabinet: An Analysis in the Period from Wilson to Eisenhower.* Cambridge: Harvard University Press, 1959.

Foraker, Joseph Benson. *Notes of a Busy Life.* 2 vols. Cincinnati: Stewart and Kidd Company, 1916.

Fuess, Claude. *Calvin Coolidge, The Man from Vermont.* Hamden, Connecticut: Archon Books, 1965.

Galbreath, Charles B. *History of Ohio.* 5 vols. Chicago and New York: American Historical Society, Inc., 1925.

Garraty, John A. (ed.). *The Barber and the Historian: The Correspondence of George A. Myers and James Ford Rhodes, 1910-1923.* Columbus: The Ohio Historical Society, 1956.

Gilbert, Clinton Wallace. *Behind the Mirrors: The Psychology of Disintegration at Washington.* New York and London: G. P. Putnam's Sons, 1922.

Hagedorn, Hermann. *Leonard Wood: A Biography.* 2 vols. New York and London: Harper and Brothers, 1931.

Hammond, John Hays. *The Autobiography of John Hays Hammond.* 2 vols. Murray Hill, New York: Farrar and Rinehart, Inc., 1935.

Harbaugh, William H. *Lawyer's Lawyer: The Life of John W. Davis.* New York: Oxford University Press, 1973.

Hays, Will H. *The Memoirs of Will H. Hays.* Garden City, New York: Doubleday and Company, Inc., 1955.

Hechler, Kenneth W. *Insurgency Personalities and Politics of the Taft Era.* New York: Columbia University Press, 1940.

Hooper, Osman Castle. *History of the City of Columbus, Ohio: From the Founding of Franklinton in 1797, Through the World War Period to the Year 1920.* Columbus and Cincinnati: Memorial Publishing Company, 1921.

Hoover, Herbert. *The Memoirs of Herbert Hoover: The Cabinet and the Presidency, 1920-1933.* New York: Macmillan Company, 1952.

Hoover, Irvin. *Forty-two Years in the White House.* Boston: Houghton-Mifflin Company, 1934.

Howe, Frederick C. *The Confessions of a Reformer.* New York: Charles Scribner's Sons, 1925.

Hoyt, Edwin P. *Spectacular Rogue: Gaston B. Means.* Indianapolis: Bobbs-Merrill Company, 1963.

Hutchinson, William T. *Lowden of Illinois: The Life of Frank O. Lowden.* 2 vols. Chicago: University of Chicago Press, 1957.

Ireland, W. A. *Club Men of Columbus in Caricature.* Columbus: Roycrofters, 1911.

Johnson, Willis Fletcher. *George Harvey: A Passionate Patriot.* Boston: Houghton-Mifflin Company, 1929.

Keller, Morton. *In Defense of Yesterday: James M. Beck and the Politics of Conservatism, 1861-1936.* New York: Coward-McCann, Inc., 1958.

Kelly, Frank K. *The Fight for the White House: The Story of 1912.* New York: Thomas Y. Crowell Company, 1961.

Knox, John C. *A Judge Comes of Age.* New York: Charles Scribner's Sons, 1940.

Longworth, Alice Roosevelt. *Crowded Hours: Reminiscences.* New York: Charles Scribner's Sons, 1933.

Lowenthal, Max. *The Federal Bureau of Investigation.* Westport, Connecticut: Greenwood, 1971.

Lowitt, Richard. *George W. Norris: The Persistence of a Progressive, 1913-1933.* Urbana: University of Illinois Press, 1971.

Lowry, Edward G. *Washington Close-Ups: Intimate Views of Some Public Figures.* Boston and New York: Houghton-Mifflin Company, 1921.

Marsh, Benjamin. *Lobbyist for the People: A Record of Fifty Years.* Washington: Public Affairs Press, 1953.

Martin, Joe. *My First Fifty Years in Politics.* New York: McGraw-Hill Book Company, 1960.

Mason, Alpheus Thomas. *Harlan Fiske Stone: Pillar of the Law.* New York: Viking Press, 1956.

_____ . *William Howard Taft: Chief Justice.* New York: Simon and Schuster, 1964.

Mayer, George H. *The Republican Party, 1854-1964.* New York: Oxford University Press, 1964.

Mayer, Martin. *Emory Buckner.* New York: Harper and Row, 1968.

McCoy, Donald. *Calvin Coolidge: The Quiet President.* New York: Macmillan Company, 1967.

McKenna, Marian C. *Borah.* Ann Arbor: University of Michigan Press, 1961.

Means, Gaston B. *The Strange Death of President Harding.* New York: Guild Publishing Corporation, 1930.

Mercer, James K. *Representative Men of Ohio, 1904-1908: Administration of Myron T. Herrick, Governor of Ohio, 1904-1905.* Columbus: Fred J. Heer Press, 1908.

Miller, Benjamin F. *The Complete Medical Guide.* New York: Simon and Schuster, 1967.

Morgan, H. Wayne. *William McKinley and His America.* Syracuse: Syracuse University Press, 1963.

Mott, T. Bentley. *Myron T. Herrick: Friend of France: An Autobiographical Biography.* Garden City, New York: Doubleday, Doran and Company, Inc., 1929.

Mowry, George E. *The Era of Theodore Roosevelt and the Birth of Modern America, 1900-1912.* New York: Harper Torchbooks, 1962.

_____ . *Theodore Roosevelt and the Progressive Movement.* Madison: University of Wisconsin Press, 1947.

Murray, Robert K. *Red Scare: A Study in National Hysteria, 1919-1920.* New York: McGraw-Hill Book Company, 1964.

_____ . *The Harding Era: Warren G. Harding and His Administration.* Minneapolis: University of Minnesota Press, 1969.

_____ . *The Politics of Normalcy: Governmental Theory and Practice in the Harding-Coolidge Era.* New York: W. W. Norton and Company, 1973.

Nethers, John. *Simeon Fess, Educator and Politician.* New York: Pageant-Poseidon Ltd., 1973.

Noggle, Burl. "Oil in Politics." *Change and Continuity in Twentieth Century America: The 1920's.* ed. by John Braeman, Robert H. Bremner, and David Brody. Columbus: Ohio State University Press, 1968.

————. *Teapot Dome: Oil and Politics in the 1920's.* Baton Rouge: Louisiana State University Press, 1962.

Official Proceedings of the Seventeenth Republican National Convention, June 8-12, 1920. New York: Tenny Press, 1920.

Pepper, George Wharton. *Philadelphia Lawyer: An Autobiography.* Philadelphia and New York: J. P. Lippincott Company, 1944.

Preston, William, Jr. *Aliens and Dissenters: Federal Suppression of Radicals, 1903-1933.* New York: Harper and Row, 1966.

Pringle, Henry F. *The Life and Times of William Howard Taft.* 2 vols. New York: Farrar and Rinehart, Inc., 1939.

Pusey, Merlo J. *Charles Evans Hughes.* 2 vols. New York and London: Columbia University Press, 1963.

Quint, Howard H. and Ferrell, Robert H. (eds.). *The Talkative President: The Off-the-Record-Press Conferences of Calvin Coolidge.* Amherst: University of Massachusetts Press, 1964.

Richberg, Donald R. *My Hero: The Indiscreet Memoirs of an Eventful but Unheroic Life.* New York: G.P. Putnam's Sons, 1954.

Rosewater, Victor. *Back Stage in 1912: The Inside Story of the Split Republican Convention.* New York: Derrance & Company, Inc., 1932.

Russell, Francis. *The Shadow of Blooming Grove: Warren G. Harding in His Times.* New York: McGraw-Hill Book Company, 1968.

Sherman, John. *Recollections of Forty Years in the House, Senate and Cabinet: An Autobiography.* 2 vols. Chicago and New York: Werner Company, 1895.

Sinclair, Andrew. *The Available Man: The Life Behind the Masks of Warren Gamaliel Harding.* New York: Macmillan Company, 1965.

Smith, Joseph P. (ed.). *History of the Republican Party in Ohio and Memoirs of Its Representative Supporters.* 2 vols. Chicago: Lewis Publishing Company, 1898.

Socolofsky, Homer E. *Arthur Capper, Publisher, Politician, and Philanthropist.* Lawrence: University of Kansas Press, 1962.

Sparks, George F. (ed.). *A Many-Colored Toga: The Diary of Henry Fountain Ashurst.* Tucson, Arizona: University of Arizona Press, 1962.

Starling, Edmund W. as told to Thomas Sugrue. *Starling of the White House.* New York: Simon and Schuster, 1946.

Steuart, Justin. *Wayne Wheeler, Dry Boss.* New York: Fleming Revell, 1928.

Stevenson, Elizabeth. *Babbitts and Bohemians: The American 1920's.* New York: Macmillan Company, 1967.

Stokes, Thomas L. *Chip Off My Shoulder*. Princeton: Princeton University Press, 1940.

Sullivan, Mark. *The Twenties*. Vol. VI of *Our Times: The United States, 1900-1925*. New York: Charles Scribner's Sons, 1935.

Taylor, William Alexander. *Centennial History of Columbus and Franklin County, Ohio*. 2 vols. Chicago and Columbus: S. J. Clarke Publishing Company, 1909.

The Federal Antitrust Laws: With Summary of Cases Instituted by the United States. New York: Commerce Clearing House, Inc., 1949.

Timmons, Bascom N. *Portrait of An American: Charles G. Dawes*. New York: Henry Holt Company, 1953.

Trani, Eugene and Wilson, David L. *The Presidency of Warren G. Harding*. Lawrence: The Regents Press of Kansas, 1977.

Vadney, Thomas E. *The Wayward Liberal: A Political Biography of Donald Richberg*. Lexington: University of Kentucky Press, 1970.

Walters, Everett. *Joseph B. Foraker: An Uncompromising Republican*. Columbus: Ohio History Press, 1948.

Warner, Hoyt Landon. *Progressivism in Ohio, 1897-1917*. Columbus: Ohio State University Press for The Ohio Historical Society, 1964.

Watson, James E. *As I Knew Them: Memoirs of James E. Watson*. Indianapolis and New York: Bobbs-Merrill Company, 1936.

Werner, M. R. *Privileged Characters*. New York: Robert M. McBride Company, 1935.

_____ , and Starr, John. *Teapot Dome*. New York: Viking Press, 1959.

Wheeler, Burton K. with Healy, Paul F. *Yankee from the West*. Garden City, New York: Doubleday and Company, Inc., 1962.

White, William Allen. *A Puritan in Babylon: The Story of Calvin Coolidge*. New York: Macmillan Company, 1938.

_____ . *Masks in a Pageant*. New York: Macmillan Company, 1928.

_____ . *The Autobiography of William Allen White*. New York: Macmillan Company, 1946.

Whitehead, Don. *The FBI Story: A Report to the People*. New York: Random House, 1956.

Wilensky, Norman M. *Conservatives in the Progressive Era*. Gainesville: University of Florida Press, 1965.

Wilson, Joan Hoff. *Herbert Hoover: Forgotten Progressive*. Boston: Little, Brown and Company, 1975.

Wolf, Harry D. *The Railroad Labor Board*. Chicago: University of Chicago Press, 1927.

Zieger, Robert H. *Republicans and Labor, 1919-1929*. Lexington: University of Kentucky Press, 1969.

Articles

"Bad News for War Grafters," *Literary Digest,* LXXXIII (May 27, 1922), 14-15.

Bagby, Wesley. "The Smoke-Filled Room and the Nomination of Warren G. Harding," *Mississippi Valley Historical Review,* XLI (March 1955), 657-74.

Bates, J. Leonard. "The Teapot Dome Scandal and the Election of 1924," *American Historical Review,* LX (January 1955), 303-22.

"Daugherty, Aegis of Justice," *Nation,* CXVIII (March 26, 1924), 333-34.

"Daugherty and His Critics," *Independent,* CVIII (June 10, 1922), 501-02.

"Daugherty Declares War," *New Republic,* XXXII (September 13, 1922), 57-58.

"Daugherty's Dud," *Nation,* CXV (September 20, 1922), 271-72.

Dunne, Finley Peter. "A Look at Harding from the Sidelines," *Saturday Evening Post,* CCIX (September 12, 1936), 24, 74-79.

German, James C., Jr. "The Taft Administration and the Sherman Antitrust Act," *Mid-America,* LIV (July 1972), 172-86.

Giglio, James N. "Harry Micajah Daugherty," in Edward T. James (ed.). *Dictionary of American Biography.* Supplement 3. New York: Charles Scribner's Sons, 1973, 213-14.

"Government by Daugherty," *Nation,* CXV (September 13, 1922), 243.

Hard, William. "Oil and Irony," *Nation,* CXVIII (March 5, 1924), 256-57.

Harper, Robert S. "Before Revelry," *Plain Talk,* III (July 1928), 44-51.

Hawley, Ellis W. "Herbert Hoover, The Commerce Secretariat, and the Vision of an 'Associate State,' 1921-1928," *Journal of American History,* LXI (June 1974), 116-40.

Hooper, William E. "General Atterbury's Attitude Toward Labor," *World's Work,* XLIV (September 1922), 505-08.

"How Daugherty Helped Harding into the White House," *Literary Digest,* LXIX (April 9, 1921), 40-42.

"How to Estimate the Daugherty Evidence," *New Republic,* XXXVIII (March 26, 1924), 112-13.

Jewell, Bert M. "The Railroad Strike: Strikers' Viewpoint," *Current History,* XVII (November 1922), 202-07.

"Labor Injunctions Must Go," *New Republic,* XXXII (September 27, 1922), 109-10.

Maddox, Robert James. "Keeping Cool with Coolidge," *Journal of American History,* LIII (March 1967), 772-80.

McKillips, Budd L. "Company Unions on the Railroads," *Nation,* CXLII (January 8, 1936), 48-50.

Mels, Edgar. "Daugherty at the Bar," *Nation,* CXXVI (October 27, 1926), 423-24.

_____ . "Daugherty's Past," *Nation,* CXXVI (May 19, 1926), 551-52.

"Miller Guilty; Daugherty Free," *Literary Digest,* XCII (March 19, 1927), 256-57.

"More Daugherty," *Nation,* CXV (October 4, 1922), 323.

"Mr. Coolidge Dismisses Mr. Daugherty," *Nation,* CXVIII (April 9, 1924), 386.

"Mr. Daugherty Comes Clear," *Literary Digest,* LXXVI (February 10, 1923), 16.

"Mr. Daugherty Out of Place," *Outlook,* CXXXVI (March 5, 1924), 380-81.

"Mr. Daugherty's Resignation," *Outlook,* CXXXVI (April 9, 1924), 586-87.

Murray, Robert K. "President Harding and His Cabinet," *Ohio History,* LXXV (Spring and Summer 1966), 108-25.

Nevins, Allan. "Warren Gamaliel Harding," in Dumas Malone (ed.). *Dictionary of American Biography.* Vol. VIII. New York: Charles Scribner's Sons, 1932.

New, Harry S. "The Senatorial Oligarchy," *Saturday Evening Post,* CCIV (May 28, 1932), 21 and 84.

"Not Proven Guilty: The Ohio Gang in Court," *New Republic,* XL (October 27, 1926), 267-68.

"Punishing the Guilty Without Admitting the Guilt," *New Republic,* XXXVIII (April 9, 1924), 165-66.

Schruben, Francis W. "An Even Stranger Death of President Harding," *Southern California Quarterly,* n.v. (March 1966), 57-84.

Slosson, Preston S. "Warren G. Harding: A Revised Estimate," *Current History,* XXXIX (November 1930), 174-79.

"Smothering a Strike by Injunction," *Literary Digest,* LXXIV (September 16, 1922), 7-9.

"Strength and Weakness of the Cabinet," *Literary Digest,* LXVIII (March 12, 1921), 7-9.

"The Attack on Daugherty," *Literary Digest,* LXXVII (February 16, 1924), 16.

"The Case of Attorney General Daugherty," *Outlook,* CXXXI (June 7, 1922), 246-47.

Thompson, Frederic L. "Morse, Charles Wyman," in Dumas Malone (ed.). *Dictionary of American Biography.* Vol. XIII. New York: Charles Scribner's Sons, 1934.

"Uncle Sam's Prosecutor Prosecuted," *Literary Digest,* LXXV (December 16, 1922), 11.

Wakstein, Allen M. "The Origins of the Open-Shop Movement," *Journal of American History,* LI (December, 1964), 460-82.

Waterman, Richard. "Shopmen's Strike— Who Won It?" *Nation's Business,* X (November 1922), 25-26.

"War Frauds and Daugherty's Impeachment," *New Republic,* XXXII (October 11, 1922), 162-63.

Unpublished Material

Alderfer, H. F. "The Personality and Politics of Warren G. Harding." Ph. D. dissertation, School of Citizenship and Public Affairs, Syracuse University, 1928.

Boatmon, Ellis Grey. "Evolution of a President: The Political Apprenticeship of Warren G. Harding." Ph. D. dissertation, Department of History, University of South Carolina, 1966.

Cinclair, Richard J. "William H. Hays: Republican Politician." Ph. D. dissertation, Ball State University, 1969.

Hauser, Robert E. "Warren G. Harding and the Ohio Presidential Primary of 1920." M. A. thesis, Department of History, Pennsylvania State University, 1967.

Himmelberg, Robert F. "Relaxation of the Federal Anti-Trust Policy as a Goal of the Business Community During the Period 1918-1933." Ph. D. dissertation, Department of History, Pennsylvania State University, 1963.

Mackin, James A. "Harry M. Daugherty and Our Text Books." M. A. thesis, Department of History, Loyola University of Chicago, 1939.

Ridinger, Gerald E. "The Political Career of Frank B. Willis." Ph. D. dissertation, Department of History, The Ohio State University, 1957.

Ruetten, Richard T. "Burton K. Wheeler of Montana: A Progressive Between the Wars." Ph. D. dissertation, University of Oregon, 1961.

Thompson, Jack M. "James R. Garfield: The Career of a Rooseveltian Progressive." Ph. D. dissertation, Department of History, University of South Carolina, 1958.

Index